THE BOOK OF JUDGES

Perspectives from the Bench

Jeffrey L. Goodman

Curator

ISBN 9798218615413 (hardcover)

Cover Design by Pete Garceau

Printed by IngramSpark, in the United States of America

First Edition: May 2025

Published by Lamont-Ogden Group
1501 42nd St. Suite 300
West Des Moines, IA 50266

Lamont-Ogden
Group

Further Praise for The Book of Judges

"*The Book of Judges* is striking in the sheer number and varied backgrounds of its contributors, all stalwarts in the legal profession. Each one shares the unique insights, personal qualities and career paths that led them to trial and appeals courts. This book will be an invaluable resource not only for anyone aspiring to the bench, but for any attorney whose practice puts them in a courtroom."

George LaMarca, trial lawyer and author

"Judging is a practical business. It is the art of deciding for others. Want to know the 'nuts and bolts' of solving people's legal problems? Read this book."

Robert J. Blink, Senior District Court judge

"An invaluable book for anyone who wants to understand why an attorney would want to become a judge… and why the role of an independent judiciary is of such urgent importance."

John C. Gray, trial lawyer and former state judicial nominating commissioner

"This invaluable new book provides a fascinating glimpse into the judicial nomination and selection process from the perspective of those who have successfully traversed it. Their candid, thoughtful, and often quite personal essays offer a master roadmap of what lies ahead for those contemplating a position on the bench."

Cynthia C. Moser, trial lawyer and former federal and state judicial nominating commissioner

This book is dedicated to those who took the oath of office and vowed to uphold the law "without fear, favor, or hope of reward." I thank you for your service in preserving liberty and ensuring that justice is dispensed by our court system.

Acknowledgements

I have so many to thank for the inspiration to begin and complete this book.

First, to my wife, Liz, who is my soulmate, my booster, my occasional critic, and my lifetime companion for the past 40 years. I love you!

To Bryan Garner, renowned legal scholar and lexicographer, who I met at a U.S. Senate confirmation hearing for a U.S. Supreme Court Justice. Since then, we have become dear friends. Over the years, Bryan has inspired me to become a better writer, and *The Book of Judges* is my tribute to his encouragement and inspiration.

To the Honorable David R. Hansen, the first judge I came to know and truly respect early in my career. Judge Hansen is a country lawyer of unmatched wisdom and insightfulness who embodies all of the finest characteristics of an excellent jurist, which is why he is the sole author of Chapter One. He was instrumental in making *The Book of Judges* what it has become.

To Judge Mark Bennett, the most prolific writer I know. Judge Bennett is a beacon of judicial independence and creativity and a dear friend.

To Judge John Jarvey, whom I met early in my legal career and quickly came to admire for his humility, work ethic, and kind nature. I count myself fortunate to share our careers in private practice since his retirement.

To Judge Robert Blink, my trial advocacy professor, an excellent writer, and lifetime friend. Judge Blink was a constant companion in the design of this book, and an incisive critic and mentor to me throughout its production.

To Michael Dolan, Doug Elmets, and John Moreland, Jr., I offer my heartfelt thanks for their creative suggestions and editorial support which made this book the best it could be.

To the late Dr. Howard Hong (October 19, 1912 – March 16, 2010), former professor of philosophy at St. Olaf College, who taught me to think and wonder about all things large and small.

To Joseph Tomain, professor of law, who instilled in me at the young age of 22 the ability to boldly ask on behalf of clients: "What do I want?" Since the summer of 1982, this simply worded inquiry has remained foremost in my mind when I counsel and advocate for clients. Without Joe Tomain, I would not be a lawyer.

To Catherine Knepper, my longtime editor and friend. *The Book of Judges* would not be the book it is nor would it have been possible without the sage advice, guidance, gentle prodding, encouragement, counsel, and most of all, skilled editing and rewriting that Catherine provided. This book is exponentially better because of her hand on the steering wheel along with mine.

To Kelly Jacobson and Brenda Ploeger, my indispensable assistants. Kelly and Brenda kept me well organized so I was able to focus on the things that matter most. They offered tireless encouragement and support throughout every phase of this book's production.

Finally, to each of the judges and justices who contributed essays for *The Book of Judges*, I extend my deepest thanks. It has been my honor to play a role in sharing these candid, compelling writings with the public and judicial aspirants alike. It is my hope that your stories will inspire others to follow in your footsteps for years to come.

Contents

The One Among the Many

Jeffrey L. Goodman

"Are you the one among the many?"

I routinely had this unspoken question in mind when meeting with attorneys who were considering a career in the judiciary. Over the past 28 years, I have attended numerous such meetings, serving on judicial nominating commissions at both the state and the federal level and offering informal guidance on the judicial nominating process to interested attorneys. In collaboration with my fellow commissioners, I have helped nominate and appoint members of the Iowa Supreme Court, the Iowa Court of Appeals, the Fifth Judicial District, and the United States District Courts in the State of Iowa. I also serve on a federal advisory committee whose members recommend judges for assignment to the United States Court of Appeals for the Eighth Circuit. Though I have been a trial lawyer for nearly 40 years and could not have chosen a career better suited to my skill set and personality, I regard my efforts to help bring excellent applicants to the bench my most significant contribution to the legal profession.

My involvement in judicial nominations and appointments began informally. Long before I was elected to serve on the District Court Nominating Commission, I wrote letters of endorsement for applicants, usually fellow attorneys who were friends or acquaintances. I was one of dozens who provided such letters, as the prevailing wisdom held that the more recommendation letters one had from the legal community, the better one's chances of success. It was always exhilarating to see which applicants made it through the process and gained admission to the bench.

When I moved from advocating on behalf of friends and colleagues to helping decide who would serve the public from the bench, I sought to school myself on the process and its intricacies. I read as much as I could find, which was surprisingly little, save for discourses on the traits of great judges going all the way back to Socrates, Plato, and Aristotle.

Before long I had a chance to test my fresh knowledge. Shortly after my election to the nominating commission, a vacancy arose on the district court bench. We commissioners were called to duty. This was the first of many vacancies during my initial tenure from 1996 to 2002, a busy period that saw many judges retire. Our commission nominated applicants who embodied qualities essential for the bench: humility, discernment, a strong work ethic, impeccable character, adherence to the rule of law, and a temperament given to patience, decisiveness, and fairness. Yet I always looked for an additional quality, a certain *je ne sais quoi* that answered the question, *Are you the one among the many?*

After all, every field of applicants seeking nomination had each declared themselves to be a cut above the rest. They had to maintain a delicate tension between hubris and humility, balancing the confidence necessary to pursue the office against the certainty that the process, long and labyrinthine, might not go as desired. Several applicants would possess not only the necessary qualifications but also that special "it factor" that makes an excellent judge. But with only two slots available, commissioners were tasked with the difficult task of narrowing the field. For these and many other reasons, it is not uncommon for aspirants to apply several times before being selected.

Given the great responsibility and power bestowed on judicial officers, the commissions I served on took their vetting responsibilities seriously. We sought candidates who were not applying out of weariness with client representation or as a career detour, or even because a persuasive voice had encouraged them to apply. We looked for those who were responding to a deep sense of calling, a conviction that their best and highest act of service would be carried out from the bench.

Even as a young attorney, I was awed by those who donned the black robe. To me, the judicial office is akin to a sacred vocation, requiring adherence to the rule of law even when it conflicts with one's personal views or desires. And like all callings, it is not without sacrifice: judging often entails isolation, public scrutiny, and criticism, not to mention financial trade-offs compared to private practice. Yet judges show up daily because they cannot imagine doing otherwise.

What leads a lawyer to feel worthy of joining this venerable company and to take on its awesome responsibilities? How do individuals confirm that they truly are called and qualified to rise from the ranks of the many to become the one to preside?

Beyond a few bare-minimum requirements—such as being a licensed attorney and under the age of 72—applicants receive scant guidance and are left virtually on their own to puzzle out the necessary steps while in the midst of taking them. In a world where nearly everything comes with instructions, or at least a how-to video on YouTube, it has long astonished me that this most consequential of public endeavors stands alone in its dearth of worthwhile advice. An internet search on the judicial nomination process yields results on controversial topics such as the Robert Bork nomination, the Clarence Thomas hearings, and the second confirmation hearing of Justice Brett Kavanaugh, along with a few obscure articles from which a persistent seeker can glean a few nuggets of wisdom. But what about help for those who wonder whether they should even apply?

Those aspiring to serve on the bench deserve a reliable guidebook. So I set out to make one. This book was born of a desire to demystify the judicial nomination and selection process and to provide guidance for applicants inspired by a sense of calling who also need concrete, actionable advice.

Originally, this book was to be a straightforward guide for judicial hopefuls. As I sought contributions from various distinguished judges, though, so many said yes that the project became much more expansive than I had anticipated—so much so that what I had envisioned as one book grew into two. In this volume (*Perspectives from the Bench*), you will find the collective wisdom of 66 experienced and dedicated judges, representing more than one thousand years of aggregate experience as lawyers and just shy of one thousand aggregate years as judges. The companion volume (*The Pathway to the Bench*), scheduled for publication in late 2027, will offer a step-by-step guide on how to navigate the judicial nomination and appointment process. Although each volume stands on its own, together they will give the most complete set of practical guidance ever assembled on what it takes to prepare for the bench, make it successfully through the nomination and selection process, and be an effective colleague and decision maker once you are appointed.

To the judges who contributed, I offer my heartfelt thanks. Your dedication to justice and public service is an inspiration, and your essays are a testament to the vital role of the judiciary in upholding the rule of law.

What Lies Ahead

Jeffrey L. Goodman

The Book of Judges is meant to be read sequentially and in full, but for those of you who prefer to turn straight to the topics that interest you most, or for those who would just like a little more detail about what lies ahead, this brief overview is for you. In Chapter 1, Senior Judge David Hansen sets the stage by elucidating what it really means to serve the public as a judge. He reflects upon the awesome powers that are bestowed on judges, and offers insight born of his decades of experience on the state and federal benches.

From there you will hear from two district court judges and one senior judge—Alan Heavens, Kevin McKeever, and Richard Doyle respectively—who describe what can be a confounding transition from "advocate to umpire." By all accounts, there is an enormous difference between being a zealous advocate for your clients and a neutral arbiter who must rule decisively and with fairness and impartiality. These judges offer advice for how to manage the transition from lawyer to judge—an act not only of the intellect but of the imagination as your self-perception, your professional identity, and your mandate must all undergo a transfiguration. Will you be able to complete such a metamorphosis? Their insight will help you determine the answer.

On a more practical level, one of the most pressing questions for anyone who is considering the bench is, "Do I have the necessary experience and skills to be a judge?" This is a broad topic that extends far beyond matters of education, publications, clerkships, and trial experience. We are fortunate to have a wealth of knowledge in Chapter 3. Retired Justice Brent Appel offers a masterful overview of the qualities that both trial and appellate judges need to be most effective—as well as what judicial aspirants can do to best prepare. Retired Associate Judge Romonda Belcher issues a pertinent reminder that the judge is often the sole representative of the justice system many people encounter, and thus bears an outsized responsibility to rule with fairness and exercise their discretion wisely. Judge Andrew Chappell confides that the "dirty little secret" of becoming a judge is that you are instantly expected to know what you are doing, despite having precious little training beforehand. Not to worry—he provides a list of cogent tips on how to "get yourself right" before taking your seat on the bench. Judge Patrick McElyea highlights the importance of openness for being a good judge—openness to new ideas, experiences, and tools, to feedback and continual self-improvement, and to handling whatever a particular day requires of you, even when it is inconvenient or unpleasant. While acknowledging that it is impossible to gain deep expertise in every subject that would be useful to you on the bench, Judge Christopher Polking offers some helpful tips to gain a wide swath of knowledge in a relatively short period of time—some of them from surprising sources. In an essay that is a study in clear, concise communication, Judge Paul Scott identifies the key attributes required to be not just a competent judge, but one who is worthy of this "highest calling." Finally, Judge Joseph Seidlin memorably relates how curiosity is "the most vital of skills" for a judge, and the necessary ingredient to make the job fulfilling over the long term.

Chapter 4 moves into the expectations that are placed upon judges from day one. Judge Joel Barrows highlights the forces that can undermine judicial independence, as well as how to avoid them. Judge Zachary Hindman expounds upon the "virtue" of judicial humility as it manifests in the personal, professional, and institutional aspects of the office. Noting Justice Scalia's wise observation that mistaking one's own predilections for the law is the worst pitfall a judge can face, Hindman makes the case for humility as the powerful corrective. Senior Judge Sean McPartland poignantly reflects on maintaining the high bar of judicial excellence while juggling the challenges of a relentless schedule, the erosion of respect for the judiciary, and an escalation in the tensions and stressors that trial judges often endure. Despite these challenges, he says, "the work is important and extremely rewarding," a sentiment echoed by many contributors. Judge Thomas Murphy poses an interesting question to judicial aspirants: do you want to do judge stuff or do you just want to be a judge? In other words, do you want to put in the hard and often unheralded work of judging, or do you want to put on a black robe and be addressed as "Your Honor"? From this rather tongue-in-cheek premise, Judge Murphy offers a mini master class in how to be a good judge who does good "judge stuff." And for anyone who wonders how extensively their life will change after becoming a judge, Judge Dustria Relph's title alone has the answer: "Congratulations! Everything is Different Now." She describes the massive transformations that take place in one's personal as well as professional life—even down to how humorous you are perceived to be.

Chapter 5 is devoted to helping you determine which type of judgeship suits you best. Retired Judge Richard Blane poses a list of self-reflection questions that can help you discern if you are more suited for the trial or appellate bench. Retired Judge Randy Hefner explains why, "at the ripe old age of 57," he sought a district court judge appointment—as well as why he was "particularly unsuited" for a position on the appellate court. Chief Judge Michael Huppert follows in kind, though he explains why he was particularly suited for the job of district court judge rather than the appellate court. Justice David May and Judge Robin Rosenbaum teamed up to write an informative overview of the duties required for both trial and appellate judges, leaving the reader to decide where they would prefer to apply their skills. In the final essay of this chapter, Judge Michael Shubatt describes why and how he found his home on the trial bench, a job he counts as a "rare opportunity" to serve his community in a unique way.

Chapter 6 describes how private practice experience benefits the judicial office, while Chapter 7 offers the same insights from the perspective of government lawyers. Initially Judge Myron Gookin worried if he had what it took to be a judge, but quickly discovered that 28 years in private practice enabled him to easily acclimate to his new role. Judges John Haney and David Odekirk both describe how their busy and intensely varied private practice experiences were invaluable for their service as district court judges, while Judge Julie Schumacher recounts how her experience as a general practitioner in a rural county prepared her for both the trial court *and* the appellate bench. Similarly, Judge Sharon Soorholtz Greer credits the "very diverse and varied" experience she obtained as a private general practice trial lawyer with preparing her well to be an appellate judge. Finally, Justice Thomas Waterman describes how he routinely uses skills he gained in private practice—such as urgency, humility, diplomacy, and writing with accuracy and clarity—on the Iowa Supreme Court.

In Chapter 7, Judge Tyler Buller writes movingly about his love for his former role as a government prosecutor and now as a judge for the court of appeals, citing the commonalities between them: ensuring accountability, fidelity to the law, and embracing the institutions that uphold democracy. Judge Margaret Reyes found that her duties as a government lawyer lent her a familiarity with the duties of being a judge; indeed it is what attracted her to the judicial office in the first place. Senior Judge Karen Romano describes how her experience in a county prosecutor office eased her transition from advocate to neutral decision maker, and how the self-sufficiency skills she gained as a prosecutor were an invaluable asset on the bench. Chief Judge C. J. Williams agrees that serving as a government attorney eased his transition to the bench, adding that contrary to expectation, such experience may provide "no finer means" for avoiding bias against criminal defendants.

Though it is true that every judge makes it to the bench by a unique path, Chapter 8 offers a collection of some of the more unconventional means judges took to get there. Despite being told repeatedly that his background as a civil rights and federal criminal defense attorney and his lack of political connections meant he had "no chance" of being selected for a federal district judgeship, former Chief Judge Mark Bennett made it through a pool of 70+ applicants and landed "this best job in the world." He recounts how it happened, and offers six valuable lessons he learned from the experience. Former Chief Judge Arthur Gamble knew from a very young age he wanted to be a lawyer, and thought he would remain a lawyer until his retirement. Even after his own mother suggested he was more suited to the judiciary than the practice of law he demurred—until a local vacancy unexpectedly became available and the Governor appointed him, despite his relative youth and inexperience. Former Chief Judge John Jarvey describes how he went to law school with the intention of becoming a tax attorney, but a professor's suggestion that he apply for a judicial internship set him on an eventual path to become a magistrate, and later, a federal district court judge. Finally, retired Judge Eliza Ovrom chronicles how a reporting assignment at a Minneapolis courtroom changed her entire career trajectory from journalism to law.

Chapter 9 contains a wealth of compelling tales from judges and justices who relate what surprised them most about being a member of the judiciary. Chief Judge Lars Anderson found that instead of being socially isolating, judging offered him a rich and fulfilling social life. Retired Judge Rob Blink offers an entertaining and unvarnished view of all "the great unknowns of judging." Former Chief and Senior Judge Duane Hoffmeyer discusses the many ways his life suddenly changed after becoming a judge, while Justice Edward Mansfield describes how he was unprepared for how political being a supreme court justice can be. Former Chief Judge Robert Pratt confesses that he found no less than "everything" surprising about serving as a judge, and that indeed, the surprises never end. With his 30 years of experience as an attorney, Senior Judge Michael Schilling did not anticipate how many revelations awaited him on the bench, but he learned to relish each one as an inimitable opportunity for growth. Judge Leonard Strand offers a valuable cautionary perspective: the office will confer upon you the weighty responsibility of issuing decisions with life-altering consequences for a defendant as well as their loved ones, and in daily life, judging can expose you to certain social and personal safety risks. Judge Ian Thornhill explains how "good lawyering makes good judging," and why this realization initially surprised him. Finally, Chief Judge Patrick Tott delivers an excellent reminder about the need for judges to put their personal feelings aside and always rule according to the law's requirements. Doing so is not always easy, he observes, but it is what your oath and your obligation to the system requires.

Chapter 10 turns to a matter of great importance for all judges—how to handle difficult decisions—beginning with the realization that what you thought to be difficult may turn out to be something entirely different. Judge Paul Ahlers certainly learned this when ruling in a custody battle to decide the fate of a flea-ridden cat named Felix. Retired Judge Bob Hanson and former Chief Justice Marsha Ternus, meanwhile, faced what many assumed would be a difficult decision involving the historic *Varnum v. Brien* case, but both independently averred that based upon the clarity of the law, the decision itself was one of the easiest of their careers. Judge Jeffrey Farrell candidly describes the challenges of maintaining consistent decision making while managing a high-volume docket, and Justice Dana Oxley relates how staying in one's judicial lane, by which she means being impartial and principled, can alleviate some of the difficulty of making challenging or controversial decisions.

Many contributors noted the fundamental necessity of excellent writing skills, and Chapter 11 is devoted to the value of the written word. Judge Sarah Crane outlines three balancing acts every district court judge must achieve in order to issue a ruling efficiently, mindfully, and with clarity. Judge Stephen Locher dives into a topic not often associated with the judicial office: humor in judicial writing. Should a judge *ever* attempt to be funny? Read on to find out. Justice Matthew McDermott, meanwhile, explains why writing for a nonlawyer audience satisfies the needs not only of litigants, but of researchers, the media, and even lawyers and judges, too. Finally, Chief Judge Mary Tabor, former editor-in-chief of *The Daily Iowan* and AP reporter, explores thc parallels between legal writing and news reporting, and offers tips of the trade for enhancing your legal writing.

It goes without saying that working with good colleagues is essential for any job, but the four judges who cover this topic in Chapter 12 examine it through the lens of the judiciary. Noting the long friendship between Justices Ruth Bader Ginsburg and Antonin Scalia despite their sharply different ideologies, Judge Gina Badding emphasizes the need to disagree without being disagreeable among deliberative bodies such as the appellate courts. Former Chief and Senior Judge Thomas Bower offers nine key practices for being a good colleague, no matter what type of organization you are in. Retired Judge Michael Moon cautions against the loss of the rich culture, history, and lore of the legal profession that can happen in the absence of ongoing collegial relationships—and does his part to counter this loss by regaling the reader with comical stories from his decades-long career. Judge Shawn Showers praises his colleagues and mentors and stresses the important role that empathy and humanity should play in judicial decision making. Supportive colleagues can also, he adds, help safeguard against the cynicism, burnout, and vicarious trauma fatigue that can come about from exposure to chronic stress, disturbing cases, and the weight of consequential decision making.

In Chapter 13, three judges address the ever-popular topic of judicial philosophy. Judge David Faith opens the discussion by asking whether he, a district court judge serving a rural district, even needs a judicial philosophy. He makes the case that every judge does, as it provides a framework for being consistent in interpreting legal writing, and helps prevent judicial bias of all kinds. Judge Roger Sailer acknowledges that an orienting framework from which one makes judicial decisions is necessary, but argues against the notion of "having" a judicial philosophy if that means having a fixed framework, especially at the beginning of your career. Instead, he says, a sound judicial philosophy must be grounded in experience and real-life utility, and thus, open to change and growth. Judge Samuel Thumma, meanwhile, attests that "judicial philosophy" can mean many things, and generously shares ten discrete judicial philosophies that have helped him over the course of his career.

Many readers will find Chapter 14 to be the most inspiring of the book. That's because it's composed of a pair of remarkable chapters by two jurists—Judge Mary Chicchelly and Chief Justice Susan Christensen—who applied to the bench multiple times before they were selected. With humor and good cheer, Judge Chicchelly shares the story of repeated applications, rejections, and ultimately, triumphs, in becoming first a district court judge and then an appellate judge. A rejection, she points out, is not necessarily a reflection on one's fitness or qualifications; instead, it merely means someone else was chosen this particular time around. Judge Chicchelly and Chief Justice Christensen agree that if you are called to serve the public in this manner, do not get discouraged if you are initially rejected and do not give up, no matter how many times it takes. In the case of Chief Justice Christensen, it took 14 attempts to become a Supreme Court Justice, and so it is no accident that her essay appears in Chapter 14.

The final chapter of Volume I, on deciding whether the robe will be a good fit, will inspire you to engage in some deeply honest self-assessment. Senior Judge Michael Mullins leads you through a series of personal reflection questions that will help determine your suitability for the bench, and underscores key realities about the daily life of judging with which you must contend. Judge David Nelmark's essay is notable for its bracing candor and keen insight into the differences between being a great lawyer and a great judge. It is must-read material for anyone contemplating the bench. Finally, Judge John Sandy illustrates how the quest to determine one's suitability for the bench begins and ends in self-awareness. He closes with three key pieces of advice for those who are considering the bench.

Chapter 1

The Essence of Judging

It's Rooted in Antiquity

David R. Hansen
Judge, U.S. Court of Appeals
for the 8th Circuit (Ret.)

Judging is hard work, especially given the high standards for it held by free societies. Writing about its essence is even more difficult.

It is important to understand that judging's essence is distinct from its goal. The goal is to bring legally correct endings to disputes that have defied all other means of resolution. Describing its essence is considerably harder. The essence of judging is the protocol that a judge is expected, indeed required, to employ in order to reach a decision that inspires public confidence in the fairness of both the system and the judge. It is to that end that Codes of Judicial Conduct, Canons of Judicial Ethics, and Rules of Court were created and continue to exist as regulators of the human tendency towards unfairness in the administration of the law.

In my view, the two most important judicial functions in resolving legal disputes are, to no one's surprise, the determination of what the facts of the case really are (not necessarily which party's version of the facts is correct), and the ascertainment of the controlling law governing the resolution of the dispute in front of the judge. Each function can be heavily daunting depending on the extent of the evidence in the record, and the complexity of the statutes, regulations, and case law involved. When it is a capital-C Constitutional issue that requires judging, the burden is greatly enhanced. In the context of both trial judging and appellate judging, what is the skill set a person must have and employ to give justice the best chance to emerge from the dry application of the law? Much has been written over the millennia in an effort to answer that question.

The best synopsis of those traits of judicial character which represent the essence of judging is ancient in origin. Some 2,500 years ago Socrates gave the following advice to those who were then judges and to those who aspire to be judges even today: "Four things belong to a judge: to hear courteously; to answer wisely; to consider soberly; and to decide impartially." These four attributes of judicial behavior are, of course, interrelated; how can a judge "answer wisely" the questions raised in the litigation, at trial, or on the appeal if one hasn't "consider[ed] soberly" all of the admissible evidence offered by the parties? And one certainly cannot "consider soberly" that which may have been missed by failing to "hear courteously" the witnesses' testimony and the lawyers' arguments. Do these important traits just naturally occur in those few members of a free society who find themselves discharging judicial responsibilities, or can they be acquired first by learning what they are and practicing them in our own private lives outside the realm of the law? Within the realm of the law, every lawyer, whether practicing, counseling clients, trying cases, or teaching soon learns that listening closely, carefully, and courteously to a client's story told across the desk, or to an opposing counsel's arguments, or to a law student's questions yields big dividends in truly understanding the legal and personal issues involved, spotting the holes and weaknesses that exist in each side's proposals, and using the nuanced opportunities (which inevitably occur, if we are wise enough to see them) to resolve the dispute in an honest and forthright manner.

An effective judge knows that there is always the other side of the story, and she understands that she must delay forming her dispositive judgment about either the facts or the law until both sides have had a full and fair opportunity to be heard. In an essay entitled "Of Judicature" Sir Francis Bacon (1561-1626), the very first designated Queen's Counsel, opined "[i]t is no grace to a judge first to find that which he might have heard in due time from the bar."

"To answer wisely" can be done only after one has "consider[ed] soberly" the whole of the admissible record before the judge in a calm, deliberate, and thoughtful manner giving each party's arguments the due consideration and weight which they merit. It also means that the judge's answer must be done in a respectful tone of voice while avoiding, to the maximum extent possible, legal jargon[1], or any belittling of the losing party's position unless it is so far beyond the pale that it can be correctly called frivolous as a matter of law. However the decision is tendered to the participants, the parties are entitled to an explanation of the judge's reasoning. Even more importantly, the words explaining the reasoning must be carefully chosen, avoiding the use of street talk or colloquialisms, but by using language that the parties can readily understand without the necessity of their lawyer's translation or interpretation. It is well that the judge considers carefully how the written transcript or record of his comments and judgment will appear in the cold hard print in front of a reader the next day. That is particularly important when the reader is an appellate judge considering whether an assignment of error has any validity. The appearance of flippancy must be studiously avoided. When drafting an opinion, it was always my practice to write so that the losing party knew why they had lost and to demonstrate to them that their side of the case had received due judicial attention and consideration. Taking the time to explain why a decision was made also provides a reviewing court with another opportunity to consider whether the judge's final judgment is deserving of affirmation or reversal. Beware verbosity in all its forms. In an oft quoted phrase, Sir

Francis Bacon also said, "[p]atience and gravity of bearing is an essential part of justice; and an overspeaking judge is no well-tuned cymbal." Neither is an overwriting judge. It was my experience as both a trial and appellate judge that the winning side really didn't care why they had won; the victory itself was more important. The losing side will read the judge's opinion in its entirety, and every page will smart. The merciful judge will minimize the sting: better to be laconic than loquacious.

"To consider soberly" is, as noted above, a necessary part of "answering wisely." It means more than just being in full possession of one's unaffected and unaltered cognitive abilities. One could substitute the word "seriously" for "soberly" and do no damage to the intent of the admonition. "Soberly" also requires impartiality (whether innate or learned), a consideration of the issues which is free from implicit or actual biases or the judge's pre-trial or pre-argument preliminary reaction to the case. The consideration which the judge gives to the case must be dispassionate, temperate, and restrained; the 18th century philosopher Edmund Burke described it as "the cold neutrality of an impartial judge."

"To decide impartially" is probably the most difficult of Socrates's four judicial attributes to successfully employ, particularly for newly commissioned judges coming to the bench from a career as an advocate where the lawyer is obligated to advance his client's cause. His focus has been on being a mercenary for his client's point of view, not on being one of society's soldiers for truth. The old adage that "the trial judge seeks the truth, the appellate judge hunts for error" continues to be believed today. To say the advocate may be "partial" is an understatement; after all he has had a financial interest (his fee) in resolving the case favorably to his client. We all know that is why courts place restrictions on how long a time period must elapse before a judge can hear cases brought by his former firm; or how soon after leaving a clerkship a former law clerk may appear on brief or argue before the court or judge for whom he or she clerked. To decide impartially means that the judge must set aside any extraneous facts or circumstances which may influence, however subtly, her decision. She must remain loyal to her oath, and that necessitates giving no consideration to friendship, prior legal relationships, any disparity in the abilities or professional reputations of counsel, the political preferences of the parties and their counsel, including the respective social or economic status of the parties. *Ex parte* communications with the parties or counsel must not occur. In short, the judge must avoid any outside influences that may, if considered, become a determining thumb on Lady Justice's scales. The judge must follow where the facts the record establishes and the applicable law lead her to make the impartial decision justice requires.

The aspiration to seek a judgeship occurs at different times for different lawyers. For some it is a thought that first arises while in law school, while for others it occurs after years of practice. For many, the decision to seek the Bench doesn't present itself until there is a vacancy that needs to be filled, and then the lawyer's personal circumstances may not permit him or her to leave a practice or firm that has been so painstakingly built. In those states where judges are still elected on a partisan ballot, the lawyer thinking about moving to the Bench may not want to enter the political arena, nor have the time or the money to mount a winning campaign. But those are practical concerns as variable as there are legally trained people thinking about becoming a judge. My concern is that before the personal practical issues are determined, the potential judicial officer must give deep and thoughtful consideration to whether he or she can discharge the heavy responsibilities that attach to the donning of the black robe. And so I offer these whisperings in the ears of all "wannabe" jurists: Am I a careful and courteous listener or am I prone to interrupt? Do I frame my answers carefully when questioned or am I a "stream of consciousness" responder? Do I have any serious difficulty expressing myself or my ideas in writing? When I speak, do I engage my mind first and then my mouth? Am I patient and respectful with others with whom I may disagree? (A very important attribute to the deliberations and collegiality of an appellate court!) Do I have the ability not only to perceive the other side of the story but also to give it intelligent, fair, thoughtful, and careful consideration, or do I quickly jump to final conclusions when deciding important questions? Could I handle and live with the fact that my decisions will affect a person's life for decades—or in the states and the federal government which both authorize and impose the death penalty, result in its termination?

Do I have the necessary qualifications of experience and knowledge to do the judge's job?

These are but a few of the many hard questions that must be addressed forthrightly by anyone considering a judicial appointment at any age or stage of their legal career. For most of my life, obtaining a judgeship was considered the capstone to a legal career, not to be sought until one had acquired years of wide-ranging experience practicing law, and the seasoning and scar tissue that come with it. From my perspective, the trend now seems to be for both Presidents and Governors to appoint judicial officers, both trial and appellate, at younger ages in order to extend the time a particular judicial philosophy has a voice on the Bench. I leave to others to debate the merits of that practice.

Finally, although Socrates did yeoman's work in reducing the essence of judicial temperament to four elements, never forget the parable of the blind men describing an elephant. One takes hold of the animal's trunk and concludes it is a giant snake, another presses on its rib cage and thinks it is a solid wall, and so on. The essence of judging is much like that. Socrates's four elements are an attempt to describe an ineffable concept. It is a heroic beginning of understanding: it is not meant to be the end of our inquiry. Muse on it yourself, and humbly begin to explore this "brave new world that has such [cases] in't!"

If lightning does strike and you are successful in your quest to be on the Bench, following the Athenian's advice will help ensure that your epitaph may be a high compliment: "he (or she) was an able judge."

Chapter 2

From Advocate to Umpire

The Near Perfect Umpire

Alan T. Heavens
Judge, Iowa District Court

Chief Justice John Roberts famously compared being a judge to being an umpire during his Senate confirmation hearing in 2005. You may recall him pledging to "remember that it's my job to call balls and strikes, and not to pitch or bat."[1]

It's true that an umpire neutrally applies the rules of baseball like a judge neutrally applies the laws of our state and country. But all umpires and all judges are not the same. Some are good at their job. Some aren't. Chief Justice Roberts' metaphor only addresses what each position requires and leaves a key question unanswered—what does it take to do the job well?

Imagine a knee-high pitch thrown over the middle of the plate. Every umpire must call that pitch a strike. And every umpire knows a pitch that's thrown three feet away from the plate, like the first few pitches that Ricky "Wild Thing" Vaughn threw in the movie "Major League,"[2] must be called balls. Umpires don't need much training or expertise to get those calls right. Those are the easy ones.

Now imagine a pitch that's down and away on the outermost edge of the strike zone. The perfect spot for a pitcher . . . if the umpire calls the pitch a strike. If the umpire says "ball," then the result is no different than the pitch that went over the catcher's head. How accurately an umpire calls the close pitches will reveal whether the umpire is elite, average, or so biased that he should consider another profession.

In 2021, Neil Greenberg, a *Washington Post* staff writer who specializes in sports analytics, wrote a column called "MLB Umpires Are Squeezing the Strike Zone, and It's Hurting Some Teams More Than Others."[3] Greenberg noted that Major League Baseball started using a pitch tracking device called Pitchf/x in the 2006 playoffs. Pitchf/x shows whether a pitch was a ball or a strike and gives data analysts like TruMedia the information they need to determine who the best and worst umpires are.

Umpire Edwin Moscoso had the least-friendly strike zone to pitchers in 2021. According to TruMedia, Moscoso called 108 balls on pitches that Pitchf/x labeled as strikes. Umpire Doug Eddings had the most-friendly strike zone for pitchers in 2021. He called 113 pitches strikes that should have been called balls. TruMedia found that Umpire Chris Segal had a different strike zone for each team.

Every bad call by an umpire has a shocking impact. For hitters facing an 0-1 count (zero balls and one strike), if the second pitch is called a ball, then the hitter's expected batting average is .339. As a reference, Hall of Famer Tony Gwynn is considered one of the best hitters of his generation. His career batting average is .338. If the same second pitch is called a strike, then the hitter's expected batting average is .142. Most Major League Baseball players who hit .142 are sent to the minors or released. Greenberg found that pitchers who receive a favorable strike zone make $700,000 to $1.3 million more per season than otherwise similarly situated pitchers. A team that doesn't receive any extra strike calls wins their game about 50% of the time. Compare that to a team that receives ten or more extra strike calls in a game. That team wins 74.2% of the time. Only one team in almost 150 years of Major League history (the 1906 Chicago Cubs) had a season-long winning percentage better than 74.2%.

While bad calls by umpires change games, bad calls by judges change lives. A bad call in a sentencing hearing either deprives a defendant of their liberty when probation was the better option or puts the community at risk by releasing a dangerous person into it. A bad call in a custody case might deprive a parent of time with their child, time that they will never get back. A bad call in a civil case could financially devastate the losing party. A bad call in a constitutional case means the most important document in our legal system was not honored. A lot is staked on the judge making all of those calls correctly. And all judges, like all umpires, will make some bad calls.

Some of the most difficult decisions that umpires and judges make are made immediately. Was that 100-mile-per-hour pitch a ball or strike? Should an objection be sustained or overruled? The answer is expected instantaneously. Human error will never be eliminated from those decisions if a human is doing the job. But a good judge, like a good umpire, understands why some *avoidable* errors are made and learns how to sidestep the traps that too many in the profession fall into.

Research indicates that some umpires have a familiarity bias—older pitchers get the benefit of the doubt more than younger pitchers. The same principle may apply to some judges—familiarity with a long-time attorney may give that attorney's client an advantage, or disadvantage, that's nowhere to be found in any law. There's also a concept known as the "compassionate-umpire effect" where the strike zone gets up to 50 percent bigger when a pitcher is struggling.[4] Might some judges be tempted to decide a dispute in favor of the more sympathetic litigant regardless of what the law says?

The list of potential biases that lead to bad calls is seemingly endless. Fortunately, all judges in Iowa receive training and continuing education aimed at identifying and rooting out unconscious bias. But good judges don't just eliminate actual bias, they eliminate perceived bias by not doing anything that creates the impression that a case was, or will be, resolved based on anything other than what the law says.

Imagine a plaintiff who files a lawsuit against a defendant based on a theory of liability which has been unequivocally rejected by the supreme court. At the summary judgment hearing, the judge smilcs and nods approvingly when the defendant's attorney speaks before frowning and glaring during the plaintiff's attorney's presentation. The judge then interrupts the plaintiff's attorney after allowing the defendant's attorney to speak without interruption. Months later, the judge issues a 70-page ruling dismissing the plaintiff's claim. An explanation of why the claim was dismissed is on page 32, sandwiched between an extensive procedural history and factual background on one end and summaries of several cases from other jurisdictions on the other end.

That case is the equivalent of three strikes right down the middle of the plate. An at bat which was resolved by the pitches that the pitcher threw, not the close calls that the umpire made. But the demeanor of the judge at the hearing, and the length and density of the ruling, probably left the plaintiff in the dark about why his claim was thrown out. That's a mistake entirely of the judge's own making.

To avoid this error, a judge first needs to have a poker face[5] in the courtroom. Attorneys and witnesses will occasionally do and say irritating things. That is a cast-iron guarantee in the same category as death and taxes. But those annoyances usually have nothing to do with how the law applies to the facts. An impatient judge gives the impression that emotion, instead of the law, is what drove the case to its conclusion.

A good judge also illuminates their reasoning and eliminates perceived bias by how they write. Short and clear opinions make it easy to understand the reasoning behind the decision. Brief and straightforward opinions are also more likely to be read.

Merriam Webster's Dictionary now includes an abbreviation, "TL;DR,"[6] which means "too long; didn't read." A one-page ruling is likely to be read entirely by everyone involved. The odds that the entire opinion will be read decreases with every page after the first. And while most contested cases are too complicated to thoroughly resolve in one page, most cases are also not so complex that they require a ruling which spans dozens of pages. Many people will quit reading before the end. Some will be so intimidated by the page count that they won't attempt to read *any* of the decision.

What happens when people don't read the judge's decision? The same thing that happens when a person reads a decision but doesn't understand it—the reader invents their own reason for the ruling. And the reasons that an unsuccessful litigant or attorney invents won't be flattering to the judge. One contrived reason from an unsuccessful participant may be that the judge is biased because of race, gender, religion, sexual orientation, or disability status.

Incomprehensible rulings open the door for this type of accusation—an accusation that had better always be false. A judge is not doing their job well when he or she does, says, or writes anything that gives the impression that an accusation of bias might be legitimate.

A concise and unambiguous ruling can still be misrepresented by anyone who is not happy with the result. But the odds are much better that the judge is seen as faithfully following the law when the ruling is short and crystal-clear.

When one side misstates the law in their briefing or oral argument, a good judge's ruling will clearly outline the law and then accurately and neutrally outline the litigant's argument. Putting the law and a legally unsupported argument side-by-side makes it easy to understand why the requested relief can't be granted. It's not you, it's not me (the judge), it's the law.

Removing every unnecessary word from a decision is important because it only takes one word to create an impression of bias. Cutting the excess is also an effective way to avoid making "undue personal observations or criticisms of litigants, judges and lawyers," a trait that attorneys rate judges on in the Iowa Bar Association's biannual judicial performance evaluation.[7]

To conclude his article about umpires, Greenberg wrote that "[t]here are few more enduring—some might even say charming—aspects of baseball than arguments over balls and strikes. They're expressed in a pitcher's glare, a batter's eye-roll, an R-rated chirp from the dugout." While many would agree with Greenberg, his observation about this aspect of baseball may not be true for much longer.

Starting in 2023, every Triple-A minor league baseball stadium used an automated ball-strike system known as a "robotic umpire."[8] MLB Commissioner Rob Manfred (a former labor lawyer) said that using robotic umpires in the majors is being "seriously considered" for the near future. There isn't much charm in an argument with a robot. But at least no one is asking for robotic judges.

The preamble of the Iowa Code of Judicial Conduct describes our judiciary as "men and women of integrity" who independently, impartially, and competently "interpret and apply the law that governs our society."[9] In practice, this means that our society expects that judges will not be plaintiff-friendly or defendant-friendly. Society insists that judges put their personal views aside and apply the same set of laws and rules for each litigant. Judges are expected to act professionally and write clearly and concisely. The hope is that judges will get the closest calls correct most of the time. And for the missed calls, the anticipation is that each litigant will have about an equal number of errors to their benefit as errors to their detriment.

That's how judges enhance and maintain confidence in the legal system. And while there will still always be "R-rated chirp" about some decisions, a judge must make sure that the fervor is aimed at the law, not the judge.

The Transfiguration[10]

Richard H. Doyle
Senior Judge, Iowa Court of Appeals

I begin with a short story. The phone call came when I was a newly minted appellate judge. My former law partner was apoplectic. How in the world could I have concurred on a recently filed opinion favoring the insurance industry? After all, we fought for years to advance the plaintiffs' side of the issue (now long forgotten) addressed in the opinion. In losing his motion in district court, it was particularly stinging to him when the judge mentioned the opinion and pointed out to him that if Judge Doyle, formerly a well-known plaintiffs' lawyer, signed off on the issue, it must be right.

Of course, my former partner did not know the full story behind my decision to concur. When it came time to vote on my colleague's opinion deciding the issue in favor of the defense, I was bothered. After all, I had spent much of my career in premier plaintiffs' firms advocating before district and appellate courts arguing the opposite side of the issue. So, after examining the record and parties' briefs, I spent considerable time doing extra research. In the end I was convinced my colleague's opinion correctly stated the current law and that the Iowa Supreme Court would not change it and adopt the plaintiffs' side of the issue. The advocate in me could have gone off on a toot and written a dissent—which would have been futile. Instead, the judge in me accepted established precedent and I then concurred. But after being so thoroughly excoriated, I began to doubt myself. I hit the books once again, and concluded again I had made the right decision. It is just one example of how I had successfully transitioned from advocate to impartial judicial officer.

I am a senior judge on the Iowa Court of Appeals,[11] a nine-judge intermediate court of appeals. I was a plaintiffs' personal injury lawyer for over 30 years before being appointed to the appellate court in 2008. Advocacy was at the core of my practice. My mentors instilled in me the values of practicing with honesty, courtesy, civility, class, and compassion. All characteristics of a good advocate—and a good judge. Following these precepts, I established a good rapport with other plaintiffs' lawyers, the defense bar, and the bench. Continuing to follow those precepts eased my transition from advocate to judge. Although I was responsible for the appellate work in my law firms, I found out quickly that being an appellate judge is quite different from being an appellate advocate. Just becoming a judge in itself is life-altering. It was odd at first. For example, someone would call me "judge" and I would look around to see whom they were addressing, for it couldn't have been me.

Was the transition from trial lawyer to appellate judge difficult? No. I embraced the change. A fair portion of my practice was devoted to appellate work. And the transition was probably a little easier because of my role in my law firm. I was the "peacemaker." When attorneys (especially those with big egos) got sideways with each other during litigation, I was often called in to calm the waters. Becoming an appellate judge had been a dream of mine for many years. I applied for a position on the court of appeals seven times over a 15-year period. I was nominated twice before the sun, moon, stars, and planets finally aligned, and I was appointed after my third nomination. Once appointed I felt as if most of the stress in my life had been lifted from my shoulders. As a trial lawyer, my time was dictated mostly by others—the court, opposing counsel, clients, and law partners. It was difficult, if not impossible, to maintain a healthy work/life balance. I can't remember taking more than one or two two-week vacations during my private practice years. Many times, when I was at the office, particularly during evenings and on weekends, I felt like I should be at home with my family. On the other hand, when I was at home, I often felt like I should be at the office working on pressing matters. All those stomach-churning anxieties dissipated upon my appointment. Although the workload of the court is high—some say staggering—I felt like I had control over my time. The legendary collegiality of the court eased my transition. Our court culture encourages family and recreational activities. I now enjoy those activities without regret.

Although when I was appointed there was no judicial training available because of budget constraints, I had eight seasoned colleagues and an extraordinary staff to guide my way. And because of various constraints, both practical and legal, the transition from advocate to impartial appellate judicial officer was not as difficult as one might imagine.

A practical constraint is in how we decide cases. Most of our decisions are decided by three-judge panels. So, before filing, my work is scrutinized and voted on by my two panel members and then reviewed by the remaining judges and staff. If I crossed that line from impartial judge to advocate, the other judges, or staff, would rein me in.

We also have legal constraints. The court's mandate "is to dispose justly of a high volume of cases" Iowa Ct. R. 21.11 (2024). Most of the cases transferred to us by the supreme court are routine cases that may be decided by applying the facts to established precedent. The supreme court generally retains cases with issues of first impression and important public interest and constitutional issues. We are restrained from ignoring or disturbing our supreme court's precedent. So our job is to not reason why, but to do and apply: "We are not at liberty to overturn Iowa Supreme Court precedent" *State v. Hastings*, 466 N.W.2d 697, 700 (Iowa Ct.App.1990). And as the Iowa Supreme Court has pointed out, "If our previous holdings are to be overruled, we should ordinarily prefer to do it ourselves" *State v. Hughes,* 457 N.W.2d 25, 28 (Iowa Ct.App.1990) (citation omitted).

A real challenge in not becoming an advocate for a party is when that party is underrepresented. Although tempting, we cannot make up for poor lawyering by becoming an advocate for a party, which an abundance of legal precedent makes clear. "[A]ppellate judges must not be cast in the role of advocates for a party who fails to comply with court rules and inadequately presents an appeal" In re Detention of West, No. 11-1545, 2013 WL 988815, at *4 (Iowa Ct. App. Mar. 13, 2013). In facing a deficient brief, the supreme court said, "[t]o reach the merits of the case would require us to assume a partisan role and undertake the appellant's research and advocacy. This role is one we refuse to assume" *Inghram v. Dairyland* Mut. Ins. Co., 215 N.W.2d 239, 240 (Iowa 1974). "It is not appropriate for us to, and we will not, initiate research or form arguments on behalf of the appellant" *State v. Alderman*, No. 19-0278, 2020 WL 2987992, at *6 (Iowa Ct. App. June 3, 2020). "Judges cannot assume the role of a partisan advocate and do counsel's work" *State v. Coleman*, 890 N.W.2d 284, 304 (Iowa 2017) (Waterman, J., dissenting). Furthermore, "[J]udges are not like pigs, hunting for [meritorious] truffles buried in briefs" *United States v. Dunkel*, 927 F.2d 955, 956 (7th Cir. 1991). Nor will we advance arguments the parties have not made

Venckus v. City of Iowa City, 930 N.W.2d 792, 806 (Iowa 2019) (citing Dunkel). "We will not speculate on the arguments [a party] might have made and then search for legal authority and comb the record for facts to support such arguments" *Hyler v. Garner*, 548 N.W.2d 864, 876 (Iowa 1996). And as a practical matter, "He who must search a haystack for a needle is likely to end up with the attitude that the needle is not worth the search" *Brown v. Allen*, 344 U.S. 443, 537 (1953) (Jackson, J., concurring).

I cannot count the number of times I have faced inadequate briefing on an issue or the lack of raising an issue on appeal. So often have I said to myself, "If only the party had raised a certain argument, I could adopt it and rule in their favor." As an advocate I would do that; but as an impartial decider I cannot. For example, several years ago, a legal issue of personal interest to me was presented in an appeal. In my heart I wanted to reverse the district court's decision and rule for the defendant. And I could have reversed if presented with the right argument, but alas, the defendant had not made that argument. My hands were tied; I wrote my opinion to uphold the district court.

Guidance by my colleagues made the transition from trial lawyer to appellate judge almost effortless for me. And practical and legal constraints keep me from veering off track as an impartial judicial officer.

By the way, some 15 years after that hotheaded phone call, my ears are still burning.

More Akin to a Metamorphosis

Kevin McKeever
Judge, Iowa District Court

The Making of an Advocate

In our society, it is common to pick sides. In our movies, plays, television dramas, and books, we often find ourselves drawn into a feeling that we want one side to prevail over another. The side we choose can be in the form of an individual or a group of individuals, and the side we root against can likewise take the form of an individual or a group. The side we root for is commonly referred to as the protagonist, while the side we root against is known as the antagonist. In our decision to select a side to root for, we often identify certain aspects of characteristics or ideals which we consider to be good in our protagonist, and likewise we find characteristics or ideals which we find to be bad in the side we identify as the antagonist. This dichotomous approach to our media and literature is present even in childhood: Saturday morning cartoons often consist of a superhero or group of superheroes struggling to contain the nefarious designs of a supervillain or group of supervillains. It is easy to understand how as adults, we might aspire to fight for the "good guys" in a fashion that mirrors or is at least similar to the literature and media that permeate our society and culture from our earliest days.

I was an officer in the U.S. Navy for seven years prior to attending law school. My decision to attend law school was a combination of a desire to improve my educational level and provide myself with an opportunity to join a profession in which I could make a positive contribution to society. In law school, I learned about the different types of cases including civil, criminal, probate, and family law. Some face a choice of whether to engage in transactional or litigation work. For me, the choice has always been litigation of some sort. In keeping with my goal of making a positive contribution to society, I wanted to pick a side and fight for that side. Naturally, my desire was to pick a side I believed in representing and felt good about representing. I wanted to fight for the good guys.

This led me to consider both civil and criminal litigation. My first internship landed me at a law firm in Cedar Rapids. I found the work to be interesting, though not necessarily inspiring in the way that I wanted. During the summer of 1999, however, I would engage in an internship that would change my life. I accepted a job at the Johnson County Attorney's office in Iowa City, Iowa, which involved prosecuting state crimes. I found great satisfaction in the work, as I believed it enhanced the safety of my community. Additionally, I learned about the principle of exercising discretion. This great responsibility involved evaluating and considering the nuances of cases and factoring in these differences in the proposed resolution of said cases. Each day, I felt in some small way that I was working for the good guys.

What is a Neutral?

Unlike nearly every show, story, and movie, which present us with a main protagonist and a main antagonist—a good side and a bad side to root for and against, if you will—a neutral takes no sides, and applies the rules evenly to both sides. Advocates labor zealously for the side they represent, but a neutral serves the purpose of ensuring a fair contest between two parties, and works assiduously to maintain impartiality.

Our narratives offer few examples of protagonists who operate from a position of complete neutrality. Other than a judge, the closest example of any significance we may have can be seen in our sporting events, in the form of the referee. Without going into too much detail, it is fair to say that the referee is almost never the hero of any story. More likely than not, if the home team loses because of a close call, the referee will get the blame. It is interesting that the individual who has the assignment of being a neutral arbiter of the rules, to the benefit of none and detriment of none, is almost certain to be seen as the villain by the losing side. It is difficult to think of any occasion in which the referee is seen as the hero; indeed, it seems the best a referee can hope for is not to be seen as an outright villain. Their purpose is not to be the hero, but to ensure the contest is fair by applying the rules equitably to both sides.

It should be self-evident that we want some degree of neutrality with our judges. I have intentionally claimed that we want "some" degree, because I do not believe that we want 100% or computer-like neutrality. Judges are permitted some discretion to account for the fact that no two cases in our system are precisely identical. The discretion afforded to judges makes it possible for our system to incorporate an individual's experience, training, and common sense into the rulings. The principle of neutrality therefore does not mean that we want robots who will always make identical choices in each and every scenario. Rather, neutrality should mean that the decisions made by the judge are devoid of prejudices, biases, sympathies, and other emotions that are not helpful in attaining equitable results within the boundaries of the rules and laws.

The Transition

When one considers the emotional, cultural, and intellectual components of making the transition from advocate to neutral, it becomes clear that it is no easy task. Again making the analogy to sports, imagine being a lifelong fan of one team, going to games as a child, buying all of the team's apparel as a young adult, and hosting parties to celebrate your team's success as an adult. Through thick and thin, your favorite team consists of the good guys. Or, put another way, your team is the main protagonist of the story.

Then, one day, you get the call to referee the big game and your favorite team is one of the contenders. How do you find the ability to set aside emotions and do the job well? What happens if there is a close call that should be resolved against your favorite team? Can anyone objectively make that call against their favorite team, the team they have loved for decades, especially if it could make the difference between a win and a loss?

For many advocates, this is a difficult situation and can elicit a plethora of emotions. An advocate is not only a fan of their side, but also a champion. Not only does the advocate feel emotionally invested in winning the case, but they have poured their energy, time, hope, and effort into winning. An advocate often fights in this manner for one side for years or even decades, all the while fully believing that the fight is not just for the represented entity, but for the "good guys." With this level of investment, the advocate takes on the endeavor to such a degree that it becomes part of their identity. A defense attorney, in other words, is not just a defense attorney by profession, but as a significant part of who they are as a person. Likewise, the prosecutor is not just fulfilling a prosecutor's role, but being a prosecutor as a significant part of their very identity. To abandon the position of advocate and take up the mantle of the neutral referee is therefore an extremely difficult endeavor because to a certain degree, one has to redefine oneself in order to accomplish the task of making the transition.

How to Make the Transition

For over a decade, I advocated for the prosecution in a variety of cases, from traffic tickets to Class A felonies. When acting as a prosecutor, I felt there was only one thing worse than failing to convict the person responsible for committing the alleged crime, namely, convicting someone who had not committed the alleged crime. A truly good advocate for the prosecution seeks not only a win and a conviction, but justice, and justice cannot be served by convicting the wrong person and letting the guilty person escape.

Then in October of 2015, I was appointed to the bench as a district court judge for the 6th judicial district. Suddenly it was no longer my job to be an advocate but to be neutral, and the question of how to be an impartial judge was fresh in my mind. How does one go from a life dedicated to fighting for one side, to a life of being the person who ensures an equitable application of the rules for both opposing sides? How does one shed the identity of being an advocate for one side to being a neutral referee? I needed to find a way to answer these questions.

Fairly quickly, I found that there are two main factors that drive the transition from advocate to neutral. In the first instance, there is the realization that within the context of being a judge, you are the only person who can ensure a fair and equitable application of the rules. Secondly, considering this perspective, one must believe that the integrity of our system, which promises a fair and equitable venue judged by a neutral fact finder, is of paramount importance.

In order to complete the transition to neutral, it is necessary to understand that your role as advocate was a special one, which helped to ensure that the system worked as it should. The system depends on two zealous and competent advocates and one fair, equitable, and knowledgeable neutral judge. Now that your role as zealous advocate has come to a close, you must take up the mantle of your new role, which requires you to leave behind any notion of taking sides.

As a neutral judge, your favorite team can no longer be the defense or the plaintiff/prosecution. It becomes evident that you must adopt a new favorite team: the integrity of the system itself, which promises justice for all. Without that integrity and that strong commitment to impartiality, there exists a significant danger of injustices occurring in a system built upon the promise of equal justice for all. As a neutral judge, you must ensure a fair and equitable application of the rules and provide both sides with an equal chance to be heard. The failure to do so not only frustrates the purpose and intent to provide a fair chance for both parties to have their complaints heard in the individual case, it interferes with the full administration of justice. Perhaps graver still, it is also a failure of the judicial system to provide an essential function promised by our democracy. Therefore, judges must realize that they do in fact advocate for a side—the side of fairness. Without fairness, one of the cornerstones of our democracy is left more vulnerable.

In the final analysis, society demands and deserves a fair and equitable system. As humans, we are not required or expected to be perfect. However, those who accept the call to be a judge must realize that the greatest enemy to fairness and equity is a referee who refuses to fairly and equally apply the rules in an attempt to help their favorite team. To be a judge means to be a symbol of the justice system itself, one that truly seeks to deliver justice for all. And to be a good judge, one must realize that the only true "good guys" are honesty, fairness, equity, and integrity—all valued traits worth advocating for.

Chapter 3

Recommended Experience and Skills

The Qualities and Skills of Good Judges

Brent R. Appel
Justice, Iowa Supreme Court (Ret.)

A Good Judge

This essay addresses two important questions. First, what qualities should we look for in a lawyer who aspires to be a good judge? Second, once these qualities are identified, how does a lawyer develop them prior to seeking judicial appointment?[1] Before diving into these interesting questions, several caveats are in order.

First, consideration must first be given to the nature of the judicial office in question. As will be seen below, the functions of a trial judge, an intermediate appellate judge, and a judge on an appellate court of last resort are not identical and to some extent require different skill sets and outlook. Some excellent trial judges would likely do less well as appellate judges, and, conversely, some excellent appellate judges would not thrive on the trial court bench. Some lawyers, though by no means all, cover all the bases and do well in either the trial or appellate setting.

Second, it would be wrong to believe that there is only one assembly-line template for the manufacture of quality judges. Every judge has individual strengths and weaknesses. Strengths in one area may compensate for shortcomings in another. Further, rigid views on a necessary "qualification" should not be used as a tool to limit diversity on the bench, particularly in light of the limited applicant pools in recent years.[2]

Third, when considering members of multi-member appellate courts, the question of diversity and balance has particular importance. These courts with broad jurisdictions consider a wide diversity of cases. Ideally, a multi-member court will have a membership with a variety of cultural and legal experiences.

Finally, though, there is one common quality that is, in fact, universally required in our judges. That is a fierce commitment to judicial independence and the rule of law. That does not mean that a lawyer aspiring to be a judge must eschew, for instance, political activity or all interaction with the political world. There is much to be learned about human nature and the performance of government institutions from past political activity. But a prospective judge must understand that abandoning any prior partisan affiliations and commitments is an essential part of being a judge. In my view, in this hyper-partisan era, all judges, upon appointment, should abandon any formal political affiliation and register as a no-party voter in symbolic recognition of critical norm judicial independence.

Trial Court Judges

Let's begin with an exploration of some of the qualities that contribute to lawyers becoming fine applicants for trial court positions. Not that long ago, lawyers would semi-seriously state that a good judge was one who would grant a continuance when a lawyer was not prepared to proceed. Those days are long gone. Today, the qualities of a good trial court judge include high-quality legal skills, sensitivity to procedural fairness, an understanding of the importance of access to the courtroom, an understanding of how to manage complex court dockets, an awareness of implicit bias and the need for cultural competence, a healthy skepticism and strong sense of fairness, an openness to judicial innovation, an understanding of the sacrifices in assuming a judicial office, and a fierce commitment to the rule of law.

High-Quality Legal Skills

At all levels of the judiciary, high-quality legal skills are a prerequisite for reasonable success. Indeed, the importance of legal skills is one of the key justifications for the involvement of experienced lawyers in the judicial selection process who are in the best position to evaluate legal skills. Included in the basket of legal skills are listening ability, analytic ability, skepticism, sensitivities to language, and firm understanding of the difference and similarities between questions of fact and law. An unskilled but ambitious judge is likely to be a real problem for the bench and bar and the public being served.

Procedural Fairness

A trial judge must be sensitive to procedural fairness.[3] That means that the trial court should seek to ensure, as much as possible, that participants in the trial process, attorneys and clients come away from court believing that they have been heard. A widely cited study shows that perceived court legitimacy may depend upon the parties' perception of the fairness of procedures.[4]

Procedural fairness does not mean that issues have to be reconsidered over and over again, but it does mean that the trial court judge should carefully consider the written and oral arguments of the parties on each substantive issue at least once and produce a reasoned order explaining the outcome based on fact and law. In other words, the trial judge should reserve judgment, be a good listener, and then clearly explain decisions.

Access to Justice

In a related vein, the trial court judge must ensure that parties who are not represented by counsel have adequate access to the judicial process taking place in the courtroom. Trial courts, of course, are not to act as advocates for unrepresented parties, but they should ensure that unrepresented parties are treated with dignity and that the basic procedures of the trial process are explained in terms the unrepresented parties can understand. So, the trial judge must have patience where patience is required.[5]

In addition, trial court judges should promote and participate in judicial innovation designed to expand citizen access to fair and impartial government-sponsored conflict resolution. An applicant for a judicial position not affirmatively interested in the access to justice issues, if not unqualified entirely, is certainly less qualified than other applicants with an interest in this very pressing problem.[6]

Management Ability

Next, considering the sheer amount of litigation and the limitation of resources, a trial court judge must be an able manager.[7] To move cases along, a trial court must exercise discretion in case management in a way that permits lawyers to litigate but not procrastinate or unduly burden the parties or the court with unhelpful shenanigans. A trial judge must have a hammer, a supply of velvet, and a good sense of when to use them.

In managing the docket, a trial judge must understand that swift rulings based on limited advocacy and information are routine and not likely subject to meaningful appellate review. Most cases, of course, are not appealed, and even when they are, many of the rulings made by a trial court judge made along the way to judgment will not be relevant on appeal. Workmanlike and timely resolution of disputed issues, clearly explained, is the goal.

Effective docket management also requires that a trial judge accurately distinguishes important issues from minor issues and recognizes the value of a good process, but also realizes that an approach that leaves every conceivable stone unturned may be astronomically expensive and not in either party's interests. A trial judge has to have sufficient knowledge of the litigation process to understand how lawyers of all stripes, and their highly variable clients, try to navigate through the relatively complicated process. In managing the docket, a trial judge must see technology as a friend. Remote hearings are becoming the norm, thereby saving time and expense without sacrificing the quality of the process.

All this said, a managerial judge must not overlook fundamental fairness through overmanagement. Quickly decided rulings piled one upon another may be "efficient" but cumulatively may also prevent a party from making a solid case on the merits.[8] The traditional notion that courts should have a strong preference for trial on the merits is especially important in cases involving self-representation or in complex cases where inexperienced counsel makes nonmaterial procedural errors.

Implicit Bias and Cultural Competence

There is now a substantial literature on the twin topics of implicit bias and cultural competency.[9] With respect to implicit bias, the scholars suggest that all of us have unconscious or unstated biases based upon our past experiences. As noted by Judge Bernice B. Donald of the United States Court of Appeals for the Sixth Circuit:

> Judges, like the rest of us, carry implicit biases . . . . [T]hese implicit biases can affect judges' judgment, at least in contexts where judges are unaware of a need to monitor their own decisions. . . . [C]onversely, when judges are aware of a need to monitor their own responses for the influence of implicit biases, and are motivated to suppress that bias, they appear able to do so.[10]

After having 133 judges take the Implicit Association Test on race, one study concluded that, like the population as a whole, a moderate to large degree of judges harbor implicit racial bias.[11] A good judge should thus have a basic understanding of the concept of implicit bias and engage in self-reflection designed to ensure fundamental fairness.[12]

Similarly, the notion of cultural competence is something of a buzzword to some, but it embraces a critical concept.[13] In order to be culturally competent, a judge or lawyer must understand nuances of culture, customs, traditions, and language. Such understanding may arise from experience, or from diligent self-education. Legal experience in the rough-and-tumble world representing members of diverse communities, disadvantaged persons, and indigent persons, or defending or prosecuting criminal defendants, however, is a plus, particularly for trial court judges. Finally, a judicial aspirant must be aware of the value of effective and active listening, not just speech-making.

It is clear, though, that in many settings, such as taking a plea or obtaining a knowing and voluntary waiver of any rights, the trial judge must be sensitive to effective communication among the diverse lawyers, the parties, and the court. Just rattling off words and getting pre-scripted nods, of course, has never been adequate, but the need to effectively communicate with persons of different cultural backgrounds is increasingly important in the diverse world of the trial court judge.[14] The court may need to do more listening, and less talking, in order to understand the reality of what is going on in the courtroom.

Healthy Skepticism and Strong Sense of Fairness

A trial court judge is, of course, often called upon to decide facts. The good trial judge is something of a skeptic. Facts are not presumed but are proven. The good trial judge consistently and by temperament gives individualized assessment to each case. Any preliminary inkling on legal matters can never morph into more until the judge has had adequate opportunity for thorough assessment. Speed must not materially trump accuracy. While exercises of discretion are rarely reversible, the lodestar is shaping a process to get to the core issues of a dispute, not the convenience of the court.

Openness to Judicial Innovation

Beyond doubt, the litigation process in American courts has become expensive and time-consuming. As a result, consideration of modification of court processes is always on the table. We may have always done, say, divorces a certain way, and may have done sentencing hearings a certain way from time immemorial, but maybe there are better ways of doing things. Certainly no one wants to go back to the days of paper filings, unnecessary billing of clients or taxpayers for the time a lawyer is driving behind the windshield, or researching matters without a search capability of an appropriate database.

Understanding the Sacrifices of Bench Membership

Many lawyers may not fully appreciate the sacrifices that are made when a person becomes a judge. Social relationships change, particularly among lawyers. You have to avoid any appearances of impropriety, evade situations that might suggest judicial favoritism, and limit your political engagement. A political yard sign brought home by a spouse is best returned to the campaign unused. Judicial parents do not permit sons and daughters to engage in fundraising for school activities for fear of giving a wrong impression.

Further, in these days of polarization, some people are going to be angry or irate with judicial decisions, large and small. Judges and their families may become unpopular among some as a result of court decisions. Confrontations at the local grocery store, unfortunately, may happen.

At a minimum, it is fair to say that a judge and the judge's family are all impacted by the decision to take the bench. It is important that an aspirant for judicial office explore the implications of becoming a judge with family members to ensure that moving into a judicial career is the right move for the lawyer and the family.

Fierce Commitment to the Rule of Law

The last quality of the good judge may be the most important, and that is that the judge must be firmly committed to the rule of law. Decisions are to be based solely on law and fact and not on external influences, past associations, or future ambition. A judge has to be a tough nut. Criticism goes with the territory. A judicial aspirant must understand that democracy depends on a cadre of judges (and lawyers) who are committed to an orderly and fair process for conflict resolution. The process demands judges who are personally and passionately committed to follow the facts and the law and not simply achieve results for some favored party or constituency, real or imagined. A brilliant lawyer who is shaky or unconvincing in commitment to the rule of law or who sees the judge as politically responsive to certain constituents or groups should not receive serious consideration for the bench.[15]

Preparation

I now turn to the second question, namely, what can an aspiring lawyer do to prepare for a potential career on the bench? Here, there is no one-size-fits-all model. But, as a general rule, a package of diverse personal and professional experience in the community is desired.

Litigation Experience

For lawyers seeking to become trial court judges, litigation experience is a plus. Public service as a prosecutor or criminal defense attorney offers substantial experience, but experience in private firms with litigation practice or other government or private entities may also be helpful. In particular, private firms should recognize the value of allowing relatively inexperienced lawyers to second chair trials even if the billing lawyer determines that any billings for the second attorney should be unbilled or discounted.

Further, the opportunity to participate in pro bono representation is available to all attorneys and would provide good background for a judicial aspirant. Many organizations providing pro bono opportunities offer more support than may have been available in the past, including training sessions, access to real-time consultation with experienced lawyers, and provision of malpractice insurance. Lawyers who participate in pro bono representation have a very high rate of satisfaction with the experience. And, of course, pro bono representation contributes to closing the yawning gap in access to justice.

But the value of litigation experience should not be overblown. First, varied litigation experience might be hard to find as we live in an age of settlement and not an age of trials. Second, a highly experienced "never give an inch" bulldog of a litigator may bring more negatives than positives in terms of performance on the neutral bench. Third, many new judges have an opportunity for intensive training either through local judicial administrative entities or through national conferences for "baby judges." Finally, we do not want our bench to be composed solely of former prosecutors and defense attorneys.

But an appointing authority would do well to determine what aspects of an applicant's legal career make the person well suited to the life of a trial judge. An applicant whose background shows at least an interest in the litigation process and an appreciation for procedural values should not be eliminated from consideration. And, on the appellate bench, while some procedural issues inevitably arise, they are not the bread and butter of the broad legal issues likely to be presented to an appellate court.

Service on Bar or Judicial Branch Committees

Service on a relevant bar association or judicial branch committee or on the board of directors of a not-for-profit organization is useful and may demonstrate the ability of an individual to participate in consensus decision making. Although our system is largely adversarial, the ability of a trial court judge to seek and obtain consensus on procedural matters minimizes costs and eliminates issues on appeal. Service on such committees is likely to be a marker for civility, too, an important part of our legal system.

Service in the Community

Service in the community can, of course, take all shapes and forms. Among other things, a lawyer may provide pro bono services through organized legal structures. A lawyer might serve on the board of directors of nonprofit organizations designed to improve the lot of the less fortunate. A good trial judge applicant has not likely lived the life of a hermit. An otherwise qualified but bookish person might be more comfortable on an appellate court.

At the same time, while a trial judge must not be a social recluse, the trial judge cannot be committed to particular community, political, or nonlegal cultural perspectives. Nor may a trial judge be bound by ideology or preconceived notions. Life is complicated. Very few cases are truly identical, and thus each case is likely to require individual treatment. So, one has to be familiar with the community, with all its pluses and foibles, without bringing preconceived notions to the bench.

Demonstrated Commitment to Continuing Education

A trial court judge must have a robust interest in keeping abreast of changes in the law. So, one aspiring to be a judge would do well to have a demonstrated record of intentional formal and informal legal education. A good trial judge does not need to have an overwhelming interest in and knowledge of legal history beginning at the Magna Carta and carried through to the most recent advance sheets, but an ideal applicant keeps aware of the changing legal world that surrounds practice as well as the courthouse. A judicial candidate who habitually selects continuing legal education to beat the calendar imposed by mandatory requirements may not be the best candidate. Rather, applicants to the bench would be well served to show how they used legal education requirements intentionally to build effective skills in their areas of practice or new areas of interest.

Intermediate Appellate Court Judges

Many of the characteristics of a good trial court judge listed above apply to persons who aspire to serve as intermediate appellate court judges and will not be repeated here. But some attention should be paid to the special role of an intermediate appellate court in our judicial system.

At the outset, we must recognize two important features of the judicial landscape. First, the role of the intermediate appellate court is to handle routine appeals that involve application of facts to established law and to permit the state appellate court of last resort to focus on cases of fundamental importance.[16] Second, it is a reality of life in our current judicial system that intermediate appellate courts have a huge volume of cases, many of which can involve complicated factual records. Third, the volume of cases and the limited ability of the state supreme court to hear cases means that a significant number of cases before the intermediate appellate court are not routine, and may involve important issues.

As a result, in addition to many of the qualities of a trial court, an intermediate appellate judge must be highly organized, have an interest in applying legal rules to a variety of fact settings, and manifest a willingness to tackle important questions left open by the higher appellate court.

High Level of Organization

An intermediate appellate judge always has a number of pans in the fire. An effective intermediate appellate judge must be able to handle multiple matters at once and to make progress according to a reasonably established timetable. Once an adequate opinion has been produced, there is no time to look back. In a volume court, the old adage that the perfect cannot get in the way of the good seems apt. If further elaboration is required, the Supreme Court can review the case.

Ability to Apply Established Law of Variety of Facts

Holmes famously said the life of the law is not logic, but experience. That is often true, but not less likely to be true on an intermediate appellate court than, say, on a court of last resort. An important task of the intermediate appellate court is to take the established principles and apply them in a wide variety of factual settings. Right-sizing the apparently applicable legal principle may be important: when does the rule begin and when does it end? Thus, determining which principle of law applies may also be important.

Willingness to Tackle Important Questions Left Open by the Supreme Court

Finally, as every intermediate appellate judge knows, the highest appellate court does take every case with open and very important legal questions. The intermediate appellate court must be willing to proceed on these substantial matters with the understanding that the approach taken will likely be given considerable attention by the parties and by the final appellate tribunal.

Preparation

For the most part, steps a lawyer might take to prepare to serve on an intermediate court are similar to those for trial courts. In state intermediate appellate courts, a familiarity with certain subject matters, like divorce, juvenile law, and criminal procedure is a plus.

A judge on an intermediate court is likely to review many cases that have at least some important common features. An intermediate appellate judge is in a position to apply general principles of law in a consistent way across fact patterns. A demonstrated capacity to view the case law from a larger, horizontal perspective is a useful skill among intermediate judges that promotes the rule of law by eliminating glaring inconsistencies in the law's application.

The Appellate Court of Last Resort

I now turn to the question of characteristics that can be useful for judges on the state appellate bench of last resort. At the beginning, it is important to recognize two important concepts. First, such courts entertain a very broad range of different matters. State supreme courts consider cases involving family law, juvenile law, criminal law, criminal procedure, taxes, real estate, estates and trusts, consumer protection, antitrust, environmental law, administrative law, constitutional law, civil rights law, banking law, and more. The diversity of cases on a state supreme court docket is far more varied than on a federal intermediate appellate court.

Second, it must be recognized that, with the exception of cases involving federal issues, the judgments of state supreme courts are final. A trial court ruling on a search-and-seizure issue is not the final word and may not even be material depending upon the outcome of the case. Indeed, most trial court rulings are either not appealed or not contested.

But a state supreme court decision is binding precedent in the jurisdiction. As a result, the supreme court's court development of the relevant law must be thorough and complete. Do-overs are possible through rehearing, but rare. In this setting, in addition to the qualities listed above that apply to judges generally, there are some specific traits that may contribute to the performance of the state supreme court justice. These characteristics include an abiding interest in the law, a profound sense of the evolution of legal history, an understanding about the law's choices, the ability to foresee the likely consequences of a decision, and an interest in writing.

Interest in Legal Structure and Relationships

I begin with interest in legal structures and relationships. For example, particularly in constitutional matters, an understanding of how various legal instructions interact is as important as an understanding of the specific constitutional concepts at hand. An excellent example of a case involving institutional interaction is Justice Jackson's famous opinion in the *Youngstown Sheet & Tube Co. v. Sawyer* case where Jackson examined the interaction of executive and legislative powers in the context of the seizure of private property.[17] An appellate court judge must understand, or at least seek to understand, how a particular decision fits in within the larger institutional framework of government.

Interest in Evolution of Legal History

In a related vein, an interest in legal history is important. You cannot understand where the law is, let alone where it should travel, without knowing where it's been. Judges must exercise great care in not simply spending a few hours cherry-picking a complex historical record to provide ex post justification for broad legal principles. And, speaking frankly, a number of important appellate courts that have explored history have gotten it quite wrong.[18] The literature criticizing courts and lawyers for cherry-picking history to achieve preconceived ends is extensive.[19]

Yet, the past can inform the present and instill a better sense of the scope and intensity of constitutional values in a particular case. As Justice Holmes said some years ago, "In order to know what [the law] is, we must know what it has been, and what it tends to become."[20]

Recognition that the Law is About Choices

A member of the appellate bench should understand that the law often involves choices.[21] Those with strong ideological commitments might think to the contrary. But Holmes was right in the sense that the law is not a mathematical exercise. A judge declaring discovery of a "correct" answer often masks the true nature of the judicial process.[22] Opinions from appellate courts ideally should identify key choices and explain why one road taken was superior to the others.

Understanding that the Law is About Consequences

Because the law involves choices, appellate judges must at least seek to understand the likely impact of decisions. Like a chess player, then, the judge must think several moves into the future when a legal piece on the board is moved. That does not mean, of course, that judging is solely or primarily a pragmatic exercise, but it does mean that a judge should seek to understand the impact of the decision and its tendency to promote, or undermine, the rule of law in a democratic society.

Passion for Persuasive Writing

An appellate judge must be more than merely interested in persuasive writing—it must be a passion. Persuasive writing should, of course, explain to the losing party, as well as the prevailing party, the reasons for a judicial decision. Where an opinion represents a question of first impression, an overview of the develop- ment of the law and the choices available to an appellate court is often helpful. The most important aspect of an opinion might not be the result, or holding, but may well be in the method or approach.

With respect to writing, I want to make several additional points. First, the process of preparing a written opinion is critical to legal decision making. In my service, there were occasions when a tentatively unanimous court completely changed its mind after the drafter of an opinion reported back that "the opinion wouldn't write." I also know that dismissals of criminal cases through conclusory statements from lawyers that criminal appeals are "frivolous," which are no longer permitted in my state, are unsatisfactory. The temptation to be less than thorough when no explanation is required is just too great to be permitted.

The same is true regarding decisions without opinions by appellate courts. Decisions without opinions run the risk of significant undisclosed error.[23] The writing process imposes discipline on the decision-making process beyond that which arises from a first impression based on review of the briefs and oral argument. A preliminary sense or impression should not drive the writing process: the writing should be driven by the law and facts. A judge who does not at least occasionally through disciplined study come to a view at variance with their initial impression is truncating the decision-making process and becoming a defender of first impressions rather than a thoughtful judge testing the validity of potential outcomes through thorough investigation and effort.

Second, legal writing must be reasonably accessible. Care must be taken to write directly, concisely, and purposefully. While I do not agree with the proposition that a legal opinion should read like a feature in *Time* magazine, I do think unnecessary use of foreign vocabulary or the use of 70-word sentences are hardly ideal. The use of fine distinctions is the essence of law and should not be abandoned, but an accurate, simpler explanation may be better than a more elaborate and extended discussion.

That does not mean writing should face some unrealistic or arbitrary page limit or be dumbed down in any way. Judges uniformly appreciate concise briefs, but a well written 75-page brief might well qualify as a good brief while a shorter but incoherent submission might not.

Third, the logic of the writing must be persuasive. I am not one who believes the purpose of an opinion is to entertain as some kind of performance. Law by metaphor, of course, is almost always unstable. Care must be taken to ensure that the use of striking verbiage in an opinion does not distort or overwhelm the legal principles being articulated and the rational argument employed.

Finally, of course, developing writing skills is a never-ending task. One's legal writing can always be improved. Certainly, many who have read my opinions think so, and I semi-joyously accept that, as should all judges.

Dealing with Scorpion Colleagues

The effective trial court judge truly presides. The trial judge runs the show. The trial judge seeks consensus among lawyers and litigants where possible, but has the authority to drive and shape the litigation process within the applicable rules. When decisions need to be made, the judge makes them and the gavel falls.

The appellate court of last resort has a much different character. Appellate judges of a court of last resort have been referred to as scorpions, aggressive and highly individual creatures with stingers.[24] The label is exaggerated, perhaps, but certainly has an element of truth. Even in courts that ordinarily seem to operate through broad consensus, disagreements may run deep, occasionally as to outcome but more often as to approach or legal method. And, in a conflict court, with outcomes routinely in doubt because of the varying judicial philosophies, disagreement will be high on the menu of every judicial conference. An ability to maneuver among colleagues in contested environments and tolerate differences among them may be more important to the outcome of a case than analytical clarity. Great care, however, must be taken to preserve maximum flexibility and avoid preconference, closed-door sessions with "swing" justices to lock in a certain outcome. The judicial conference in a court of last resort should be free-flowing and uninhibited, not scripted.

Finally, the appellate judge on a court of last resort will believe that some of the majority opinions are completely wrong. Writing strong dissents without crossing into personal attack is for most of us a learned art. On the other hand, a trial court judge can only disagree with themselves.

Preparation

How does one prepare to be a judge on a court of last result? The short answer, perhaps, is one doesn't. Even for the most qualified applicant, there are elements of luck and circumstance. When does a vacancy appear?

What is the make-up of the appellate court at the time of a vacancy? What is the likelihood that the appointing authority will look with favor on an application? Who are the other applicants? Is the applicant in a position to take what is likely to be a substantial pay cut? Nonetheless, there are a few steps a potential applicant might take to support a possible pursuit of a judicial career on the appellate bench of last resort.

Become a Judge

One of the obvious avenues to an appellate court of last resort is service on a lower court. Experience in the judicial branch is certainly a plus. But there are several qualifications. First, not all excellent trial judges are suited for the bookish and rarefied atmosphere of the appellate court. First, if research and writing are not in a lawyer's wheelhouse, the lawyer might think twice about moving from the trial court to an appellate court. Further, some judges might be more comfortable as the leader of a group effort in the trial court rather than as a mere member of the group of judges on appeal.

Hold Supervisory Positions in a Law Firm or Other Entity

This kind of experience will give one an ability to work with other persons in solving problems. An appellate judge often works behind closed doors with law clerks laboring on opinions, but the conference room is always down the hall. Holding responsible positions in the private sector likely cultivates personal skills of value when dealing with legal disagreements or variance of policy.

Engage in Meaningful Legal Research and Writing

Demonstrating an interest and skill in legal research and writing would be helpful. A writing portfolio might include a brief in support of motion to dismiss or motion for summary judgment, an appellate merits brief, a law review article, a comprehensive outline for a continuing legal education program, or a combination of the above.

A Rueful Observation

In looking over my modest contribution here, I feel somewhat rueful. In Iowa state courts, at least, applications for judicial positions are down. When I retired from the Iowa Supreme Court in 2022, there were only five applicants for the vacancy. We have had occasions where the number of applicants for district court judicial positions has been very small.

There are multiple reasons for the lack of applicants, but it is hard to observe the small applicant pools without having a sense of foreboding. Fortunately, there have been enough good candidates to fill vacancies, and I do not in any way wish to disparage recent appointees to any court. But I am concerned, over the long run, that very high-quality candidates and candidates from diverse backgrounds have made the decision to not apply. Relatively low pay is likely a factor. Limited staffing (like one law clerk for four district judges) may be a deterrent. Lack of public support and disparagement of judicial officers may be part of the problem. And, of course, the process of selection may be viewed as politicized to the point of choking down applications.

My fear is that all the dignified and high-minded narrative about the qualities of a good judge may be for naught if the applicant pool becomes inadequate. We are not yet at this point, but it might not be far away. The rule of law will be undermined if the ability and integrity of our judges declines. It may be time for friends of the judiciary and the judiciary itself to engage in some serious soul searching about the future.

The Impact and Weight of Discretion

Romonda D. Belcher
Associate Judge, Iowa District Court (Ret.)

As a judge, you will encounter individuals from all walks of life. You may be the only "face" of the justice system they encounter, and how you treat individuals could leave a lasting impression on their perceived fairness of the system. Those individuals may be of a different race, gender, sexual orientation, political affiliation or religious belief, or may come from a different socio-economic or educational background. Their lived experiences are going to be quite different from your own.

We not only need to preside in a manner where justice is perceived, we have to ensure justice is attained. In Iowa, and perhaps in every other state, the criminal and juvenile justice systems are filled disproportionately with minorities and those who are disenfranchised.

While the inequality starts long before they appear before the court, there are many interactions with those in authority who may have a different world view. There are those who may believe judges do not play a role in the disparate representation of minorities who are incarcerated. I beg to differ. Even where we have discretion, our decisions are often influenced by our own biases, or more subtly put, our preferences. Having an understanding of trauma also impacts our impartiality, and being able to prevent compassion fatigue through engaging in self-preservation practices influences our decision making. These things may make a difference in whether the court imposes a jail sentence or grants probation. They may impact who is referred for diversion programs and who gains access to treatment or mental health services. They may make a difference in whether the court, as a fact finder, makes a finding of guilt. In short, your world view, your understanding of trauma and your commitment to self-preservation will be key in how you treat those appearing before you and how you exercise discretion.

World View

While every judge in Iowa has obtained a law degree, not everyone comes with the same world view, which shapes your perception and is influenced by your biases and past experiences. It is absolutely imperative that you have an awareness of your biases, or your preferences, and have a willingness to broaden your lens on how you view others, especially those who may have some fundamental differences from you. In acknowledging your biases, you have to ask yourself why you have those views or opinions, and how your upbringing, lifestyle, and exposure to various social and cultural factors have persuaded or influenced your beliefs.

We all often gravitate to what we were taught, what we know, what we are familiar with and what makes us comfortable. If you were not taught to see those who may be less fortunate than yourself differently, then ask yourself what of your own choices have played a pivotal role in forming your view of others. I challenge you to challenge yourself. How often do you engage with someone who does not look like you, has not attained your level of education or has a different belief system?

How often do you pay attention to what you take in on a daily basis from news outlets, social media, and television programming that projects others in a negative light? Have you ever made an effort to broaden your understanding of another's culture, political viewpoint or religious beliefs? What is your level of commitment to just getting to know someone different from yourself, providing them with encouragement and learning from their lived experiences?

While our lived experiences, race, gender, sexual orientation, religious beliefs, socioeconomic status and education may differ, everyone desires the same basic core things: to be loved; to be healthy; to be happy; to be seen and heard; to be respected; and to be safe. If you could be purposeful in this truth and, instead of seeing the differences in those appearing before you, relate to everyone from this shared set of desires, then perhaps you would view them as you see yourself, your family member, or a loved one as you are exercising your discretion.

After acknowledging your biases or preferences, be open and willing to engage in an honest dialog regarding it. Be aware of the microaggressions that have too often become commonplace. Actively participate in training, hold yourself accountable, and be courageous enough to hold your colleagues and peers accountable. Follow the old adage: when we know better, we do better. Live by the golden rule: treat others the way you want to be treated.

Trauma Informed

Understand, a considerable majority of the people appearing in court have experienced some level of trauma, which may stem from substance dependency, mental health disorders, domestic violence, homelessness, or poverty. Often, many suffer from dual diagnoses and multiple traumatic experiences. It is important to have an understanding of trauma and recognize how untreated trauma affects or manifests into behavior. Do not identify individuals by their bad actions. Endeavor to understand what has happened to them, instead of questioning what is wrong with them. Recognize the need for services to address their trauma, and identify available resources to meet their needs. Understanding trauma allows you to view a person's perceived noncompliance or resistance to services as a product of the trauma they have experienced and not a lack of desire to receive help or get better.

Being trauma-informed allows you to avoid the revictimization of those appearing before you in both the language and practices utilized in your courtroom. You have to be intentional in the words you use to address individuals and to create a safe space. Recognize it is not business as usual, and be thoughtful in making adjustments to ensure that individuals feel respected, safe, seen and heard.

Some specific changes I utilized in my courtroom were as simple as rearranging the seating assignment to eliminate any perceived unfairness; referring to individuals by their surnames; advising individuals of warrants and impending arrest from the courtroom; speaking of a substance dependency, rather than addiction or substance abuse; speaking of drug screens that simply reflect use, rather than referring to them as "dirty" or "positive;" asking individuals if they have questions or understand the court's ruling; exercising motivational interviewing techniques to engage individuals; and encouraging and allowing individuals to have a voice in their outcomes. As you exercise your discretion, be mindful of both an individual's childhood trauma, adverse childhood experiences (ACEs), and any ongoing trauma, and how those experiences have played a role in that individual's behaviors and responses to assistance.

Self-Preservation

Being trauma-informed is the best barometer in ensuring your own self-care. While some believe "work-life balance" is a misnomer, again, I challenge you to believe it is attainable. It, too, requires intentionality. In a highly stressful profession where compassion fatigue can be present, it is important to recognize your own traumas and ensure your experiences include a conscious commitment to taking care of yourself, both mentally and physically. A failure to do so, in a profession that can be plagued by alcohol and substance use if not properly addressed, could lead to substance dependency. Working in a profession where you see and hear the worst in individuals on a daily basis makes it easy to be drained with compassion fatigue, having experienced vicarious trauma.

Compassion fatigue can in turn lead to exercising discretion without patience, active listening, respect, or kindness, and certainly, without sufficient empathy. Patience is a necessary quality to prevent becoming easily frustrated with individuals who may appear to be uncooperative or resistant due to their trauma. Active listening allows you to be thoughtful and insightful in meeting the need to ensure equal justice under the law. Respect, kindness and compassion are absolute musts when an individual's life, livelihood, children or freedom lie in your hands.

Commit to achieving and maintaining a healthy balance in your life. Tap into who you are "outside of the robe." Do things that bring you joy. Take a break, go for a walk, read a book, take a nap, have a massage, connect with friends, spend time with family, or enjoy a hobby—and do not take work home! Your discretion is best exercised fairly and impartially, with thoughtfulness and decisiveness, when you take care of yourself first.

Getting Ready by Getting Yourself Right

Andrew B. Chappell
Judge, Iowa District Court

Introduction

Judging, being a judge, is a job. It is a job that is different from many others in a number of particulars, but it also is a job that, like most others, requires preparation in order to be done well. When you make the decision to attempt to become a judge, there are things you can do to ready yourself, and ideally to improve your chances of achieving your goal. Judging, especially as a trial judge, ideally requires a broad knowledge base. It requires the respect of your peers. And it requires a certain mentality. Finally, it requires realistic expectations.

Get Your Experience Right

Obviously, there is no specific, required experience for becoming a judge. You have to be a lawyer, of course, but beyond that the precise job requirements are more sparse. Iowa trial judges preside over courts of general jurisdiction and come from all walks of lawyer life. Civil litigators. Family law attorneys. General practice lawyers. Prosecutors and defense attorneys. The bench is a kaleidoscope of practitioners.

There is no reason you can't be a specialist and then go straight to the bench. But, the dirty little secret of becoming a judge is that as soon as you are selected, and certainly as soon as you sign the oath, you are expected to know what you're doing. I've known new judges who were shocked by the lack of real training they received prior to being expected to take their seat on the bench. Once you are appointed, people will start calling you "Judge" and they will mean it. You will suddenly, rightly or wrongly, be expected to be the person in that courtroom who best knows what is going on and what should be happening. You should try to be as prepared as possible for what awaits you.

Moreover, having some more varied experience will never hurt your chances with the judicial nominating commission. The commissions are often made up of lay people from all walks of life and lawyers of wide-ranging experience. Any addition to your knowledge base, and any area of professional experience you gain, gives you a better chance of connecting with the members of the commission as they consider your qualifications and whether you are one of the best candidates.

So, before you apply to become a judge, get your experience right. Most lawyers specialize to one degree or another, and we have gaps in our professional experience. Before you apply, try to identify those gaps and think about how you might fill them. If you've never handled a criminal case, consider taking on a few cases as a court-appointed attorney. (Trust me, we need you!) If you're able to accept pro bono civil work, take on a pro bono dissolution case. If your practice for some reason does not allow you to do any volunteer work, get to the courthouse and watch it being done—preferably by those who know what they're doing. If you've been in practice a while, you likely know who has a reputation for doing good work. Watch them do it. Ask them questions. And, if the gaps in your knowledge base are not those that can be filled by taking a trip to the local courthouse, fill them by reading cases, the Code, and the Rules. Chapter 598 of the Iowa Code is enlightening to someone who has never handled a divorce. The Rules of Civil Procedure can be downright foreign to the prosecutor who hasn't read them since law school. Do your best to prepare yourself.

Get Your Reputation Right

Before I made the decision to apply to be a judge, I always looked with interest at the list of candidates for any open judicial position. Often, the names fell into one of several categories. First, there were those applying that one would expect to be applying. I knew them, or knew of them. They had solid reputations and I was not surprised to see them throwing their names in the hat. Second, there were lawyers applying whose names were unknown or only vaguely familiar to me, but usually because they practiced in areas outside my own area of specialization. As judicial candidates they were intriguing, perhaps, but unknown qualities. Third, there were often a few names of lawyers that I knew of but, because of their reputations, could not imagine them serving as judges. You don't want your name to be one that people read on the list of judicial applicants and place into this third category.

It really is difficult to overestimate just how much your reputation as a lawyer impacts people's impressions of you. Every experience you have with another lawyer incrementally impacts that reputation, which is ultimately a product of your complete body of work. You also must realize that judges, by the nature of their profession and the limits placed on them by the ethical rules, are a somewhat insular bunch. They will talk amongst themselves about their experiences, and that includes any experience they have with you. In fact, you should assume that any bad experience you have with a judge will be shared with several of her or his colleagues.

Lawyering the right way, maintaining your professionalism, requires work. It is easy, especially in our electronic world, to let things get personal. Many young lawyers in Iowa seem to lack real mentors, either because they're practicing on their own or they are in a firm whose partners are just too busy to help them. And many more experienced lawyers fall prey to getting caught up in the adversarial system and a version of zealous advocacy that is sometimes over the top. We are quick to see slights and microaggressions that may or may not be there, and can be quick to respond in kind.

Before you apply to be a judge, you need to put in the work to get your reputation right. That is, if you have developed bad habits with regard to your professionalism, you need to replace them with better behavior. In fact, not only do you need to replace your bad habits, but your colleagues need to *notice* that you have replaced your bad habits. Preferably, you need to establish a new body of work that other lawyers, and maybe even judges, can call upon when they see your name on that list of applicants. If your prior dealings with people have left a bitter taste in their mouths, you can assume the commission and maybe even the Governor will hear about it, one way or another.

Get Your Mind Right

Judging is different from advocacy, and being a judge takes a different mindset than being a lawyer. So, prior to becoming a judge, you need to get your mind right.

As a lawyer you always have "a side." Sometimes you've been able to pick your side (or your client), so you can be fully behind the position for which you are advocating. Sometimes the circumstances (or your employment) dictate which side you are on and for which position you must advocate. While it might not be a position you would personally embrace, you still are able to focus exclusively on advocating for that position.

When you become a judge, you will no longer have a side that you are advocating for. The judicial mindset requires you to be neutral—fair to both sides—regardless of your personal likes or preferences. That does not mean all positions are equally correct, or that you cannot favor the position that the law and your experience tells you is the correct one. But even then, you are not really picking "a side."

You have to be professional in all of your dealings with counsel. You have to be respectful toward both sides and their advocates. You have to be patient in listening to their arguments and evidence. You must avoid allowing your prior advocacy, or your history of being an advocate, to hasten you toward one position or another. There likely will be a time when the scales have tipped, but you must make sure it is the law or evidence that has done the tipping and not the fact that you may have been predisposed toward one position or another.

This will not always be easy to do, or even easy to remember. It can be difficult to transition from advocate to neutral, but as you are working toward becoming a judge you can and should prepare for this mindset. It requires looking at your cases in a different way, and seeing the issues from a disinterested set of eyes. Doing so will prepare you for thinking like a judge, and in any event will help you know your own cases better.

Get Your Expectations Right

Being a judge is an incredible honor. After appointment you are immediately showered with respect, and very likely an undeserved amount of praise. But there's a reason it's called public service. People's expectations for you will change instantly, and you need to have realistic expectations about what comes along with the job.

People, the public, will suddenly expect more of you and view you differently. Your behavior in and outside of the courthouse will be scrutinized. You may become somewhat of a novelty to friends or family, and some acquaintances can become suddenly enamored of their relationship with you. You will have come to represent something of an institution. None of this is, in and of itself, a bad thing, but you should contemplate how you will deal with it and whether you are ready for it.

Good judging, like good lawyering, is hard work. It can require long hours and, unlike when you are used to billing your time, you won't experience an added financial benefit the more you work. Many judges, especially state court judges, have relatively little in the way of administrative support, especially compared to some lawyers or law firms. With all of that judicial independence comes the need for you to be a self-starter and fully capable of managing your workload on your own.

You also will lose a fair amount of independence and ability to control your schedule. If you've worked hard to become a partner at a well-established law firm, or you're a solo practitioner, you may have become used to setting (or at least impacting) your own schedule. As a judge, with some exceptions, you will have relatively little control over your schedule or, for that matter, what type of work you are doing from day to day or month to month. While we are able to plan for some things, it is not uncommon to receive a text on your last day of a vacation letting you know you'll be in trial the next day. You will have to be able to roll with this and be flexible.

Make sure you have realistic expectations for what things will be like if you get the position, and whether you are ready for it all at this point in your life.

Closing

I love being a judge. As I wrote above, it truly is an honor. And I like to think I work very hard to earn the respect that is so freely given to the position I hold. If you, too, want to become a judge, I encourage you to prepare yourself in all of the ways that will help you to first, get the position, and second, to excel in it. You need to get yourself right in order to be a judge who will uphold the expectations and responsibilities of your appointed office.

Embracing Openness

Patrick A. McElyea
Judge, Iowa District Court

This chapter is focused on skills and experiences that prepare you to become a judge. Having served as a trial court judge for the last six years I can safely say that there is no magic set of skills or experiences a lawyer must have to become a judge. All my colleagues bring their own story as a person and a lawyer to the bench. None of them are better or worse than the other. The variety in those experiences allows each one of us to be a resource for our fellow judges and makes our bench more complete.

As I reflect on what experience or skill makes a good judge, my thoughts turn to what I call "soft skills." And the word that continually comes to mind is "openness." Openness is a personality trait that makes one receptive to new ideas and new experiences. It may be ironic to think that someone whose job it is to judge people would need to avoid sitting in judgment, but this is an important skill and trait to foster as you seek to become a good judge. Openness impacts all facets of being a judge.

Not surprisingly, people have varying degrees of openness. For example, I love the show "Cheers," and would enjoy nothing more than to show up at my local watering hole and greet everyone as I grab my corner stool. I'd order the same thing every single time with a simple nod indicating "the usual." My wife on the other hand would describe this as an epic failure in life. She always wants to order something different on the menu and try the new places in town. So far she's winning; I've eaten more foods that I can't pronounce and have yet to be on a first-name basis with a server or bartender in town.

Not only has my level of openness increased in my personal life but it has also increased in my professional life. I am hopeful that being open to new ideas and experiences as a judge makes me a better jurist. One of the challenges of being a lawyer and a judge is that people rarely come to see you with good news. There is a reason we celebrate adoptions so much—it is a rare time when we put a family together at the courthouse. My challenge to readers of this essay is to be open with yourself, open to serving others, and open to new ideas for the justice system.

You will undoubtedly read other essays in this book about the change that happens when you become a judge. You are expected to have all the answers and you will get very little constructive feedback on your work. Don't get me wrong, I appreciate our appellate judges, but sadly their job is not to soothe the trial court's ego when they write their decisions. As you take on the role of a judge, you must be willing to take a hard look at your skill set, experiences, and your weak spots. Then, be open to feedback, criticism, and insight from lawyers and colleagues on the bench. Imposter syndrome is a real thing when you get this job, and hunkering down in your office trying to do it all on your own will only make it harder to understand the job. So be open with challenges you might be facing in making certain decisions or understanding an area of the law. Your colleagues understand what you are facing and will do their best to provide feedback and point you in the right direction.

One of the central themes that arose when I applied to become a judge was intellectual curiosity. Our system is better when judges are curious about the law, the facts, and the process. Asking questions and seeking to understand an area of the law you may not have experience with is vital to your success. I have a quote in my office that says, "It takes less time to do things right than it does to explain why you did it wrong."[25] It is far better to ask the dumb question and make sure you are on the same page with the lawyers, than to "fake it 'til you make it," and miss the issue completely, costing the litigants time, money, and possibly liberty. I have found that litigants respect and appreciate a judge who works hard to reach the right result, and a big part of that is being open with yourself about what you know and don't know.

First and foremost, judges are public servants, and being a public servant has presented new challenges throughout my tenure as a judge. It is no secret that in many places there are fewer attorneys to serve clients. The public has grown increasingly impatient with governmental institutions, and the people who face the brunt of this attitude shift are our court staff. They work hard to insulate the judges from many of the behind-the-scenes issues that go on at the courthouse. In order to return the favor, we have a duty to not only bring a positive attitude to the courthouse each day but we also have to bring a public servant mindset each day. "Public service must be more than doing a job efficiently and honestly. It must be a complete dedication to the people and the nation."[26]

I came to the bench from the public sector and one of the main reasons I applied for this job was to continue to serve the public. Since becoming a judge, I have learned how significant of an impact we can have on people's lives with what used to be the stroke of a pen and is now the click of the mouse. I am fond of telling people that judges have to be mindful that even though it might only be Tuesday and you have a full schedule ahead of you, every hearing on the day's docket will have an impact on the lives of the litigants. In my opinion, it is important to adopt the philosophy of hearing the cases before you and rendering a decision. Resolving disputes and allowing people to move forward is one of the best ways we can serve the public. But it doesn't end there. Being pleasant in the courthouse, courteous to litigants and jurors, and always willing to do our best to help people when they ask are all ways that we can be public servants.

How does this connect to openness, you might ask? I think it is a mindset of addressing the problems before you, being open to talking to strangers, and being willing to assist when you otherwise may want or need to be doing something else. It can be tempting to kick the can down the road and continue a case when you may not want to deal with it. It is far easier to walk quickly through the courthouse and rush into the secured areas to avoid interacting with people in the hallways. And it would be easier to write a decision if you said "no" to the judicial specialists who ask you to sign those urgent orders. I view this position as one that requires you to approach every day with a willingness to be open to handling whatever the day throws at you. By keeping an open mind and being prepared for the not-so-infrequent curveball, you are better able to meet the needs of everyone in the courthouse and serve the public.

The final area of openness relates to new ideas for the justice system. Iowa was on the cutting edge when we transitioned to an online court filing system. It is a phenomenal tool that allows judges and practitioners to streamline their processes and remove barriers around access to the courts. Our courts have embraced further technological changes since the pandemic. We have allowed for remote appearances, explored new methods to report proceedings, and enhanced the technology in our courtrooms. Perhaps the most significant benefit of embracing technology has been to allow attorneys to represent indigent litigants in our more rural jurisdictions.

The ever-changing landscape of our justice system requires judges to be nimble. Increasingly that means embracing technology and learning to be more self-sufficient. But it does not end there, being open to new ideas is not confined to any one area of being a judge. We owe it to the litigants before us to consider new arguments and new ways of making decisions. Having a high degree of openness frees us to be critical of our own decision making and how we can improve it. When you are open-minded as a judge you ask questions like "how can I help?" Or, "why are we doing it this way?" When a judge asks these questions, they are creating space for reflection and change.

As judges, we have the opportunities and challenges that come with making very significant, life-altering decisions for people we barely know. Because of that, I believe we have a responsibility, in fact a duty, to cultivate openness. That is, to hone our ability to look ourselves in the mirror and ask how we can improve, to seek out opportunities to serve the public, and to embrace the inevitable changes that come with the passage of time. As you finish this essay, I encourage you to think about who you are and what you bring to the bench, and how you can challenge yourself to remain open throughout your career.

Sources of Valuable Experience for the Bench

Christopher C. Polking
Judge, Iowa District Court

If you aspire to become a district court judge, there will inevitably be areas of your background you feel confident are strengths. There will also be areas of your background (or lack thereof) that concern you.

A wide range of experience in different topical areas of the law can be very useful, as the district court hears a broad range of matters. However, that range is so broad that no one can have deep and meaningful experience in every subject that will be encountered. In addition, even in areas where one's knowledge and experience are deep, novel situations will come before you. It may be a unique set of facts, or an aspect of law that rarely comes up.

That being said, there are three main areas where judges spend the majority of their time on a day-to-day basis. They are criminal, family law (divorce, custody, child support), and probate. Overarching all of the areas is the ability to manage the courtroom and communicate effectively, both verbally, during the hearing, and in writing, when the order is being drafted. Many people these days specialize in an area of the law. A person aspiring to be a judge with a general jurisdiction docket should consider widening the type of cases they currently handle, if that option is available to them. All the better if it can be in one of the three areas just mentioned, as that is where it would have the most application to the work in the district court.

In addition, one should consider areas where a lot of courtroom time can be gained in a relatively short period of time, and that are easily accessible to beginning representation: criminal defense, juvenile court, family law, and mental health and substance abuse committals. Even though juvenile court and committals are different jurisdictions from the district court, they not only maximize courtroom time, but are also more likely to offer valuable experience regarding how to handle difficult people in the courtroom.

Courtroom time in any subject area can be valuable. However, to have the most benefit, the person should keep in mind their ultimate goal of being a judge. What does this mean? In general, we tend to focus only on our own roles in hearings. Attorneys naturally pay the most attention to their clients, for instance, but much can be learned by paying *full* attention—in particular to what the judge is doing and saying, but also what others are doing, including any pro se parties. How does the judge introduce the matter? How does the judge control the hearing? How are objections handled? How are pro se parties handled by the judge? How are any difficult parties, attorneys, or witnesses handled by the judge? Every observation will be valuable to the attorney who is giving serious consideration to pursuing the bench.

I remember my first hearing as a magistrate judge, a mental health committal. Despite having represented the respondent dozens upon dozens of times in such hearings, I stumbled to introduce the case. While I felt confident with the subject matter, I realized I had not paid close enough attention to every aspect of the hearing from beginning to end. When I later decided to apply to the district court, I began paying more attention to everything the judge was doing at hearings and in their rulings.

Another area that a person can seek to add to their practice and that can have benefits as a future judge is to become trained as a mediator. A mediator tries to assist the parties in coming to a resolution that they feel is their own. A judge decides the resolution to the problem. So how is mediation still helpful?

Mediation training requires building one's listening skills, and making sure that the positions and arguments of the parties are quickly understood, and can then be turned around and communicated effectively to the other party. A huge part of what a judge does is listen. Sit through a two-day divorce trial and the person who talks the very least will be the judge. But the judge must always be listening closely to hear and understand the facts, to hear and understand the arguments, positions, and requests for relief of the parties, and to hear and respond to objections.

In addition, mediation builds skills in how to remain in productive control of the process, even if the parties are emotional, highly charged, or highly contentious. More and more litigants, particularly in family law, are representing themselves. Mediation builds skills that are very useful in working with pro se litigants. While there are different processes for mediation, in some situations the mediator drafts into writing the agreement that was reached by the parties. This gives good practice in making sure that you understand the situation clearly enough to then write it out in a form that makes sense to all involved.

Finally, mediation gives insight, particularly in family law, into how there are common and recurring patterns of emotional responses to the legal issues. This aids in understanding how the parties pick, describe, and press their issues and concerns. This view of the process from the inside out is valuable in understanding the parties' ultimate positions and requests for relief. Or as one of my mediation trainers once said, the argument over the couch is never really about the couch.

There is also useful experience to be gained in areas outside of the law—some of which may surprise you.

Imagine you are about to preside over a murder trial. Between the jury pool, attorneys, family members of the defendant, family members of the victim, media, and others, there may well be over 100 people in the courtroom. A television camera may be set up. A photographer is quietly taking pictures. Are you used to acting out your role in front of a crowd? How will you handle it when things inevitably go "off script"?

At times like these, I rely on what has unexpectedly become one of my greatest teachers: my experience performing in my high school musical every year, as well as in the chorus and swing choir. Things like plays, musicals, chorus, and dance give great experience in performing your role in front of an audience. They also give very valuable experience in calmly moving forward in the face of unscripted "mistakes" that occur in public and in a high-pressure environment. If you didn't do these activities in high school, do not worry. Such options are still available through community theater, choruses, and other groups.

Another area I found surprisingly helpful was the many years I spent coaching middle school and high school mock trials. On many occasions during an actual trial, I have been able to quickly respond to and rule on an evidentiary objection due to my experience coaching mock trials. The reason? If you can break down the rules of evidence such that teenagers can understand and use them and make and respond to objections, then you have learned the material very well yourself. This is an easy place to get involved. Just ask, and I bet you'll have a local team that would be thrilled to have an attorney helping out.

Whatever your perceived strengths and weaknesses, issues will regularly come up where you either have no prior knowledge or no experience in the matter. The desire to add to your knowledge and to find the solution to novel issues will help you in diving in and discovering how to address the matter. A general intellectual curiosity is necessary for both, as it is for listening attentively to a case and doing the research needed to write the ruling. You may find yourself knowing more about a construction process, a medical issue, or how certain products are manufactured then you ever knew. While certain subjects will repeat themselves, each week something new is also likely to come onto your docket. Rather than find that intimidating, you and the people you serve will derive the greatest benefit if you find it interesting. Whether you end up as a judge or not, taking on some of the experiences noted above will make you a better attorney and a more well-rounded person. There is nothing to lose and only opportunity to gain.

What it Takes to Be a Judge

Paul D. Scott
Judge, Iowa District Court

To me, becoming a judge is the highest calling of a trial attorney. It is important work and it's a prestigious position. Judges are given respect by lawyers, litigants, and the public. Judges have enormous authority, which comes with great responsibility. Judges are tasked with making grave decisions that, at a minimum, have great importance to the litigants and may have enormous public consequences.

A trial judge does more than research and grind out ruling after ruling. Trial judges make decisions every day that can have a far-reaching impact on those involved. They listen to testimony, sometimes gut-wrenching, sometimes boring, sometimes humorous. Being a trial attorney requires a special set of skills. Some should be had when seeking a judgeship, others will be earned on the bench.

What skill set should you have to take on this job? What experience is important to be competent?

Experience

You need to have trial experience. Obvious? No. But it seems to me that without that rudiment, without the prior experience of trying cases, presiding over a trial would be challenging at best.

The application of the law occurs in the courtroom, not the classroom. Litigation experience is key because it teaches you how it's done. You need to have made sausage before you can tell someone else how to do it.

Because you wear the robe, lawyers and litigants alike are required to give you respect in the courtroom. When you exclude evidence or rule on an objection, the lawyers may disagree with you, but because you've been in their shoes before, you and your decision have credibility. Just like the way Smith Barney made money; the best judges gain credibility the old-fashioned way—they earn it.

Patience

Patience is a virtue for most, it is an absolute necessity for a judge. Days on the bench are often filled with long, tedious, mind-numbingly boring testimony only to be interrupted by objections, sidebars, and arguments over evidence. Interactions with self-represented litigants are often trying and sometimes contentious. A judge must maintain his composure while being assaulted by these outside forces. Keeping one's frustration in check can be a difficult undertaking, but a judge must have this skill.

Explaining legal concepts to people who have no idea what you're talking about, lawyers and self-represented litigants alike, goes with the territory. But whether you are discussing points of law with a particularly dense attorney or explaining to a witness the meaning of a "yes or no answer," a judge needs to be patient.

Humility

We all know judges who, once they "ascend" to the bench, become something more: more intelligent, more arrogant, more condescending, more of everything. It's hard not to have a big ego as a judge. People stand when you enter the courtroom, you are addressed as "Your Honor," you have the last word (at least until a higher court looks at your decision). Judges must have a healthy and modest view of their own importance. "Black robe syndrome" is off-putting to attorneys, litigants, staff, courthouse personnel, basically everyone. Simply put, a judge must be humble.

A judge needs to understand that he is not infallible. He must recognize that every decision he makes can have significant and far-reaching consequences. A good judge needs to be open to new information and be able to admit when he is wrong. Changing a decision is not a sign of weakness, but rather of strength to have the confidence to correct a mistake.

A judge interprets the law; he does not make it. He must respect the separation of powers and know the boundaries of his authority. He must have the humility to recognize his role in the larger legal system and our government. A judge must stay in his lane.

Resilience

Judges get criticized, it comes with the territory. You need to be thick-skinned enough to take it. Judges work hard to get it right. When an order is entered, or an objection ruled on, or a verdict rendered, judges naturally believe they have it right. But not everyone will agree.

Every ruling will leave at least half of the parties unhappy. Sometimes the unhappy party files motions criticizing your wisdom. Sometimes they appeal to higher court and, again, your wisdom is criticized. You must have the confidence in yourself to accept criticism, incorporate constructive feedback, and set the rest aside—it's important to your success and your mental health.

There are also times when you preside over high-profile cases. Cases that attract media examination will subject your rulings to heightened scrutiny by the press and the public, which will almost certainly lead to harping and nitpicking and produce criticism of your rulings. Some may even challenge your qualifications and abilities. Presiding over high-profile cases is not for the squeamish; thick skin is a must.

Efficiency

Judges have a tremendous workload; cases require time and consideration. Litigants generally want a decision from you quickly. You may have deadlines that require you to work swiftly. It's essential to balance the need for efficiency with the obligation to give each case the attention it deserves.

A judge must consider every aspect of a case before ruling to ensure all voices are heard and all the evidence is evaluated. A timely and effective resolution of cases is critical to instill and maintain confidence in our judicial system. The dilemma: a rushed decision can undermine the pursuit of justice, yet, as Martin Luther King Jr. paraphrased, "Justice too long delayed is justice denied." It's easier said than done, but a judge must be efficient, working hard to achieve maximum productivity with a minimum of wasted effort.

Decisiveness

To be an effective judge you must be decisive. Judges make decisions every day, some of which you can ponder and ruminate over and some you cannot. A trial judge must know the rules, and he must act upon them. There is no time for hand wringing when an objection to a question is made or the attorneys ask for a sidebar arguing a motion *in limine* has been violated.

You must have confidence to make the call. A judge must make a decision and stick with it. That is not to say that a judge can't or shouldn't reconsider rulings. But in trial, rulings must happen on the spot in real time. Judging is often compared to umpiring; you have to call balls and strikes.

Impartiality

Impartiality is the cornerstone of our judicial system. To be a judge you must be impartial. Juries are often admonished with something similar to: "Personal prejudices have no place in court. You must set aside and disregard any personal feelings of bias or prejudice you may have based on sex, race, religion, national origin, age or disability. You must decide this case only upon the basis of the evidence admitted and the law as I explain it to you." This applies equally to judges who must make decisions solely based on the law and the facts.

Just like everyone else, judges have implicit biases—feelings, assumptions, perceptions, fears, and stereotypes that they may not be aware of. These hidden thoughts can impact what a judge sees and hears, or how they remember what is seen and heard. Ultimately, implicit biases can affect the way we make important decisions. Judges must evaluate each case carefully and resist jumping to conclusions based on personal likes or dislikes, generalizations, gut feelings, prejudices, sympathies, stereotypes, or biases.

Judges also may have professional biases. Judges come from the bar where they have friends and colleagues who they have worked with for years. It goes without saying, but I'll say it anyway: if a judge cannot be impartial because of a friendship, he should recuse himself.

Judges may also form opinions about lawyers based on past experiences. The temptation to ignore legal arguments from those who a judge considers a dunce is great. Of course, this too is a bias that must be overcome to ensure that all voices have been heard and all arguments considered.

Listening

Better to remain silent and be thought a fool than to speak and remove all doubt. Often attributed to Abraham Lincoln or Mark Twain, but, either way, it's often the case. Judges are first and foremost trained lawyers, and lawyers advocate. Sometimes it can be almost impossible to remain silent, but often the best thing a judge can do is listen. Knowing when to let lawyers argue and when to interject is a fine art.

Authority

It seems obvious, but a judge must have control over the courtroom. The judge maintains decorum in the courtroom. Lawyers will attempt to control their environment; it's part of the art of being a trial attorney. A judge must temper the lawyers' instinct through the authority of the bench by enforcing the rules, requiring civility, and ensuring that things run smoothly. There is a fine line between authoritarian and authoritative and it's one that should be walked carefully.

Humor

Maybe the most important of the skills or attributes a judge needs is a sense of humor. The law is serious. Many cases that you hear are sad at best, horrific at worst. It has been said that the only happy events at a courthouse are weddings and adoptions; everything else is wrongs against someone, criminal, tortious, or contractual. The decisions a judge makes are life-altering for litigants, which adds to the pressure. Without a sense of humor, the intense weight and nature of a judge's work would be overwhelming.

So despite the serious nature, a joke, friendly banter with an attorney, or a smile can make all the difference. Funny things happen in the courtroom. Witnesses say crazy things, facts can be ridiculous. It's okay to laugh. Wit and humor can also defuse edgy situations where lawyers are at each other's throats. Humor puts nervous jurors or parties at ease and reminds everyone that the law is administered by people.

Close

There are a great many attributes that a judge should possess. A trial judge needs the experience of trying cases. A judge needs to be patient with lawyers and litigants. A judge must display humility. A judge should have thick skin. A judge should be efficient and decisive.

A judge, above all else, must be impartial. A judge must know when to speak and when to listen. A judge must use the authority vested in him to control the courtroom. And, to remain sane, a judge should have a sense of humor.

Curiosity, Communication and Patience

Joseph W. Seidlin
Judge, Iowa District Court

When I was appointed as a district court (general jurisdiction) judge, I looked forward to occasional strolls outside of my "comfort zone." I soon found out that my comfort had been "rezoned." There are times when judges are placed into the realm of things they do not know or understand on an almost daily basis. That never goes away—the unknowns just keep coming. What can go away is the pit in your stomach when faced with them.

I think there is one trait that can become the most vital of skills for a judge seeking to remove that pit. The possession or lack of this skill does not necessarily make or break a successful judge. It's more important than that. To me, this skill means the difference between enjoying and hating the job. The skill is curiosity: the desire and ability to ask "how and why" as opposed to just "what, where and when." We all come with some sense of curiosity. The key is to not let this job kill it. Perhaps more positively stated, the key is to feed it and let it grow.

My father had the biggest sense of curiosity of anyone I have ever known. He embarrassed my brother and me regularly with his questions to our friends, teachers, coaches, neighbors, plumbers, electricians, bank tellers…well, everybody. He was simply fascinated by what other people did and how, and by what other people thought and why. His curiosity reached new heights when I became a lawyer. It was like walking into a bar exam whenever I went home. Thankfully, he accepted my answers, not having quite enough grasp of the subject matter to grade them.

Having learned at the feet of the master, I was able to inject a healthy sense of curiosity in my law practice, and enjoyed having a practice involving a wide range of people, situations and law. Still, my wide-ranging practice did not prepare me for what I would encounter as a judge. After all, there are now eight volumes of the Iowa Code, and each appellate decision expands the limitless expanse of law we are called upon to apply. And apply it we must, to the vast expanse of people, cultures and endeavors that we encounter. I remember thinking about three months into my experience as a judge that at least my dad could choose what he was curious about, as I could in my law practice. Judges don't have that choice.

It is enough for any sense of curiosity to give way to that pit in the stomach.

So what can we do to cope with and embrace the daily discomfort, to further develop and sustain this vital skill of curiosity and not let the job kill it? I suggest that there are two things that we can do. First, learn to communicate with people on their level. Second, learn patience.

Communicating "On the Level"

Please don't assume that I mean learning to communicate on a *lower* level. It is pointless to try to assess where on the hierarchy of "levels" someone is compared to you. Trust me, as a judge that will only serve to point out how often you find yourself having to talk *up* rather than *down*. No, there are levels all around us. Developing the ability to communicate "on the level," then, requires education and preparation. Let me give you just one example of each.

Education

Criminal, divorce, child custody, domestic abuse, and juvenile, among other cases, often involve parties with significant histories of exposure to trauma. The brains of people with significant exposure to trauma do not work the same as those without it. Exposure to trauma is often responsible for the things that they do and the things that are done to them that result in their need for court. People with significant exposure to trauma often have difficulty understanding and following court processes and orders.

There are myriad educational opportunities and texts teaching the brain science of trauma and behaviors tied to trauma exposure. Failure to take advantage of these opportunities to study in this area will result in barriers to understanding and effective communication between a judge and a significant percentage of the people who need to understand and follow judicial directives. The how and the why will give way to the what, where and when, resulting in a judge's frustration with a party's inability to understand and follow court processes and orders. If you are that judge, you will dread having hearings and trials with these people. The pit in the stomach will grow.

On the other hand, if you actively seek education in this area, you will not only learn a fascinating area where science meets the law, but you will learn how to communicate in ways that improve understanding and adherence to court processes and orders. The how and why pull even with the what, where and when. Enjoyment increases. The pit shrinks.

Preparation

As general jurisdiction judges, we encounter countless business, contract, and regulatory law cases. The possible subject matter is as limitless as the business and governmental interests within our state. Some are familiar. Most are not. The subject matter in these cases usually comes with its own terms of art, acronyms and rules which must be applied pursuant to law. Being able to communicate on the same level as the lawyers and parties to these cases goes a long way to helping a judge understand the subject matter and apply the law to it. This takes some digging-in on the front end, not just after the case or arguments have been submitted. I found that the pit in my stomach in these cases came from not even knowing what I didn't know. My curiosity had nowhere to go if I didn't know the questions to ask. Preparation by learning the basics of the subject matter helps the judge to rise to the level of communication occupied by the attorneys and parties. It helps to frame the right questions during arguments on discovery and summary judgment motions, administrative appeals and fights over jury instructions. When I am able to at least converse in the same language as the litigants, I can actually get something out of these arguments that will help focus my analysis and decision making. This "digging-in" once again pulls the how and why even with the what, where and when. I hope that these two examples show that learning to communicate "on the level" is not just an abstract concept, but a real tool in freeing and feeding a judge's curiosity. You can almost feel the pit in the stomach fading away just thinking about it.

Patience

What does patience have to do with curiosity? As judges, patience boils down to listening. How can our curiosity survive if we don't listen to what people tell us?

Without patience, the judge assumes the how and why rather than learn it from the people who really know it.

As a lawyer, I handled a lot of family law cases. These cases involve all kinds of hearings in front of judges—injunctions, temporary matters, contempts, and trials. Almost nothing irritated me more than when the judge, after knowing the parties for only a few hours or even minutes, proceeded to scold them on all their shortcomings as parents or even human beings, presuming to know the how and why of what they did. Often, I would feel embarrassed for the judge who got it so wrong. The problem is that in all cases—bar none—judges are the least informed persons in the room when it comes to the litigants and litigation in front of them.

The judge has to learn everything, not just the what, where and when, but the how and why, from everyone else in the room. By speaking too soon or saying too much, the judge's ignorance is exposed. All—the litigants, lawyers and judge—leave frustrated.

Patience, then, is just realizing how dependent I am upon the parties and lawyers to learn. It's suppressing the need to feel like the smartest person in the room so that I can shut up and listen. The more I talk, the less curious I become, and the pit in my stomach grows larger for having to deal with people I don't appreciate, respect or understand. Don't get me wrong; patience does not mean having to suffer fools gladly or constantly run behind schedule. It just means allocating more of the available time to the people who know more about their case than I do.

Curiosity, fed by the ability to communicate on the level with those in front of me and patience, goes to the core of what makes being a judge fulfilling. As I look around at my colleagues after over ten years on the bench, I can tell you that those who exercise and feed their sense of curiosity love their job. Those who do not, no matter how skilled a judge they are, hate it.

Chapter 4

What Judging Expects of You

Resisting Pressures that Erode Judicial Independence

Joel W. Barrows
Judge, Iowa District Court

How do we maintain judicial independence and, as important, show the public that we maintain that independence, thus preserving respect for the courts and the rule of law when they are under unprecedented assault?

Judicial independence is being questioned as never before. While some of this is the result of posturing by politicians, it also stems from legitimate inquiries into investments, gifts and favors bestowed upon judges and justices, and the extent to which they could compromise impartiality, or the public's perception of it.

In most instances the characterization of bias is unfair, but in others the perception is a self-inflicted wound. Witness recent news stories about the failure of some federal judges to make appropriate investment disclosures, or those concerning gifts or favors bestowed upon several Supreme Court justices. While the evidence of direct conflicts is limited, the perception created is possibly even more damaging. And, it is ammunition to those who would use these accusations to further their own agenda under the guise of "judicial reform."

But threats to judicial independence come in many forms, and from many sources. The impact can be manifest, subconscious or simply perceived by others, fairly or not. Much of the public now sees judges as aligned with one political party or the other, depending on who appointed them. This is particularly true as to our federal courts. It is a recent, and dangerous, phenomenon. In my experience, judges are almost uniformly nonpartisan in their approach. This is something that must be emphasized to the public and to potential judicial applicants. The bench is no place for someone with policy goals. While it is certainly acceptable to have a judicial philosophy, it is not appropriate to have a judicial agenda.

Historically, Iowa's judicial selection process has been noted for its independence and the quality of candidates selected. This has given Iowa one of the most respected court systems in the nation. Additionally, Iowa's Code of Judicial Conduct is strict and greatly limits a judge's outside activities. These factors have combined to give our state a judiciary noted for its independence from external pressures. It must remain so. Other states have not been as fortunate, thus eroding their citizens' confidence in their courts.

Obviously, no judges should rule in a case in which they have a financial interest. Nor should they participate in any case in which their independence of judgment could be reasonably questioned. The key word is "reasonably." There is a duty to recuse when appropriate, but there is also a duty to sit and hear the assigned case. Recusal too freely taken can encourage judge shopping, which also erodes confidence in the bench. Each judge must decide for themselves when recusal is appropriate, while remembering that, at times, the perceived conflict of interest can be nearly as damaging to respect for the courts as an actual conflict.

As to that duty to sit, becoming a judge does require a degree of dissociation from former colleagues, groups and activities. This is an important aspect of becoming a judge, and one of the sacrifices one makes in accepting the position. A judge cannot simply maintain these relationships and always expect another judge to hear the case. Of course, some relationships will always require recusal, but after a period of time a judge will be expected to hear most cases involving former colleagues. Were this not the case, court administration's job of juggling the docket would be far more difficult than it already is. And if there is any question on the issue of recusal, a record should be made to allow the parties the opportunity to object, or waive objection and consent. Nonetheless, the decision on whether to recuse rests with the Court. If a judge does not feel they can be objective, they should recuse regardless of whether one or both parties consent.

When the court does hear a case, the judge must not only carefully consider the evidence and arguments offered by each side, but must also manifestly appear to do so. If both parties feel that they have been heard, whether successful or not, it will enhance their respect for the rule of law and the court's reputation for fairness.

Litigants watch the judge and notice even the subtlest gestures. The court must be vigilant in its recognition of this fact and govern itself accordingly. This can be challenging when one of the parties or their counsel breach decorum, but it is the essence of judicial temperament.

A judge must always be reasonable and fair in their dealings, compassionate when warranted, and sensitive to the widely varying backgrounds of the many people they encounter.

Our district courts are where justice is done at the most fundamental and important level. This is where the citizen has their most direct encounter with the guarantees of our Constitution. Each case is probably the most important thing in that particular litigant's life, a fact the judge must always remember.

Judicial Humility

Zachary S. Hindman
Judge, Iowa District Court

A good judge is a humble judge. This concept—judicial humility—might at first glance seem strange, or even paradoxical. Certainly, the authority of the judicial office is anything but humble—judges exercise immense power over the property, the liberty, and the many aspects of the lives of litigants who appear before them. So, too, do accouterments of the office—the black robe, the imposing bench, the majestic courthouse—encourage respect and even awe, and exalt not only the law and our system of justice, but also the judicial office itself. Indeed, the names of our judicial offices—"magistrate," "judge," "justice"—connote not humility but gravitas and solemn grandeur. But notwithstanding the eminence of the *judicial office*, perhaps the most important quality in a *judge*—what judging most insistently expects of you—is humility, properly understood. By judicial humility, I mean the considered submission of certain aspects of one's self—one's emotions, efforts, pride, and personal preferences, among other things—in the service of something greater than self: the judicial office. This self-effacement requires not only a dedication to the duties of the judicial office, but also a commitment to the preservation of the legitimacy of the office, a recognition of the distinction between the office and the person who holds it, and an acceptance of the institutional limitations of the office. All of which is often easier said than done.

This virtue—judicial humility—comes in three somewhat overlapping flavors. One of those, which I call personal or temperamental humility, requires balancing the authority inherent in the judicial office against the human tendency to self-aggrandizement. Put simply, while a judge must exercise the authority of the office, the judge must never lord the office or its power over litigants, lawyers, or anyone else.

Putting this aspect of judicial humility into practice often requires a somewhat delicate balancing act. Consider, for example, those courtroom formalities directed most obviously toward the judge—the requirements that parties and lawyers address the judge as "Judge" or "Your Honor," that they stand when the judge enters and leaves the courtroom, and the like. Such formalities can easily go to a judge's head. Most judges, of course, are likely to be on guard against that possibility, but experience shows that such guard is not always effective. And a subtler danger arises from the opposite extreme. Such formalities, like all courtroom formalities, serve several purposes: they encourage respect for and compliance with the law, which the judge will be applying; they foster the appearance (and the reality) of procedural fairness, by identifying the judge as distinct from the parties and thus neutral; and they function as a system of enforced manners, promoting self-control among even parties in fraught disputes whose emotions are running hot. So an overly informal judicial style runs the risk of undermining those purposes. Indeed, a judge's excessive informality may well arise from a *lack* of humility, in that the judge prioritizes popularity with those who appear before him or her over and to the detriment of the dignity of the judicial office, and of the law.

There is no sure guide for balancing these competing concerns, except that a judge's robe, and the exercise of the power of the office that robe represents, should always weigh heavily. A wise judge should always feel at least a twinge of discomfort at being called "Your Honor," even while recognizing the necessity of that appellation. And a judge should always remember that judging is a human enterprise, which means (among other things) that a judge must, in exercising the authority of his or her office, respect the human dignity, and make due (though not undue) allowance for the human frailties of those who are subject to that authority. To put the matter more bluntly, the least pleasant part of a judge's job should always be the bossing around of other people. Judges are called public servants for good reason—we are servants of the law, and our offices exist to provide the people of our society with a means to peaceably resolve their disputes. And so while we must exercise the authority with which we have been entrusted in order to resolve the disputes presented to us, even when doing so requires making litigants do things they do not want to do, we must do so with the mindset of a servant, not a superior.

A second aspect of judicial humility—one which relates more directly to a judge's judicial duties—entails an honest recognition of one's professional limitations, and a willingness to put in the work to counteract them. Most new judges are experienced lawyers, but few begin the job with a knowledge base as broad as the jurisdiction exercised by their new office. And the law is so vast, and the facts underlying the disputes we see so varied, that new and surprising issues are certain to arise, even within the scope of a new judge's—or, for that matter, an old judge's—experience. So a judge must, through a perhaps uncomfortable process of self-reflection, habitually assess his or her knowledge base, and study hard to close any gaps.

This is especially important for district court judges, who in addition to writing rulings with the luxury of time to research the issues, also often must make split-second decisions in the heat of trial. A trial judge must therefore have an immediate command of the law that governs the resolution of all issues likely to come up at trial. And with regard to the more unusual issues, the judge must (to the extent possible) learn each case inside and out prior to trial, and must also follow the trial closely, in order to anticipate and prepare for such issues, to the extent that it is possible to do so, before the issues arise. Doing all this requires that the judge maintain a sufficient knowledge base to spot approaching potential issues, foster the research skills necessary to quickly study an issue while simultaneously presiding over a trial, and accept the frustrating fact that he or she will prepare to rule on many potential issues that never actually arise.

And while a judge should take comfort in the availability, to parties, of appellate review to correct the judge's mistakes, the judge must not become too comfortable. For one thing, appeals take time and cost money, and so litigants are much better off if lower-court judges get their decisions right in the first place. And for another, even where appellate review is technically available, a trial court judge's decisions often are final as a practical matter—for example, parties may adjust their settlement positions in light of a trial court's preliminary rulings, resolving the case and thereby precluding an appeal, or they may decide that an appeal, even if likely to be successful, simply is not worth the cost and effort.

In short, a judge must have the humility both to recognize his or her intellectual weaknesses and the shortcomings in his or her knowledge, and to put in the never-ending hard work necessary to minimize them.

The third variety of judicial humility—institutional humility—is perhaps the most important. By institutional humility I mean, in part, a respect for our adversarial system of justice, and for a judge's proper role in that system. While a judge ought not to hesitate to ask questions of parties about their arguments, and while a judge is not limited by deficiencies in a party's research on an issue, the judge must avoid raising issues or making arguments not raised or made by the parties. For one thing, a judge rarely knows behind-the-scenes details about his or her cases, and so there may be good reasons why a party does not raise an issue or an argument that seems to the judge like a good one. And for another, both procedural fairness and the continued legitimacy of the adversarial system demand that judges allow parties to suffer the consequences of their mistakes—judicial help for one party is almost always detrimental to the adverse party, and our system of justice is based on the belief in vigorous disagreements presented to a *neutral* arbiter as the surest means of reaching the truth. So in most cases, a judge should become almost like a part of the scenery, and should never be the star of the show, acting only when asked to do so, and never searching out dragons to slay.

Institutional humility also means something even more fundamental to our system of justice: a judge must apply the law carefully and honestly, and must not—consciously or otherwise—substitute his or her own preferred result for the result which the law requires. This is essential to the preservation not only of our system of justice, but also of our system of government as a whole. The people of our State made the law of our State, through their ratification of our State's Constitution, and through the statutes passed by their representatives in our General Assembly. And we judges were appointed to apply that law as written, with fidelity to the text of that law, and without regard to our personal preferences. So we must have the humility to play our proper role, and to foster the proper role of the judicial system, and we must not usurp authority that properly resides elsewhere.

Of course, all judges understand this reality, and most judges try to abide by it. But as recognized by the late Justice Antonin Scalia, "[a]voiding th[e] error" of "mistak[ing] [one's] own predilections for the law . . . is the hardest part of being a conscientious judge." And this is especially so for the skilled advocates who so often attain the bench—for many lawyers, after years of zealously representing clients, it becomes second nature to view a source of law in the light most favorable to the result which the lawyer desires for the client. Hence the need, mentioned above, for judges to apply the law both carefully and also honestly. Since most good judges were once clever lawyers, those judges must constantly engage in careful and honest self-reflection, in order to ensure that any subtleties, refinements, or other cleverness in their rulings is employed in the service of the law, and not as unwitting cover for a results-oriented ruling.

In putting these principles into practice, a judge can put to good use some of the formalities discussed above as potentially dangerous. For example, no good judge who applies those principles will be happy with the results of all of his or her rulings. And so I often find it useful to distinguish between "Zach," who dislikes a particular result, and "Judge Hindman," who will do his duty and apply the law, regardless.

All that said, it is also important to recognize what judicial humility, properly understood, *is not.* Judicial humility is not indecisiveness or an excuse not to do the hard work of judging—after all, a judge is not permitted to render a judgment of undecided. Nor does judicial humility mean timidity, since judges must control their courtrooms, announce their rulings, and enforce those rulings with confidence. And judicial humility does not necessarily mean submission to the political branches of government, since where a careful and honest reading of a higher law (*e.g.*, the State Constitution or the United States Constitution) conflicts with the actions of a political branch, that higher law must prevail.

But properly understood, judicial humility in all its facets—personal, professional, and institutional—is perhaps the most essential judicial virtue. And from those who seek and hold it, the vocation of judging expects nothing less.

The Pursuit of Judicial Excellence

Sean W. McPartland
Senior Judge, Iowa District Court

No one completes an application to become a trial judge with the thought of performing judicial duties with anything other than excellence. Excellence in performance of judicial duties after appointment to the bench, however, is affected by many circumstances facing a judge once appointed. Moreover, the landscape in which judicial officers must perform their duties has changed over the years, adding challenges to achieving excellence in the performance of the duties of judges. The expectation of excellence nonetheless is a privilege which should be embraced and considered by those contemplating an application to serve as a judicial officer.

Serving on the district court bench can be an isolating and solitary experience, compounded by the current workload and lack of resources available to district judges in Iowa. I have described many days serving on the district court bench as analogous to "Lucy on the chocolate line."[1] The "chocolates" keep coming, and sometimes the line speeds up.

The performance of judicial duties has also always been complicated by the adversarial nature of judicial proceedings, the emotions involved in judicial proceedings, and the need to be fair to all participants. Although not all of Rudyard Kipling's writings have aged well, his poem, "If," has several stanzas which provide food for thought for a trial court judge. My favorites include the following:

> If you can keep your head when all about you
> Are losing theirs and blaming it on you;
> If you can trust yourself when all men doubt you,
> But make allowance for their doubting too;
>
> * * *
>
> If you can talk with crowds and keep your virtue,
> Or walk with Kings—nor lose the common touch;
> If neither foes nor loving friends can hurt you;
> If all men count with you, but none too much;[2]
>
> * * *

In my pursuit of judicial excellence as I have tried to define it, I have always tried to serve the litigants and lawyers before me with attention, empathy, and clarity. In courtroom settings, in conferences in chambers, and in written rulings, I have always tried to let the litigants and lawyers know they have been heard even when the relief they have requested is not carrying the day. I have tried to be clear in communicating not just the "what" of judicial determinations, but also the "why." In other words, I strive to provide not just clear rulings and determinations, but also clarity in the reasoning for those rulings and determinations. I acknowledge that I have not always achieved excellence in these pursuits even by my standards, and that some lawyers and litigants may believe that I did not achieve excellence even when I thought I did. Still, the pursuit of excellence remains an important goal for any trial judge.

I have come to believe that judges often perform their best and most important work outside of public view. Although the vast majority of our proceedings are matters of public record and are open to the public, in reality many proceedings take place in small courtrooms where the public never will be present and/or will never take the opportunity to read the trial transcript. That the public may never attend or become aware of such proceedings does not lessen the importance of the proceedings and the judicial determinations to the litigants and to the system.

As merely one example, I once conducted a hearing involving a civil domestic abuse petition filed by a woman who included in her petition the chilling statement that her partner regularly "would punch me for what I felt was not a reason to hit me." Both parties appeared as self-represented litigants. The hearing was not attended by any member of the public and no one requested a transcript, so no member of the public likely learned about the petition or the outcome of the hearing.

The hearing may not have had the attention of the public, but it was enormously important to the litigants, and obviously stuck with the judge. In short, despite most matters being open to the public, much of a judge's work is performed in relative isolation when only the litigants are present, and only the litigants will know of or be affected by the outcome. A trial judge's need to act with wisdom and appropriate empathy, but also fairness and adherence to the rule of law in such situations is sobering, grave, and important.

I believe the performance of the duties of a trial judge is an art and not a science. There is no one way to perform the duties of a judge, and therefore no one right way. Often the work of the trial judge involves the ability to improvise and handle curveballs, fastballs and, all too frequently, screwballs. The assessment of excellence in the performance of duties in such circumstances is usually a subjective one.

Indeed, even assessments of judicial performance by criteria often characterized as objective, such as through the lenses of "originalism" and fidelity to the "intent of the drafters" of the Constitution, are fluid and have evolved over time.[3] If the understanding and command of originalism has changed over time, how is a judge to adhere to notions of originalism at any given time?

Rather, it seems clear that the work of a trial judge most often involves the solitary and important job of exercising judgment with creativity but also clarity, sometimes "when all about are losing their heads and blaming it on the judge." The trial judge has the obligation to perform the job in a variety of ways and contexts, recognizing that "all litigants count, but none too much."

External forces in the recent past have added stress and tensions to the job of a trial judge, making the essence of judging more challenging. Over the last decade, I have seen an erosion of respect for the judiciary and the judicial process, and sometimes defiance of and disrespect for the rule of law. On a national level, there have been threats to judicial staff and families of judicial officers. Around the country, litigants increasingly and publicly do not feel the need to obey judicial determinations and orders with which they disagree. Moreover, proceedings conducted by courts around the country have more frequently been disregarded or dismissed as not binding on the parties. Prominent people, including elected officials and lawyers whose jobs require adherence to the rule of law and belief in and support of our system of justice, more frequently criticize regular performance by judges and juries of their duties in a usual and ordinary fashion. Such criticisms have included reference to convicted defendants as "hostages" despite their convictions following usual and proper due process, and sometimes after guilty pleas.

In Iowa, a serious reduction in the number of candidates for judicial positions in the last 15 years has coincided with these external forces. While one cannot conclude the external forces are the sole cause of the reduction in judicial candidates, the correlation is striking.

The rule of law commands respect not for the judge as a person, but for the system, including obedience to orders of the court with proper opportunity for review. If our respect for and support of the judicial system and the rule of law continues to erode, who can we expect will be willing to serve in judicial positions? Moreover, if any one person or group of people on a national level are not obligated to follow orders of a court, or to follow the rule of law generally, how can we ask or expect individuals appearing before local trial courts in "flyover country" to respect the obligation to comply with judicial orders?

I recognize that honest and regular criticism of the judicial process not only is healthy but is essential to the proper functioning of judicial procedure and the rule of law. Such criticism can and should include exposure of and challenge to inappropriate influences on prosecutors and judicial officers, perceived unreasonable discrepancies in prosecutions, failure to adhere to due process and other judicial procedures, and other outcomes of judicial proceedings based upon race, political affiliation, or other factors which should not matter. Criticisms and threats to the rule of law and the judicial process, however, intended solely to affect the outcome of a particular case or to sway or chill the very judicial system on which we all rely, are dangerous and destructive. It appears that threats to court staff, families of judicial officers, and even jurors are occurring more frequently without disapproval by those who should be defenders of the court system and the rule of law. Silence by people who should be defenders of the rule of law, including lawyers, elected officials, and members of the press, can be deafening and catastrophic.

In August 2017, I participated in a three-day conference, along with several other Iowa judges, hosted by the Iowa Judicial Institute, titled "Portraits in Judicial Courage." The program was one of the most valuable continuing education programs I have ever attended. It included extensive presentations by Dr. William F. Meineke, Jr. and Ann O'Rourke of the United States Holocaust Memorial Museum, with an accompanying booklet, "Law, Justice and the Holocaust." Their presentation and materials included discussion of how the judicial system in Germany gradually contributed to the rise of the Third Reich. Judges in the German system had historically valued judicial independence, and "rendered judgment based on such fundamental Western legal principles as the equality of all citizens, the right of an accused person to a fair trial, and the concept that there could be no crime or penalty without prior law."[4]

The booklet provided interesting and disturbing context for the eventual reaction of the judiciary in Germany to political and legislative action in Germany in the 1930s. The following quote from the booklet may seem alarmingly benign, unless considered in the context of what followed:

> The National Socialist movement will try to achieve its aim with constitutional means in this state. The Constitution prescribes only the methods, not the

> aim.... We shall try to gain decisive majorities in the legislative bodies so that the moment we succeed we can give the state the form that corresponds to our ideas.
>
> - Adolf Hitler, testimony before the Supreme Court, September 1930 (*Justiz und Nationalsozialismus: Katalog zur Austellung des Bundesministeriums der Juistiz*, Cologne: Verlag Wissenschaft und Politik, 1989, 53)[5]

As we now know, judicial independence, and "rendered judgment based on such fundamental Western legal principles as the equality of all citizens, the right of an accused person to a fair trial, and the concept that there could be no crime or penalty without prior law," over time, changed in grave and despicable ways.

> I am totally indifferent as to whether a legal clause opposes our actions.... During the months when it was about the life or death of the German nation, it was entirely irrelevant whether other people whined about breaking the law.... They called it lawless because it did not conform with their notion of the law. In truth, through our labors we laid the foundations of a new law, the right to live of the German nation.
>
> - Reich Leader of the SS and Chief of the German Police Heinrich Himmler, speaking to the Committee of Police Law of the Academy of German Law, October 11, 1936 (Hans Adolf Jacobsen and Werner Jochmann, eds.

> *Ausgewählte Dokumente zur Geschicte des Nationalsozialismus 1933-1945*. Bielefeld:1961)[6]

It is always good to be mindful of and to reflect on history, even when it is uncomfortable and difficult to do so.

> How was this possible? Why did it happen? It seems clear that the Nazi period presented individual judges—as it did so many others—with intense personal and ethical dilemmas. And while it is all too easy to condemn them in retrospect, oversimplifying their circumstances and declaring moral absolutes from a safe historical distance, it is more difficult and, ultimately, more useful to examine critically and objectively the pressures they faced. Moreover, it is neither the outright heroes nor the obvious villains whose stories are the most deeply challenging. Rather, it is through studying the actions of the ambivalent, conflicted and ordinary individuals that the realities of ethical struggle become accessible.[7]

While it is not my intention to be hyperbolic or alarmist, the experience of the changing role of the justice system in the 1930's in Germany, which had been based on Western legal principles, provides a cautionary tale worth reconsidering and studying. New judges are wise to be mindful of, and indeed have the obligation to consider, past precedent and the implications of the ordinary performance of judicial duties. A system of justice governed by the rule of law once lost can be difficult to recapture.

Despite the regular challenges facing the judicial system, and even considering any increased challenges in the recent past, service as a judicial officer in Iowa is a great and fulfilling job. The "chocolates keep coming," and sometimes the "chocolate line" moves faster, but the work is important and extremely rewarding. I am proud and grateful to have been appointed to the trial court bench. It is a wonderful job, involving important work with direct, serious, and real effects on the litigants appearing before the court. While judicial officers may not always achieve excellence in every proceeding or ruling, the expectation of excellence comes with the job and is a privilege.

How to Be a Good Judge

Thomas P. Murphy
Judge, Iowa District Court

Attorneys contemplating becoming judges often seek my advice. I view each of those attorneys as potential colleagues. I tell them to ask themselves if they "want to do judge stuff" or "just want to be judges"?

Doing "judge stuff" requires attorneys who are humble, confident, and competent. "Judge stuff" requires personal and professional sacrifices, working hard, solving problems, and serving others. Judges who want to do "judge stuff" are good colleagues.

Attorneys who "just want to be judges" are those who seek status, want to be called "your honor," and look forward to having everyone stand when they enter the courtroom. They have "black robe syndrome." They are not good colleagues.

Good colleagues are good judges. Being a good judge is not easy. To good judges, judicial robes feel very heavy. They come with the weight of tremendous responsibility. The responsibility is inherent in the oath Iowa judges take when we swear or affirm that we:

> . . . will support the Constitution of the United States and the Constitution of the State of Iowa, and . . . without fear, favor, affection, or hope of reward, [we] will, to the best of [our] knowledge and ability, administer justice according to the law, equally to the rich and the poor.

The oath requires us to maintain the integrity of the judiciary. To do that requires vigilance and sacrifice.

The oath requires us to be confident, and competent. Confidence and competence come from learning, hard work, and experience.

The oath requires us to humbly serve others. To administer justice to people equally, regardless of their status, requires humility. Humility makes good judges work hard. It makes us realize that our work is not about us; it is about the people we serve. It makes us respectful of others.

Maintaining the integrity of the judiciary is a full-time job. Judges are leaders. We represent the judiciary, and other judges. Everything judges do becomes an example. Our colleagues rightfully expect us to always be good examples.

Absent occasional media coverage, most citizens do not regularly think about judges. Most people will never meet a judge. Many litigants only see one or two judges. People's views of all judges are based on their impressions of the judges with whom they have experience. Judges' conduct must be impeccable in, and out of, the courtroom.

In the courtroom, we must exercise emotional and judicial restraint. All litigants and attorneys must feel that their judges are treating them with dignity and respect. We must endeavor to fairly apply the law to their cases.

Judges expect their colleagues to follow the law. We must research the law as we apply it to our cases. We should continuously review new decisions from the Iowa Supreme Court and the Iowa Court of Appeals. Judges must follow changes to the Iowa Code. When we all do our best to follow and apply the law, litigants can count on consistent justice.

We are not just judges in the courtroom. Our personal lives matter. We must never use our positions to impress people or to curry favor. We all suffer from a colleague who, regardless of whether it ends up as a YouTube video, plays the "judge card" with a law enforcement officer during a traffic stop.

We owe it to our colleagues to refrain from participating in political activities. The best thing the public can know about our preferences regarding candidates for public office is nothing. Likewise, judges must be careful not to engage in activities that suggest we have an opinion one way or another regarding any legislation.

We must exercise good judgment in our personal lives. Our conduct must be above reproach. For example, public intoxication or operating while intoxicated charges brought against one judge are unacceptable. They reflect poorly on all of us.

Again, protecting the integrity of the judiciary requires vigilance and sacrifice. Judges must be aware of situations that might create appearances of impropriety. We may have to forsake events that could call our behavior or integrity into question.

Colleagues who are confident and competent are essential. The oath requires judges to do their "best." We are at our best when we keep learning, work hard, and seek new experiences.

Good judicial colleagues set high standards for themselves and others. Judges must make timely decisions, begin trials and hearings on time, maintain dignity in judicial proceedings, demand that attorneys produce good work, and require attorneys and litigants to be respectful. Judges who do not set high standards for themselves and others undermine the efforts of their colleagues who demand excellence and respect.

Good colleagues are judges who actively seek their share of tough assignments. At my investiture, the judge who administered my oath said:

> [J]udges will be required to spend more time on the bench hearing contested cases and doing

court service and will forfeit, at least during working hours, much of the time necessary to decide cases and write rulings. The result is that judges will continue to find it necessary to work on the rulings at night, on the weekends, and even to the extent that some will forfeit vacation time to prevent a delay in filing decisions.

No attorney can, or should, take the bench with the expectation that judges work five eight-hour days a week. Our dockets are becoming increasingly busy. Legal issues are often complex and time-consuming. Good judges handle a fair share of tough trials and motions.

Good judges should not continue trials or tough motion hearings because of unease with the subject matter. When that happens, it puts an increased burden on colleagues. It creates scheduling backlogs. Worse, it denies litigants timely access to resolution of their cases.

We have a tough job. Everyone needs occasional time away from work. But good colleagues should not take vacation on short notice to avoid a tough jury trial, a difficult divorce case, or a tough motion hearing. When those things happen, another judge must ignore pending rulings to preside with little time to prepare.

We must recuse ourselves from cases in which we have conflicts. But we should closely examine whether we have real conflicts. For example, having once presided over an unrelated case with a litigant may not create a conflict for a judge assigned to preside over that litigant's divorce trial.

Good judges always remember that we serve others. We serve the public. We are not supreme beings because we wear the robe. We should not consider ourselves better than the attorneys and litigants who appear before us.

We have significant power. But we must be humble in our uses of it. The robes we wear are heavy because of our responsibility to use our power appropriately and refrain from using it when necessary. Good colleagues respect and support other judges' exercise of power.

Humility allows judges to treat everyone fairly and respectfully. Judges expect their colleagues to treat everyone well. That means judges must be kind to other judges, attorneys, litigants, and court staff. Even-temperament is a non-negotiable requirement for judges. One temperamental judge reflects poorly on the rest of us.

Judges need their colleagues to be available. We have lonely jobs. When a judge is on the bench in a jury trial, and decisions need to be made quickly, there is no one to turn to for advice. We have to be decisive and maintain control of the courtroom.

Most of the time, for those of us who work in rural areas, we are the only judge in a county on any given day. But, when time allows, it is often helpful to run things by a colleague.

Few, if any, judges are appointed with experience in all aspects of the law. General jurisdiction judges "drink from fire hoses." We cannot know everything. Good colleagues realize that about themselves and other judges. Fortunately, many of us have diverse backgrounds. Good judges are available to their colleagues in the morning, during lunchtime, and in the evening.

Our social circles are limited. The tough subject matter of many of our cases makes fellowship important. A judge presiding over a two-week child death or a sexual abuse trial benefits from unwinding with colleagues who understand the stress of the job. Good colleagues meet for lunches and other activities. For example, in our district, we meet somewhat regularly on Saturday mornings for coffee. Showing up for each other lessens the weight of our robes.

Doing "judge stuff" is a privilege. Doing "judge stuff" with good colleagues is a blessing.

Congratulations! Everything is Different Now

Dustria A. Relph
Judge, Iowa District Court

As an attorney, I held numerous judges in high esteem and hoped to emulate them. Some due to the seemingly endless breadth of their knowledge, some because of their remarkable patience and composure with litigants and inexperienced attorneys like I was starting out, and others for a host of reasons.

One judge was particularly aspirational to me. I did not appear before her often, as she presided in a neighboring district that I did not routinely have a lot of cases in. But when I did, she was exemplary—knowledgeable, kind, patient, and ever professional. Our husbands were business colleagues, so we had a few opportunities to socialize outside of work. Those occasions were mostly in public and fairly superficial, but she was still warm and courteous. I understood that she had to maintain boundaries to avoid any ethical concerns for my future appearances before her. When I did appear in her chambers or courtroom, she always made a record to inform opposing counsel or litigants of our husbands' work relationship to avoid any appearance of impropriety and to mitigate any perceived bias.

When the opportunity arose for me to apply to become a district court judge, she was one whose advice I sought. She enthusiastically encouraged me and generously shared her wisdom about the application process. She gave me valuable tips about completing the written application and navigating the intimidating interview process. Her advice was incredibly helpful to this newcomer to the course, and she delivered it in her ever professional, ever classy way.

I was appointed to the bench a few months later and my mentor promptly extended an invitation to dinner. I'll never forget her broad smile and sparkling eyes as she shook my hand with both of hers and said, "Congratulations! Everything is different now!"

Of course my response was a wholehearted, "Thank you," but I recall wondering at the time, "What exactly does that mean?" After all, I didn't feel any different, other than incredibly shocked and honored, which I humbly remain today. It felt awkward and made me blush that people were already calling me "Judge" instead of "Dusti" like I was accustomed to, but other than that, I failed to see that much changing. Unfortunately, I failed to ask for further explanation. I surmised that she must be referring to our ability to communicate and socialize in a more open, relaxed manner and not be as on guard about appearances. Well, I would soon learn that while my assumption was true, it was only the proverbial tip of the iceberg.

Believe it, like it, understand it or not, becoming a judge transforms more than just your career; it reshapes one's personal and professional life in profound ways. Many former peers and colleagues begin to see you differently and social interactions change, including how you socialize in public and online. New judges often find themselves under the scrutiny of the public and even those they consider friends in ways they have not experienced before. New expectations are placed on your behavior that sometimes feel stifling. Navigating the transition can be challenging.

Two of the earliest transformations I noticed in myself were a sudden broadening of my intellectual horizon and the enhancement of my wit at least tenfold. Of course, and to my dismay, this did not actually occur. But a less keen observer would have thought so.

For about a year after their appointment, new judges in my largely rural district are typically assigned to courthouses that are not within the geographical areas they most often practiced in. I was no exception, and that meant I was meeting many new people every day for some time. I enjoy meeting people and developing relationships, but I've never thought of myself as particularly witty. So, imagine my surprise when my jokes seemed to become instantly funnier and drew raucous laughter like

I'd never experienced before. It did not take long to recognize what was happening—my material was fresh to my new audience—and my tiny bubble burst, though I still tried.

Similarly, attorneys would come to me with legal questions that I had no idea how to answer, assuming that because I was a judge, after all, I must be in possession of the answer to every legal question. Sadly, becoming a judge does not instantly confer upon one all the knowledge necessary to navigate every possible obscure legal scenario. Fortunately, my experienced colleagues on the bench have never failed to graciously accept my requests for phone-a-friend consultations. This humbling experience underscored the importance of supporting new judges as they navigate similar challenges. I cannot think of another career that would better exemplify Aristotle's quote, "The more you know, the more you know you don't know." On the other hand, I'm all about being here to help my new colleagues out because, in the words of the venerable Red Green, "We're all in this together."

One of the most difficult professional changes for me, still after nearly ten years on the bench, has been the shift in relationships with attorneys and others in the legal community who were once my peers. In addition to getting legal work done, pre-Covid court service days provided at least weekly opportunities to observe and learn from more experienced attorneys, brainstorm challenges, and develop meaningful professional relationships. In the relatively small legal community of south-central Iowa, fellow attorneys, social workers, probation officers, and many others became my friends.

Then, almost literally overnight, those relationships changed out of necessity. While still a colleague, I was no longer a peer. I was suddenly thrust into the position that my mentor judge had been in with me before my appointment, and navigating the necessary professional boundaries to avoid any appearance of bias was a challenging task. It was no longer acceptable for me to join counsel in courtroom banter about pending cases, trial strategy, difficult litigants, or the like. And if I did happen to walk through on my way to chambers during such discussions, the tone changed immediately. Counsel sat straighter and light conversation became more serious as they waited for me to pass. While I treasure my relationships with fellow judges, I miss the camaraderie of my attorney friends and others, and to this day find it difficult to resist the pull to the courtroom to join the conversations. Striking a balance between professional boundaries and collegial workplace relationships will be my goal so long as I am on the bench.

Inevitably, there are shifts in social and public engagements. Circles of friends become smaller and more close-knit, with only the most understanding adaping to the changes. Social outings take on a different nature, often concluding earlier, and inquiries from newly made friends turn into exercises of evasion to keep one's profession undisclosed. Judges who were once extroverted may find themselves tempering their behavior to avoid drawing attention to themselves and to steer clear of any semblance of impropriety. The effort to do so affects not only our professional conduct but also permeates our personal lives.

Social media presence can become almost non-existent in an effort to avoid scrutiny, and resisting the urge to comment on current hot topics can sometimes be unbearable! Every comment, photo, meme, or page must be carefully scrutinized before sharing to ensure that it won't impact public confidence in either myself or the impartiality of the judiciary.

Even simple trips to a store can be a challenge when a vaguely familiar face causes you to wonder where you know someone from. Is it someone who appeared before me? Did I sentence her, or perhaps her family? Did I rule against him? Was that a victim, or a witness, or any number of possibilities? Many people appear before a judge for a short period of time, and we may not remember their faces, but litigants seem to remember their judge forever.

To this point, you may be left wondering if all the changes are worth it. My answer would be, "Yes." The differences have not been solely negative; there have also been immeasurable positive changes as well. Reflecting on my journey, I am sincerely grateful for the growth and wisdom I've gained, as it has been a profound honor and privilege to serve my community in this esteemed role.

The work of a judge is both challenging and rewarding, especially for those who enjoy learning. My mind and intellect are consistently stretched by time spent researching and contemplating subject areas or peculiar fact patterns that I previously had no experience with. Moving from an environment where success was measured by the ability to persuade and win, to one where success is defined by the fairness and integrity of one's judgments has been a profound and positive difference.

Though adjusting to changes in associations with prior coworkers has been a challenging phase, the most fulfilling part of my journey to judgeship has been the bonds I've established with fellow judges. We each have unique approaches, peculiarities, and methodologies, but above all, we support one another unconditionally. Sharing our experiences, reinforcing each other's values, and learning from our collective wisdom has not only enriched my personal growth but also enhanced the professional camaraderie within our judicial community.

Overall, the journey to the bench is a transformative one that requires adapting to new roles and responsibilities. It reshapes personal and professional retionships, brings new challenges in navigating legal scenarios, and places one under public scrutiny. However, the journey is also filled with growth and invaluable learning experiences, underlining the importance of mentorship and support within the legal community.

My mentor was right. Though perhaps not everything is different now, many, many things are.

Chapter 5

Which Judgeship Suits You Best?

So, You Are Thinking About Applying to Be a Judge?

Richard G. Blane, II
Judge, Iowa District Court (Ret.)

I have been asked to provide some insight on what a lawyer might want to consider in applying for either the trial bench or an appellate position. The first thing I recommend is to ask yourself a series of questions.

The first question to ask is, Am I right for the job? Be honest with yourself. Foremost, is it in your make-up to make a decision? Bottom line, the job of being a judge is making decisions. Sometimes, literally hundreds of decisions each day. I have seen firsthand a number of judges who were miserable in their role. Some simply were not decision makers and had difficulty "pulling the trigger"—it ate them up. Others did not want to "hurt anybody's feelings." Although as a judge your ultimate goal is to do justice, in doing so you determine winners and losers—whether it is ruling on motions, evidentiary objections, entering findings, rendering civil judgments, sentencing criminal defendants, or even writing appellate opinions. Judges will always disappoint one or more parties (and their attorneys). Is it within your make-up and personality to handle this? And obviously you should not apply if what you are seeking is simply the prestige of a black robe and the title. Being a judge on any bench is hard work. It is not for slackers or someone who wants to "retire" from the practice.

Second, is the job right for me? You need to find out what the job of judge really entails and what is expected for the particular judicial opening you are considering. Do this by talking to judges about the position. Which judges you talk to depends on what court you are considering and what kind of cases are handled: trial court—general jurisdiction versus specialized dockets—e.g. criminal (felony, misdemeanor, traffic), civil, juvenile, probate, small claims—or appellate court.

Third, am I prepared to do the job? Do you have sufficient training and experience for the judgeship you are considering? Be realistic; don't oversell or undersell yourself. Seek advice from others. Make an honest list of your pros and cons.

Next, here are some things to consider when trying to decide which bench to apply for—trial or appellate.

Attributes for Both Trial and Appellate Bench

Do you have a good sense of right and wrong? A good moral compass? This is valuable in both trial and appellate work, but probably more so on the trial bench.

Do you have a strong academic background? Consider data points such as your law school class rank, any awards you received, and whether you participated in law review. (This can be helpful in seeking any judicial position, but probably more important when applying for an appellate position). Are you published? Did you participate in law school moot court and mock trial? (That experience is probably more conducive to the trial bench.) You may be able to make up for a lack of academic credentials with practical trial experience, particularly for the trial bench.

Do you have a broad background of experience in the areas of law you will be applying? Do you have a specialized law practice that is suited for a particular court? Are you recognized as an expert or leader in a particular area of the law?

Are you a good writer? Are you able to convey a result and the logic that supports it?

Do you like to do legal research? This is necessary at both the trial and appellate levels. You may have limited or no access to a law clerk on the trial bench.

Are you ready for the "cloistered" life required of a judge? You will be required to abide by the code of judicial ethics. You will have limitations on your public activities. There will be expectations on how you conduct yourself in public.

Are you a perfectionist versus a "get 'er done" type? As a trial judge, sometimes you just have to make a call and move on to keep a docket or trial moving. Appellate work, however, requires more perfection.

Do you have a good reputation in your community as well as the legal community? Have you contributed to public service, served on court or bar association committees, or offered pro bono representation? Are you recognized for your trial experience, appellate advocacy, or legal expertise? Have you received awards for your legal ability?

Do you have the appropriate temperament? Do you treat others cordially and with respect? As an attorney have you been timely and reliable? Is that your reputation among the bar?

Attributes and Considerations for the Trial Bench

Are you a "quick read"? (I do not mean do you read fast, although that helps.) Do things come to you quickly? Do you process information rapidly? Can you make decisions on the spot (e.g. ruling on objections during a trial; rendering decisions from the bench)?

Are you a "people" person? Do you have good "people skills"? The trial bench is the "peoples' court" where you will be dealing with litigants, attorneys, jurors, witnesses, law enforcement and court staff. You will also be dealing with numerous individuals within the judicial branch.

Do you like to fly solo—can you make decisions on your own as required on the trial bench? You can discuss a case with fellow judges, but it will be your signature alone on the ruling or order.

Do you have sufficient courtroom experience to recognize, understand and handle procedural issues you will face during a hearing or trial?

Do you prefer the action of the courtroom to solitary appellate work?

Are you able to verbally articulate your thought process and conclusions in a way people understand when called on to announce an oral ruling or decision from the bench?

Do you have strong time management skills? Are you organized? Are you able to multitask? Can you establish priorities and stick to them? Or are you a procrastinator?

How well do you handle pressure? You will be faced with crowded dockets, complicated trials and legal issues, controversial issues of public interest, the press, a backlog of cases needing rulings, pushy lawyers, self-represented litigants, insufficient staff, and a lack of adequate time.

Are you willing to sacrifice your personal time? You may have to drive to various courthouses (a.k.a. windshield time) that will require you to leave home early and get home late. Issuing timely rulings and preparation for hearings and trials will likely require work at home during evenings and weekends. Overall, you will have less control over your time and schedule. Your workdays will be controlled by court administrators and case coordinators.

Attributes and Considerations for the Appellate Bench

Do you have a familiarity with the appellate court, its process and decision making? Did you serve as a judicial law clerk for an appellate court? Do you have significant appellate practice?

Do you like to write? Edit? Proofread? Do you have a background in legal writing? The primary work of an appellate judge is reviewing the record and briefs and drafting opinions. Secondarily, as an appellate judge, you may be asked to serve on committees or commissions to review, draft or edit court rules.

Do you function well in solitude? The appellate bench is more isolating than the trial bench. There is less contact with lawyers and the public in general. You will spend considerable time looking at a computer screen as opposed to sitting in a courtroom.

Is your thought process more deliberate? Can you maintain your focus for longer periods of time? Because appellate opinions are usually viewed by more than just the parties, and may serve as precedent cited by others, the drafting process requires more precision. Generally, writing appellate opinions is more tedious than drafting trial court rulings and orders as there is more redrafting and editing.

Do you work well in a collaborative setting? You will be working with law clerks (or staff attorneys) and the other judges on your panels. Opinions may require conferencing and redrafting to satisfy requirements of the other judges on the panel.

The decision of whether to apply for the trial or appellate bench—and indeed, whether to pursue a judgeship at all—is a consequential one that requires thoughtful deliberation and an honest assessment of your temperament, skills, strengths and weaknesses. The work is demanding, and the burden of justice is not a light one. But if you were able to answer most of these questions in the affirmative, it is a good indication that you are well suited for the role of either a trial or appellate judge. Being a judge imposes great responsibility, but with the right people on the bench, it also allows great personal reward while serving justice.

From Pigs to Practice to Presiding: My Journey to the Bench

Randy V. Hefner
Judge, Iowa District Court (Ret.)

My longtime friend and colleague, Jeff Goodman, asked me to write an essay about why I decided to apply for a district court judge position but never sought an appellate court appointment. I told him the answer was easy enough. I wasn't smart enough and I wasn't that great a writer. He pressed on (as Jeff does), and asked what I would have done if I had been smarter (which also begged the question of what I would not have done). Would I have applied for an appellate court position? He argued that some lawyers who are considering applying for a district or appellate court position may be interested in my perspective. After all, as Jeff said, "You are old, retired, and can say anything you want." So I hope this may be helpful to someone considering applying for a position as a judicial officer.

To understand my perspective, you need to know a little about me. I hail from Cushing, a very small town in northwest Iowa. If you know where Cushing is you are either from there or at some point you've been lost in northwest Iowa. My parents were truck drivers (yes, even my mother) and later janitors at the local school. Brother Rod and I played basketball in high school, and after a home game, win or lose, Rod and I were on the floor again, this time to sweep and clean the gym for the next day's PE classes. As was true with most boys in rural Iowa in those days, I made spending money shoveling manure out of hog houses, baling hay, and walking beans.

For some reason, I was told from a young age that I was going to college. In hindsight, I think that arose because of my lack of more practical skills, such as the ability to hammer a nail into a board without smashing my fingers or the ability to overhaul a truck engine in the middle of the night with only a flashlight for illumination, skills my father and brothers possessed but which had eluded me. The thought must have been, "If Randy doesn't go to college, he'll starve and the rest of us will have to take care of him." I attended UNI and obtained a degree in history. Summers were spent working construction, painting barns or erecting grain storage bins.

So after years honing my skills in menial labor and obtaining my history degree from UNI, law school seemed to be the next logical step. Up until then, I had never met a real lawyer. In my family, you would never admit you knew a lawyer because that would be interpreted as meaning you did something, probably criminal, that required a lawyer's services.

The first lawyer I ever met in person was Father Jerome Petz, a Jesuit priest and law school instructor. Imagine my relief when the first law school professor I met was a priest! (I made a point to tell Fr. Petz that I was married to a good Catholic girl.) While a first-year student at Drake, I worked at the pretrial release program, which in those days was staffed with law school students. While in law school, I also clerked for one of the larger Des Moines firms and ultimately for Jim Van Werden and Greg Hulse in Adel, which at that time was a rather typical rural county seat.

Following graduation, I worked for David Shaff's firm in Clinton for one year. Though my tenure with his firm was brief, the lessons David taught me about professionalism and the practice of law stuck with me throughout my career. My wife Connie and I returned to Adel, and I practiced there for over 30 years. As a young attorney, and then as an old attorney, I did what county seat attorneys typically do—a little bit of everything. By the end of my career, I was spending most of my time in courtrooms, trying civil jury and non-jury cases and a few criminal cases. By my count I represented clients in 40-50 appeals in both state and federal courts. I wrote more than my share of appellate briefs and argued more than my share of appeals.

Connie and I lived in Adel for 44 years. Connie taught elementary school in the ADM District for over 30 of those years. We were active in the community, as most rural attorneys and teachers are. And as small-town lawyers do, I joined a number of organizations and served on a number of boards, ranging from the local Rotary Club to the ADM Scholarship Foundation board to the ICLU board. I started my own small firm in 2000. My staff consisted of good friends who were also exceedingly competent.

Over those many years, I had the good fortune to represent clients in many different types of cases. I represented a gay state employee who was harassed at work before sexual orientation was a protected class. I represented a cocaine addict who was fired after he bottomed out, went to his employer (a bank) to report his problem and what he was doing to address it. I represented women who were passed over for promotions in favor of less qualified men. I represented farmers who were seriously injured operating equipment that was unnecessarily dangerous. I represented clients whose medical insurance claims were denied because of preexisting conditions or honest mistakes made in filling out an application. I represented many clients in family law cases. And yes, I also represented banks in foreclosure actions during the '80s farm crisis, and I represented insurance companies defending claims.

Through all of this, I discovered something about myself. I liked helping people—real people with real problems, issues or goals. I found that I could communicate effectively with lawyers, judges and clients from different backgrounds. In the process, I made a pretty good living and a lot of friends.

Which brings us to 2010. Judge William Joy from Perry retired creating a district court vacancy. I submitted a letter recommending a colleague and friend for the position. Then after submitting that letter recommending someone else for the position, I asked myself a question that I had never before thought about. Would I like to be a district court judge? Did I have the skills to do the job? Was I too old? At the ripe old age of 57, I was ancient as a first-time district court judge applicant.

After talking with Connie and Mark, brother Rod, and my close friend and former law partner, Judge Greg Hulse, I decided that I would like to serve and that I probably had the experience and background to do the job. I may have been a bit long in the tooth, but I decided to apply anyway. Senility was still a few years away—at least that was what Governor Culver thought when he appointed me.

In addition to never coveting a judicial appointment, there were other reasons I applied relatively late in life. Rural district court judges are required to travel, and you may not know today where you'll be sent tomorrow. This makes it difficult to consistently participate in or even attend your child's school and extracurricular activities, help with doctor appointments, or help with pickup and drop-off at daycare. But by 2010 our son Mark was out of college and gainfully employed, and being involved with his activities was no longer a consideration. Connie and I were financially stable, and the cut in pay was not a concern. Though I very much enjoyed working with the staff at my office, and I enjoyed the flexibility and autonomy of the practice, I also felt I was getting a bit stale. Age 57 was the right time for me to apply.

I had a pretty good idea as to what district court judges did when I applied, but there was still a learning curve. By my rough calculations, district court judges spend 80% of their time handling or trying family and criminal cases. I was familiar with family law cases and the issues commonly arising in those cases, and I worked to become more familiar with the criminal law issues and processes. Rural judges must efficiently handle busy court service days and, as with every judge at every level, even-handedly control the courtroom during contentious trials. I was unaware of the extent of administrative responsibilities of a rural district court judge, such as chairing courthouse security committees and magistrate selection commissions and filling clerk vacancies in the rural counties. I was appointed shortly before the state judiciary converted to electronic filing, a worthwhile but nonetheless challenging project for all.

There were unexpected benefits as well. My best decision as a judge was my first decision—hiring Lisa McCarville as my court reporter. As a district court judge, your staff consists of your court reporter and clerks you share with other judicial officers. Lisa, as with all rural court reporters, was not only a court reporter, but she also managed court service days and trials, helped me with technology issues, served as a valuable sounding board, and proofread rulings. She became a good friend. Likewise, I was always impressed with the professionalism, efficiency and friendliness of the personnel in the clerks' offices, our schedulers, and district court administration staff.

Another unexpected benefit was having a front row seat to watch good lawyers try cases or argue interesting legal issues. At times it was downright humbling! And at times I was mildly amazed that I was getting paid to watch!

Despite the challenges of the position, my mission as a district court judge was essentially the same as when I practiced—bring each case to a fair and just conclusion and ensure that the lawyers and litigants have their day in court. As a judge my role changed, but the mission was essentially the same. As an attorney, I appreciated a judge who took time to prepare detailed written rulings in non-jury cases. Specifically, detailed findings of fact assured the attorneys and the litigants that you had in fact listened to them.

As I envision the work of appellate judicial officers, they read briefs and at least pertinent parts of the record, listen to oral arguments, conduct research with the assistance of clerks, discuss cases with their fellow judges or justices, write opinions, and otherwise think deep thoughts. They also perform administrative tasks, which are generally not visible to the public but are underappreciated.

As a lawyer and later as a judge, some of this sounds appealing, but these tasks are not what I enjoyed the most about either the practice of law or serving on the district court bench. I do occasionally enjoy thinking deep thoughts, but I have tried to not make a habit of it. On an appellate court, you do not get to watch good lawyers try cases. Your opinions are based on the trial record and not parties and witnesses you have actually seen. Your opinions must by necessity be written for a larger audience.

Not to stretch too far for a comparable, but district court judges, district associate judges and magistrates are a bit like emergency room doctors. We try to fix a problem as best we can as quickly and efficiently as we can. Appellate courts are a bit more like plastic surgeons—they try to make what we did look better.

You can also think about it this way. How many good movies or television shows do you remember about trials, attorneys trying cases or even trial judges overseeing those trials? A lot, right? How many of you read *To Kill a Mockingbird* and wanted to be Atticus Finch? How many good movies do you remember about appellate judges or justices thinking deep thoughts and writing opinions? The action, the drama, and the intrigue all happen at the trial court level.

Without question an appointment to an appellate court is a laudable accomplishment, and the work of appellate judicial officers is critical to a functioning judiciary. Simply due to longevity, I have known quite a few appellate judges and justices over the years (though most may understandably deny they ever heard of me). Chief Justice Marsha Ternus, Chief Justice Mark Cady, Justice Daryl Hecht, Justice David Wiggins, and Judge Richard Doyle are a few that come to mind as appellate judicial officers whom I have known and deeply respect. But the skills required to be a good appellate judge differ from those required to be a competent district court judge, district associate judge or magistrate. I also deeply respect the dozens of district court judges, district associate judges and magistrates I appeared before and worked with over the past 45 years.

Time to circle back to the original question: Why would I have been particularly unsuited for a position on an appellate court? I think I've answered the question. The law for me was always a path to a goal, not a goal in and of itself. It led to a career and a satisfying life in rural Iowa. It provided me with the means to help people resolve disputes, achieve justice, plan for the future or improve their lives by simply buying a house or starting a business. The logical capstone for my career was a district court judgeship.

Allow me to finish my story. After 45 years practicing law and serving on the bench, I became a grandfather to identical twin girls. When Connie and I heard that Mark and Nichole were having twins, we decided that I would retire, and we would move to Minnesota to help care for the girls. As it happened, I applied for a judicial appointment when my daily duties as a father were over, and my judicial career ended when my duties as a grandfather began. I have made my share of mistakes and committed reversible errors often enough, but I have never doubted these decisions.

Why I Never Considered the Appellate Court

Michael D. Huppert
Chief Judge, Iowa District Court

The focus of this chapter is to look at why someone would pursue an appointment to the trial bench, and once appointed make the decision to stay there. I have had the opportunity over my 25-year career as a district judge to better understand what brought me to the bench and to see others come onto and move through the judicial branch as judges or justices. My purpose in contributing to this book is to provide some insight from those observations that may be helpful to those who will come after me who may be considering a career on the trial bench.

To begin with, the pursuit of a judicial appointment is as amorphous a process as could be imagined. The stated qualifications are pretty minimal—you have to be a licensed attorney and (at least in my home state of Iowa) you have to be young enough to serve a partial term after your appointment and one full term before reaching the mandatory retirement age of 72. Other than that, it's frankly pretty murky. Anyone who meets these requirements can apply and be interviewed by a commission, who in turn selects two finalists to ultimately be appointed by the governor. The selection process at all levels turns on such nebulous concepts as judicial temperament and philosophy, as well as more pragmatic concerns such as time management and the extent of one's experience in all areas of the law. To be able to navigate this process successfully requires a combination of luck and hard work. I had to apply several times before I was appointed, which is not uncommon. To be successful in the pursuit begs the ultimate question, however—why is someone attracted to the trial bench in the first place?

I don't think a lot of law school students are thinking about a judicial career; that motivation, if it arrives, comes after several years in the practice of law. I believe there are two forces at play when someone contemplates going onto the bench: something is pushing you *away* from what you contemplated as your career in the law, and something is pulling you *toward* the appeal of being a judge. Ultimately, those who are successful in getting onto the bench respond more to the pull than the push; they discover something about themselves that attracts them to taking on the role of an impartial arbiter of a dispute rather than a zealous advocate for one side.

Looking for a new pursuit to take the place of disappointment in one's career path (the "push") may be the reason to put your name in the first few times, but if you can't see yourself in the role (the "pull"), it is unlikely that you can be successful in convincing a commission and the governor that you are the right choice. To be serious about the process requires a tremendous amount of self-examination—to not just be able to talk about your accomplishments, but also look back on those accomplishments and determine whether you really have what it takes to be a judge. Some lucky applicants are able to undergo this process successfully the first time; typically, it takes several attempts before it comes together (and of course, for some, it never does).

Just being appointed is no measure of a successful, rewarding judicial career. This is because not only is the process of appointing a judge nebulous, but most judges come onto the bench with only a rudimentary notion of what is required of them. The interaction between an attorney and a judge is really quite limited—an occasional hearing or trial, perhaps being involved in a professional group or committee, etc. Other than that interaction, and receiving the end product of a judge's work in the form of a written decision, a lawyer really can't prepare for what is awaiting them once they become a judge.

A judge immediately receives a level of respect and autonomy that you just do not see in other professions. The organizational structure of the court system is designed to serve the needs of the judge, and he or she is allowed to do their job with relatively little oversight or criticism (except when their work product is the subject of an appeal). While there are some opportunities for mentoring, most of the time a judge is on their own to figure out the granular details of the position. The harsh reality of the situation is that the work of a judge involves dozens and dozens of decisions to be made on a daily basis. These decisions can run the gamut from the quick decisions one has to make during a trial on motions and objections, to the more contemplative decisions resulting from complicated motions or trials.

I believe that the best barometer on how a new judge will develop into their new position is how they are able to handle the need to make these decisions. Some of this just takes time to become comfortable with the need to make quick decisions, especially when it seems time is standing still while everyone is waiting for you. It also takes time to develop a writing style that allows for the proper analysis of a complex or emotional dispute to not only get to the right result, but let the losing side know that you heard what they had to say. To be a successful trial judge, one has to be able to master both types of decisions and be comfortable in the different skill sets they require.

Unfortunately, this is not always the case. I have seen far too many colleagues labor under the weight of difficult decisions and the self-perceived burden of coming to the right result. Sometimes, this is just plain indecisiveness; sometimes it is allowing the perfect to be the enemy of the good. Whatever the source, the inability to make decisions on a regular, consistent basis is probably the singular reason trial judges become disenchanted and burned out in their job. It may seem counterintuitive—why wouldn't someone be able to do the precise work everyone knows a judge has to do? In reality, it is simply the realization that despite one's best efforts and preparation, they are not a good fit for the job. Thankfully, this is rare, but it occurs more than people may realize.

This notion of "being a good fit for the job" is at the heart of this essay. How a person comes to the bench and then progresses through a judicial career is not the same process. The latter relies more on where the judge can find their fit. I know for me it became quickly apparent that the job of a district judge was a good fit—I enjoy the decisions made in real time and the back and forth with counsel, while at the same time enjoying the contemplative pursuits of crafting a summary judgment ruling or a divorce decree (yes, even a divorce decree). It has allowed me to be heard on issues that are important to the litigants in court and sometimes important to the public at large. To be an effective trial judge is to experience the realization that what you thought you could bring to the job was accurate. I, as well as many of my colleagues, have been blessed to know that sense of realization.

This is why I've never seriously contemplated an appellate appointment. I simply have come to enjoy my work as a trial judge to the point that I cannot see myself anywhere else. Since I've never served as an appellate judge, I really can't speak to the motivation for those who pursue that position. I assume it involves the same self-examination one must go through when pursuing any judicial career, focusing on the specialized skills that an appellate judge must possess and the desire to shape the jurisprudence in their jurisdiction for generations to come. I also assume that appellate judges come to their job facing the same learning curves that their trial court colleagues encounter, and that their ultimate success or happiness on the appellate bench is tied to how they reconcile what they thought the job was about with how it actually unfolds. In other words, they must find their fit. I have been saddened when a colleague leaves the trial bench to take an appellate position, but I know that ultimately we all need to be where we feel the most fulfilled. On those occasions when our abilities mesh with the rigors of the job, that fulfillment is easily obtained.

Trial or Appellate Court?

David N. May
Justice, Iowa Supreme Court

Robin S. Rosenbaum
Judge, U.S. Court of Appeals for the 11th Circuit

A kicker and an offensive lineman both play football. They both know the rules, and they both contribute to the game in important ways. But a kicker and an offensive lineman have very different jobs. A great kicker may not be a great offensive lineman, and a great offensive lineman may not be a great kicker. After all, a kicker's primary duty—kicking—and an offensive lineman's primary duty—blocking—require different skills. And even if both players are terrific at both jobs, they may not enjoy them equally: a player who loves kicking may not find blocking so enjoyable. And one who likes to block may dislike kicking.

Maybe you wonder what kickers and offensive linemen have to do with judging. To be sure, a judge is unlikely to be asked to protect a quarterback or kick a field goal. But the differences between offensive linemen and kickers are much like those between trial and appellate judges. Trial and appellate judges' jobs require different skills. So an outstanding trial judge may lack the capabilities or temperament to be a top-notch appellate judge. And an appellate judge who is well-suited for her position may be a poor trial judge. Plus, even those "ambidextrous" judges who perform equally admirably in each position almost always prefer one over the other. In this chapter, we'll discuss the skill sets each position requires, the peculiarities of each job, and why you should think long and hard about whether you're better suited to be a trial or appellate judge.

About Each Position

We'll begin by summarizing each position.

First, the official duties: Trial judges, of course, preside over trials and evidentiary hearings. And when they're not in trial, they may take criminal pleas and conduct sentencings. But they do much more than that. Trial judges must also stay on top of their entire dockets. That often includes resolving a sea of substantive written motions, like motions to dismiss, motions for summary judgment, discovery motions, motions *in limine* to admit or exclude specific evidence at an upcoming trial, and other motions—including motions for the release of vessels or other property. Sometimes parties file these motions on an emergency basis that requires expedited resolution. All these motions are important to the parties who file them, and trial judges owe a duty to resolve them correctly and expeditiously.

Of course, trial judges must also handle non-substantive motions, like motions for extensions of time and for continuances. And they must rule on warrant applications and, in federal court, wiretap applications. Not only that, but trial judges often have other official responsibilities. For instance, a federal trial judge (U.S. district judge) may have to preside over the empanelment of a grand jury or over Naturalization ceremonies, or both. State trial judges may also have grand-jury duties, as well as other tasks like presiding over weddings and approving name changes. In performing all these duties—motions and other responsibilities alike—trial judges act as the sole judicial officer presiding.

Beyond these official responsibilities, trial judges often must also serve their courts in an administrative capacity. That is, they must work on committees that further the business of the court, such as committees that review and revise court rules or those that address security issues in the courthouse.

Contrast these official duties of trial judges to those of appellate judges. Unlike trial judges, appellate judges (generally[1]) do not preside over trials. Rather, they review the record of the trial-court proceedings and the briefs on appeal of the parties who complain about or defend those proceedings. Sometimes, appellate judges also hear oral argument on those matters. But oral argument differs substantially from trial proceedings. Oral argument is not an evidentiary proceeding. Rather, it is a discourse between a panel of three (or more) appellate judges and the lawyers who represent the parties in the appeal. After oral argument, the judges privately discuss the case—a process called "conferencing." Here, the judges share their views of the case and try to build consensus about how the case should be decided. Because of the nature of their job, though, appellate judges spend most of their time working alone or with their clerks. This work includes reviewing the trial-court record and appellate briefs, researching the legal issues on appeal, preparing for oral argument and oral-argument conference, and writing opinions that resolve the appeals before them, explaining the reasons for the particular disposition.

Unlike trial judges, though, appellate judges cannot issue substantive rulings on their own. Rather, they must do so as a panel, which usually consists of three judges. Or in an en banc proceeding, they must deliberate with and issue their rulings as part of the entire court with all other active appellate judges on that court. That's a lot of minds an appellate judge must persuade that her position is correct. Sometimes not all of those judges can agree on the correct answer. In that case, a judge who finds himself in the minority may choose to issue a separate opinion—whether a concurrence or a dissent.

Appellate judges also participate in court administrative business. They may be appointed to either appellate-judge-only committees or committees that may include trial judges, court staff, members of the community, or some combination.

Add to these official duties all judges' unofficial responsibilities: a good judge should engage with the community. For instance, he should attend and support bar programs that help improve the quality of the bar that practices before him. And he should engage in civics education to help ensure a knowledgeable citizenry that appreciates the rule of law and the principles of our democratic republic.

The Ideal Skill Sets for Each Position

The different responsibilities of each position require skills unique to each. From the list of a trial judge's daily responsibilities, you may be able to imagine the varied and often-hectic nature of that job. A trial judge may sit in court all day, every day, for weeks at a time, but she must still find the time to correctly resolve the motions on her docket so other cases can continue to move forward. That means a trial judge must be highly efficient because she always has a lot of balls in the air at any one time. And she rarely enjoys the opportunity to ponder for long over any given legal issue. Still though, a trial judge must be proficient in legal research and writing, so she can reach the correct legal answers and explain them in her orders—whether written or oral.

A trial judge is also the leader of his courtroom. He must be able to command the respect of all who visit his courtroom. Without that respect, a courtroom can become chaotic, and justice may suffer. At the very least, the appearance of justice will suffer in those circumstances. A trial judge earns respect by being knowledgeable in the law of evidence, being well prepared for his proceedings, treating those before him with dignity and respect, being fair, and being cool-headed under pressure. And an extroverted personality can be a real plus for a trial judge in running his courtroom.

Trial judges conduct considerable work inside the courtroom. They empanel juries. And trial judges must work closely with juries and lawyers to use court time efficiently. Trial judges hear and review evidence and often must make factual findings based on that evidence. Because appellate courts often defer to the trial judge's factual findings, those findings can drive any legal analysis that follows. So trial judges must carefully judge witness credibility and assess evidence.

Finally, a trial judge must also be able to make decisions. Though some trial judges enjoy the help of law clerks, the presiding trial judge is the only judge who makes the final decision. She receives no input from other judges. So she must be comfortable pulling the trigger on her own.

Appellate judges, on the other hand, generally work in panels. As a result, they enjoy both the benefits and burdens of others' views in reaching and issuing their final decisions. To get the most out of this conferencing exercise, appellate judges must be well prepared to go toe to toe with their colleagues and should enjoy the intellectual give and take of discussing what can be complex legal issues. They should have the maturity to consider their colleagues' positions and honestly reevaluate their own. When this happens, sometimes a colleague's explanation of her position will modify or even reverse another appellate judge's view of a case. Other times, a colleague's position may solidify another appellate judge's different position. But in all cases, honest consideration of a colleague's position challenges each judge to think more deeply about the correctness of his position. So a judge who does not like the dynamics of collective decision making should not be an appellate judge.

The exchange of ideas among appellate judges also emphasizes the deliberative nature of the appellate judge's role. To be sure, like trial judges, appellate judges carry heavy caseloads. But compared to trial judges, an appellate judge's narrower duties allow him much more time to research the legal issues, deeply ponder them, and consider the most effective way to write his legal opinion. Indeed, appellate judges spend the bulk of their time doing legal research, legal analysis, and legal writing.

Those who don't love these three activities should steer clear of an appellate judgeship.

And appellate judges' courtroom work likewise differs substantially from trial judges' courtroom work. While trial judges enjoy frequent (and sometimes prolonged) formal and informal courtroom interaction with others—like jurors, lawyers, parties, and witnesses—appellate judges' courtroom work is generally more formal and limited to meticulously timed oral argument with lawyers. So unlike in the courtrooms of the trial courts—which can see unanticipated developments during a witness's testimony or other trial-level proceedings—few surprises (at least for the judges) grace the designated oral-argument period in appellate courtrooms.

What This Means for Those Considering Serving as Trial or Appellate Judges

As we hope we've clarified by now, the positions and duties of trial and appellate judges differ in significant ways. And as a result, so do the skills necessary to perform each job well. Similar to the kicker and the offensive lineman, not every lawyer who would make a great trial judge would excel as an appellate judge. Nor will every outstanding appellate judge be well-equipped to handle the duties of a trial judge.

More than that, even, not every trial and appellate judge will enjoy working in the other's position. Indeed, many judges have had the privilege to serve in both capacities. Some much prefer their later positions. Others not so much. But appointments or elections to a particular judgeship are not fungible. So it's wise to think long and hard about your skills, interests, and preferences and to conduct a thorough and honest self-assessment before deciding whether to seek a judgeship at all and, if so, whether to seek a trial or appellate judgeship.

Why I Never Left the Trial Bench

Michael J. Shubatt
Judge, Iowa District Court

A colleague who recently lost his latest bid for an appellate position told me he dealt with the disappointment by finding perspective from the movie *Field of Dreams*. In the film, Archibald "Moonlight" Graham got to play half an inning of a major league baseball game, but never got to bat. He gave up baseball, became a doctor, and moved back to his hometown of Chisolm, Minnesota, where he took care of the community's residents for 50 years.

Amazed at the peace the doctor had found given the way his life played out, the protagonist, Ray Kinsella, remarks that getting so close to your dream without being able to touch it is a tragedy that would kill most men. Recognizing how many lives he touched as a small-town doctor, Graham replies, "Son, if I'd only gotten to be a doctor for five minutes, now *that* would have been a tragedy."

I had no aspirations of becoming a judge when I went to law school, nor did I even consider it for most of the 18 years I spent as a trial lawyer. I built my practice and became a partner in my firm, as one does. While I was not unhappy with my career, I was intrigued when a local trial court judge announced he was retiring earlier than expected. Judge Shubatt? What would that look like? Suddenly I found myself thinking about it a lot, to the point I decided to change course and pursue the position. I got it on my first try.

I took to my new role quickly, feeling refreshed and rejuvenated. For nearly two decades I had been focused on winning day in and day out. Now there was no winning or losing—only getting it right. It was an entirely different kind of challenge, but one I still enjoy more than the pressure I felt as a litigator. For the first time in years, I was passionate about my work and excited for what the next day would bring.

Even though I was enjoying life as a trial court judge, I decided after only a few years to pursue an appellate position. Like most people of my generation, I was wired to believe that any promotion, real or perceived, was an opportunity that should be pursued. I was doing well, so an appellate position was the logical next step, right?

I did not get that position. I never tried again. And I've lived happily ever after.

An appellate position was never truly a dream of mine, but it is for many. And that's OK; some people are better suited for that job than one at the trial court level. The important thing for new judges and anyone thinking about becoming a judge to realize is that the trial court should not be viewed as a stepping stone. While it serves a proving ground for many who ultimately want to be appellate judges, it is also a destination in and of itself.

I have been blessed to spend so many years in the legal system as a trial court judge. Like Archibald Graham, trial court judges witness the human condition daily, up close and personally. They see the world in living color. They watch the movie, whereas appellate judges only read the screenplay. The job has a richness and texture that is difficult to fully explain to others in the legal profession, let alone to people in other fields.

My court reporter marvels over my ability to recall the minutiae of so many of the cases we have heard together. Perhaps it is because I love a story with a good plot and interesting characters. Who doesn't? That's why I can remember, after many years, the specific fast food a teenager ate on camera as he chillingly confessed to murdering his grandparents, the divorce where the wife wanted her "Cruella DeVille coat" and the husband wanted their two dogs (an easy decision that worked out well for the dogs), the funky glasses an expert witness wore on the stand, a beautifully executed leadup to a "gotcha" question on cross, the self-professed witch who used her powers mainly for good but knew how to curse someone if they needed it, and of course having to adjourn a trial because the little old lady who got picked for the jury and did not come back after lunch, thinking, as we later found out, that we were done for the day. When she showed up the next morning, her fellow jurors did not have the heart to tell her of her mistake, and neither did I.

When it comes to work settings, the county courthouse is unmatched in its uniqueness. It is the epicenter of conflict resolution in the community. Every day one cast enters and another leaves. Even in the age of electronic filings, you still have many opportunities to interact with attorneys and litigants face to face. A social-minded appellate judge I know once told me she missed the local bar so much that on days when she worked in her hometown courthouse, she was notorious for seeking out conversation with any lawyer she could find in the halls—jogging after him or her if necessary. There certainly are days when the monastic life of an appellate judge has some allure, but in the long run it would not have suited me. I just like being around people too much.

As a trial judge your dockets vary as much as the people you deal with. One day you may be a short order cook going from hearing to hearing in unrelated cases. Another may be spent in the bubble of a weeklong trial. There are days you are blessed with the peace and serenity of chambers, where you close your door, put on your favorite music, and draft that decision that has been weighing on you. Some judges will tell you that the three best words in the English language are "Your case settled."

I have always been a puzzle solver. I love a challenging crossword and usually begin my day with coffee and the Wordle. Decision writing is a form of puzzle solving. It's also an art form. Crafting a ruling on a difficult issue to the point that you are confident in its factual and legal correctness is incredibly satisfying. I experience this satisfaction whether I'm filing a one-page decision on a motion to compel or a ten-page ruling on a motion for summary judgment.

One of my favorite things about making decisions, even the tough ones, is that they're mine and mine alone. Autonomy is one of the under-recognized blessings of being a trial court judge. I never fully appreciated this until a Supreme Court justice I spoke with during my one and only run at an appellate position asked me, "Why in the world do you want to go to the Court of Appeals?" I did not understand where the question was coming from and started to go on about how I enjoyed research, which I sometimes do, and writing, which I always do. I talked about it just making sense in terms of career progression. He listened for a minute before cutting me off with another question: "Don't you realize how much authority you're giving up?"

Again, I was confused. Don't appellate judges have more authority than trial judges? Yes and no. An appellate judge can reverse a trial judge's ruling, but the appellate judge cannot do it on his or her own. Since appellate judges operate as one member of a panel, there is no guarantee the decision will be what they believe it should be. Such is not the case with the trial judge, who is solely responsible for every one of his or her rulings. That is something I cherish—the knowledge that, at least at the trial level, I am vested with the unilateral authority to make procedural and substantive decisions and, at least in bench trials, decide the case based on what I see as the applicable law and facts.

Had I moved to the appellate court, I would have missed presiding over trials. There is nothing like the feeling of taking the bench the first morning of a trial. This is especially true when both sides are represented by good lawyers. As a former practitioner, I am still fascinated by the craft of trial practice and enjoy watching lawyers make strategic decisions in real time. To keep the trial moving at a reasonable pace, most of my decisions must be in real time as well.

If it is a jury trial, I enjoy keeping the jurors informed about the process and watching them from time to time as they observe the evidence, remembering that many of them have never been in a courtroom before let alone sat in judgment of a fellow citizen. I also enjoy my interactions with them after the verdict has been rendered, educating them about the process by sharing things they were not told during the trial itself.

The best trial court judges have a rare skill set that includes intellect, empathy, patience, presence and eloquence. They can command a combustible courtroom with their voice and countenance. They keep their head about them when everyone around them is losing theirs.

Most of all, the best trial court judges do their job in a way that makes attorneys and, hopefully, the litigants, trust the process and understand and respect their rulings. This is not to say a judge's goal can or should be to make everyone happy; it is more often the case that you'll make no one happy. Rather, your goal must be procedural justice, or procedural fairness as it's sometimes called.

Through the years I've developed a special relationship with members of the local bar. Some I admire, some can drive me a little crazy at times—but I view them all as fellow travelers on my journey. There is now a generation of local lawyers who will say they had their first trial in front of me, and another generation who will say they had their last trial with me. If you stay on the bench long enough, you get to watch bright young lawyers become seasoned old(er) ones, helping them along the way with a word of encouragement and positive feedback. Had I become an appellate judge, I would have missed out on all of those relationships.

I am now well into the autumn years of both my legal career and my time on the bench. When I look back, I am grateful that I was given the rare opportunity to serve my community in this unique way. I am happy to remember the faces I encountered rather than just names on a page. I am happy to remember the things that happened before my eyes during the many trials I presided over rather than the dry transcriptions of what unfolded. I am happy that as a trial court judge, I have always been able to live in a case's present rather than its past.

As a trial judge, you too will impact your community in many ways, most of which you will never see. You will keep your community safe from some people and give others an opportunity to get their lives back on track through probation and rehabilitation. You will write the obituary of countless marriages, making custodial decisions that hopefully help children move on from a rough situation. You will tell neighbors where the boundary between their properties truly lies and both people and businesses whether their contracts say what they think they say. You will pose for pictures after many an adoption ceremony. You will make sure that everyone who comes into your courtroom has a fair trial or hearing, regardless of whether it ends the way they wanted it to. You will not always be able to solve problems, but you will always be able to give people answers.

You should not assume from my words that a position on the trial bench is inherently better than one on the appellate bench. It has been for me, but different judges are wired differently. They have different personalities, different talents and different desires. If you are thinking about becoming a judge, think about what position would be a good fit for you and allow you to provide the maximum benefit to your judiciary.

There are a lot of good trial judges, some average ones and a few bad ones. What the judiciary needs, and will always need, is more excellent ones. Where I fall in that category is for others to say, but like Archibald

Graham I think it would have been a tragedy if I'd moved on to the appellate court after only being a trial judge for a few years. The trial court is where I belong. Before you look to what you might consider greener pastures, consider whether it is where you belong as well.

Chapter 6

How Private Practice Experience Benefits the Bench

A Judicial Aspirant's Most Valuable Preparation

Myron L. Gookin
Judge, Iowa District Court

Many years ago, as I pondered going to law school, one disturbing question kept running through my mind: "Can I do it?" Having no lawyers as family or friends on whom I could rely for input or support, I had no idea if I had the aptitude and fortitude to be a lawyer. Thankfully, I did well in law school and experienced 28 years of successful private practice experience.

Then I began considering applying for a district court judge position. Once again, I kept wondering, *can I do it? Do I have what it takes to be a judge?* I forged ahead and applied. And, on September 16, 2011, I took the oath of office as an Iowa district court judge.

As I began my judicial journey, it did not take long for me to feel unexpectedly comfortable in my new role. I attribute this comfort to 28 years of private practice in a county-seat general practice law firm of five lawyers. In saying this, I do not mean to dismiss the qualities and skills my judicial peers bring to the bench from specialized legal careers, whether civil or criminal, or legal careers outside of private practice (administrative, corporate, etc.). However, as a judge of a general jurisdiction court who is authorized to hear or preside over nearly every kind of legal dispute, I am convinced after 12 years on the bench that a general private practice background is the best preparation for becoming a judge.

My private legal practice involved all aspects of the practice of law, including civil and criminal trial and appellate practice, contract, debtor/creditor, banking, family (pre-marriage planning, divorce, adoption and juvenile), estate planning, probate, business planning, real estate, personal injury/tort and municipal (I served as city attorney for two small towns). I represented banks, local businesses, local churches, municipalities, and individual clients in all manner of civil and criminal proceedings. I routinely examined abstracts and issued title opinions, prepared transactional documents, did estate and death planning, performed probate and non-probate estate matters, opened guardianships and conservatorships, performed business planning, including setting up corporations, partnerships, and limited liability companies, performed abstracting, prepared tax returns, prepared documentation for secured transactions, advised banks on debtor-creditor matters and internal policies and affairs, advised municipalities on their operations and procedures, and advised one of the largest religious denominations in Iowa on their internal policies and procedures. This broad and general legal experience was a tremendous advantage to me when I became a district court judge. It helped me have an instant understanding and context for the legal disputes presented to me for decision.

Being a private practice lawyer also helped me in my judicial career in ways beyond the day-to-day practice of law. Being a lawyer in a county-seat town in Iowa opens many doors to meet and interact with people in many different contexts. Having communications skills and legal knowledge results in being asked to participate in many different aspects of community life. You are asked to serve on numerous boards and committees in which you learn much about topics you would not otherwise experience.

Before going on the bench, I served on my local city council for 14 years. I learned about city finance, city planning, human resources, potholes in roads and probably more than I ever wanted to know about sanitary sewers. Like formulating legal arguments in trial and appellate practice, I formulated specific reasoning for my city council decisions and tried to convey that reasoning in a common sense, straightforward manner to help my constituents understand why I voted a certain way. They might not agree, but I wanted them to understand the basis for my vote. This was invaluable training for writing judicial rulings that litigants could understand. They might not agree with my decision, but, hopefully, they would believe they had been heard and could understand the basis for my decision.

In the day-to-day rush of court service days, trials and getting rulings filed as quickly as reasonably possible, it is incredibly important that a judge has the knowledge and experience in the law and in life to make good decisions in a timely manner and to communicate those decisions effectively to his audience, both lawyers and nonlawyer litigants. Private practice, especially the general practice of law, affords a lawyer the opportunity to experience many different areas of the law. Before becoming a judge, I was always slightly jealous of my lawyer peers in larger firms who had the luxury of focusing on and becoming an expert in a specific area. Now, I realize the importance of a broad background and experience in the law and life to properly do the job of a judge.

Such a broad background gives a lawyer the advantage of learning from experience while he or she is practicing, and putting that experience to work making good decisions when he or she dons the robe and becomes the decision maker. With all due respect for my peers on the bench who did not have a broad, general practice background, I believe it is the most valuable, practical, real-world education a lawyer can obtain in preparation for the bench.

How a County Seat Practice Prepared Me for the Bench

John J. Haney
Judge, Iowa District Court

My name is John Haney. While I was not born in a small town (Pittsburgh, PA), I have lived in a small town, Marshalltown, Iowa, most of my life. I have been married to my wife, Carol, for 40 years. We have four adult children and close to a football team of grandchildren. I have been asked to share some thoughts on how my experiences as a "small-town" private practice attorney helped prepare me to serve as a judge.

My journey to the district court bench was not linear. I think it would be remiss to not share a bit of "small-town" history about myself as part of this story. I believe these life experiences have helped me in my role as a district court judge. I believe that others with ambitions to serve as a judicial officer bring their own legal skills and life experiences to the bench. These experiences form where we came from, who we are, who we aspire to be, and how we go about solving problems and making decisions. Having insight and knowledge about yourself and your history, including all your strengths and weaknesses, are invaluable tools in being a better person, and naturally being a better judge.

I was not a fan of school in my younger years. I graduated from high school early to make my way into the working world. The path to being an "adult" in a small town was typically college, the military, or taking a job at a local factory. My venture into adulthood began with working for the railroad. I worked as a track laborer and brakeman-switchman for four years after high school. These experiences certainly helped me to appreciate the value of demanding work, long hours, and crossing paths with many intriguing characters along the way.

Shortly after my wife and I met, I shifted my career path and moved on to become a youth services worker at the State Juvenile Home in Toledo. This job gave me an opportunity to experience psychology, behavior modification, and the court system, and to encounter a wide range of troubled young people, as well as adults interested in helping others.

Being a lawyer was something that slept within me from the time I was in high school. My parents used to toy with me about my tendency to argue and debate. Of course, that often resulted in the unsatisfying parental admonition, "because I said so." My wife would sometimes end my arguments and debates early in our marriage by letting me know that "it is lonely being right." These experiences may have been early premonitions for my becoming a judge.

In any case, I decided to return to school a bit later in life and earned an AA degree from our local community college. I went on to receive a bachelor's degree from Grinnell College, and a law degree from the University of Iowa in my late twenties and early thirties. Balancing my roles as a husband, father, youth worker, and student during this period of my life certainly helped me develop a sincere appreciation for time management, or controlled chaos, depending on the day. These experiences also provided me with an even greater appreciation for the support people in my life, including my wife, family, friends, teachers, and colleagues.

My desire from the time I decided to pursue a career in law was to return to my hometown and work as a lawyer in my community. I interned and clerked for a small firm while I was getting my undergraduate and law degrees. George Hinshaw, the elder attorney of the firm, offered me a job when I completed my first year of law school. He told me not to rule out other options, but if I wanted a job, he would find a place for me. While toying with the idea of moving to a larger city, my wife and I decided small-town life was where we wanted to land. I cannot think of a time in my life when I ever regretted that decision.

I worked in a small law firm with three to four attorneys from 1996-2014. George Hinshaw, and my future partners Brian Danielson and Steve Kloberdanz, served as my colleagues, mentors, and friends during this journey. I will never forget my first day after being sworn in as attorney. George walked into my office and put a real estate abstract in front of me and said, "You might as well learn how to do this right from the start because it will help you a great deal on down the road."

I had to review the firm's "title opinion file." I looked at the other attorneys' notes and studied their methods for examining abstracts, and then bothered them all with endless questions. My memory is seared with what became a common response: "Have you looked in the Code?" or "Have you looked in the title standards?" I developed my own method for examining titles, combining the various methods of my mentors. This process was invaluable to me in learning real estate law.

In my experience, small-town practice required a wide array of diverse work. I was blessed, or cursed, to manage civil, criminal, probate, tax, real estate, and a variety of other legal matters on a day-to-day, and sometimes hour-to-hour basis. On any given day, I might work on a farm family's tax return, and then represent one of their children for an OWI or dissolution. I represented clients in civil, criminal, and juvenile litigation, in addition to examining abstracts and doing title opinions, preparing wills and trusts, and closing real estate transactions, among other things. I used to joke that small-town private practice often required you to be a jack of all trades but a master of none. Nevertheless, there was a certain romance associated with the ideal of a small-town, county seat, "Marcus Welby, M.D." type of law practice.[1] I had daily contact with clients in my community, at the café, school, sporting events, church, and other community activities. Our local judges and professional colleagues shared advice and feedback that helped me improve and develop my skills as an attorney throughout this journey.

I was quite content with my station in life as a small-town practitioner. I had a successful practice and was incredibly happy. In 2007, several colleagues approached me to seek a magistrate judge position in Marshalltown. I politely declined. I never aspired to be anything other than a small-town attorney. They persisted. I gave in. I applied for and was lucky enough to get the job.

I found great enjoyment in seeing the legal world from the windshield of the bench. The work was diverse, fast-paced, and challenging. I spent seven years balancing private practice and serving as a part-time magistrate judge. These experiences inspired me to pursue a position on the district court bench. In 2014, after several attempts, I was appointed as a district court judge.

Working in a busy, small-town practice, and serving as a part-time magistrate, helped me to develop a variety of skills and character traits over the years. These included: legal research and writing skills, communication and listening skills, cultural awareness and tolerance, self-awareness, patience, humility, independence, honesty, integrity, a sense of fairness, and empathy. Serving my clients, as well as working with judges, attorneys, and others in a small-town setting, has been invaluable to me as a judicial officer. These opportunities permitted me to observe and adopt skills and attributes from others I found valuable, while disregarding those practices I found ineffective or objectionable.

I can say without hesitation that working in a small-town practice provides an outstanding foundation for anyone with aspirations to be a judge.

The Invaluable Advantage of Private Practice

David P. Odekirk
Judge, Iowa District Court

Private practice experience has been invaluable to me as a district court judge. The reasons for this are many and varied, as I am reminded on a daily basis interacting with the wide variety of matters that come before me and the wide variety of people with whom I interact. It is my hope to encourage attorneys considering applying for the bench to embrace private practice as an opportunity, not only as a wonderful and fulfilling career path in itself, but also as an opportunity to develop and enhance those professional skills necessary to excel as a judge at any level, whether on a trial or appellate court.

Private practice experience is by itself a very broad topic, therefore it may be helpful for the reader to have some understanding of my background and the perspective I bring to it. I entered private practice in 1995 with a small law firm in Waterloo, Iowa, composed of two partners and two associates with a handful of support staff. The firm was truly general practice and handled criminal cases, family law, civil litigation, employment/labor law, real estate, wills and probate, etc.

My first day at the firm I was handed case files and was signed up on court appointment lists. I was in the courtroom almost from my first week, in family law and criminal matters. In addition, I was meeting with clients to prepare wills, title opinions, real estate contracts and deeds. Gradually, I began to do more substantive civil litigation for both plaintiffs and defendants, including personal injury, contract disputes, debt collection medical malpractice, products liability, workers compensation and insurance defense. I was also involved in many cases resolved through alternative dispute resolution, including mediations and arbitrations.

My clients included individuals, corporations, employers and unions. During my 20 years of private practice until taking the bench in 2015 I was exposed to a wide variety of legal matters, and, more importantly, people.

From 1995 to 2015 our firm expanded from four attorneys to approximately 20 attorneys and associated support staff with locations in Iowa and multiple other states in the Midwest. This required the development of other professional skills such as management, financial and human resources. Further, as a private practice attorney I had the privilege of volunteering to serve on government and nonprofit boards. These experiences were invaluable in helping me develop my professional skills and qualifications to be a judge.

Ultimately, the work of an attorney in private practice centers around clients. A client typically seeks out the assistance of an attorney to solve a particular problem or set of problems. The skill set of a competent private practitioner must include the ability to spot and analyze the legal issues presented by a client. The attorney must then be able to take that analysis and formulate a plan to solve the client's particular problems. Likewise, a judge, especially a trial judge, must also be able to quickly identify and analyze the legal issues presented by the parties to a particular case. A judge with a varied private practice background has honed the skill of identifying the relevant legal issues over many years. A judge has finite time to devote to any given legal matter and it is imperative for the judge to be able to determine the relevant legal issues quickly in order to know what must be decided in each case.

Like the private practitioner, the judge having identified the legal issue to be decided must then be able to identify the proper legal framework to analyze the issue. Most clients do not give their attorneys unlimited funds to research every legal issue. Private practice attorneys must generally perform legal research within very strict budgetary constraints. This forces private practitioners to be organized and efficient researchers. Further, years of private practice will likely have equipped the attorney with a broad knowledge of the law and rules of procedure.

This knowledge is beneficial not so much to recall specific statutes or cases, but to know where to find an answer quickly. Likewise, a judge may preside over any number of different criminal and civil matters in a given week, if not a given day, and it is impossible for any judge to know all the law applicable to every case. However, the experience as a private practitioner will equip a judge with the ability to quickly research a particular legal issue and formulate the appropriate analysis to apply to the case.

Again, clients seek out an attorney to solve a particular problem. Similarly, the litigants in each case want and deserve a resolution to the legal issue they have entrusted the judge to decide. Good private practitioners communicate the law to their clients in a clear and concise manner. A great deal of a private practitioner's time is spent communicating in written form with other people. It may be writing letters and/or emails to clients, opposing counsel, or a variety of third parties. It may be drafting pleadings, legal briefs, wills, or contracts. Good judges are also able to clearly craft their written decisions so that the litigants can understand the judge's reasoning. Clearly written decisions are more likely to be accepted by the litigants and may help avoid the expense for the parties of further litigation or appeals.

Further, an experienced private practitioner has been faced with many strategic decisions and has developed an ability to chart a clear path amongst competing strategic choices, and cannot afford to endlessly agonize over which direction to go. This is ultimately the judge's job—to decide. A judge with private practice experience will be able to draw upon the confidence gained from that experience to act decisively in resolving pending legal matters without undue agonizing.

Private practice requires attorneys to be able to interact with a wide variety of people. This requires those attorneys to be skilled oral communicators as well as written communicators. Even more than being good speakers, private practice requires an attorney to be a good listener. Listening is key to the attorney understanding what a client needs them to do. Listening is key to an attorney understanding the position of an opposing party or the competing goals of parties to a contract. During most court proceedings, the judge's role is primarily that of a listener and not a speaker. A judge with extensive and varied private practice experience is likely already a skilled listener and listening attentively will be second nature.

People skills, or what is sometimes popularly referred to as emotional intelligence, is sometimes an innate skill, but more often a skill developed over many years. Attorneys in private practice have often had the opportunity to hone this skill through dealings with a broad spectrum of humanity. The important skill of listening also requires these attorneys to be both empathetic and patient. These are both traits of a good judge. It is fair to say that most people entering a courtroom would rather be almost anywhere else—they likely enter the courtroom with a great deal of anxiety and even fear. A judge, while maintaining the necessary formalities and solemnity of the courtroom, must also be able to convey to the litigants that they are being fully heard. Despite the real time constraints for judges to hear matters, the judge must engage patiently with the parties and their attorneys.

Unlike empathy and patience, short tempers and angry outbursts rarely, if ever, serve anyone well. Generally, attorneys who successfully navigate the challenges of private practice have done so without temper tantrums, screaming, yelling, or otherwise abusive treatment of others. No doubt some successful attorneys, and even some judges, may have legendary bad temperament. However, it has been my experience that in the long run such a trait is incompatible with real sustained success. Attorneys in private practice are tested by a variety of difficult situations which often bring out the worst in many people.

Attorneys who are able to remain calm and keep their heads when everyone else is losing theirs are not only more likely to serve the interests of their clients, but to also adhere to the highest standards of ethics and professionalism expected of all lawyers. Attorneys learn quickly that their professional lives are enhanced by following the golden rule when dealing not only with their clients, but also with their employees, opposing counsel, clerks, court staff, and especially judges. Perhaps the greatest virtue to be learned by an extensive and varied private practice is that of humility. Humility is a respect and understanding of oneself that allows us to fully respect and understand the humanity of others. There may be no more important trait for a judge than humility.

The successful private practitioner likely brings to the bench a reputation for exemplary behavior, both personally and professionally. Judges must set the example they wish others to follow, showing both respect and equanimity regardless of the circumstances in the courtroom. Drawing on extensive past experience dealing with a variety of difficult people and situations allows the judge coming from private practice to meet the ever-changing challenges of the courtroom in a way that inspires respect not only for the judge but more importantly the rule of law and the judicial system itself.

Attorneys in private practice have also learned to adapt quickly and well to change—changes in the law, technology, the economy, and ultimately the needs of their clients. Change is a constant part of private practice and the successful attorney is nimble and agile in adapting. Judges are not immune to the changes around them, including changes in the economy which may necessitate the ability to find ways to do their work with fewer resources. In addition, technology has greatly changed the work of judges over the last several decades, and these changes will likely accelerate with the advent of artificial intelligence. Judges will be required to adapt to these changes and will be much better positioned to do so if they have the agility demonstrated by attorneys coming from private practice.

The judiciary is greatly enhanced by judges with private practice experience. Judges who understand the challenges and needs of the attorneys and parties appearing in their courtrooms. Judges who demonstrate industriouness and an admirable work ethic. Judges who appreciate the importance of an efficient judicial process because they understand the expense of the legal system for the attorneys and their clients. Judges who exemplify civility and embody the highest standards of the legal profession.

It is without hesitation that I encourage attorneys in private practice to consider being a judge. Cultivate a reputation for the finest legal work, hard work, collegiality, fairness, and the highest standards of integrity and character—doing so with humility. I am confident that the pursuit of these traits will not only result in a successful and fulfilling legal practice, but in the kind of attorney other attorneys will happily nominate as a candidate for a judicial position.

The General Practice Advantage

Julie A. Schumacher
Judge, Iowa Court of Appeals

As a newly licensed attorney, I arrived at my county seat office in western Iowa early on my first day of work in September 1993. Although the sky was still dusky as I stepped out of my car, I noticed a middle-aged man leaning against the front door of the law office, a cup of coffee in one hand, a cigarette in the other. He was wearing what looked like a work uniform. And he looked tired. I later learned he had just finished the graveyard shift at one of the local packing plants. As I approached the front door, he quickly put out his cigarette and extended his hand. Simultaneously, he fired a rapid series of questions: Did I know a lawyer? Was I a lawyer? Was I old enough to be a lawyer? Did I handle divorces? Could I help him out? When I responded that I was indeed a lawyer, my first day in fact, perhaps a little too earnestly, he nodded and said, "Good. I will be your first client." He was there that day to initiate dissolution of marriage proceedings. But he also wanted to visit about a possible revision to his will, a new farm lease for land he owned with his father, and the implications of his upcoming tax return.

And so began life as a rural county practitioner, a role that prepared me for both the trial court bench and the appellate bench. I consider myself fortunate to have been able to practice law for 20 years in the rural county seat town of Denison, Iowa. The nature of a general practice was attractive to me, as was the ability to be a hands-on practitioner within my first year of practice. What I was unaware of at the time I graduated from law school was how being in a general practice required expertise in so many areas. Call it luck, good fortune, or the alignment of stars, I was able to practice in a small firm with larger-than-life attorneys. The senior partner, Michael R. Mundt, was a seasoned litigator and had a reputation as a solid trial attorney. My second partner, Derrick R. Franck, was a highly respected municipal lawyer, taxation and real estate practitioner, with a deep knowledge of education law, having represented school boards, superintendents, and teachers across Iowa. Neither were gatekeepers but rather enthusiastic mentors, sharing their knowledge and passion for the law with me. My judicial career was no doubt benefited by practicing in their areas of expertise. Having two attorneys with their breadth of knowledge accessible to me every day was invaluable. And they encouraged me to develop my own unique practice, which morphed into an expansive family law and adoption practice within our firm. During my private practice, I also prosecuted for the county, which allowed me to further develop trial skills both to the bench and to juries. I was appointed early in my career as a hospitalization referee, which placed me in a judicial role in the first few years of my legal career.

And I would be remiss if I failed to mention how my legal and judicial career benefited from an active local bar association. When I arrived in Denison, I was the only practicing female lawyer in the county. But that was never an issue with the local bar. Although I do not have any biological brothers, I imagine the relationship I had with those attorneys matured much like that of an older brother and younger sister—they were patient to a point, willing to box my ears back on occasion, and then as time passed, we developed a mutual respect and referred clients to each other. I also "grew up" in the law before the implementation of our electronic docket management system, so every Monday morning was a motion day. I cannot emphasize how much these Monday morning interactions with other attorneys benefitted my own legal and judicial career, along with providing an opportunity to sit in the back of the courtroom while waiting for my cases to be called, observing and learning from others. Every Monday was a "mini CLE." Sitting in the back of a courtroom watching two seasoned lawyers pick a jury would still be one of my top five favorite pastimes.

I also had the great fortune of being located in a county where the chief judge of the district, Judge Richard J. Vipond, resided. He was a constant source of wisdom and guidance for me in his quiet, unassuming way. Although as the chief judge he was extremely busy with administrative duties and a full docket, he always took the time to share his thoughts with me when I ran over to the courthouse to get an order signed. I also benefited from considerable time spent with the two local magistrates, Arlo Schoenfeld and Joe Boddicker. Although many young attorneys, or perhaps the managing partners of the firm that they work for, are reluctant to take on court appointments, I accepted as many appointments as I could manage. The time I spent in the courtroom was extremely educational.

Most everyone that has joined the bench from a general practice will say that the ability to practice in diverse legal areas is invaluable to the bench. Agreed. My exposure to the variety of areas of the law was an immense help when I joined the bench. But my experience in private practice instilled in me another attribute critical for a judicial career, the value of service to others through the law.

It is easy to forget in the demands of private practice, deadlines, and trials that there are real people with real problems behind the issues we are litigating. On the bench, it is perhaps easier to lose track of the human nature of the law. And perhaps it is even easier to be more critical of litigants and lawyers when reading a cold record in an appellate role.

Twenty years in private practice made me more empathetic, not only for the litigants but for the attorneys. Attorneys have difficult jobs that should not be made more difficult by the judge. Prior to my appointment to the bench, I had the privilege to appear in front of judges in nearly every district in the State. The lessons learned were immeasurable and solidified in my mind what kind of judge I wanted to be through observations of various judicial temperaments.

Private practice also provided opportunities to engage in multiple Supreme Court Commissions. I was fortunate to have opportunities to serve on the Grievance Commission, the Unauthorized Practice of Law Commission, and serve as a temporary bar exam grader. These experiences not only pulled into focus the impact of judicial decisions but also the importance of service to my fellow lawyers and to Iowans.

Both of my partners were heavily involved in volunteer organizations within the community and supported my efforts in that regard as well. I served on many volunteer boards and committees for various causes, all of which further solidified my commitment to service. It is through these shared experiences with those who had a passion for service—fellow lawyers, judges, and Iowans—that I was prepared to assume the great responsibilities as a trial court judge and an appellate judge.

How My Work as a Trial Lawyer Serves Me on the Bench

Sharon Soorholtz Greer
Judge, Iowa Court of Appeals

Imagine my first day in private practice in a small town in northwest Iowa after marrying my lawyer husband and joining him in the practice of law at a firm with seven male partners. First there were not many women practicing in the area; second, my firm was not excited about adding yet a "Greer-by-marriage" to the roster. With that background, I carried tremendous pressure to prove myself to the community but also to my colleagues. But with the advice I often tell young lawyers today, I knew I could do my best work by being myself. And to carve out my insight over how private practice helps me on the bench today, I cannot ignore the steps taken to even get to a private law practice. Those steps form the foundation of my attitudes and outlook.

First, I trusted my instincts from years of living in a small town in central Iowa where I interacted with people of all ages and economic backgrounds. Even as a youngster, I was often called upon to problem solve, which I loved doing. And as a "tomboy farm kid," my parents instilled in me that there were no limitations to what I might do simply because I was a girl. But I learned something else that helped me in the private practice and has stayed with me in my role on the bench —we are all motivated by the same basic desires, and you must never assume you know what someone is going through.

Drawing on those lessons learned, I found myself in a very diverse general practice that allowed me to experience several areas of the law. Within months of starting my practice, I tried a felony criminal case solo because I was the only one in the county that had not represented this defendant and the bar said it was "my turn!" That was not my only "throw them into the water to swim" experience. As I took on more assignments to defend indigent criminals, I found I really enjoyed the trial practice. Working in a small-town community offered me opportunities to try family law matters, handle juvenile cases and do other office practice tasks, making my experience very diverse and varied. But, I found I loved the courtroom and could tell a story that a juror or judge found convincing, I was drawn to litigation. Gradually, I focused on primarily civil litigation, although until my appointment, I was still serving as defense counsel in the occasional criminal trial. My exposure to the general practice of law with all of the variety, has helped me with my work on the bench. I observe there are few issues that I have not seen in the time during my private practice life.

Early in my career, I was still often the only or one of the few women in the room. Because of the limited number of women litigating back at the time, my lack of status and power was palpable. For example, I was asked to leave the court chambers so the judge and male attorneys could tell a joke or told to sit in the hallway to wait for my lawyer until the judge realized that I was the lawyer! To compensate for that disadvantage with other litigators, I developed a secret power that allowed me to move into the "club." When I sensed I was not included or respected, I pulled from my innate ability to address my opponent's or the witness's needs and feelings. I often would use straight talk but with humor to point out my point of view and expose the offensive attitude. I knew that a person who showed disrespect often came from a place of insecurity. Thus, if someone disrespected me, I could turn that attitude into a strength for my side and perhaps coach a new path for the person to do the right thing in the next encounter—such as teasing the judge who said he did not trust a female witness because she wore black hosiery. That skill set translated into an ability to handle a male witness or a judge who might have biases, but retain my relationship with the offender. Now, as an appellate judge, I recognize and view with more tolerance the actions of litigants, lawyers, and our judiciary. As I know people often are not the master of their experiences but the recipients of what may have come their way.

My husband and I moved back to my hometown central-Iowa community after a few years in his father's firm to have the support of my family in raising our children. Although my trial practice was intense in this somewhat larger community, I found that my survival depended upon my ability to address stress. By allowing my brain to roam when I ran mile after mile, I became a better advocate and a better person. During the solitude of a run, I crafted arguments, let anger and stress go and found solace in what I could do for my clients. With friends in the community, I trained and ran road races to combat stress and stay fit. I have continued to do competitive running and added other fitness options to my routine. On the bench, I am convinced that I am a better judge because I have these outlets. That outlet was essential in a private practice pressure cooker climate, and I am thankful I could learn that early in my career.

Even though my litigation practice was state-wide, I maintained a general practice addressing a wide variety of areas of the law because I had old friends and neighbors that sought my help for all sorts of problems. I had folks come in to see me who were frightened for their lives because of an abusive spouse, scared about the future if they were convicted of a crime and some who mourned a split family over an inheritance fight. Each time I stopped and thought about how I could manage my client's stress and fear. Often, I counseled that I was not a therapist because clients would seek my help with these mental struggles, but I know that I did serve as a resource beyond just the legal advice. In the end, I was so proud when I could identify a solution that could work for what I perceived to be justice for my clients. I use that mindset each time I look at a case that comes before us on the appellate bench. Although we do not see or hear the litigants in person, that background of relating to the emotional components of a client's experience plays into how I pick words to decide the dispute.

In the civil litigation world, I was typically serving as an insurance defense attorney and my clients were people unknown to me until I was assigned the case by the insurance carrier. In the first call to them, I sensed a deep fear of what being sued meant to them, including comments like "am I going to lose everything?" To alleviate concerns and make them a better litigant, I began our relationship with a mantra that we were now a "team" and they would help me do the best that "we" could do. I often had close relationships develop from my legal ties to these assigned clients, but that translated into our presentation of their case to the judge or to the jury in a positive way. Now as an appellate judge with excellent staff working along my side, I work to create that same team approach and I feel we are better together. The ability to work closely with other legal staff without ego and with a positive message of teamwork is something I learned from my practice.

Finally, in a small-town practice I was blessed with many opportunities for public service and worked with charities in many roles. Again, those experiences helped formulate my desire to end my career in a public-service setting and overall, my livelihood does not depend on this appellate job, but is based on my need to serve my state. With that need to do service, I also became extremely active in trial groups and won a national award for my leadership in our state defense counsel organization. I hope others saw my leadership style in these groups as one of creativity and collaboration. Moving to the appellate court, I draw on that style often—both with colleagues and in oral argument where we are trying to problem solve the litigant's concerns.

Now, as an appellate judge, I especially appreciate how my small-town private practice and the skills developed in a litigation role were refined when I stepped into settlement mode. Whether it was a mediation in a family law case or a mediation in a high stakes civil case, I learned how to identify the decision makers in the room, what they really needed from the resolution (sometimes the money was not the first need) and how I could move the case to that middle ground where everyone was a winner. In my judge role, I pride myself on still being able to access from the facts presented as applied to the law, how I can resolve everyone's needs if at all possible.

Finally, from the technical standpoint of being a good trial attorney, I had mentors that pushed me and trained me on the importance of making a record, how to object without damaging your case or your position and how to write persuasively and clearly. All of those skills translate straight into my career as a judge. And because I dealt with clients from all walks of life and from all economic levels, I understand how important the decision is to them. I take that seriously and work very hard to write for the litigants first, the lawyers second. I feel very strongly about that and know that sometimes, the sting of a loss was less when a judge did an excellent job explaining the reasoning. My family values, along with the associations I had with excellent attorneys across the state, gave me confidence to step into the appellate role without insecurity. As a judge it is critical not to get into trying to prove how smart you are to the world, but instead, to work without ego to a solution that can resonate with the consumers of the court—the litigants.

What Prepared Me to Serve on the Iowa Supreme Court

Thomas D. Waterman
Justice, Iowa Supreme Court

Our seven-member state court of last resort is enriched by the experience most of my colleagues bring from their judicial service on the district court and court of appeals. Like several other justices, however, I was appointed to the Iowa Supreme Court directly from a law firm.[2] How did my private practice experience prepare me to serve? To answer that question, I'll first describe my 28 years of civil litigation at Lane & Waterman, LLP (L&W) and my mentoring and training at that regional law firm. Then I'll address how the skills and work ethic developed there have helped me serve Iowans as a justice on our state's highest court.

I graduated from the University of Iowa College of Law in 1984 and turned down a "big law" job offer from Willkie Farr & Gallagher in New York City in favor of L&W in Davenport at half the starting salary. Why? I saw this Midwestern law firm of 45 lawyers as offering the best of both worlds: the opportunity to work on cutting-edge litigation under top trial lawyers, but with much faster client contact, jury trial, and appellate oral argument experience than one could expect at Willkie. Indeed, within my first year at L&W, I argued before the Iowa Supreme Court and second-chaired partners in jury trials where I learned by watching, and soon by doing, under demanding task masters. They drilled into L&W associates the importance of taking the high road ethically. They emphasized the value of thorough preparation, careful research, writing and rewriting to hone *all* our written submissions. And they encouraged us to give back to our profession and to our community with volunteer service.

My mentors, most notably my father Robert Waterman Sr., my brother Bob, and senior partner Bob Van Vooren, led by example while trusting me with significant brief writing in major litigation. They inculcated in me the importance of building trust and credibility with the bench and bar through exemplary lawyering. And they included me in high-stakes, multi-party cases with and against top lawyers in Iowa and nationally, including former justice Mark McCormick. I briefed and argued emerging issues in products liability as Iowa counsel for target defendant Philip Morris; in environmental coverage suits defending the target insurer for Superfund pollution cleanup costs; and as co-lead counsel prosecuting one of Iowa's largest class actions, which I argued to the Iowa Supreme Court three times with co-counsel before attaining a $130 million settlement. At times I was the lead brief writer reconciling edits from co-counsel and sophisticated clients; at other times I helped edit the briefs primarily drafted by others. Sometimes I shared oral argument podium time with co-counsel; at other times I argued solo or helped co-counsel prepare for their arguments. These all were wonderful opportunities to develop my legal writing and appellate advocacy skills.

Most importantly, I was blessed to marry the love of my life, Maria, a family law practitioner. We learned time management skills raising four daughters, including triplets, while practicing law full time.

Although I never served on the trial bench, I appeared before many different judges in state and federal trial and appellate courts in Iowa, Illinois, and other states. Those experiences sensitized me to the challenges judges face day-to-day and the opportunities for good advocacy to make their jobs easier. I developed a PowerPoint presentation on brief writing and oral argument. My L&W partner Jason O'Rourke and I co-taught appellate advocacy annually at the firm. Good advocacy requires understanding strengths and weaknesses of your case and your opponent's case, and putting yourself in the shoes of the decision maker (judge or jury).

My volunteer service included the Iowa State Bar Association (ISBA) Jury Instruction Committee, where I worked collaboratively with other lawyers and judges to revise uniform jury instructions in response to new appellate decisions. I served on the State Judicial Nominating Commission from 1999 to 2005. In that capacity, I interviewed and reviewed the submissions of many accomplished judges and lawyers applying for appellate vacancies. Their input sensitized me to concerns that justices had grown isolated from the bench, bar and public, and took too long to decide cases. At that time, most justices worked exclusively in the Judicial Branch Building.

So how did these experiences prepare me to serve as a justice? Our court's core mission is to decide appeals. We write for publication, setting precedent for similar cases. I understood how accuracy and clarity are vital qualities as justices write opinions to resolve cases, settle issues, and persuade multiple audiences—the parties, the bench and bar, and the public—that we reached the correct and just outcome. I knew from private practice that lack of clarity and predictability in supreme court decisions would generate uncertainty that breeds additional costly litigation. With the help of veteran colleagues (Chief Justice Cady early on told me to try a more "deliberative" tone), the legal writing skills I developed at L&W translated well to opinion writing.

The diplomatic skills and collegiality I learned writing briefs with other lawyers equipped me for collaborative decision making as seven justices work together. Importantly, as a neutral decision maker, I regularly draw on my nearly three decades of private practice experience to evaluate issues from all sides, and I draw on my private practice group writing experience when offering edits to colleagues' opinions and when revising my assigned opinions at their request.

The substantive knowledge I gained litigating issues as a lawyer has provided a running start on many cases. Oral advocacy does not end with appointment to the bench; while lawyers may get 15–20 minutes at our podium, there is no time limit on a justice's effort to persuade colleagues during and between court conferences. Private practice sharpened skills that I use routinely on the court.

That said, representing clients ingrained in me a sense of urgency I bring to the position. Lives may be on hold as the litigants await our decisions that can be enormously consequential. Justice delayed is often justice denied. The Court in 2010 had a two-year backlog and *averaged* eight months from oral argument to filing the opinion. As one of three new justices appointed in 2011, we quickly cleared the backlog, moved to an annual term system ensuring all opinions argued each year are filed by June 30, and we reduced the average wait from submission to filed opinion to under 90 days. My service on the Nominating Commission, and the 2010 retention vote ouster of three justices, taught me the value of transparency. We responded by taking the court on the road to over 36 Iowa cities and live-streaming and archiving our oral arguments.

At L&W, I mentored junior associates and supervised their legal research and brief writing. That experience has helped me leverage my time and work efficiently with my outstanding judicial law clerks (one per year) and externs (one per semester).

The Iowa Supreme Court effectively functions as the board of directors of the judicial branch. My private practice experience in commercial litigation has helped me select the judges for the business specialty court. My experience doing Ironman triathlons, ultramarathons, and other endurance events, and a midlife decision to quit drinking, made me a natural liaison for the ISBA Well-Being Committee. Maria's experience as a mediator and divorce lawyer served as a reliable guide as I chaired several supreme court task forces on family law case processing. Relationships I developed as a lawyer and nonprofit board chair taught me the importance of seeking input from those affected by our court's rulemaking and supervisory decisions. Often the best expertise is found on the local front lines outside the Des Moines beltway. Task forces and committees need representation from all affected parties to facilitate the collaborative testing of ideas. An echo chamber won't produce the best decisions. As my father was fond of saying, "no one has a monopoly on wisdom."

Finally, humility is a vital trait for justices and lawyers alike. At L&W, we were taught to phone opposing counsel to offer congratulations for their wins, to learn all we could from our mistakes, and to lose gracefully, traits useful for dissenting justices. And by remaining mindful of what it feels like as a lawyer losing an appeal, I strive to write opinions that show their arguments were carefully considered. Overall, private practice sharpened skills that I use routinely on the court.

Chapter 7

What Government Attorneys Bring to the Bench

Good Prosecutors Make Great Judges

Tyler J. Buller
Judge, Iowa Court of Appeals

During and after the interview process for becoming a judge, more than one person told me they had an aversion to selecting government lawyers for judicial office. These folks did not mean it as an insult, and I'm grateful for their candor. But those comments floated in the background as I sat down to write this essay, the core of which is simple in my mind: good prosecutors make good judges.

Before my appointment to the court of appeals in 2022, I worked as a criminal prosecutor in the state department of justice (better known as the state attorney general's office) for more than a decade. In that role, I handled criminal trials and appeals, which gave me the opportunity to try big cases in all corners of the state's district courts and represent the people in hundreds of cases before the state supreme court and court of appeals. Although I had frequent and close contact with crime victims and police officers, I didn't have clients in the traditional sense. But my background offered something else—a shared thread of common purpose and fidelity to the law that dovetails nicely with the work I do now as a judge. And I want to highlight that commonality, both with some of my own observations and by sharing some of the best advice I gave and received in my career as a government lawyer.

For me, there is something distinctly sacred about being a prosecutor or judge. And that's not to downplay any other type of lawyer, many of whom do important, noble work and go on to be outstanding jurists. But the cord that tethers a prosecutor or judge to the law is different from that of a lawyer with a client. Whether representing plaintiffs, civil or criminal defendants, corporations, or non-profit entities, lawyers with clients are ethically bound to advocate for those clients' interests. And sometimes that advocacy is to the detriment of the court system, makes bad precedent, or undermines just outcomes. Prosecutors and judges are instead bound to justice and the law, rather than the disposition of any single case for any particular person or entity. And that fealty to the broader public interest, rather than a single client, makes prosecutors think and act differently than other lawyers.

Prosecutors and judges both work in what I call the accountability business. Just like waiters and line cooks in a restaurant are both in the food business but have different roles within it, prosecutors and judges both serve the ultimate goal of accountability in slightly different ways.

Prosecutors—within the confines of the law—seek justice by bringing appropriate charges. Judges—again within the bounds of the law—resolve those charges against facts and precedent. Neither is a roving justice commission, and both are firmly cabined in by our existing legal framework. Perhaps most importantly, the top concern of both roles is following the law, even if the consequences are occasionally uncomfortable.

In recent years, judicial writers have focused on "procedural fairness," which is basically the idea that by giving litigants a fair hearing and letting them feel heard, they are more likely to accept the legitimacy of the court's decision. Prosecutors don't use the same vocabulary, but it's a core tenant of how good prosecutors look at their cases. Shortly before one of my first big trials, my co-counsel—one of the very best trial lawyers I know—told me: *"Sometimes you try a case to lose."* I remember staring at her with a deer-in-the-headlights expression; as a brand-new lawyer, I didn't quite get it. Over the decade that followed, I prosecuted many cases with child victims of physical and sexual abuse. Every case I filed was supported by proof beyond a reasonable doubt, but sometimes that proof came from the testimony of a little girl who would rather be at basketball practice or a little boy who brought a Spider-Man action figure and stuffed dog to the witness stand. Some of these cases resulted in acquittals, but that doesn't mean they shouldn't have been charged or shouldn't have been tried. This procedural justice—getting a fair day in court, with a prosecutor who believed them, and a jury empowered to hold the offender accountable—was nearly as important to these victims as the result. In the same vein, I tried cases mindful of my obligation to treat defendants fairly, ensuring I obtained my convictions justly and only after a defendant exercised his or her right to due process.

As a judge, I remind myself every time I enter the courtroom that making sure both sides feel heard and are treated with dignity can be just as important as the outcome in my written decisions. And I recognize that, much like when I was a prosecutor, showing litigants that I have heard them and understand them, even when I do not or cannot rule for them based on the law, is an integral part of being a good judge. Procedural fairness isn't everything, but it's my experience that whether someone feels treated fairly in the courtroom is the most important factor in whether they feel justice is done in our courthouses.

For better or worse, I am well-known (perhaps infamous) for the crass vocabulary that comes from a career working primarily with dark-humored prosecutors and police officers. One of my crass observations fit for print is a piece of advice that I gave frequently in my former career, and one that prosecutors and judges uniquely understand: *"Sometimes the law sucks."* More than once as a prosecutor, I helped investigate behavior I found morally and ethically reprehensible, but a thorough review of the law convinced me there was not a legally sound charge. Coming to that conclusion is jarring for someone who believes deeply in the court system, especially when the conduct was clearly culpable or victims deserved justice in the courtroom. But good prosecutors don't file charges that aren't supported by the law, and I strove to live by that standard. As an appellate prosecutor, I encountered similar situations when reviewing convictions obtained by other prosecutors. More than a few times, I vacated convictions and sentences on appeal that violated controlling precedent, despite angry phone calls and tense meetings with county attorneys or hard conversations with crime victims. But my job as a prosecutor wasn't to do everything I could to put people in prison or keep them there; my role was to follow the law and do justice, even if that meant a corrupt public official might never serve jail time or someone factually guilty may get a new trial.

Like prosecutors, judges are no strangers to the law offering an outcome we disfavor or find occasionally unjust in application. An early case I handled as a judge involved a will contest where our court had to decide between following the letter of a family matriarch's will or trying to carry out her intent by rewriting or changing the terms she had written. The latter was the more "just" or ephemerally "equitable" option—we knew the matriarch probably wanted things evenly divided among her kids. But the former was unquestionably the right legal choice, as reflected by the unanimous opinion I authored for a five-judge panel of my court. A month or so after deciding that case, one of my former colleagues from the attorney general's office told me that if anyone ever asked him what it means to be a judge, he would point to that opinion. It's one of the highest compliments I've been paid as a judge and something I think about often. And the reason is that sometimes following the law isn't easy, but judges—like prosecutors—have to do it anyway.

Another watchword of both prosecution and judicial work is "discretion," and both roles require insight on how different kinds of discretion fit within our many-layered system of government. As a trial prosecutor, I had almost unfettered discretion on my cases: I worked closely with victims and law enforcement, but I was essentially the sole decider on what charges to bring. As an appellate prosecutor, I also exercised tremendous discretion, but within the bounds of a statutory duty to defend the district court and jury verdicts absent clear legal error. Now as an appellate judge, the level of discretion afforded to me or the court I'm reviewing varies by case and applicable standard of review. These distinctions are meaningful; they reflect considered choices in our democracy on the allocation of power. For example, in criminal cases, the elected prosecutor has virtually limitless discretion on whether to file a charge, the sentencing judge has tremendous discretion within limits set by the legislature, and the reviewing appellate court defers to the sentencing judge absent egregious legal error. But in a pure constitutional challenge to a statute, the appellate court pays no deference to a ruling below and considers the issue anew. There is no other job, beyond prosecution and government lawyering, that can prepare you for donning and doffing these different hats daily. I have seen other judges struggle to recognize where each layer of government turf begins and ends, but as a former prosecutor I see the value in separation of powers and differentiated boxes of discretion. These restrictions on power are part of why our criminal justice system—flawed as it may be—is one of the best the world has ever seen.

Last, a moment on the adjectives in my observation that good prosecutors make good judges. The modifier "good" matters. The type of prosecutor who wants to win at all costs, knowingly buries exculpatory evidence, or can't bring themselves to dismiss bad cases has no business in a prosecutor's office, let alone the judiciary. I acknowledge there are bad prosecutors out there who fit these descriptors and see themselves solely as an advocate for punishment rather than a minister of justice. No one is magically transformed by putting on the black dress that comes with judicial office, and anyone who would abuse their power as a prosecutor is just as likely to abuse their power as a judge. But this isn't to say that a prosecutor you disagree with is a bad prosecutor, any more than a judge whose rulings you disagree with is a bad judge. There is a parallel in these roles: it's intrinsic that neither prosecutors nor judges can make everyone happy. By default, one of the parties in nearly every case will be displeased with the result. But it's important to differentiate between good judges or good prosecutors you disagree with and bad judges or bad prosecutors who aren't doing their jobs in the accountability business. This is the type of nuance that should inform scrutiny of prosecutors seeking judicial office—not a blanket preference for or against them.

I'm blessed that my legal career offered roles I am called to and feel deep responsibility for. It's no secret that I loved being a prosecutor. Or that I love being a judge now. And the reasons why are these common threads: the accountability business; fidelity to the law—warts and all; and embracing the institutions that undergird our democracy. My sincere hope is that others who feel this calling to the law, especially good prosecutors, consider applying to become a judge as a continuation of their public service.

How Representing the Government Prepared Me for the Bench

Margaret J. Reyes
Judge, Iowa District Court

I spent 15 years working as an assistant county attorney in a county with both urban and rural issues. I didn't prosecute criminal cases, but rather worked as a civil legal advisor to county officials and litigated the county's civil (not criminal) cases. Across the state, many of my judicial colleagues are also former government attorneys (both prosecutors and public defenders). While cynics suggest that government attorneys, especially prosecutors, are attracted to the power of a judicial appointment or the desire to maintain a public retirement account, I found the duties of government lawyer to be uniquely similar to those of a judge. It was that familiarity that piqued my interest in becoming a judge.

First, as an assistant county attorney, I worked in a county courthouse every day. I saw judges and courtrooms frequently. I was familiar with the courthouse building, court offices, and court staff. Working as a government attorney, I was familiar with the quirky gift and spending restrictions for government employees and the budget cycles that come with working for the government. Just as government attorneys work for a city, county, or state, judges work for Iowa's judicial branch whose budget—including judicial salaries and benefits—must be approved by the state legislature each year.

The work of judges and government lawyers is not only subject to public funding, but also public criticism. As a government attorney, or judge, your work may be subject to open records laws. And, since government attorneys represent citizens of the local community or state—taxpayers may remind you that they "pay your salary" and expect to weigh in on the work you do. Unfortunately, public scrutiny can also be accompanied by political or public pressure to decide a case in a certain way. Unlike most lawyers, a government attorney is not bound to the interest of a single client or individual, but rather to the community, state, or governmental entity they serve. This responsibility can lead to disagreements with citizens, government officials, or government employees. As a government attorney, I learned to make independent, sometimes unpopular, decisions despite public or political pressure. Now, as a judge, I rely on the courage, integrity, and fortitude I developed working as a government attorney to make decisions without concern of political pressure or public criticism.

Both government lawyers and judges work on cases that make the news. As a former government attorney and now a judge, I have been assigned cases that generate public interest and have been in the news. In many small towns in my district, the local newspapers routinely publish the decisions that judges make in court, sometimes garnering comments from citizens. But, as a former government lawyer, I was prepared for the public nature of a judge's work. In Iowa, both county attorneys and judges have a similar ethical obligation to avoid making extrajudicial statements about cases they are working on. Judges, like government attorneys, also have an ethical obligation to avoid impropriety and the appearance of impropriety in both their professional and personal conduct. This means not considering personal views, political pressure, or public opinion when deciding cases.

In Iowa, a county attorney's official duties include providing legal advice to county officials on policy matters that impact employees, citizens, and the public at large.[1] As a civil legal advisor to the county, I advised officials on county operations, policies, litigation, legislation, and similar matters. Similarly, judges in Iowa work on a variety of Iowa Supreme Court and judicial branch committees and commissions to develop policies and procedures for the court system. In criminal cases, county prosecutors must look to the unique facts and circumstances of each case to determine whether criminal charges should be filed. Likewise, as a judge, I must look at the specific details of a criminal case and exercise a similar discretion in arriving at a proper decision or imposing an appropriate sentence.

As a "civil" county attorney, my practice was that of a "generalist"—I worked on a wide range of legal issues. I was a "jack of all trades, master of none." But, this generalist background prepared me for my work as a district court judge where I handle civil, criminal, and family law cases, among other matters.[2] As a government attorney, I was expected to communicate professionally and effectively with people from a variety of backgrounds such as county officials, community leaders, members of the public, and self-represented litigants. As a judge, I must also communicate effectively and respectfully with self-represented litigants as well as attorneys and litigants in a wide variety of cases.

In Iowa, a criminal prosecutor has the ethical responsibility to ensure that a defendant is "accorded procedural justice."[3] Similarly, as a judge, I must ensure that court proceedings are conducted fairly. In the courtroom, I am responsible for maintaining decorum to ensure that every case is handled fairly and that each litigant is given a full and fair opportunity to be heard. Most of what I do as a judge, however—reviewing evidence, researching the law, and drafting sound legal decisions—is conducted outside of the courtroom. Whether in court, or behind closed doors, judges—like government attorneys—must perform their duties with honesty and integrity and a sense of fairness. As a judge, I took an oath to perform my duties fairly and impartially "without fear, favor, affection, or hope of reward."[4] Both judges and county attorneys take a similar oath of office and swear an oath to support the state and federal constitution.

As a government attorney, I was keenly aware of the government's power to affect people's lives whether through the collection of taxes, regulation of property, criminal investigations, or passing and enforcing legislation. Working in a prosecutor's office, I saw people on their worst days. I saw the harm that people inflict on themselves, on their children, on their spouses, and on strangers. A friend of mine who served on a federal jury told me that the experience gave her nightmares. She asked how I could work as a judge and see people suffering every day. While at times it is difficult, as a former assistant county attorney, I was uniquely prepared for the worst that I would see as a judge. As a judge, litigants come before you on their worst days, depending on you for the best outcome.

Government attorneys apply to become judges not to become wealthy, but because they respect the legal system. Government attorneys in particular are acutely aware of the heavy burden that comes with a judicial appointment, and most choose to become a judge because they want to make the system better. They choose to become a judge despite the personal security and safety risks that come with the job. In 2021, the U.S. Marshals Service reported over 4,500 threats against federal judges, prosecutors, and court officials, a 400% increase from 2015.[5] While working in the county attorney's office, I took steps to protect my physical safety and to safeguard my personal information available in the community and online.

While the inefficiencies and often divisive political nature of government work were sometimes frustrating, I also enjoyed playing a small part in making a positive difference in my community. Despite the downsides, I was always drawn to a legal career in public service. I began my career working as in-house counsel for an urban public housing agency and finished working 15 years as an assistant county attorney. Because of the unique perspective into the role of a district court judge I was afforded as a government attorney, I am now honored to continue my public service career from the bench.

My Path from Prosecutor to Judge

Karen A. Romano
Senior Judge, Iowa District Court

Every person who takes the bench at any level of court brings their own life experiences and background to the position. No two judges have the exact same background. Some come from a long line of lawyers and judges, some are the first college graduates in their family, some are from privileged and wealthy backgrounds, some are from poor or middle-class backgrounds. All these different life experiences have a role in forming how a person approaches being a judge. Having judges with a variety of backgrounds and experiences is important so that the judiciary looks like the people it serves. With this in mind, a little of my background is important to know.

Some people grow up with a big dream like becoming a judge. I was not one of those people. My dreams were all over the board—from veterinarian, journalist, and author to being a labor lawyer. Lawyer was the dream that stuck with me. I grew up in a middle-class family where helping others less fortunate and being accepting of all was demonstrated daily by my parents. My father was a labor leader and very involved in many community boards and activities. My siblings and I would often be called into service to assist with the project at hand, be it stuffing envelopes for a mailing or filling boxes with gifts and food for those having a tough time at Christmas or walking a picket line. My mother stayed at home with her five children (I was the third of the five) until I was about 14 years old, when she began a long career at the Iowa House of Representatives and the Legislative Computer Support Bureau. She held several positions but what stood out to me was she learned (and then taught) computer skills to legislative secretaries when computers were new and she had no formal training in computers or teaching. She showed me through her work that you can do anything if you put your mind to it and work hard. It is with this background of hard work and caring for fellow human beings that I went off to college. And then on to the University of Iowa College of Law.

I was not certain what I wanted to do after law school, but through my father I came to know several lawyers who were involved with unions and politics. I felt labor law would be a good fit. I started down that path and after about a year felt restless for a different challenge. I began working at the Polk County Attorney's

Office in the Juvenile Division. I had no experience in this area but quickly learned and enjoyed the work. The feeling of making a difference in the life of a child or a family was very rewarding. I interacted with child abuse investigators, police officers, doctors, and mental health professionals, as well as Juvenile Court Officers and many attorneys. I then transferred to the felony criminal docket prosecuting general felonies with an emphasis on child abuse and sexual abuse. This work was rewarding, and my focus was on the victims and making sure their voices were heard. However, I also focused on arriving at a fair disposition on each case. I oversaw a sexual abuse treatment program for intra-family abuse cases. This gave me insight on the rehabilitative role of the courts. As a prosecutor I had certain obligations, and primarily among them was my ethical obligation to "find the truth and do justice." In making prosecutorial decisions, I regularly pondered what was the right decision. I believe a primary tenet of prosecutors is "Just because you have the right to do something does not mean it is the right thing to do." I conducted myself with this in mind.

Experience in a county prosecutor office prepared me for my years on the bench in several ways. I was an advocate representing the people of the State of Iowa but also entrusted with the ethical obligations set forth above—to do the right thing and see that justice was served. This differs from the role of attorneys in private practice or criminal defense. Their obligation is to zealously advocate for their client's position within the bounds of the law. How an attorney transitions from an advocate to a neutral decision maker is different for every person. I believe my transition was less drastic than some because of my work as a government attorney. I had always considered what course of action would lead to a right and just result. The ability to look at a situation from the victim's perspective, society's perspective, as well as the defendant's perspective, especially as to rehabilitation versus punishment, enabled me to understand those issues as a judge more readily than an attorney without this background.

As a prosecutor, I tried many cases to the court and to juries. Courtroom experience and knowledge of how a trial judge manages a courtroom is invaluable when taking the bench. Prosecutors, in general, have more trial experience than many, if not most, attorneys. My trial experience was a great asset when I became a judge. I had seen many skilled and well-respected judges manage their courtrooms. While each judge had different procedures and methods for conducting a trial, I found it essential to have all those examples to draw upon when presiding over hearings and trials as a judge. During a judge's first trials there are many things the judge needs to learn to focus on. Having knowledge and familiarity with the procedures of selecting a jury and conducting the procedural aspects of the trial allows a new judge to focus on the particular details of the case, including the law, evidentiary rulings and the attorneys. A judge without courtroom trial experience will have a much steeper learning curve when managing a trial.

An aspect of being a government lawyer which may be overlooked when seeking judicial appointment is working with a lack of resources. As a prosecutor, I needed to be self-sufficient in many respects. At the time, support personnel were limited, law clerk assistance was non-existent, and I needed to take care of things many attorneys in other practices have staff to do for them. This experience of taking care of myself, so to speak, was an asset when joining the judicial branch. In over 25 years on the bench, I typed all my own rulings and orders. Federal judges may have access to additional resources, but as a state court judge you share a law clerk with up to seven other judges so you must be very selective as to what case you ask a law clerk to work on. I did most of my own legal research. I kept my own calendar and kept track of what cases I had under advisement to rule upon. I typically made my own copies, got my own supplies, got my own coffee, and managed my email inbox, which increased exponentially over my years on the bench. I have seen some judges from private practice really struggle with the lack of staff and the necessity to do many tasks themselves which were done for them in their practice.

Similarly, as a prosecutor I had a very large caseload. All lawyers have to manage their caseloads but as a prosecutor I often did not have control over how large of a caseload I carried. Managing a large and varied caseload was good training for the workload of a district court judge. The organizational skills I learned to keep track of all my cases as a prosecutor were the skills I employed to make sure I was tracking my court docket. The limited staff available to state court judges requires a judge to have a system to know what cases need ruled upon, what cases are coming up, and on what cases the judge is waiting for filings from attorneys. Without these skills, a judge can quickly become overwhelmed by the caseload assigned.

Attorneys in private practice often must deal with difficult clients. As a prosecutor, dealing with victims of crimes can also be difficult. Victims have their ideas of what the prosecutor should or should not be able to do in a case. Typically, clients and victims are interacting with an attorney/prosecutor because of something bad that has happened to them or will happen to them. Dealing with people at their lowest is a common factor for both private practice attorneys and government attorneys.

Coming from a background in criminal and juvenile law, I did have a learning curve in civil cases. I served as a district associate judge when small claims, traffic, mental health and misdemeanor cases were all handled at that level. Presently, much of that is handled by part-time magistrates. My time in small claims court was very helpful in learning the ropes of civil procedures and law. While the dollar amounts at stake were less, the legal issues were the same as in civil cases in the district court. It was a great education on products liability, medical malpractice, car accidents and other torts, as well as landlord-tenant issues. By the time I became a district court judge I had a firm understanding of the law, rules and procedures in civil litigation. One area a prosecutor may find it difficult to maneuver is attorney fees. When attorney fees are recoverable is simply a matter of a little legal research. The more difficult matter is the amount of attorney fees. I believe even attorneys from private practice who take the bench can struggle with this issue. Judges continue to learn and study this issue and it becomes less challenging as time passes.

A growing issue in the courts is the proliferation of self-represented litigants. Some judges enjoy working with them and others detest it. I found it rewarding to be able to help a self-represented litigant through the court system, and once again my background came to bear. My time as a prosecutor brought me in contact with many people from many walks of life, as I met with victims, parents, family members, witnesses, service providers, probation officers, juvenile court officers, doctors, police officers, and more. That work taught me that everyone has a story, and it may or may not be what you thought it was at first glance. It helped me be more empathetic and respectful of self-represented litigants. Certainly, every person deserves to be treated with respect, and an ability to respectfully interact with the people who choose to represent themselves is an essential attribute for a judge. A judge must be cautious not to provide legal advice, but there are many ways to move a case without crossing that line. I have had self-represented litigants who have received an adverse ruling from me but have thanked me for allowing them to be heard. When a litigant feels unheard, that litigant leaves with a bad impression of the courts. It is important to always remember that how any individual judge treats a litigant is the litigant's impression of the entire judicial system.

Rather than your background as an attorney, I believe a person's life experiences, background, compassion, and empathy is more important when taking the bench. Interacting with litigants, attorneys and witnesses will be based on who you are as a person, not what you did before becoming a judge.

Taking the Bench as a Government Lawyer

C. J. Williams
Chief Judge, U.S. District Court
for the Northern District of Iowa

I practiced law for almost 29 years before becoming a judge, during all but seven of which I served as a federal prosecutor. In 2016, I was first appointed as a United States magistrate judge, then a couple of years later as a United States district court judge. When going through the interview processes for both judicial positions, I was asked several times about whether I would be able to be fair to criminal defendants, given my long career as a government attorney. There were also questions about my ability to comprehend, understand, and empathize with issues unique to civil practice and practitioners. These were fair questions, and I was happy for the chance to allay any concerns about my background.

In fact, I would posit that serving as a government attorney eased my transition to the bench and better equipped me for its responsibilities than perhaps any other attorney role could, while at the same time acknowledging that my additional years in private practice has given me a distinct advantage.

Some more details about my particular background would be helpful to understand my views. My path to the bench was the result of a series of fortunate events. I did not come from a family of lawyers; my father was a haberdasher and my mother a newspaper editor. I majored in business as an undergrad and applied to law school only because I happened to take a business law class that I found fascinating. I attended law school thinking I would become a corporate attorney. But after law school I clerked for a United States district court judge, where I had greater exposure to criminal practice. On one occasion, I observed two Department of Justice attorneys argue a case before my judge. I was overwhelmed by their performance and told myself that I wanted to be as good as them. That led me, after my clerkship, to join the Narcotics and Dangerous Drug Section of the United States Department of Justice in Washington, D.C. I worked as a trial attorney in that section for about two years, but when it looked like I was going to be relegated to policy work, I decided to try private practice. I moved to Kansas City, where I joined a large law firm and practiced complex civil litigation and white-collar criminal defense. After five years, I found that I didn't cotton to private practice like I thought I might, so once my final trial was over, I rejoined the Department of Justice, this time as an Assistant United States Attorney in Cedar Rapids, Iowa. There I remained for the next 20 years, prosecuting just about every type of criminal case imaginable. Through this circuitous route, I found that I had developed a breadth and depth of experience that couldn't have better prepared me for the bench if I had planned it all along.

Which brings me back to the questions I faced as a judicial candidate. The premise underlying the first one—would I be able to be fair to criminal defendants—is that my background as a prosecutor might bias me against criminal defendants. I can't speak for all prosecutors, but for good prosecutors, this is a false premise. The United States Department of Justice inculcates in its career prosecutors a core belief that a prosecutor's job is to do justice. Good prosecutors, then, recognize and fulfill their role in a criminal justice system, the object of which is to dispense justice fairly to all people in every case. In short, to do what is right.

Prosecutors—especially federal prosecutors—are granted enormous discretion to exercise decisions in criminal cases with the only goal of doing justice. That means that prosecutors can, and should, exercise discretion to charge only cases for which there is proof beyond a reasonable doubt, and then bring only those charges that are supported by the facts and that advance the goals of justice. As a federal prosecutor, I exercised my discretion to decline to charge some people, or to decline to bring some charges against people I did prosecute, when I thought the evidence wasn't sufficiently strong. That's not to say that a jury might not still convict. Rather, it means that I personally wasn't satisfied that the evidence was overwhelming. I also exercised my discretion not to bring charges, even when supported by the evidence, if the punishment didn't fit the crime, or to refer the case to a county prosecutor when the state punishment was more in line with the seriousness of the offense and the history and characteristics of the offender.

My goal in every case was to get at the truth and seek a just outcome based on the facts and the law. I didn't have an agenda. I didn't have a bias against offenders. I wasn't out to get every bad guy or seek the longest sentence in every case. It was my experience that most offenders were decent and good people at their core who, for various reasons, had made bad decisions. Over my career, I prosecuted more than 900 offenders; I can count on one hand the offenders who I thought were evil.

So no, I don't believe having been a government attorney made me biased against criminal defendants. Quite to the contrary, there may have been no finer means for avoiding such bias. There may also have been no finer preparation for taking on the responsibilities of the bench. Attorneys have an ethical obligation to zealously represent their clients. They are ethically bound not to seek justice, not to seek the right answer, but to seek the outcome that is best for their clients. The adversary system works well that way. But judges are not advocates. Judges must not choose sides. Judges must be neutral and seek to do justice in every case. As a prosecutor, I didn't have a client, per se—I served the people, the system, justice itself. I became accustomed to evaluating cases seeking the right answer. In that sense then, my job now as a judge is similar to my job then as a prosecutor.

What surprised me most about becoming a judge was how I stopped being invested in cases. As a trial attorney, you live and breathe the cases you work on. You think about them when you lie in bed trying to fall asleep. You think about them when you're watching your children's baseball game. The cases consume you. You care about the case, you care about the outcome, you care whether you win or lose on appeal.

As a judge, however, I learned very quickly that I am not invested in any case. What I care about is making a decision on the matter in front of me to the best of my abilities; I care about getting the answer right. After I make my ruling, the matter is out of my control, no longer my concern. For that reason, I don't care what happens to the case on appeal. That's not to say that I don't care what an appellate court may say if they overturn my decision on appeal. I care a lot. I want to get the answer right and I want to learn from my mistakes. But whether one party or another prevails is not my concern. My job—my only job—is to apply the law to the facts of the case before me and render a decision consistent with the law as I understand it. Again, my service as a federal prosecutor in search of the right answer, rather than the best outcome for an individual client, helped to form the proper mindset I needed as a judge for seeking justice in every case.

If there is one concern I could cite about a background as a government attorney, it would be that lacking a client could potentially blind judges to the nuanced difficulties of private practitioners who serve clients. Judges who have never been in private practice may not fully understand or appreciate the difficulty of attorney-client relationships. These judges may not realize that criticizing an attorney in open court, before the attorney's client, could jeopardize the relationship that attorney has with the client. These judges may not fully appreciate the difficulty of representing an obstreperous client who demands that attorneys file motions or take positions that, left to their own judgment, the attorneys wouldn't file or take. These judges may not empathize with attorneys struggling to represent clients who are not current in their payments, or with attorneys encountering other financial difficulties inherent in the private practice of law. As a result, government attorneys who have never been in private practice come to the bench at a disadvantage, lacking the insight necessary to appreciate the unique struggles of attorneys in private practice.

Thankfully, I had five years of private practice. I represented human and organizational clients. I had to console clients' families as my client was sentenced to prison. I had to deal with clients who failed to pay their bills, but still expected my representation to continue unabated. I made arguments I didn't believe were the best because my client insisted. And I was embarrassed when dressed down by a judge in front of my client. I have never forgotten those experiences, and painful as they may be, they equipped me to be a better judge. Judges who have never been in that position will need to learn quickly through other means, such as careful observation, close reading, and probing questions. Empathy, generally, is a valuable attribute for any judge, from any background, and being exposed to the nuances of private practice is one reliable means of increasing it.

Having never set out to become a judge, I can glance back now at my career and recognize that my service as a government attorney—in addition to my other experiences—prepared me well for the position. I am proud of my years as a public servant, and take pride now in continuing to serve the public. Service as a government attorney in whatever capacity may not be the only, or the best, path to the bench. But neither is it a disadvantage, nor discordant with the judicial role.

Chapter 8

My Unique Path to the Bench

My Path to the Federal Bench

Mark W. Bennett
Former Chief U.S. District Judge
for the Northern District of Iowa (Ret.)

On my first evening at new federal judges' school in 1994 I had dinner with seven other new federal district judges. One suggested we go around the table and describe our path to this best job in the world. The first judge gave us a wicked smile. "I was working for my father-in-law, a U.S. Senator," he said, "and he asked me to draft a letter from him to the President asking the President to nominate me for an opening for a federal district judgeship. I eagerly agreed!" The next judge said his law school roommate was a U.S. Senator, so when the Senator called and asked if he wanted to be a federal district judge, he wholeheartedly agreed. The next was a primary fundraiser for a buddy who just happened to be a U.S. Senator. The remaining four had similar tales of close encounters with U.S. Senators.

I was last to explain my path. I told the group I had never met my U.S. Senator until the day of my interview at the Federal Building in downtown Des Moines, Iowa, after he and his staff had chosen 12 candidates from a pool of 70+ applicants. I explained I had not been involved in politics since college and was now too busy as a civil rights and federal criminal defense lawyer to be politically active. They did not believe me and thought I was downplaying my connections to the Senator. Nothing could have been further from the truth. Here is a little bit about the rest of the story.

As my interview approached, several of my closest friends and confidants had repeatedly warned me that while I was the most qualified, I had done nothing to help the Senator, who was in a tough reelection campaign, so I should not get my hopes up. I agreed on all counts and thus never expected to be selected. Adding to my long-shot status were two other factors. As a civil rights lawyer I had represented many, many controversial and often despised clients, ranging from Rev. Moon and the Unification Church to the Hare Krishnas, the Christian Nudist Church (whose motto was "Go Naked if the Holy Spirit Moves You"), the Communist Party of America, the Socialist Workers of America, and hundreds of civil rights clients challenging everything from handing out bibles in public schools to a new mall owner dismissing the longstanding mall Santa because she was a woman. And more importantly, I had never contributed a dime to any of the Senator's political campaigns.

When I arrived for my interview I was relieved to discover I was first on the schedule, and would be meeting with the Senator at 8 a.m. I would not have to sit in the waiting room while the other candidates were interviewed, worrying that I would not be selected. My interview with the Senator went extremely well. He was impressed that I had personally argued a major employment discrimination case in the U.S. Supreme Court barely three years out of law school, and had had three more cases accepted for U.S. Supreme Court review before I was 32.

He also seemed impressed that I had litigated cases in over 25 federal district courts, several of the Courts of Appeals, and several State Supreme Courts. I was very surprised but delighted when the Senator asked me what I thought of the Supreme Court's jurisprudence on habeas corpus—and I was loaded for bear. I explained in detail how the court had turned "the Great Writ" on its head, making it virtually impossible to ever address the merits because of all the judicially crafted hurdles which often were insuperable barriers to relief even when there were egregious constitutional violations in the accused criminal trials. He listened very carefully and asked excellent follow-up questions. When I looked at my watch and realized I was 20 minutes past my allotted 25 minutes, the Senator indicated he wasn't ready to end my interview. I reminded him that he had 11 other qualified candidates waiting for him, and said, sincerely, that I had very much enjoyed my time with him. I stood up to leave and shook his hand.

In the ensuing days I told my close friends and confidants that I thought the interview had gone surprisingly well—and they dutifully reminded me I had no chance because several of the 12 candidates were very well connected politically to the Senator. I assumed they were right. Indeed, a sitting federal court of appeals judge called me to his chambers to discuss who was my "campaign manager." I had no idea what he was talking about, so he explained that I needed to run a full-fledged campaign to become a federal judge, which required a campaign manager. I thanked him for his advice and immediately discarded it. If I was selected on my merits, fine, but I certainly had no desire to run a campaign, and I did not.

Several months after the interviews I was informed by the Senator's Office that mine was one of four names he had sent to the President. After another several months I learned that two of us were invited to Washington D.C. to interview with the Department of Justice. It's impossible to say who was more surprised, my friends or me. Seven top DOJ lawyers interviewed me for about 90 minutes. The interview went well except for one answer I gave. They did not like it and suggested that if I was nominated, I needed to change my answer. Unflinchingly, I told them I did not covet the position badly enough to change my position. They seemed chagrined by my response, and I assumed my chances were now zero as I left the interview to fly back to Iowa.

Many months went by and I heard nothing, and I continued to assume I was out of the running. One day I was driving back from a case in another city and stopped at a payphone to check in with my office. My secretary indicated that the Senator had called and wanted me to call him back. As I dialed his number from the pay phone, I thought about how nice it was that the Senator was going to tell me personally I would not be nominated. The Senator greeted me warmly and said he wanted to give me a heads-up that the President would be nominating the individual later that day—and that it would be me. Shocked, I told the Senator I had done nothing for him politically and understood if he wanted one of the others. He laughed and said he had known since my interview that I was the one who would be nominated.

The rest is history. I served 24 years as a United States district judge and seven years as the Chief Judge of the Northern District of Iowa. I tried over 400 jury trials in five different districts, sitting by designation in districts spanning the Middle District of Florida to the District of the Northern Mariana Islands in Saipan. I also sat frequently, again by designation of the Chief Justice of the U.S. Supreme Court, on the U.S. Court of Appeals for the Ninth Circuit.

At age 68 I retired after being recruited to teach by the Dean at my alma mater, the Drake University Law School, where I remain as the first Director of the Institute for Justice Reform and Innovation. I also have a nationwide mediation, arbitration and legal consulting practice.

Here are six lessons I've learned from the experience:

- If you want to be a federal judge, hope a roommate becomes a U.S. Senator.
- Failing that, even though the selection of federal judges is a political process you don't have to be actively engaged in politics to become a federal judge—just become the best lawyer you are capable of.
- To that end, work harder and more efficiently than other lawyers to consistently achieve excellent results for your clients. Don't brag—let others be your cheerleaders.
- Many lawyers, especially for state court positions, try several times before they are selected for a judgeship. Be gritty and determined, and never badmouth your competitors.
- Work well with lawyers on the other side of your disputes—remember they have a duty of zealous representation as well. Former adversaries are often the best proponents on your behalf for judgeships.
- Remember it takes a lot of tireless effort to develop a superb reputation, and one minor incident can tarnish it. Always be honest and candid with

your clients, opposing counsel, and the court. Your reputation is your calling card. It's priceless.

What Do We Do Now?

Arthur E. Gamble
Former Chief Judge, Iowa District Court (Ret.)

Judging is in my blood. I was privileged to be born into a multi-generational family of judges and lawyers. My great-grandfather was a circuit-riding lawyer in Alabama after the Civil War. My grandfather was a judge of the same circuit during Jim Crow. My uncle served as circuit solicitor during the civil rights movement and was a circuit judge for many years. My father was an attorney in an Iowa law firm founded by his uncle, and my brother practiced in the same Des Moines firm until it dissolved, when he joined another practice. My son is a lawyer in a successor firm.

Given this history, one might wonder if an eventual place on the bench was a foregone conclusion. What I do know is that in the Sixties, when I was about eight years old, I started to accompany my dad to his law office on Saturday mornings. I loved the smell of musty law books and the energy of the office. It whetted my appetite. When I was 14, a young Iowa law professor visited my junior high on a recruiting trip. By then I already knew I wanted to grow up to be a lawyer, but the professor inspired me to set my sights on the University of Iowa College of Law to make it happen. Several years later, I was a student in his class.

In the Seventies, after graduating from law school and passing the bar, I achieved what I believed to be my highest ambition—practicing law with my father and brother at the law firm where I spent the Saturdays of my youth. I thought I was going to be a business lawyer, but I ended up in a litigation practice doing transportation law, employment law, and a myriad of civil matters. I worked nights and weekends feeding the beast of billable hours. Eventually, I found the practice of law to be more stressful and less fulfilling than I expected. Something was missing.

My mother put her finger on it. Pointing to my grandfather and uncle as role models, she tried to convince me that my personality was more suited to the role of a judge than a trial lawyer. She had an old-fashioned view of the prestige of the judiciary. She described it as a calling. She felt that over the course of a lengthy career, helping others resolve their disputes in the courtroom doing the work of justice would be more rewarding than slugging it out every day in private practice.

I began thinking about what life would be like on the bench. But I needed more seasoning, and I worried about the financial sacrifice and isolation of a judge's life. The judiciary was a dream to be put off for another day. But before I was ready, a local judge was elevated to the appellate court and a district court judgeship was available.

In the Eighties, like today, judicial salaries did not keep up with the compensation of lawyers in private practice. Some middle-aged lawyers contemplated the difficulty of supporting a family on a judge's salary and chose not to apply. Others thought a career in the judiciary was too much work, too structured, and too stressful. As a result, younger lawyers were appointed to the bench with increasing frequency, and at my stage of life it seemed realistic.

To gain an understanding of the position and to seek advice on how to proceed, I visited a younger judge before whom I had appeared. The judge shared his experiences with the nominating commission and described the governor's process for appointment. He was candid about the challenges. He suggested I should apply to become acquainted with the commissioners and to get my name out there. But, given my relative youth and inexperience, he observed, "Mr. Gamble, you have a snowball's chance in hell of being appointed!" (This fortune teller later became one of my best friends on the bench and I enjoyed lording that comment over him for years as his chief judge.) After some soul-searching, I decided to apply.

The merit-based judicial nominating commission consisted of lawyers elected by the bar from Polk County and the surrounding rural area together with citizens appointed by the governor. The longest-serving district judge was the chair. I spent hours obtaining well-placed references, polishing a persuasive application, and traveling around the district meeting commissioners. The interview with the commission was my opportunity to make a positive impression and to convince each one I would make a good judge.

It worked! The commission nominated me along with an older lawyer whom some of my supporters described as one of the "good old boys." The *Des Moines Register* said I was supposed to be his "stalking horse" as the legal establishment lobbied a newly elected governor for the appointment of this more experienced attorney. But my plan was to convince the governor that my work ethic, temperament, and legal ability outweighed my relative youth and inexperience. I recruited influential attorneys and businesspeople who knew the governor and me to write letters of recommendation. It helped that the governor was also a young lawyer, and this was his first district court appointment. In the end, the governor resisted the old business-as-usual approach to judicial appointments and took a chance on me.

After the governor called to notify me of my appointment to the district court, my brother, stealing a line from the classic movie, *The Candidate*, incredulously asked, "What do we do now?" Good question. I wondered the same thing when the governor swore me in at the age of 30, one of the youngest district judges in Iowa history. But a wise chief judge established a new mentorship program and assigned me to a stint on the Polk County family law bench and a ride-along on the circuit with an experienced rural judge for several weeks of training.

After showing me the ropes, the chief assigned me to distant courthouses far outside my comfort zone. It was trial by fire. But presiding over criminal, civil, juvenile, and probate matters on country court service days in 15 different rural courthouses taught me valuable lessons about the fabric of rural life.

When I became a judge, Polk County was in the same judicial election district as surrounding rural counties. Several years later, the legislature established Polk County as a separate judicial election district and required judges to reside in their election district. I eventually rotated to my home county to preside over everything from misdemeanors to murders, complex lawsuits, delicate domestic matters, and the everyday business of a metropolitan trial docket. Over the years, this combination of rural and urban courts provided both the legal experience and the life experience I lacked when I was appointed to the bench.

Mom was right. Judging suits me. It has been the honor of a lifetime. It has opened the door to opportunities for leadership and public service that I never thought possible as a young lawyer in private practice. I served the citizens of Iowa for over three decades as a trial judge, including two-plus decades as chief judge of Iowa's largest and most diverse judicial district.

In a nod to longevity, I also served as chair of the judicial nominating commission of our election district. This gave me the opportunity to see what commissioners are looking for in a candidate for judicial office. In my view, our nominees for appointment to the district court share three essential qualities. First, successful candidates possess an overarching desire for public service. Second, they hold sufficient knowledge of law and procedure to be competent and comfortable in the courtroom. Third, the best candidates command the capacity for demanding work along with the character, temperament, and wisdom necessary to make tough decisions and explain their rulings to the parties in a manner that makes them feel heard.

Our nation needs great judges who possess these qualities. My story is just one example of how the process works. A person does not have to be born and bred to be a judge. I have seen lawyers of every demographic, background, and practice area become excellent judges. Diverse perspectives contribute to a collaborative judiciary and a collegial bench. Everyone has different experiences, and all are welcome.

So, if you think you want to be a judge someday—or in the words of my mother, if you hear the call—don't let anything hold you back. Now is the time to do it.

Something in Me I Could Not See

John A. Jarvey
Former Chief U.S. District Judge
for the Southern District of Iowa (Ret.)

I went to law school in 1978 with the thought of becoming a tax lawyer. I had received a Bachelor of Science degree in accounting and thought it could nicely combine with a law degree to handle "problems of the very wealthy," or something equally noble. After a difficult first year of law school and an excruciatingly boring summer as a financial analyst, I quickly shifted my focus. In my 2L year, one professor took note of my new zeal for law school and, after getting an A in his class (my first), he saw something in me that I had not. He told me that I needed to apply for a judicial internship. I confessed I did not know what that was. So after asking where I wanted to be that summer, he drove to St. Paul,

Minnesota and persuaded the newest federal judge to take me on as an intern.

I walked in the back door to the courtroom on my first day, right behind Judge Robert Renner. He had steely eyes, silver hair, and an incredible intensity about him. The problems I encountered in that courtroom were real and big and important and difficult. It got my attention immediately. Everyone impressed me—the law clerks, the prosecutors, the defense attorneys, the case agents, and all the civil lawyers. After about a week, I said to myself in 24-year-old foolishness, "I wonder if I could ever do that?"

I already had a little experience "climbing the ladder" from years working at a country club—from caddy to busboy to barboy to bartender—so in my youthful naïveté I figured the same process could apply here. So I set it in motion in 1981, starting on the entry level as a law clerk with Judge Donald O'Brien in federal court in Iowa. It was the best two years ever. I felt valuable but had no ultimate responsibility for the decisions. I knew that the next step was to become the best trial lawyer I could be. I wanted the most experience in the shortest time possible, and I wanted to play in what I considered to be the big leagues. So with the help of two judges who had both been federal prosecutors, I was hired in the criminal division of the United States Department of Justice.

It was 1983, before the internet, email, and texting. We wrote letters back then, and I wrote many to Judge O'Brien about what I was doing. Soon, I began addressing the return address portion of my envelopes like this:

John A. Jarvey
Future Magistrate
Northern District of Iowa

There was no opening for such a position and the incumbent magistrate was just over 40 years old. I had another 15 to 20 years before anyone would consider me for a judicial position anyway, right? But partially in jest and partially not, I wanted Judge O'Brien to see me in that light. And that little experiment might hold my very best advice for how to become a judge. For I had already been the beneficiary of a professor who saw something in me that I could not. That event caused me to stop and, at least briefly, see myself in a light that I had not yet entertained. Why couldn't it work the other way too? Ask someone else to see you in a light that they have not yet entertained—and then give them plenty of time to ponder it.

So, with the Department of Justice I was off trying drug cases, and it was crazy fun for a 26-year-old. I was in Indianapolis, Phoenix, Miami, Ft. Lauderdale, West Palm Beach, Augusta, Des Moines, Chicago, New York, Atlanta, and many points in between. In 1985 I traveled 46 full weeks with three weeks for vacation and only three weeks in the home office in Washington, D.C.

I tried a bunch of cases, too many to keep track of. My memory bank is mostly filled with great experiences with judges, and a few not so great experiences—and every single one made an impression. I was publicly honored in Indianapolis by an amazing judge and Truman appointee, for briefs he deemed "perfectly accurate." I was held up as an example by the United States Attorney in Miami for taking on and winning a case thought to be unwinnable. Judges appreciated my efficiency and professional demeanor. Against the wishes of a number of colleagues, I confessed error in a court of appeals argument because there had been error committed by a close friend of mine. Maybe my best letter of recommendation to become a judge came from a Washington, D.C. Superior Court judge who later became my colleague on the federal bench.

Oh, and I was yelled at two or three times when I had done nothing wrong at all.

The point is, if you want to be a judge, start acting like the ones you admire. My experience as a trial attorney gave me a firsthand understanding of the importance of judicial temperament, ethics, ability, motivation, fairness, and efficiency. Never, ever raise your voice. Let your calm voice take the lead and be way more powerful. Work harder than anyone else so that even when others disagree with you, everyone will respect that it is a legitimate difference of opinion. Ask rhetorical ethics questions constantly. And call out incivility every time you experience it, no matter who is the culprit.

I would also advise that you begin preparing now for the questions you will receive as a judicial candidate. When I applied for judicial positions, people would ask me for my "judicial philosophy." Usually this is asked in such a perfunctory and vague way that it is like asking what golf clubs you prefer (I play PINGs). I did not understand the question and I was seldom convinced that those who asked the question did either. They seemed to want some satisfying, one-sentence sound bite that could encapsulate everything you believe about judging.

And when the appointment process is political, it seems like the peripheral political players (often non-lawyers) just want to know if you identify more closely with Justice Antonin Scalia or Chief Justice Earl Warren. Others are only concerned with where you stand on abortion and the death penalty (I never handled either question in 34 years on the federal bench). This reductionist line of questioning is both annoying and unhelpful, because it does not get at where the fights are every day in court, nor does it capture what distinguishes one candidate from another.

I was interviewed twice at the White House by some of the most brilliant lawyers I have ever met. Their questions about the Ninth, Tenth, and Eleventh Amendments to the United States Constitution were so difficult that one of the panel members actually interpreted another member's question for me. When I turned my answers to what a federal judge actually does in court day in and day out, they suddenly became much quieter and anxious to hear about me.

From my experience, a judicial candidate should be well prepared to express views generally on the following topics:

1) What modality do you think best describes how the Constitution should be interpreted?

2) What principles are most important when interpreting statutes? Regulations?

3) What is the role of stare decisis? When should prior decisions not be entitled to deference?

4) What is your philosophy on case management? Who should be in control of the pace of litigation? How involved should the judge be in that process? What if the clients disagree with their lawyers?

5) What are your most important beliefs about sentencing? Who needs as much prison time as possible? What factors suggest that prison is not the answer for a particular case? Should white collar defendants spend at least some time in prison? Why?

6) What have been your best and worst experiences in trials that were driven by judges?

7) What will you do for juries and the public to show them that the system is fair, effective and efficient?

8) How will you fulfill your obligation to promote respect for the law outside of the courthouse?

My final piece of advice is to live your life in a way that you will not have difficult questions to answer in a background check. After the incredibly difficult interrogation I endured at the White House, one panel member remained, and for 15 minutes asked me questions that were designed to see if my appointment might embarrass the President. They began with inquiries into any criminal history I may have, including traffic tickets, and then went downhill quickly. Had I ever hired an illegal alien, had I withheld employment taxes on domestic workers, had I been unfaithful to my wife, and on and on it went, ending with a series of questions about drugs. ("Ever done a line of coke?" Answer: "No.") Apparently unsatisfied with my repeated denials, my interrogator then spent quite a bit of time explaining that many candidates had experimented with drugs in the past and they got through the process without difficulty, but that truthfulness was key. Then came three or four more questions about drugs, followed by three or four more denials—followed by two men blankly staring at each other in awkward silence.

Finally, I explained it in a way he could understand. I had lived my entire life as a nerd, I said, and it was finally paying off. And it did.

The Accidental Jurist

Eliza J. Ovrom
Judge, Iowa District Court (Ret.)

I was honored to serve as an Iowa district court judge in District 5C (Polk County) from 1999 to 2018. I loved being a trial court judge.

However, when people ask if I always wanted to be a judge, I have to say of course not! Growing up in southeast Iowa in the 1950s and 1960s, I did not know women could be lawyers, let alone judges. Most professional women at that time were teachers or nurses. I was lucky because I had two role models: my mother, Mary Hamblin Ovrom, was a newspaper reporter, columnist, and photographer, and her sister Dora Jane Hamblin wrote for LIFE Magazine. I dreamed of following in their footsteps. I wrote for my high school newspaper and yearbook, and I wrote for and edited my college newspaper, *The Coe Cosmos*. I used to fill in for Mom when she was out of town, writing news stories for the local papers. I remember taking photos of all the prize-winning animals (and their owners) at the Van Buren County Fair, and calling the sheriff's office every morning so we could report who had been arrested overnight. After I graduated from college in 1975, I entered a master's program in mass communication at the University of Minnesota.

A funny thing happened on the way to becoming a journalist. One of my journalism classes required me to go to the Hennepin County Courthouse in downtown Minneapolis to cover a trial. I chose a criminal trial—I cannot remember the charges—and it changed my entire career trajectory. I interviewed the two attorneys, both young, one female and one male. They were smart and funny, and the presiding judge was kind enough to sit down with me and discuss the trial. As I sat in the courtroom it struck me that I would rather participate in the trial than write about it.

I dropped out of journalism school, took the LSAT, and was accepted at the University of Iowa Law School. My father, Art, had graduated from the Iowa law school, but was a banker rather than a practicing attorney. He was a fairly conservative guy, and although he could not have known many, or any, women attorneys, he strongly encouraged me to go to law school. I always joked that it was because I was so argumentative growing up.

I started law school in the fall of 1976, in the midst of the decade when the numbers of women in law school exploded. There were only seven women in the Iowa law school class of 1971. By the time of my graduation in 1979 our class was approximately one-third women. The number of women attorneys has continued to grow over the years.

I was lucky enough to have wonderful clerking experiences while in law school. I clerked for an attorney in my small hometown, Keosauqua, who had a private practice and served as part-time county attorney; I clerked for a small law firm in Iowa City; I did a semester's internship in the U.S. Attorney's office in Des Moines with Roxanne Conlin; and I clerked for a summer with a large Kansas City firm. In all those clerkships I sought courtroom experience, tagging along whenever I could to court proceedings, and jumping at the chance to attend trials.

In my third year of law school I was offered a position with the Kansas City firm where I had clerked, and I also received an offer from Iowa's new Attorney General, Tom Miller. I chose to pursue public service over private practice. Financially it was not a wise decision; my salary was literally half of what I would have made at the law firm. However, personally it was one of the best decisions I ever made. I loved the work and got courtroom experience right away. I met a coworker named Mark Schuling who would become my husband, and made many lifelong friends in the A.G.'s office.

While at the attorney general's office, I did mostly environmental and conservation cases, representing the Iowa Department of Natural Resources. I brought enforcement actions against polluters and tried cases over ownership of public lands. I had hearings and trials in state and federal courts, I argued in state and federal appellate courts, and I was counsel in a large environmental case involving the Missouri River that ended up in the U.S. Supreme Court. I did not argue that case, but I worked on the briefing and I was at counsel table with Iowa's solicitor general, Elizabeth Osenbaugh, when she argued the case.

One of my coworkers and mentors at the attorney general's office was John Sarcone, who was elected Polk County Attorney in 1990. John offered me a job heading up the civil bureau of the county attorney's office. I held that position from 1990 to 1999. During that time, I handled complex litigation concerning the Prairie Meadows racetrack and casino, and the collapse of a large municipal investment pool called the Iowa Trust (it had been managed by a scam artist and many local governments lost significant amounts of money). Of course we handled more routine cases involving zoning, employment law, public records and open meetings, and all the myriad legal matters that arise in local government. I thoroughly enjoyed working for Polk County. I felt privileged to represent many dedicated public servants who were working every day to handle property taxes, mental health issues, elections, real estate records, county parks and public lands, county streets and roads, and law enforcement. There was never a dull moment.

During those years of attending court proceedings in state and federal courts, I felt a call to become a judge. It is difficult to explain, but when I watched judges at work, I felt that I could do that job and that I would be good at it. In the early years of my practice I did not always feel welcome in all rural courthouses. After all, I was a young attorney, a woman no less, and from the Attorney General's Office in Des Moines, which made me a bit suspect in rural Iowa. I vowed to myself that if I ever became a judge, I would emulate the good judges I had appeared in front of; I would show everyone professional courtesy, be prepared for hearings, and listen to all sides with patience.

I began applying for judgeships in the mid-1990s. I was not very successful at first. I think I threw my hat in the ring six times before finally being appointed to the district court in the summer of 1999 by Governor Tom Vilsack. I was discouraged at times, but several of the nominating commissioners were kind enough to provide encouragement, and my boss (John Sarcone) and my family were always supportive. I was also practicing the martial art of Tae Kwon Do, whose tenets are courtesy, integrity, perseverance, self-control, and indomitable spirit. I especially called on the tenets of perseverance and indomitable spirit in my quest to become a judge.

I doubted whether my background as an attorney for the State of Iowa and Polk County would be good experience when I became a judge. However, after I got on the bench I realized that I had great experience in civil litigation. And because of my work in state government, I was very familiar with administrative appeals from state agencies, which comprise a significant caseload in Polk County. I could jump right into those cases with a good basic knowledge. I had volunteered for some criminal work at the county attorney's office and I attended criminal law seminars through the County Attorneys' Association, so I had some experience in that area as well. When young attorneys tell me they can't apply to be a judge because they lack experience in a certain area of the law, I tell them that no one comes to the bench with expertise in all areas. Actually, one of the joys of being a trial court judge is the opportunity to learn new and different areas of the law. I found that, as a judge, every area of the law was interesting when it was my case to decide. Lack of experience in an area of the law should not discourage people from applying for judgeships. But you do have to work hard to get up to speed in areas of the law that are new to you.

I will always be grateful that I achieved my goal of becoming a district court judge. I served from September 1999 through May 2018. I was especially lucky to spend much of my time in Polk County, which, in my opinion, is the best place to be a judge in the entire state. Polk County has a wide variety of cases, including litigation between private parties, appeals from state agency actions, interesting cases involving local governments, and fascinating criminal trials. And overall the Polk County bar is outstanding. Lawyers are prepared for their cases, and skilled in the courtroom. It was a joy to preside over a trial with two good attorneys going head-to-head. And, unlike my rural colleagues, I did not have to spend hours each day on the road driving to faraway courthouses. I also had the benefit of working with wonderful colleagues right there in the courthouse. I never applied for another judicial position after I was appointed to the trial court. I absolutely loved working where I was.

My guiding principle as a lawyer and as a judge was to follow the law to the best of my ability. This came into sharp focus when I was counsel to the Polk County Board of Supervisors. There were five supervisors with often differing agendas and opinions. They were politicians; I was their legal advisor. County Attorney Sarcone always told me to stick to the law when giving advice. I think this gained me the respect of the supervisors and other county officials. They knew that although they might not always agree with my advice, it was based on my best legal opinion. This principle—following the law—also guided my work as a judge. Although I was presented with numerous difficult legal issues (after all, gray areas in the law are one of the main reasons lawsuits do not settle), my guiding light was to fairly and impartially interpret the law. This led me at times to rulings that might not have been in accord with my own personal views of a case, but were my best attempt to apply the law to the facts of the matter before me.

After I became a judge I started volunteering for additional assignments that would improve the judicial system. I helped institute the 5th Judicial District's family law mediation program, along with Judge Jack Levin. I was appointed to the Child Support Guidelines Review Committee, which evaluates and recommends changes to child support guidelines every four years (I eventually co-chaired the committee). I was appointed by the Iowa Supreme Court to civil justice review committees that revised Iowa's civil procedure and civil discovery rules. And I was a member of the Iowa State Bar Association's jury instruction committee, which reviews and recommends changes to Iowa's proposed jury instructions. I also taught at the Iowa new judges' school, and I served on the board of directors for the National Association of Women Judges. One project near and dear to my heart was the renovation of the historic Polk County Courthouse, and construction of two new court buildings to handle the expanding caseload of the courts. This was a years-long effort that included two bond issue ballots, trips out of state to view court buildings, and many, many planning meetings with architects and county representatives. I felt that my relationships with county officials helped in that effort. I also started a mentoring program for new judges in the 5th District, pairing an experienced judge with a new judge in a formal mentoring partnership.

All of these projects were extra work, but they allowed me to see the "big picture" of the state judicial system in a way that was not available when I was just in my courtroom deciding cases assigned to me. They also allowed me to have collaborative experiences with attorneys and judges from around the state and in other parts of the country. And I hope that I contributed to improving the legal system in the state of Iowa and in the 5th district.

Chapter 9

What Surprised Me Most About Judging

Is Judging Socially Isolating?

Lars G. Anderson
Chief Judge, Iowa District Court

One of the things that has surprised me most about being a judge is the richness of the social life. This was entirely contrary to what I expected, as I was warned that the nature of a judge's work, to say nothing of the workload that often requires hours alone in chambers, can be inherently isolating. Further, certain ethical rules may indeed limit judges' social interactions with former colleagues, and though new technologies have increased efficiency, they have often done so at the expense of social interaction. In short, people told me that I would be lonely as a judge, that I would lose friends, and generally that the associated social isolation was a significant downside to the job.

Thankfully, I have not found any of this to be the case.

This is not, however, to dismiss any of the real concerns about the social isolation associated with the bench. A quick internet search leads to an abundance of materials on judges and social isolation. Former Supreme Court Justice Abe Fortas said, "Judging is a lonely job in which a man is, as near as may be, an island entire." As this quote suggests, Iowa trial court judges do not decide cases with colleagues, nor does our budget allow for sufficient law clerk resources to enable us to routinely engage in a collaborative process with a law clerk when writing a decision. At best, we might discuss an issue or two with a judicial colleague to get their feedback.

Ethical rules and location also play a role in judges' isolation. Judges have codes of conduct which, in broad terms, require them to avoid doing things that might undermine public perception of judicial independence and impartiality. Sometimes, this means a judge must limit social activities and constrain or even cease interactions with friends and former colleagues. Some judges, especially those in more rural settings, can feel like they are in a fishbowl, needing to watch what they say and do in almost all social interactions. In such cases, judges may find it easier to not socialize at all. Judges working in a more rural setting are also less likely to have colleagues available with whom they can have in-person interactions.

Finally, there is technology, which has contributed to increased isolation in society as well as specifically in the legal community. In Iowa, lawyers of a certain age talk fondly about the days before online filing. EDMS (Electronic Data Management System) started as a pilot program in 2010 and has been operating statewide for well over ten years. Pre-EDMS, lawyers of all types would regularly appear at the courthouse to get orders signed. There, they would visit with other lawyers and judges, discussing issues with their cases, and catching up on families, vacations, local legal gossip, etc. Many of these same lawyers have now told me they have not been inside a courthouse for years. Further, many lawyers who continued coming to the courthouse post-EDMS are doing so less as we increasingly utilize technology to conduct court proceedings remotely.

Despite all of these concerns, however, I have found that being a state court judge in Iowa is socially rewarding. Forewarned, as they say, is forearmed, and with a few simple measures, one can not only avoid professional isolation and loneliness, but enjoy a socially enriching experience on the bench.

Just as I did in my private practice experience before becoming a judge, I still spend a lot of time each day in my office working. However, there are now always court staff around, and, in the urban courthouses in our district, there are other judicial officers in the building. As I was with a small firm, my daily social interactions with the people I work with have increased tremendously since becoming a judge. It is not just the quantity; the quality of the social interactions is also generally high. I have colleagues with whom I discuss issues, bounce questions off, and commiserate about shared aggravations. Work is also not the only focus of these interactions. I have gotten to know many of the people I work with on a more personal level and have made several long-lasting friendships.

In addition to districtwide social interactions, I also have had the opportunity to interact with many people statewide. Judges can be involved in workgroups, committees, and task forces where they interact with other judges and Judicial Branch staff across the state. Twice-yearly judges' conferences and CLEs are another chance for judges to interact with each other. These interactions have also been more numerous and meaningful than I anticipated, in part because of the sense of a shared mission.

I have also continued to have meaningful social interactions with lawyers. I see lawyers at the courthouse (even after EDMS), and I interact with them at continuing legal education events, bar association events, and other similar events. In my case, the frequency of these interactions also increased after I became a judge. Certainly, my relationship with most lawyers I knew has changed, and I now generally avoid socializing with lawyers outside of work-adjacent events. But when I do see them, I can still talk to them and discuss happenings in the local legal scene, how their families are doing, sports, etc.

Also, my relationship with lawyers I was particularly close to has not changed for the worse. Many lawyers who become judges will have a few former colleagues in the area, maybe a former partner, a law school roommate, the one whose wedding you were in, etc., whose cases they will never be involved in as a judge. I had a few such friends who were attorneys, and my relationship with them has changed little after becoming a judge.

I also have not found that being a judge impedes my social life more broadly. I can and do go to restaurants, movies, sporting events, and the like with friends and family. Living in a larger metropolitan area helps with my comfort level. In the two areas where rules and other factors significantly impact my social life as a judge, those being active political involvement beyond voting and social media use, I cannot say that I mind much. In fact, less of the latter probably helps with my overall social engagement.

Overall, I cannot say my social life has suffered since becoming a judge. Quite to the contrary, I have found being a judge to be socially enriching rather than socially isolating. The people I work with, the shared sense of mission, my past experiences, and my location in an urban district all play a role. I hope it continues to be the case.

Be Careful What You Wish For

Robert J. Blink
Judge, Iowa District Court (Ret.)

When dreams become fact, the reality is often unexpected. Much that has been anticipated is joyfully experienced, a little is less friendly, and some things come as a complete surprise. Aesop's caveat is true: "Be careful what you wish for, lest it come true." Decades of working in the well, before the bench, bar and jury box, should prepare a person to sit on the bench, right?

You Don't Know What You Don't Know

I entered my tenure on the bench like a ship slipping into a fog bank—knowing just enough to realize I was in real trouble. There were hazards all around me, but I would not know what they were until I crashed into them. After a year of floundering in the mist, I began to see my way clearly. Then, of course, I was assigned to a different docket with its own Scylla and Charybdis. Thus ends the lesson: extensive trial practice is the best teacher of future trial judges but inadequate, nonetheless. Let me share with you the great unknowns of judging. For no good choice can be made without appreciating the consequential risks and benefits.

Impersonal Opinions

Judges and lawyers work in the same room, but their roles are far more different than I imagined. After 20 years of watching and listening to judges, I figured, "How hard could that be?" I failed to appreciate how 20 years of being a trial lawyer had molded me—made me set in my ways. In the litigation process I always evaluated both sides of the case—the opponent's so I could destroy it. I wanted to win. That was my role and my goal. But on the bench, my job became: "I don't care who wins." My new role was to advocate for "the process"—undeterred by what verdict might result except that it be fairly delivered.

Because I had spent my professional life practicing in courtrooms before judges, I errantly assumed that transitioning from the mindset of an advocate to that of a jurist would be seamless. It was not. In my early days on the bench, I expected the jury to find in a manner consistent with the verdict I would render. More often than not, they did. But when they did not, the difference between my opinion and theirs made me question the soundness of their verdict. I had to learn that just because I evaluated the facts differently than the jury did not make their verdict unfair. In fact, the judge's opinion of what verdict should be rendered rarely has any relevance. I developed a greater appreciation of my role in the judicial process: conduct a fair trial and let the chips—verdicts—fall as they may.

When I tried my first bench trial and was confronted with being both jurist and "singular juror," reaching exactly the right verdict was more of a challenge than I expected. Bench trials require more work than jury trials because they necessitate a detailed ruling, not a one-liner like a jury verdict. But deliberating the verdict itself was not as easy as it appeared. The ease with which I had been critical of a jury's duties, in retrospect, caused me chagrin.

There is a corollary to the "I don't care who wins" rule. This is the "they don't all try a case like you did" rule. Twenty years of courtroom work formed personal litigation techniques—my unique trial style. It worked for me, won my cases, got the verdicts. Once on the bench I tended to expect the lawyers to try their case the way I would have. They didn't. What might have taken me a minute to prove a point might take them ten minutes to "get around the barn." In jury trials I had to learn to focus on the legal process, not be distracted by the style of the lawyers. In bench trials, if the point was belabored or unclear, I became more comfortable with simply telling them to "move on" or asking them to clarify their point.[1]

These "personal opinion" rules took me by surprise. My career as a trial lawyer ingrained in me the spirit of a competitor. It took time to completely change my perspective—to watch trials as a neutral manager unburdened by personal preference for verdict or lawyering style. I had to learn to be an un-advocate. Having played on the field for decades does not equate to being a good referee. They both know the rules but only one carries the ball, in their own way, and one throws the flag. The change from player to referee was far more challenging than I anticipated.

The Judge in the Mirror

If Aesop gave you fair warning, Socrates' *Protagoras* dialogue provides the defense: you must "know thyself." Judicial realism is real. The best advocates seek to understand the decision maker as much as they appreciate the law and the facts, and tailor their arguments accordingly. To maintain neutrality a judge must know their own strengths, weaknesses, foibles, and biases—they must understand who and what they are. As Dirty Harry said, "A man's got to know his limitations." This is harder work than you would expect. No one wants to concede their opinions might rest on feelings, not facts; personality, not proof. A judge must admit they possess these human failings, relentlessly seek to identify their faults, and affirmatively push back against them. This must become a daily, and sometimes hourly, habit. Among the characteristics of good judging, few require greater personal energy. It is the only way to check oneself and neutralize lawyers' attempts to persuade based on the judge's beliefs and not reason.

Judging is a particularly tough job for a perfectionist because the key to fairness is the judge as a person. Great responsibility magnifies human frailties. Justice in your courtroom will only be as good as you are. And you are responsible for you. The greatest challenge is "thyself," not the law, facts, or others. Lawyers don't think about this when they contemplate applying for the bench—or the exhausting antidotes for perfectionism: patience, tolerance, and self-forgiveness.

Workload

The lawyer's simplistic expectation of judicial duties is embarrassing in its ignorance. Most who ascend to the bench are people of high energy and professional industry. Whatever their deficits, the common denominator of "hard work" is intrinsic to their personality. The workload of trial judges is staggering—far beyond what could be imagined as the judicial application is written. Ceaseless motions, incessant writing obligations, grave decisions with little time to contemplate resolutions, covering colleagues' benches for vacations or illnesses, 24/7 access through electronic filings, communications, warrants, and emergency orders were never on my radar screen. Most successful lawyers who seek the bench come from well-run law firms with adequate support staff, associates, and clerks. Not so with the government judicial position. So, while the attorney's mantra of "work harder to get the job done" is not cast aside when assuming the bench, the judicial workload and its gravitas are demonstrably greater.

This enormous demand for thoughtful effort compresses time and requires physical stamina. Judicial decisions are most difficult in the ratio of their number, their gravity, and the time available to resolve them. Judges must constantly balance the efficiency and empathy the docket demands. They must be approachable to counsel and the public when they would rather be writing in chambers. Intellectual work takes its toll. Suppressing your emotions takes stamina. It is difficult, consuming work, much more strenuous than I envisioned.

A Universe of Law

After years of drafting pleadings, taking depositions, sending and responding to discovery, preparing witnesses, arguing pretrial motions, selecting juries, making opening statements, direct and cross-examining witnesses, handling exhibits, giving closing arguments and perfecting appeals, I had been schooled in evidence, procedure, legal analysis, courtroom human nature, and "making the record." These tools of advocacy were hard and well learned. To that extent I was well equipped to take the bench. But there were many substantive areas of the law that I witnessed as a jurist that had not been part of my practice. As a lawyer I honed my skills and kept abreast of developing law pertinent to my fields of practice. You get the picture. While I was skilled in reading the law and legal parsing, the bench plunged me into unfathomable waters with all the subtle nuances and currents of the common law. Legal learning does not end when assuming the bench; it burgeons ten-fold. Every appellate decision must now be critically studied, not just those in your areas of practice. My years in "the pit" taught me the basics of procedure, evidence, and personalities, but the challenge of learning unmeasured fields of substantive law was overwhelming.

A humble judge is rare, but that persona draws out the best in lawyers. In your early days, do not hesitate to cry "mea culpa" and admit to the lawyers that they are taking you into unfamiliar law. Ask them to "spoon feed" you. This allows them to make a better record and allows you to decide based on the correct legal principles. In time, your experience will fill the gap. The general legal concepts will be mastered. You will never know them all. Knowledge of procedure and trial practice I took to the bench. Yet after nearly 30 years in a robe, I still went to school every day. Wisdom is the trait of admitting personal ignorance.

Roads Without Maps

The common law is an evolutionary process. Creative trial lawyers regularly pull and tug and stretch and squeeze legal principles. They contort precedent to fit their client's needs. Once you are daily endorsing or nullifying these novel concepts, you are struck by the limitless number of cases of first impression. They are as numerous as the ingenuity of all the lawyers multiplied by the number of dockets. There are never clear answers to these questions.

One of the greatest unanticipated treasures of the bench is the opportunity to craft a path in new legal terrain. The art of creating and preserving a good record to make law is the reward for the unforgiving dearth of work. You not only solve case-specific issues, but facilitate the dynamic accretion of the common law.

The Weight of Lonely Responsibility

Good judges are addicts to responsibility—the trait of doing that which must be done, though you wish not to. It is the courage to make hard choices that others would avoid or ignore. Such jurists tend to be industrious perfectionists, expecting similar qualities of lawyers. They are driven to make trials fair and "reversal-proof." Judging is a profession, a fine one, but a profession, nonetheless. Like the practice of law, it can take too much of you. What appeared from counsel's table as a simple task of sitting on the bench listening is far more demanding than being a lawyer. Judges are responsible for the legal, and sometimes personal, welfare of a multitude of people, not just one client. Every decision a judge makes affects the lives of others—a community or society as a whole. Judges are required to know more about the law and know it better than anyone else in the courtroom. They are required to be adept students of human nature.

The weight of the robe is so very heavy, so much heavier than I could ever have imagined. And there is no one to share the burden. There is no second chair. There are no "law partners." All the gravity—all the responsibility—falls upon one person: the judge. The love of family and embrace of friends helps strengthen your resolve to shoulder the load, but only you shoulder it. Once on the bench it is too late to learn this lesson. The weight will be too much if you *want* the bench. It will be manageable if you are *called* to the bench.

Judicial challenges are met alone. While judicial applicants appreciate that the bench will constrain social interaction, the breadth of this deprivation, like the limitation on speech, is woefully underestimated. The solitude spreads beyond the courthouse to your home and friends. Ethical proprieties preclude sharing the onus of the job, even with loved ones. The scrutiny that attends the robe is cast upon those loved ones as well, sometimes to their frustration or misunderstanding.

The cloistered lifestyle has been dramatically increased by the implementation of electronic docketing. It has reduced the personal interaction between lawyers and the bench. The days of daily "chats in chambers" when motions and proposed orders were delivered are gone. In our "business of humanity," we have chased efficiency and lost our humane exchange. The only remedy I found was to share the load with my colleagues, make their burden my burden, and let them ease my load. Share coffee in chambers each morning. Dine together. Stop for a drink on the way home. There are few social restraints among colleagues. Together you must be "a few, a happy few, a band of brothers and sisters."

Insolubles

The problems a judge faces are more difficult than those of attorneys—sometimes seemingly insoluble. Yet they must be solved. An answer must always be given. A judge cannot not decide. The oath requires a judge to address issues they would sidestep if they could or reach results that are anathema to their heart and soul. The cup cannot be passed. Judging often requires you to endorse a political, ethical, or moral view with which you disagree. Unlike the lawyer who advocates for such a position and need not believe in it, a judge is compelled to put their imprimatur on concepts they personally think are wrong. Before you seek the bench, if you think of nothing else, think long and hard upon this.

There are cases that present questions with no good answers, where everyone loses, or the wrong person prevails. These arise most often in matrimonial cases involving children, juvenile cases, or in criminal cases involving the death of an innocent or a victim's horrendous injury. The tools given to the judge may seem inadequate to assuage human suffering—where every road leads to unpleasant ends and where there is no fair result. Your oath may require you to enter a judgment without reliable precedent, or facts and law that guide you to inevitably unpalatable conclusions. They may present a choice between the law and your faith. Regardless of religious conviction, you are sworn to judge your "fellow man." Save your conscience. Judge conduct, not people. Applicants do not see this dilemma. This duty casts a pall over chambers.

Errors of Injury

With responsibility comes the satisfaction of knowing you can, must, and do positively affect the lives of many. You solve the most difficult of human questions without violence. The reverse side of that coin is accepting the fact that you will err. You will make irreversible mistakes—even if you labor long and are well-intentioned. Your mistakes will adversely affect the lives of others till their death. A judge must accept this human truth as part of the calling. While on balance your life effort will do good to those you serve, some will inexorably and irretrievably be harmed.[2] Even with due diligence you will make decisions that are, in hindsight, wrong, unfair, or unjust. You will find yourself applying the law in a manner that you recognize is hurtful because you must follow that law, because the power of your office limits your ability to treat a litigant more justly. If you cannot live with this, you should not be a judge.

You must learn to forgive yourself for being a judicial human. You must not rethink or dwell on past decisions. Instead, put adequate time and energy into contemplating an opinion before pronouncing it. Learn to be satisfied in doing your best, appreciating that people will suffer regardless of your efforts. Be accepting when shown you are wrong and correct the error if you can. Move on if you cannot.

Personal Restraint of Judicial Power

Applicants for the bench see the position as one of near limitless power. Judicial restraint, self-governing the power bestowed, is a skill they do not often contemplate. The difficulty of managing the power of the bench is amplified by the restraints imposed by statutory and ethical requirements: no political activity, a limitation on the freedom of speech, suffering the "slings and arrows" of public comment without remark—whether it be by knowledgeable journalists or ignorant opinion-holders—and disassociation from persons or groups who were part of the lawyer's past social life. A judge's behavior and speech are under constant scrutiny when in public. Except at home or with family, a judge carries the burden of "always being on." Every public action, word or deed is graded and evaluated by society. You must decide whether the power granted is worth living your life this way. Self-control is critical.

Judging should be a calling, not a want. Ego and power, of course, are involved, but if money, power, or political aim are the reasons for seeking the bench, you are traveling down the wrong path. Every judge succumbs to the "power trip" at some time. "Black robe fever" is real. It is stealthy and creeps into your chambers imperceptibly. As a lawyer I could not stand "that type of judge." As a judge, my greatest regret was those times I had been overbearing, impatient, sharp, or intolerant, like "that judge." It caught me off guard when it happened. I thought I had more self-awareness. I thought I had more self-control. The power of the robe is so great that it must be met with the equal force of self-discipline. Know your temperament well. It may be your greatest challenge on the bench.

Judicial Hats

Perspective is the primary difference between practicing law and presiding over cases. The lawyer's priority is the case at hand. The judge views the extant case as one part of a whole—as a portion of the docket, as a time allotment on a daily calendar, as a cause for requisite ruling time, and as a single paving brick in the ever-expanding roadway of law. The lawyer cares about who wins; the judge only cares that the process is fair.

It was a rude awakening to find that I was not appointed to just make wise judgments, resolve difficult legal issues, and preside over jury trials. The chores attendant to these roles were self-evident. I was unprepared for the larger aspects of the job. I had become an air traffic controller: keeping all the planes in the air, on the right flight paths and on time without mid-air collisions, preventing mechanical breakdowns, calming angry passengers, fixing decaying runways and terminals.

Judges manage an incredibly voluminous and diverse system of "people problems" as well as the processes by which they are solved. Every docket has thousands of cases in differing stages of gestation. Each one must be managed efficiently because time wasted on one is justice delayed to another. The cases are graduated by urgency, importance, rights, and remedies. Overarching all is the fact that these are not really "cases," but human disputes. How myopic I was, blissfully sitting in my counsel's chair wondering why the judge spent limited time on my client's case. If you are a lawyer who is "organizationally challenged," the bench might not be right for you. If you are not punctual in responding to your client's needs, the bench might not be for you. If you do not manage your work time well, the bench might not be for you. This is not a reflection on your legal acumen. But a judge who cannot be efficient and contemplative will, by definition, provide less justice.

The judicial perspective includes a variety of roles beyond decision maker. Judges are the best teachers of how to be a good trial lawyer. They have a duty to improve adversarial skills, trial practice and ethics. There is no manual on how this is to be done. But there is a truism: A judge deserves the quality of lawyering they are willing to tolerate. Lawyers soon learn the nature of the newest judge on the bench. Judges with higher expectations of the lawyers receive better lawyering, those willing to accept sloppy lawyering get it. Surprisingly, a few lawyers need to be told that the judge is not their law clerk, and that counsel are required to know the rules of evidence and procedure before entering the well. Punctuality, preparation, and professionalism are learned behaviors. My judicial office allowed and required me to impose them.

The bar, like every other profession, is stratified. Not all attorneys are equal in intellect, industry, diplomacy, experience and the qualities of integrity, patience, and professionalism. If "suffering the fool" is not a line item in your personality, you had best learn to live with it. Watching a train wreck in a courtroom that unnecessarily injures a party because of poor lawyering is a painful experience. To watch it without flinching as if nothing happened is a learned technique. Over the years the most common phrase heard from new judges at their first judicial conference was, "I can't believe all the bad lawyering."

Younger lawyers are best educated in chambers face to face. Or the lesson might also be taught in written rulings that parenthetically identify the practitioner's errors in a passive voice. If they ask for a critique, this is the sign of a promising lawyer. Sometimes the lesson must be unsolicited. In either event, the instruction must be given with care because the confidence of a trial advocate is one of their greatest tools. With the advent of mediation and arbitration, fewer cases are tried, limiting the judges' ability to teach the lawyers. I found mentoring lawyers to be one of my most enjoyable unexpected duties.

Diminishing trial experience among the bar presents judicial candidates less skilled in trial management. New judges are stratified too. Like teaching attorneys, I discovered that mentoring new judicial appointees was a pleasant surprise. The same can be said of helping attorneys considering judicial vacancies.

Disliked Lawyers

Not everyone is teachable. There were lawyers with whom I did not get along well in practice. It made cases doubly difficult. I did not consider the fact that those same lawyers would appear before me. They made my duties as a judge appreciatively harder. Having authority over someone who personally dislikes you or whom you dislike or do not respect heightens the duty to treat them and their clients fairly. It makes setting aside your personal feelings an arduous task. This was a rare occurrence, but more than uncomfortable. I discovered it was one of the most difficult aspects of judging.

Difficult Litigants

Being fair to disagreeable people takes other forms. The bench presented a variety of parties and witnesses foreign to my private practice: primarily unrepresented and mentally ill people. It required "people skills" and patience beyond anything I had needed in my practice. This reflects the paradigm shift in who now avails themselves of the legal system. Domestic abuse protection suits invite litigants without lawyers. Increasing legal fees, the availability of internet legal forms, and the general willingness of the public to represent themselves also contribute to the problem. The deluge of cases without lawyers is staggering.

Sheltered in a successful trial practice with paying clients and the right to decline cases, the onslaught of litigants without lawyers and troubled souls representing themselves caught me off guard. Client control as a lawyer is far different from trial management of people unschooled in legal proceedings and often imbued with high emotion or mental instability. I soon learned the bench carries great power, but not the power to make the fool wise or the mentally disturbed well. There are categorically unreasonable people. I found that I could not change them. At best I could guide them. The price was personal, physical, and intellectual fatigue.

What Goes Up

Trial lawyers, by their nature, do not like to lose. They learn it is part of the business. The same is true of judges being reversed on appeal. Sometimes you will, upon reflection, see the wisdom of the appellate court. Sometimes you will just have to grin and bear it. And, on occasion, you will not even recognize that the appellate court is talking about a case you tried. Like adverse verdicts, reversals sting—more than you might want to admit. While judges become steeled to reversals, I must admit there were some appeals I followed more closely —ones that were important to me because I was convinced my decision was right and just. Some pills are easier to swallow than others.

Unlike other professions, judicial "mistakes," or poor judging, are published for the world to see and become part of the jurisprudence of your state in perpetuity. You must assuage yourself that only a few cases are appealed and only a few of those are reversed. The odds are in your favor. The appellate court might change the law you applied at trial. The error might be the conduct of a lawyer or party that was out of your control. And there are times when you "just get it wrong." Do not dwell on that which you cannot change. Be pleased when your jurisprudence is affirmed for all to see. Good judges are like good quarterbacks: they forget the last interception and just throw the next pass. Judges who brood over past rulings only make their ability to decide more difficult.

Don't Send Flowers, Send Cement

Lawyers just want a timely decision, not erudite verbiage. This can be a challenge for those, like me, who enjoy writing. It is also a challenge for those who are indecisive, simply cannot help themselves and write too much, torture themselves with revisions, or equate quantity with quality. Rulings should be prompt and correct, not perfect. Brevity is the soul of wit. If I could rule from the bench, I would. Not haste but deliberate speed to move cases along is a good thing. I found sitting on rulings frustrated the lawyers and created stress for me. It is better to deliver a brief, well-reasoned and legally sound ruling than one that is clever or verbose. You always looked at the last page of a ruling first. Lawyers do the same thing with your rulings. Lawyers need a concrete record upon which to build their case for verdict or appeal. Concrete blocks are not beautiful, but they are practical. I had to teach myself to produce a more timely than literary ruling.

Sneaky Ex Parte

Like black robe fever, you are only one slip of the tongue from an ex parte conversation. It is a constant threat to the judiciary. Lawyers discuss all manner of cases. Judges also discuss all manner of cases, but their discourse is best confined to their colleagues. Vigilant self-discipline is necessary to prevent the cordial greeting of the first lawyer to a hearing from becoming a discussion of the issues to be heard. With fewer hearings and trials, judicial solitude begs for chats with those of the law. With the significant decrease of in-person proceedings, the solace of the bench naturally starves a judge of social contact. It is a slippery slope from discussion of one case to the case at hand.

Conversations between lawyers and judges present heightened ethical problems if one party is unrepresented. With the significant upsurge of litigants without lawyers, any conversation between the court and counsel outside the presence of the pro se party raises the possible appearance of impropriety and at least suspicion by the uninformed. Even being seen together causes distrust by the laity.

A judge can satisfy the need to chat with attorneys, one-on-one, with talk of family, sports, travel, or hobbies. In cases where one party has no lawyer, forgo any talk with counsel unless the other party is present.

Ex parte communication's little brother is flattery. It usually comes in the form of laughing at your bad jokes or commentary on rulings you have written, or cases that have been affirmed. Flattery is a slippery fellow too. In my whole judicial career, whatever tie I wore was always "nice" or "beautiful" to a certain lawyer every time he entered my courtroom. What a coincidence.

Closing

These observations are a cautionary tale, offered to encourage contemplation before assuming the mantle of "judge." Regardless of the unforeseen challenges of the bench, there is no joy like an affirmance where your rulings or bench oratory are quoted. There is no satisfaction like solving a problem and giving people peace through a decree that is not just legal but just. There is profound gratification in making a "tight" record and learning the skill set of limiting or avoiding grounds for appeal. There is the pride in shouldering the responsibility for other people's lives, hopes and needs. There is fulfillment in knowing you have dedicated your life's work to concepts that serve the greater good. Would I accept my appointment again if offered to my younger self? Yes. Without hesitation.

So Long Duane/Hello "Your Honor"

Duane E. Hoffmeyer
Former Chief & Senior Judge,
Iowa District Court

Introduction

Becoming a judge is a remarkable milestone in my career, marking a culmination of almost 20 years of private practice as a general practice attorney. I believed I had a comprehensive understanding of the judicial system. However, upon donning the robe and taking a seat on the bench, I quickly realized that being a judge came with its own unique set of challenges and surprises.

I served as a general jurisdiction district court judge for over 20 years. I presided over many criminal and civil jury trials. It is what I liked to do and felt I was best at it. For 13 years, I had additional administrative and statutory responsibilities as chief judge.

As an attorney I had the opportunity to appear in front of many fine judges in Iowa, Nebraska, and South Dakota. In the year before going on the bench I tried criminal jury trials in the United States District Court for Iowa, Nebraska, and South Dakota. I was able to see and experience different judicial personalities and philosophies.

In this essay I will share some surprises I encountered when becoming a judge.

My Name Is…

The theme song of the popular sitcom *Cheers* was "Where Everybody Knows Your Name" by Gary Portnoy. At some point in most, if not all episodes, George Wendt's character, Norm Peterson, would enter and be greeted by a resounding "Norm!" from the bar patrons. In the courthouse I did expect to be called "Judge." A plaque with my name was outside the courtroom or on the bench and my name was announced by the court attendant or court reporter. Being addressed as "Judge" is a long-standing sign of respect, and a humbling experience. What I did not expect was my public recognition to increase and my name outside the courthouse to almost disappear and be replaced by "Judge."

This happened in part because Iowa allows cameras in the courtrooms. I presided over many jury trials and was interviewed often during my time as chief judge. Further, a former district court administrator encouraged me to attend local seminars involving other court family entities, and whether you say anything or not, they will see and know you are there. Her words were prophetic. Attorneys and other court family employees still call me "Judge" outside of the courthouse. I can live with that.

So, what is the problem? I am good at recalling case details, but not particularly good at remembering names. When I'm greeted outside of the courtroom as "Judge" it invariably prompts several questions. Do I know you? Should I know you? Is this an attorney to whom I have been previously introduced to? Is this person a party in a case I presided over? A person who served on a jury or jury panel? Should I exercise caution in my response?

It is easy enough to acknowledge people and say hello in passing. The more difficult encounter is in a setting where they want to engage in a conversation. My wife is adept at introducing herself in these situations, knowing (correctly, most of the time) I do not recall their name. This coping skill avoids those awkward situations when I should know them and be able to introduce them to her. Thanks to her, no issues.

A. Are You a Judge?

All the same questions run through my mind when I'm asked this question, but my usual response here is, "Depends, is it good or bad?" This question can arise in some unusual circumstances. My wife and I were walking through a farmers' market when a vendor asked if I was a judge. I said yes and the vendor responded, "I thought so, I have your picture in my living room, I see you every day." Whoa! Red flags in my mind and looks from my wife quickly followed. Then the vendor said I had presided over the adoption of one of her children. When I began, adoption hearings were very private affairs held in a judge's office. They may now take place in a courtroom teeming with friends and family and be video-recorded for posterity, and often, there are photo requests with the judge. I have had my picture taken many times. I may indeed be in many photo albums or living rooms.

As the most senior district court judge, I served as chair of the district judicial nominating commission for several years. At one of the commission meetings, a commissioner asked to speak with me privately. She told me I had sentenced her son to prison, and she quoted the statement I had made at the sentencing: that I did not believe he understood the seriousness of his offense (child pornography). She then told me he was doing well and gave me an update. I did not get the impression that she thought I had made a misjudgment. I believe the commissioner was simply letting me know her son had become a successful law-abiding citizen.

I was in San Antonio, Texas for a college football bowl game on the famous Riverwalk when I was asked if I was a judge. OMG! A steady stream of folks and this happens! After saying yes, the woman asked if I knew so-and-so, and pointed him out. I told her I did not recognize the name or the individual. She then proceeded to tell me I had sentenced his daughter to prison. She gave a brief description of the facts and I immediately recalled the case. I had accepted a plea agreement with an agreed-upon prison sentence for a young girl in an abusive relationship who had tried to harm herself and her boyfriend by intentionally colliding with an oncoming motor vehicle. The other driver was seriously injured. The charge carried a mandatory prison sentence. I could not have granted probation. This was one of the most uncomfortable and awkward situations I encountered as a judge. Nothing further was said, and after a short pause I kept moving with my group of friends.

B. Are You THE Judge?

I hear this question in social settings from friends of friends, at the gym, while playing pickleball, and so on. Usually, the person asking has been told by other individuals that I am a judge, or have heard others call me "Judge." When I confirm that I am, soon they too are calling me Judge.

Later, when I became chief judge, my colleagues got in on the act too. I became known to my judicial colleagues as "Chief." My first name is seemingly relegated to family, childhood friends and a few past clients, replaced almost entirely by Judge or Chief.

Emotional Impact

Courtrooms can be the setting for tense encounters. For litigants and their loved ones, drama and pent-up frustration can come to the surface, or even boil over to verbal and physical altercations. A courtroom is where the action is.

Less known is the emotional impact that judges can sustain. No two cases are the same, and I found that a judge can learn from every case. In my first months on the criminal bench, a young individual was before me with an agreed-upon prison sentence, and I was disappointed to see that no family was present. For all intents and purposes this young individual was on their own. This gave me pause to determine how I could help this young person not come back into the judicial system.

Some individuals simply haven't been dealt the best hand, and no matter how heart-wrenching the stories and tragedies they hear, a judge must maintain an impartial demeanor. Witnessing the emotional toll that legal proceedings can take on individuals and families was a constant burden. Striking a balance between empathy and objectivity is a constant challenge, but essential for upholding the integrity of the judicial process. Despite these difficulties I enjoyed being a trial attorney and trial judge, and I also had the opportunity to see good attorneys exercise their craft and to learn from a wide variety of expert witnesses testifying at trial.

The Decreasing Number of Applicants for a Judicial Position

Deciding to apply to be a judge is a difficult decision. Sometimes, vacancies for judicial positions become available unexpectedly, prompting individuals to apply even if they had not considered it previously. I had no career aspirations to be a judicial officer. I was very happy in my private practice. An older attorney approached me and suggested I should apply for a current district court judge opening. I did not do so but it did plant a seed, and I made an application when the next district court judge opening occurred. As I recall, there were around 15 applicants, and I was fortunate to be one of the two names forwarded to Gov. Tom Vilsack, though ultimately I was not selected. A couple of months later another district court judge opening occurred, and again mine was one of the two names forwarded to Gov. Vilsack. On this occasion I was selected.

Making an application depends upon timing and some good luck. Are you at a stage in your career and your family to make an application when a vacancy occurs? Some applicants are hesitant because they do not practice criminal law. A colleague of mine with no criminal law experience stated it is easy to learn criminal law. Most cases result in plea taking and sentencings. I think it is harder to find an individual who has some civil litigation experience who can step into the unusual and sometimes quirky situations that arise during complex civil litigation. As the number of individuals making applications for judicial opening decreases, I urge trial attorneys to encourage individuals to make application to be a judicial officer. There are few things more satisfying than when an individual tells you that what you said or did changed the direction of their life in a positive manner.

Safety Awareness

Lastly, I was surprised by the number of threats made to judicial officers. Some can be expected. I received threats as an attorney. Depending upon your area of practice, some attorneys may not be able to tolerate or adjust to receiving threats. Most are nothing more than words with no follow-up, though sometimes law enforcement may deem a threat credible and investigate. It sets you back when law enforcement tells you that your name was mentioned at roll call for an individual's threat to kill you. It is a topic that needs to be discussed with your family when considering whether to apply for a judicial vacancy. Do they want to know about the threats? That is a question I posed to my wife that gave her pause. This is a job you are applying for, but it will have consequences for your family. A judge must live their life. The way you lived your life was probably a contributing factor to your selection as a judge. But you must develop an awareness to recognize an uncomfortable or dangerous situation, assess the degree of danger, and decide what action you should take.

Conclusion

Becoming a judge was a transformative experience that brought numerous surprises. The burden of responsibility, drama, emotional impact, the complexity of some legal analysis and the degree of public recognition are some of the significant revelations I encountered. Embracing these surprises allowed me to grow as a judge and strengthen my commitment to upholding justice and the rule of law in our society. The journey into the world of a judge is an ongoing process of learning, adapting, and striving to ensure that justice prevails for all.

The Politics of Serving on an Appellate Court

Edward M. Mansfield
Justice, Iowa Supreme Court

Nearly 50 years ago, having just graduated from college, I had the privilege of working on Capitol Hill for a group of Republican congressional representatives known as the House Wednesday Group. The members of the group were not well known, but they were dedicated and effective public servants. Today few people remember Representative M. Caldwell Butler of Virginia, Representative Bill Frenzel of Minnesota, Representative Bill Gradison of Ohio, or Representative Joel Pritchard of Washington, but I recall them as capable and principled legislators.

I viewed the Wednesday Group members as politicians in the best sense of the word. They got along well with their colleagues and listened to their constituents, but they also stood by their core beliefs. They were noticeably lacking in ego; what mattered was the legislative outcome, not who got credit for it. I remember being reprimanded once when I answered the phone and asked a caller to identify themselves before putting them through to Representative Pritchard. That was not how he did things. Most of all, as members of the minority party, the representatives in the Wednesday Group sought attainable victories, and they were willing to compromise in pursuit of that goal. Never did the perfect serve as the enemy of the good.

Having spent this post-college year in Washington DC, I went on to law school in the fall of 1979. I filed away what I had learned as a research assistant for the Wednesday Group and really didn't draw on that experience during 26 years of private practice. I came to view my year on Capitol Hill as a source of some good jokes and stories, and a nice historical window into a less partisan era, but not an essential part of my professional training.

That changed when I became an appellate judge in 2009, and especially when I joined the Iowa Supreme Court in 2011. Until then I had not realized how political being a supreme court justice can be. Again, I mean political in the good sense of the term. All of us on the supreme court take our jobs seriously, and we do not decide cases based on public opinion, legislative or executive pressure, or personal whims. So "bad" politics isn't a problem for our court. But "good" politics is one of its attributes. And this came as a surprise to me.

In appellate courts, as in legislative bodies, the majority rules. And even though judges don't think of themselves as "legislating," our opinions have the *effect* of legislation. So it would follow that legislative talents are to some extent also *appellate judging* skills, even though I didn't realize this at first.

Let me describe a few examples. After an oral argument conference, I would find in a number of instances that I was now on the losing side in a case. I soon came to realize that there were times when switching sides made sense. By voting with the majority, I could shape the rationale for the decision. Almost any appellate decision can be written more or less broadly. It wasn't a matter of adding or removing "dicta"—an overused and misunderstood term. Rather, I would be using my vote to recraft in some way the reasoning that supports the actual decision.

On other occasions, I might be with the majority from the beginning but I would have misgivings about some of the language in a colleague's draft. I quickly learned that the best way to fix something was to propose the fix yourself without insisting on total success. I still follow the practice of marking up colleagues' drafts with proposed changes. I prioritize my requests, and signal carefully how much I care about those changes and which are deal breakers. Depending on their importance, I may enlist an ally or two for one or more proposed changes.

Of course, I also discovered early on that my colleagues would request many changes to my drafts. I came to appreciate that this too is a political process. Typically, changes are substantive and make the opinion better. But it is important to swallow one's pride and be willing to make non-substantive changes almost reflexively. Even if I might be attached to my own words or might prefer not to include particular language in something bearing my name, an effective appellate judge has to give as good as they get.

In addition, our court pre-assigns the presumptive writer for every case we hear. Sometimes, when I was the pre-assigned writer, I realized after oral argument and post-argument conference that getting four votes for my position was going to be a difficult slog. I soon learned that it might be best to sit on that case for a while, and circulate an opinion later. Perhaps a fresh look at the case later on would enable me to sound more persuasive. Or perhaps a reluctant colleague might be more willing to go along as the court term wound down.

Even dissents are frequently part of a process of negotiation. Many don't end up being filed: they are dropped when the author of the majority steps back from part—but by no means all—of their central reasoning.

These are all political lessons I learned early on in my judicial career. Just as legislatures contain both workhorses and showhorses, so too do appellate courts. I have tried to model myself after the behind-the-scenes professionals who belonged to the Wednesday Group. Many of the court opinions that I'm proudest of during my tenure do not bear my name.

Even after 15 years as an appellate judge, I continue to learn political lessons, although unfortunately I don't always follow them. Because nonunanimous appellate decisions, like legislative votes, ultimately just have a "yea" and a "nay," anything beyond the majority opinion and the principal dissent is usually just baggage. There are a few exceptions. Sometimes a case has no majority opinion, which means there have to be three opinions. Sometimes, there are two strongly held but irreconcilable views on how to get to the consensus outcome, necessitating what we call a "special concurrence" or what other courts describe as "concurring in the judgment."

But generally, less is more on an appellate court, as in a legislative body. Appellate judges are as suspicious of grandstanding by their colleagues as legislators are. Therefore, I have slowly learned that it's best to avoid writing extra dissents, "wingman" concurrences that exist primarily to criticize dissents, and "keep your distance" concurrences that imply the author possesses more exalted wisdom than everyone else.

When I was in law school, the prevailing view was that appellate opinions should emerge from a pristine intellectual process. A tell-all book about the United States Supreme Court came out during my first year,[3] and indicated that this wasn't exactly how the Burger Court decided cases. Law school faculty and students alike took this as confirmation of their cynical view of that Court.

Now I see things differently. Appellate judging is inherently political. Politics is inescapable when a group of people make important decisions collectively that will affect how others order their lives. What the Supreme Court was going through in the 1970's wasn't unusual. The important thing is to aim for good politics. One can sacrifice one's effectiveness in the overall process and write beautiful and memorable separate opinions. Or one can be like the members of the Wednesday Group. That means getting one's hands dirty, pursuing what's possible, and in the end making our body of law hopefully somewhat better.

The Surprises Never End

Robert W. Pratt
Former Chief U.S. District Court Judge
for the Southern District of Iowa (Ret.)

When I was first nominated to become an Article III federal judge—a "judge of the United States of America"—a reporter from the *Des Moines Register* called to ask my reaction. This was a time, of course, when Iowa's largest newspaper had a state-wide readership, with a masthead proclaiming it was "The Newspaper Iowa Depends Upon." I responded that I felt much like Harry Blackmun immediately after he was sworn in as Associate Justice of the Supreme Court. Standing in the conference room with the likes of Potter Stewart, William J. Brennan Jr., and William O. Douglas, Blackmun thought to himself, "What am I doing here?!" That exact feeling of incredulousness would stay with me from the moment I was nominated, to the day I was confirmed in 1997, as both a Chief and Senior judge, and on the day I entered inactive service in 2023. It stays with me still, as I reflect on my 26 years of service in the Third Branch of government.

I've been asked many times over the years what was most surprising to me during my experience as a judge. The honest and simple answer is, "Everything." With the benefit of what I hope is the wisdom that comes with age and hindsight, I understand now that I was completely naïve about what it truly *meant* to become a federal district court judge. I did not appreciate how intense or diverse the work would be, the public nature of the job, or the media attention that would accompany so many of my decisions. I was unprepared to work in a small court chamber, suddenly cut off from my busy legal practice and my very active social and politically involved life. I underestimated completely the mental and emotional burden that would come with making life-altering decisions, day after day, about people's livelihoods, interests, and freedoms.

Yet, I have also been positively surprised by the consensus on important issues I often discovered among legislative, executive, and judicial branch authorities, based upon our shared experiences. I underestimated the education I would receive, both professionally and personally, from working with brilliant young law clerks, and from talking with jurists, scholars, and other professionals across the country. I misjudged how moving an experience it would be to learn the difficult life stories of criminal defendants, to hear the pain of victims and family members, to observe the joy of newly minted citizens, or to watch reluctant potential jurors embrace, and sometimes even come to praise, the inherent duties of American citizenship.

My path to the federal bench began in Emmetsburg, Iowa, a small Irish Catholic town, where I grew up on a farm with my three siblings. While our father farmed a very small farm, our mother—college-educated at a time when few women were—worked full-time: first as an Extension Director, then as an Iowa educator, then again as an Extension Director for Iowa State University's Extension Service. My mother was a remarkable woman, who believed fervently in equality, justice, and civil rights. Her views impacted me profoundly, and from an early age, I was interested in politics, social justice, and in working for causes that would help change or reform the law in socially positive ways.

After graduating high school, I attended Loras College in Dubuque, Iowa. My experience there was life-changing for many reasons. Most importantly, I met Rose Mary Vito, who would later become my bride, as well as my official partner in the many, many life adventures we had no clue were yet to come. I also became active in the College Democrats, doing whatever I could to help the party in relation to elections and issues of the time. A highlight of my college career was when I was selected as one of 16 students to fly to Washington D.C. for a chance to observe all three branches of government at work. The "Week in Washington" program was sponsored by Fred Schwengel, a Republican Iowa Congressman and Lincoln Scholar who served in Congress from 1955–1965 as well as 1967–1973. Amongst countless incredible experiences that week, including my first-ever airplane flight, the most memorable part of the trip was attending the last "Decision Day" of Earl Warren's Supreme Court. It was also a week in which the Senate was debating President Nixon's nomination of Warren Burger to succeed Chief Justice Warren. Occurring in the context of the '60s civil rights movement and a war in Southeast Asia, I made up my mind right then that I would be a lawyer. I had absorbed into my DNA President John F. Kennedy's words about activism: that every person has an obligation to change the status quo, or at least to try. I was young, idealistic, and excited to be part of it all. I was convinced I could, and would, change the world or at least, try.

I earned my law degree from Creighton University School of Law in 1972, where I had the good fortune to intern at a neighborhood Legal Aid office in Omaha. After graduation and passing the bar, Rose Mary and I relocated to her hometown of Des Moines, Iowa, where I worked as a staff attorney at the Legal Aid Society (now Iowa Legal Aid). At the time, before the passage of the Legal Services Corporation in 1974, the national Office of Economic Opportunity funded Legal Aid programs across the country, and Iowa's Legal Aid programs also received funding from the United Way Agencies. I quickly learned two things: one, Legal Aid services were not well-regarded by established Bar Associations, and two, broad legal and judicial "reform" was not something that happened quickly and without hard work. My Legal Aid colleagues and I thus tried our best to make the law more "fair" for our clients individually and generally, helping them navigate a wide variety of housing, domestic relations, and civil rights matters. I was fortunate to have a wonderful director of Polk County Legal Aid, Bob Oberbillig, who served as a mentor to me and who devoted almost his entire career to the representation of poor people. The Legal Aid work that was performed by the program during a part of my service is detailed in an article I published in the *Journal of Gender, Race & Justice*, a publication of the University of Iowa College of Law, Volume 15, No. 3 entitled "Remembering our Roots: HELP Legal Assistance, Forty Years of Service."

In 1975, I transitioned to private practice, where I represented indigent criminal defendants on a court-appointed basis in both federal and state court. I also did work representing organized labor and continued what I would call a "general practice." By 1978, I had started specializing in social security and worker's compensation law, trying whenever possible to take cases I perceived might help change the fields in positive ways. The social security practice was especially beneficial to me. The jurisdiction of the Article III Courts to review these decisions let me practice frequently in both the district courts of the United States as well as the Eighth Circuit Court of Appeals. So with both the indigent criminal defense work and the social security cases I became quite familiar with the federal court practice. Because of this I learned from other practitioners in primarily urban areas about how to build a practice in this rather unique field. This type of a practice had frankly never been established in Iowa before, and the work became both my passion and my calling.

At least a couple of fortuitous occurrences helped me. The social security administration began terminating disabled people, claiming they were no longer disabled, and the legal services budget was dramatically reduced by the Reagan administration. Secondly, my administrative law and judicial review practice began to flourish after Congressman Neal Smith (D-IA), then chairman of the House subcommittee on small business in 1979, ushered into law the "Equal Access to Justice Act," codified at 28 U.S.C. 2412. The act allowed people who, for example, had been wrongfully denied social security benefits, to *shift* attorney fees to the government upon proof, in both adversarial and non-adversarial proceedings, that the "position of the United States" was "without substantial justification." The EAJA dramatically increased the ability of ordinary citizens to obtain legal counsel to help them challenge harmful and unwarranted governmental actions. And of course, this permitted me to petition judges to have my fees paid for by the government for their wrongful legal positions. Unfortunately, the law "sunsetted" by its own terms in October 1984. Senator Charles Grassley, who would later play a role in my confirmation, introduced legislation providing for the act's reauthorization. It unanimously passed both chambers of

Congress, but was vetoed by President Reagan, who according to Senator Grassley, supported a position "impl[ying] that no matter how outrageously improper the agency action, the statute has no application as long as the employees of the Department of Justice act reasonable when they appear in court." Fortunately, Senator Grassley reintroduced the legislation the following year and prevailed in getting it enacted. The EAJA has, ever since, continued to help countless people and companies wrongly denied social security or other governmental benefits in obtaining both agency decisions as well as judicial review decisions, which included remuneration, attorney's fees, and costs.

I encountered Senator Grassley once again in 1990, when he was part of the Senate Judiciary's subcommittee on the jurisdiction of the federal courts. In 1990, federal criminal case loads were skyrocketing, in varying part due to increased administrative caseloads, the "war on drugs," and a recent Supreme Court decision that ordered review of around 10,000 social security disability cases for improper terminations of benefits for mentally impaired individuals. In response, Congress passed legislation known as the Federal Courts Act of 1990, calling for a study of federal court jurisdiction. At a full day hearing on the issue held at the United States Courthouse in Des Moines, Senator Grassley, First Circuit Court of Appeals Judge Leven Campbell, and Third Circuit Court of Appeals Judge Joseph Weis, took testimony about the appropriate scope of federal court jurisdiction. I personally testified about the importance of preserving jurisdiction over the review of social security claims, as supported by statistical evidence from the Administrative Office indicating nothing but continued and increasing positive benefits. Ultimately, a proposal to create a special Article I court to hear social security cases was rejected, and jurisdiction remained with Article III judges to hear the cases. As a federal judge, I thus conducted judicial review of hundreds of social security and other administrative agency decisions thanks to the EAJA.

In my years at Legal Aid and in private practice in both state and federal courts, I tried approximately 40 cases to verdict, argued 35 appellate cases, and represented hundreds upon hundreds of clients in need, often, though of course not always, obtaining positive results. Throughout my career, I was also proud to be involved in the political life of both my state and the nation, working on election campaigns for candidates I admired and believed in, and supporting the Democratic party and its causes. I had countless close relationships with the many attorneys I'd worked with over the years, themselves engaged in all manner of civil, criminal, private, and governmental practice. In 1997, I was honored when my former Legal Aid colleague, Tom Harkin, then a United States Senator (D-IA), recommended me to President Bill Clinton for a federal judgeship. I received amazing support from family, friends, and colleagues, all of whom assured me that they would keep me from getting "Judge-itis." Put another way, they ensured that I would not "forget where I came from" and somehow lose sight of the very real challenges of being a party, lawyer, litigant, or worker in the judicial system.

In March of 1997, not long after President Clinton officially nominated me to the Southern District of Iowa Article III position recently held by Harold D. Vietor, I and two other newly nominated colleagues from Florida and California were taken to the Administrative Office of the United States Courts (the "AO"). We were promptly shown a movie about the murders of Southern District of New York Judge Richard Daronco, Western District of Texas Judge "maximum" John Wood, Jr., and Eleventh Circuit Court of Appeals Judge Robert Vance, all of whom were slain because of rulings they issued in cases before them. I am sure that, up to that moment, I had been dismissive of security concerns for federal judges, especially because I lived in a Midwest state like Iowa. That film, however, brought home to me the notion that dangerous people from all political persuasions are "out there," and that listening to federal court officials with security experience was imperative for the safety of me, my staff, my family, and every single person who walked into our federal courthouse. As nominees, we also had the opportunity to talk with Ralph Mecham, who is best described as a "ward healer" appointed by former Chief Justice Warren Burger to run the AO in 1985, and who did so very effectively until his retirement in 2006. Mecham introduced us to the Judicial Code of Conduct, and explained at length how it was essential to our work to understand the AO's role, which includes legislative lobbying that ensures implementation and execution of Judicial Conference policies.

The day before my confirmation hearing, I had the opportunity to meet up again with Senator Grassley —this time, just the two of us, with no staff in attendance. By now, of course, he had earned a reputation as being unafraid to protect whistleblowers, or to criticize the other two branches of government, regardless of who held any official title (you'll perhaps recall his lambasting of "$100 hammers" and overly "expensive toilet seats" while criticizing the Pentagon's budget). The Senator and I had a fulsome discussion about the respective roles of the three branches of government when it comes to the law. He told me that Justice Scalia had once sat in my very seat, and discussed with him congressional and judicial relationships. This fascinated me because I was fully aware Justice Scalia strongly disfavored using legislative history and congressional intent to decide contentious cases, instead focusing on a statute's plain "text" as the best evidence of Congress's intent. At the end of our meeting, Senator Grassley asked me if there was anything I thought he *should* ask me about my work or career during my confirmation hearing. I told him about a client of mine that had greatly benefitted from the EAJA, and how pleased I was by its extension. The next day, Senator Grassley indeed brought up the EAJA, eschewing the more "hot button" issues that are the typical grist of judiciary confirmation hearings. The Senate confirmed my nomination, and I received my commission on May 27, 1997.

I was formally sworn in as a district court judge for the United States District Court for the Southern District of Iowa on July 1, 1997. A few months later, the week after Thanksgiving, I attended "Orientation for Newly Confirmed Judges" in Fort Worth, Texas, affectionately referred to by most as "Baby Judges School." It was a fascinating experience where I, along with 14 other newly appointed federal judges and two mentor judges, participated in educational sessions and heard from ethics advisors, case administrators, and representatives from the U.S. Sentencing Commission and U.S. Judicial Conference, amongst others. More than 25 years after I graduated law school and passed the bar, the seminar provided the best learning and refresher course I could imagine. For all practical purposes, we learned how to be federal judges in just one week, which of course only scratched the surface of what we eventually would learn in our new work. While there, I met mentors and lifelong friends, all of whom I could call on for advice throughout my career. I was also introduced to the amazing resources provided by the Federal Judicial Center, which I took advantage of more times than I can count during my tenure, *anytime* questions arose in complex criminal or civil cases.

Amongst the education and camaraderie, my "baby judge" experience was also sobering in many ways. One example comes from our visit to the women's federal prison in Fort Worth. Even knowing the women were specially pre-screened by the U.S. Marshal's Service and the Bureau of Prisons to meet with us and were likely some of the lowest-level offenders there, each and every one of their stories was compelling. I was saddened to hear the Warden explain how holidays at a men's facility are often crowded and active with visitors because women always show up when their husband, boyfriend, or partner is incarcerated. The opposite, however, is true at women's facilities, i.e., men do not keep up visitation and relationships with their imprisoned female partners to nearly the same extent. Seeing firsthand the reality of institutional life in a BOP facility also made me promise myself I would never forget my decisions directly impact the lives of *real people*—people who love and are loved, and people whose lives are as valuable as mine, no matter their history or offense.

The surprises would not be complete without detailing my involvement with the sentencing guidelines, which I consider the single most important part of my work on the district court. And it fits in with my naivete that I have described earlier. Shortly after starting I had, like all district judges in the Southern District of Iowa, a large criminal case load. Since I had "been away" from federal criminal trial work I "discovered" that Congress had radically changed the criminal law, especially the sentencing procedural and substantive law. Mandatory Guidelines were now the law. I felt these guidelines were unfair and produced much injustice. I detailed my discomfort with the law and wrote an article entitled "Senseless Sentencing" that was published on January 10, 1999 by the *Des Moines Register*. What the "Sentencing Reform Act of 1984," better known as the Mandatory

Guidelines, had done was to have eliminated or "cabined" the discretion of district judges. This was described by numerous scholars and judges as the biggest transformation in American law since the founding of the country. The act was part of or perceived as an extension of the war on drugs from the 1970's and was seen as necessary by the Congress to bring "law and order" to the country. While passed in 1984 the impact of the law did not become effective until November 1, 1987. During this interim time a Sentencing Commission established by the SRA issued mandatory guidelines that detailed the ranges within which judges must sentence defendants, regardless of any other factors that might bear on a defendant's case, including his or her personal characteristics.

Regardless of ideology, district judges for the most part rebelled against this law. The restrictions as to what sentencing options were available struck at the very heart of what judging was supposed to be about. Additionally, the SRA rejected the rehabilitation model as an inappropriate consideration, and the act required that the parole system be abolished entirely. Without detailing all the complaints about this system, eventually the Supreme Court in 2000 determined that enhancements in sentencing law had to be determined by juries and not judges.

After several other cases made their way to the court regarding the guidelines, the Supreme Court eventually in what scholars described as an "eclectic" group of Supreme Court judges declared that the mandatory nature of the guidelines had deprived defendants of their rights to a jury determination of the facts in their case; as a result the mandatory portion of the guidelines were severed, and the guidelines were now "advisory" and not mandatory. The "eclectic" group seemingly consisted of Supreme Court justices who rarely agreed on most issues, including Justices Scalia, Ginsburg, Stevens, Souter, and Thomas. This Supreme Court decision was handed down in January of 2005. As a result of this decision, I began "varying" from the advice I received from consulting the guidelines. The Government appealed my sentencings to the Court of Appeals, arguing that my sentencing variances had been "unreasonable," and the Court of Appeals agreed with the Government almost every time. In fact, between January of 2005 and December of 2007 the Eighth Circuit Court of Appeals reversed me seven times and sent the cases back to me after their review. In the case of Brian Michael Gall, their stated rationale was that the extent of the variance I made from the advisory guidelines was extraordinary while the facts of the case were not extraordinary, and did not justify a sentence of probation when a prison sentence of between 30 and 37 months was indicated by the guidelines. I had noted that Mr. Gall was a young person, he had voluntarily withdrawn from a drug conspiracy and had in effect turned his life around, and that a prison sentence would not bring respect to the law but rather disrespect for its harshness, given the very compelling facts that I had found.

Justice John Paul Stevens reversed the Eighth Circuit in an opinion filed on December 10th, 2007.

Regarding Gall, *New York Times* columnist Linda Greenhouse quoted Professor Doug Berman of Ohio State University's Moritz College of Law, an expert on sentencing, who called the decision a "stinging rebuke of circuit court micromanagement of district court discretion." Justice Stevens found that the Eighth Circuit had failed to give my "reasoned and reasonable decision" the deference my judgment was entitled to. The Supreme Court said district judges have an institutional advantage in that they see and hear the defendants and do many sentencing proceedings, as opposed to the court of appeals who only review the sentences. Therefore, district judges had an institutional advantage regarding sentencing. As a result of this decision defendants were now entitled to have their sentences determined on an individual basis with the advisory guidelines having no presumption of reasonableness. Additionally defendants were now under no obligation to show "extraordinary circumstances" to receive a non-guideline sentence. The Gall case became the standard that appellate courts now were to rely on in reviewing district court discretion.

The decision itself greatly impacted my work as a district judge. I was now given the opportunity to engage in many educational opportunities to discuss all the ramifications of criminal sentencing. These opportunities included teaching with other judges, prosecution, and defense lawyers as well as other parts of the legal community about the case of *United States v. Michael Gall* and how the law had changed because of the Supreme Court's decision, and their affirmation of my work meant a great deal to me. I believe that this was the single best part of my 26 years and two months being an active judge.

As my years on the bench progressed, I always found my experience as a judge educational, inspiring, and rewarding. I made many mistakes, but did my best to accept responsibility, and be a better jurist as a result. Life as a federal judge, however, had many difficulties. Unlike the state courthouse during my practice days, which was nearly always bustling with nearly a dozen judges, their staff, and a wide array of lawyers and citizens attending various hearings throughout the day, federal court was much more sedate and, for lack of a better word, tedious. It had fewer judges, fewer in-court hearings, and far more written litigation material. Though I had several law clerks to help manage the workload, none of my responsibilities could ever be "outsourced" completely because the final responsibility for *every* decision was *always* mine. It had never occurred to me that a federal judge must spend virtually *all* his time reading: reading jury questionnaires to prepare for jury trials, reading briefs on suppression or summary judgment; reading presentence reports; reading daily slip opinions; reading emails and updates; reading administrative notices; and reading case law to try to come to the right conclusion on a contested legal issue. Though I knew full well of the declining rate of both civil and criminal trials, I grossly underestimated how all-consuming, and sometimes overwhelming, the sheer *volume* of motion practice in federal court would be. Eventually,

I learned that holding hearings on motions was a smart use of my time, because the lawyers in the case have lived with it and knew best any factual and legal nuances. Many times, they were my best resource, along with my law clerks, to make sense of the varied and complicated legal questions I bore responsibility for deciding.

One thing that was especially unexpected to me was the feelings of isolation that would accompany my federal judgeship. There were many days over the years where I spoke to no one outside of my small chambers. Friends and colleagues I had known for decades became deferential toward me and remote. When we did get together, we had to either tread lightly on, or avoid entirely, topics we'd previously spoken freely about. I could no longer attend political functions, or even voice publicly my political views. Even a decision whether to attend a wedding or simple social function now required careful thought, as I needed to consider *anything* that might raise a potential appearance of impropriety. Having been a very active and social attorney, there were times I was unsure I could continue because I so missed the "practice" of law and the sense of collegiality that formerly attended my personal and professional relationships. My spouse, thankfully, was particularly understanding of my struggles in this regard. More times than I can count, she "talked me down" and put things in perspective for me, reminding me of the importance of my Article III responsibilities, and assuring me that no one else was likely to do the job better. We eventually carved out a new type of social life, enjoying time with the many judges and court colleagues I have encountered through the years, my many law clerks and their families, and our own, ever-expanding family, which today includes our three grown children and nine grandchildren. Despite my adaptations, my emotional struggles with the monastic environment of chamber life never fully ceased.

Perhaps what surprised me the most as a federal judge was how uncomfortable being in the "public eye" can be. I knew intellectually that the press is an integral and important part of our government and legal system. But knowing something intellectually does not prepare you for radio talk show criticisms and letters to the editor about you. Nor does the implied, or sometimes even direct, criticism of a Court of Appeals reversing your judgment feel good, no matter how thick one's skin. Over time, I had to work hard to diminish my "sensitivity" to criticism because my constitutional obligations *required* me to be a "neutral arbiter." I could no longer be an adversary, favoring my personally preferred position over any other. Perhaps this transition would have been easier had I sooner taken to heart Judge Richard Arnold's advice in *United States v. Samuels,* that the judiciary is a "passive branch of government" that does not "sally forth solving problems," but which instead "wait[s] until problems are brought to them and then they decide only what the parties want to be decided." It took time and persistence to abandon my instinct to "reform" the law, and even more time and persistence to learn to tune out (mostly) public criticisms. Thankfully, today, training on media preparedness, public criticisms, First Amendment press concerns, and similar topics are the subject of training for *all* federal judges, helping us embrace the media as the "eyes of the people," with an obligation to inform the public about the existence, impact, and possible repercussions of our judicial decisions.

Despite its difficulties, I can recount endless "good" experiences from my time as an active federal judge. From the start, I endeavored to learn from every possible source, and to grow from every experience including those where I made mistakes or managed to enormously embarrass myself. And I did. Beyond the fine training I received from the AO, the FJC, and other sources, I count myself as fortunate to have received wisdom and guidance from my more-experienced Southern District of Iowa colleagues, including three district court judges and three highly skilled magistrate judges. The U.S. Marshals kindly explained to me their security needs when it comes to handling detained criminal defendants and holding secure jury trials. The jury and court clerks helped me figure out the procedural complexities of case management, and impressed me with their polite, yet persistent efforts at encouraging reluctant citizens to serve on juries. I learned from and was impressed by those who form the "infrastructure" of the federal court system: law clerks, staff attorneys, Federal Public Defenders, United States Attorneys, United States Probation Officers, Criminal Justice Act attorneys, private attorneys, Eighth Circuit and other appellate court workers, Sentencing Commission members, and employees at the FJC and AO, amongst so many others. And most significantly, my humanity increased by my interactions with accused persons, victims, litigants, and jurors, as I observed, and sometimes shared in, their struggles, triumphs, frustrations, and joys.

Being an Article III judge was ultimately both an immense honor and an enormous burden. At root, though, its greatest surprise was that judging is a *team* effort, made possible *only* because so many people are devoted to our constitutional system of justice. I am so thankful to each and every member of my own Article III "team" that helped me so much.

Surprises Are Open Doors to Growth

Michael J. Schilling
Senior Judge, Iowa District Court

I was 55 years old and had practiced law for about 30 years when I was appointed an Iowa district court judge in 2006. Because of my age and experience, I did not anticipate that I would encounter a wide variety of life-enhancing surprises as a judicial officer. My expectations were short-sighted. The surprises have been many, and each one sprung open wide the doors to growth.

Surprises can be small or large, funny, serious, temporary, or enduring. As a judge, I have experienced all types of surprises. One of the most compelling surprises I learned early on is how little I knew about the work judges did behind the scenes. I remember feeling embarrassed that, even after practicing law for 30 years, I did not understand precisely how my actions or inactions as a lawyer could affect the work processes of the judges before whom I argued cases. Having now observed first-hand how late filings or last-minute requests for a continuance can, and often do, negatively affect a judicial officer's orderly work processes, I know I made the work process of judges less efficient. I created more work for them.

I also learned how much judges prepare for hearings and trials. Judges aim to be the most prepared person in the courtroom. As one of my mentors told me, a judge needs to think of what issues, problems, questions, and challenges might occur before the trial begins so that she/he is prepared to meet the moment when it occurs.

I learned how judges labor over the search for the correct answer. I also discovered the importance for a judge to hold lawyers to a high standard because the work of judges and lawyers is bound together. Good lawyering and good judging are necessary parts of the effort to find the best solution to legal challenges. Justice is more likely to be attained when both the bench and bar recognize and appreciate the challenges that the other grapples with.

Another surprise in my judicial career was recognizing the precious freedom I enjoyed taking the time I believed I needed to devote to research, writing and editing rulings. This is a privilege; some would say a luxury. Most lawyers do not enjoy this freedom. A related surprise was learning of the high quality of the law clerks and externs who worked with the judges. With the help of these coworkers, judges strive mightily to learn the law and determine the facts. Getting the correct answer, fairly and impartially, is the target every judge aspires to.

I often experienced surprises when working with juries. Serving as a trial judge with community members is one of the greatest privileges of a judge. First, I was surprised to learn that the fear of the jury that I sometimes felt, as a lawyer, was misplaced. Persons summoned for jury duty are stepping outside their comfort zone. They are apprehensive. They want guidance and assurance. They are much less judgmental of litigants and lawyers than I believed them to be when I was practicing.

Occasionally, I was surprised by a jury verdict or the reaction to a verdict. I have seen humor and tears in the eyes of jurors. I watched a tender, compassionate court attendant console a tearful juror following a particularly difficult criminal trial. At the other end of the emotional spectrum, the jury in a civil case sent out a note to me, complete with the word HELP written in large block letters, asking me how soon I would release them after I took their sealed verdict. I still have the note!

Jurors often feel the psychological weight of the deliberation and decision-making process. You may see tears, fear, or anger from jurors, or the need for confirmation of their verdict. Witnessing this range of emotions helped me be more observant of the needs of the jury.

Each of the surprises I experienced as a judge caused me to grow personally and professionally, but two surprises stand out above all the others. Both were positive, enduring, and life-changing, and catalyzed the most inspirational growth I experienced: the joy of public service and the opportunity to influence others in a positive fashion.

The first surprise centers on the uplifting feelings that flowed naturally from public service. Judges are public servants. We work for others, and for a common good that transcends who we are as individuals.

We also work with others. The Iowa Judicial Branch consists of hundreds of people committed to one goal: serving fairly and impartially the citizens who need help resolving a dispute. I worked daily with people who demonstrated patience, compassion, and joy while serving. Watching my dedicated coworkers sometimes caused me to question whether I measured up.

The public service workplace is not limited to a courtroom. Our workplace is much larger. It is part of a system that is larger than a law firm, or bar association, or a judicial district. Our public service is to the justice system. The justice system is committed to the rule of law and achieving justice for all. Our common goal is greater than any individual person's goal. Indeed, we are part of something that is bigger than all of us.

I first enjoyed a taste of public service in 1976 when I became a member of Volunteers in Service to America (VISTA). Fresh out of law school, I was assigned to work as an attorney for Inter-Tribal Legal Services in eastern Nebraska, which provided a broad range of legal services to the Omaha, Winnebago, and Santee Sioux Indian tribes and their enrolled members.

Now, over 45 years later, I still recall many of the life-changing experiences and opportunities I had in that role. I witnessed open and obvious hostility toward Native Americans by some members of the court system. At the same time, I know that I was part of a team that pushed back and made at least small contributions to eliminating that hostility. I was able to represent a group of Native American ranchers and accompany them on a trip to Washington D.C. to lobby the Bureau of Indian Affairs for funding. Memories of this public service remain and fill me with a special kind of spirit and pride.

This spirit and pride were rekindled doing public service as a district court judge. Day in and day out, judicial officers work with other professionals, including court reporters, clerks, court administrators, court attendants, and support staff to help resolve important, significant legal disputes between the citizens we are sworn to serve. By my observation, the Iowa Judicial Branch is filled with hardworking, dedicated, conscientious, highly competent, and compassionate public servants at all levels. I firmly maintain that Judicial Branch employees take no back seat to private sector employees.

I have served with clerks and court reporters who extended their task-filled workdays and sacrificed their own needs so that justice and the public could be served efficiently, competently, and conscientiously. I have worked with court attendants and jury managers who consoled fearful, intimidated jurors, and tended to their needs. Of my fellow public servants, my admiration and respect are high. To a person, these fine people embrace the principles of "servant leadership." Each serve driven by a motto described by best-selling author Laurie Beth Jones in this way:

> I see my work with people as being my greatest joy, my greatest gift, and my greatest accomplishment.

In addition to bringing me extraordinary joy, public service work presented me with the opportunity to positively influence many others. I had no idea before taking the bench that I would enjoy so many opportunities to influence others and, in some instances, affect real change. This has been the second great surprise of my career.

Judicial officers have many opportunities for influencing people, including citizens called for jury duty, litigants (particularly self-represented litigants), clients who participate in specialty courts, persons with mental health issues, and youthful offenders. Furthermore, judicial officers enjoy considerable discretion to use creative means to communicate with and influence these groups.

In his book *The Gift of Influence*, Tommy Spaulding writes that a person will influence about 80,000 people during a lifespan of 78 years. Of course, many of those people do not tell us of our influence or are not known to us. Judicial officers, I now know, have the potential to positively influence more than 80,000 people. And we have so many ways to do it. It all begins with our attitude.

Spaulding offers excellent guidance on the mindset we need to use to positively influence others. He writes:

> If you knew, right now, that every person you have ever influenced would be waiting for you in a stadium at the end of your life, how would it affect you today?

These words inspire. My favorite groups of citizens to engage with are those who appear for jury duty, clients in specialty court, youthful offenders, and those with substance use and mental health issues. With the group of citizens who report for jury duty, I take time to explain the jury process, the constitutional right to jury trial embedded in the Sixth and Seventh Amendments to the United States Constitution, and the concepts of the presumption of innocence, proof beyond a reasonable doubt, and privilege against self-incrimination. In discussing these matters, I often mention James Madison, author of the first ten amendments to the Constitution, known also as the Bill of Rights, and George Mason, one of the statesmen who refused to sign the Constitution out of concern that it did not expressly provide for the right of trial by jury in the states.

Sometimes, I discuss the "Boston Massacre." I note that lawyer John Adams, who later became president of the United States, represented and successfully defended Captain Preston, a member of the British army, charged with firing at and killing colonists in Boston. At the same time, I will mention that during the trials of members of the British army, a judge instructed a jury of colonists—for the first time on American soil—that the government had the burden to establish the guilt of the British soldiers "beyond a reasonable doubt."

Sharing these bits of history, I believe, allowed me to positively influence the prospective jurors and educate them concerning the awesome importance of jury duty. A juror participates in a process—a jury trial—guaranteed by the Constitution. As such, the juror becomes a "constitutional actor."

During a jury trial, I remind the jurors of the critical role they play in the justice system. A favorite message of mine comes from *To Kill a Mockingbird*:

> I'm no idealist to believe firmly in the integrity of our courts and in the jury system—that is no ideal to me, it is a living, working reality.... A court is no better than each of you sitting before me on this jury. A court is only as sound as its jury, and a jury is only as sound as the people who make it up.

Opportunities to positively influence are also plentiful for judges who preside over specialty courts, including drug court, mental health court, business court, and veteran's court. I served about nine years as a drug court judge, and this role in particular presented me with unparalleled opportunities to positively influence clients in need of a helping hand, but also to expand my personal and professional knowledge. The influence here was certainly a two-way street.

I saw mothers and fathers who had struggled with addiction for decades. Few people understand the difficulty and the complexity of addiction, and I learned how difficult it is to overcome. I also discovered that each person in drug court was at his/her core a good and decent individual. I learned so much from the clients, and am confident that they made me a better person and judge.

During the 18 months a client needed to complete drug court, I had many opportunities to positively influence them. Holding them accountable for their actions in a treatment setting was the first goal. Letting them know that I cared for them was a necessary component of holding them accountable. Reminding them that relapse can be a part of recovery was needed from time to time. And for those who fell, encouraging them to get up, admit to their mistake, and try again was critical. Teaching life lessons gave me many opportunities to influence them.

One important lesson is that the opposite of addiction is not sobriety, but rather connection: with family, community, probation officers, substance use providers, sober friends, and coworkers.

When I granted probation to youthful offenders, I tried to influence their outlook on their future by requiring them to draft a paper. The offender might be asked to author a paper discussing the emotional and physical risks of regular use of marijuana. Or I might ask an offender to explain why he/she thought carrying a gun was necessary. Occasionally, I would have a youthful offender keep a gratitude journal for a few days. From time to time, I required the young offender to read his/her paper in court weeks after sentencing so we could discuss it together.

Judges can have considerable influence in the lives of the citizens they take an oath to serve. Every judge enjoys a unique opportunity to positively influence the citizens they encounter. The ability to positively influence others is a natural byproduct of resolute and compassionate public service. The joy of serving the public as a district court judge and the opportunities I have had to influence the public have been the most profound surprises of my judicial path, and opened the door to personal and professional growth that I hope enabled me to better serve my community.

How the Bench Will Change Your Life

Leonard T. Strand
Judge, U.S. District Court, Northern District of Iowa

Before taking the bench, I was a civil trial lawyer for 22 years, practicing before many judges in various state and federal courts. I also had numerous opportunities to interact with judges in social settings. Based on these experiences, I thought I had a pretty good idea of what it would be like to be a judge. In some ways, I was wrong. Making the change from lawyer to judge is a much greater transition than simply changing jobs within the legal profession.

At the outset, I want to make it clear that I do not intend for this article to be negative or whiny. I have no regrets, and my job satisfaction is quite high. Indeed, I cannot imagine a scenario under which I would return to the private practice of law. I submit this article simply to provide some insight for those who may be considering a position on the bench.

Some of the changes my family and I experienced were entirely expected. We were well aware that accepting the position of United States magistrate judge would require that we move across the state, four hours away from our established home, friends and careers. Thus, as fresh "empty nesters," my wife and I would be starting over in a different city after spending more than two decades in Cedar Rapids. All of that required some adjustment, but it was not unexpected or surprising.

By contrast, some aspects of being a judge have been surprising. I will focus on two categories in this article. One involves a core duty of the position that still managed to surprise me. The other involves day-to-day life away from the courthouse.

Judging Others

It probably seems obvious from the title alone that the job of "judge" necessarily requires judging other people. However, as a civil trial lawyer with virtually no experience in the criminal justice system, I did not fully appreciate how difficult it is to be in a position in which my decisions will profoundly impact the lives of others. I had (and still have) general beliefs that crime is bad and criminals need to be punished, but I did not realize that specific situations are often more nuanced. Nor did I ever give much thought to the fact that those convicted of serious crimes may have parents, partners, children, family members and friends who will suffer serious consequences if a long term of incarceration is imposed.

As a United States magistrate judge, one of my duties was to determine, under the Bail Reform Act, whether a defendant should be released or detained pending trial. Of course, the defendant is always present at a detention hearing, waiting anxiously to learn whether he or she will have to remain in custody while the case proceeds. In addition, detention hearings are often attended by supportive family members and friends, with some submitting letters (or even testifying) about the defendant's positive qualities and the harm that would arise from ordering pretrial detention. In many cases, the defendant is the sole or primary source of income for a household that may include children or other dependents. Moreover, the timing of the charge and arrest is rarely within a defendant's control, making it impossible to plan ahead for a prolonged absence. Nonetheless, and despite the presumption of innocence, various factors may require the judge to consider ordering pretrial detention. Even when detention is warranted, it is sometimes (but not always) a difficult and highly-charged decision—and one that is generally announced in open court.

In my current role as a United States district judge, which requires imposing sentences on convicted federal felons, the stakes are even higher. Defendants regularly submit letters of support from parents, spouses and others who beg the court for leniency. Many of the same loved ones then attend the sentencing hearing, sometimes crying audibly throughout. The impacts on children and other dependents may be even greater. In addition, the presentence investigation report prepared in advance of each sentencing hearing contains a wealth of information about the defendant, with some of it being quite mitigating. A significant portion of our defendants have suffered from traumatic, abusive childhood experiences, serious mental health issues, and other terribly sad circumstances. Of course, many offenses create victims, who have the right to attend hearings and to be heard at sentencing. Their statements can range from understandable demands for maximum retribution to stunning pronouncements of forgiveness. When an offense has substantially impacted the lives of others, the sentencing situation becomes even more complex. Regardless, among the various lawyers, parties, victims and probation officers involved in the sentencing process, the task of weighing the mitigating and aggravating factors, and arriving at the ultimate sentence, falls entirely on the sentencing judge.

None of this means a defendant who committed a serious crime should not face serious consequences. Nor, however, does it change the fact that being a judge requires looking another human being in the eye and announcing a decision that may have life-altering consequences on not only that person, but many others. Nothing in my past prepared me for such a weighty responsibility. Perhaps prior service as a prosecutor or criminal defense attorney would have helped. However, I suspect that one cannot fully appreciate the gravity of the task without actually serving in the role of judge. It is, at least in my experience, harder than it looks.

Daily Life

1. Threats and Personal Safety

As a lawyer, I had no real concern that I might be targeted for simply doing my job. However, as I prepared to take the bench, personal safety was one of the first issues that was presented to me. For good reason. As news reports reflect (on a seemingly increasing basis), judges and their families can be targets, sometimes with tragic results. Many criminal cases involve defendants with gang or cartel ties, or who otherwise associate with dangerous individuals. And while only a very small percentage of pro se civil litigants are likely to react violently to a disappointing outcome, that percentage is not zero. Simply put, some individuals are motivated to consider carrying out attacks on members of the judiciary. However, there is no way to predict, in advance, which of those individuals will actually do so. Nor, of course, can the date, manner or location of any such attack be determined in advance. While the odds of any particular judge ever being targeted remain low, the risk is real.

Because of this risk, a new judge will have to consider difficult issues such as whether to carry a firearm and whether to have a home security system installed. Basic security steps, such as altering the timing and the route of the judge's commute and generally being vigilant in public, are likely to become second nature. A new judge will also have to consider whether to talk with family members about security issues and train them on various scenarios. For example, what should they do when an unexpected package is delivered, or when a stranger comes to the home? If a threat is made, the judge and the judge's family may need to live under strict security while it is investigated. For many lawyers taking the bench as well as their families, all of this is likely to be new and different, and not a little disconcerting. It certainly was for me.

2. Social Situations

In many settings, being known or recognized as a judge is weird and awkward. Lawyers and nonlawyers alike tend to act differently when they know a judge is present. And when meeting new people, the topic of employment inevitably comes up. Disclosing my status as a judge often has a drastic impact on the dynamics of the discussion. Despite having been a regular person just moments earlier, I am suddenly treated as important, and perhaps even scary. Much of the subsequent discussion focuses on my position and the justice system in general. Comments like "be careful, there's a judge here," are common.

This is not all bad. It sometimes gives me the opportunity to educate others about the justice system and to correct misperceptions. However, the awkwardness is almost impossible to avoid. I'm rarely eager to be the center of attention and find it uncomfortable to be treated as special or important because of my job.

In addition, being in social situations, or even generally out in public, may bring a judge into contact with someone who has a personal connection to a case the judge has handled. A question such as "Aren't you Judge Strand?" (or, more generally, "Aren't you a judge?") can be jarring, as there is no way to know which direction the conversation is about to go. And it seems that the longer I am on the bench, the more often these encounters occur. While I have not yet had any truly unpleasant interactions, a few have bordered on uncomfortable.

Conclusion

As I noted above, I have no regrets about my decision to take the bench. Being a judge is interesting and rewarding and has given me the opportunity to spend much more time in the courtroom. The "surprises" I have described do not detract from any of that, but are simply factors an attorney may wish to consider in making the important decision about whether to pursue a career on the bench.

Good Lawyering Makes Good Judging

Ian K. Thornhill
Judge, Iowa District Court

Some of the names you will recognize. Some you may not. Margaret S. Briles, John A. Nahra, Clark A. Price, John W. Rolph, Tommy E. Miller, Rebecca Beach Smith, Raymond A. Jackson, John A. Jarvey, Mark W. Bennett, Linda R. Reade, and many others—judges whom it was my honor, and sometimes my petrifying duty, to appear before—all share a special place in my psyche. That special place is one of admiration, reverence, and grandeur. A large part of my success as an attorney and a judge comes from the experiences I had and lessons I learned while practicing in the courts of these jurists. The way I manage my courtroom and the manner in which I operate as a judge is, in large part, a reflection of things I experienced in court as an advocate. After 15 years on the bench one of the things that surprises me most about being a judge is that, despite my evolution from advocate to judge, I in no way view myself the same way I viewed these great judges.

Don't get the wrong idea. I did not become a judge so that others could "admire" or "revere" me. Nor did I come into this job expecting to be elevated to a position of "grandeur" within the eyes of the Bar. Frankly, I did not know exactly what I expected, but I know I did not expect that, in my mind, I would be unable to see myself as a judge in the same way I viewed "judges" before becoming one. Does this mean I have an inflated opinion of the judges in front of whom I practiced? Absolutely not. Does this mean I lack confidence in my own abilities as a judge? It does not mean that either. What it does mean, I believe, is that whether by appointment or election, when a person's first name is changed to "Judge," you cannot accurately predict what effect that will have on that judge, but how that judge operates with this title will certainly have a profound effect on many others.

I cannot speak for other judges, but in my case, when I received the call from Governor Chet Culver in September 2009 that he had selected me for appointment to the Iowa District Court, multiple feelings simultaneously swept over me. I felt tremendous pride and honor in having been selected to serve the people of Iowa in such an important position. I felt a sense of personal and professional accomplishment in achieving a prominent position within the legal profession. I also felt a little panic and fear, and thought to myself "Dear God, what have I done?!" How is it possible that I will now be carrying the same title, and doing the same work, as the numerous outstanding judges before whom I have litigated? Will I be able to make the easy decisions, let alone the tough ones? There is no possible way I know as much as these great jurists, so what do I do?

Over the years the feelings of pride, honor, and personal achievement have not diminished, but my understanding of one factor that makes a judge successful has grown. Although one of the responsibilities of a judge is to give answers, a judge does not magically have all the answers. Many answers come from experience, which the judges I mentioned certainly had and used expertly. But many of the answers, and a significant number of the hard ones, come from the lawyers. Good lawyering makes good judging. In hindsight I don't know why this surprised me. Lawyers know their cases much better than judges. Lawyers, through their advocacy, frame the issues and construct the questions that judges are tasked to answer. That is why hearings are important, and that is why it is important to let the lawyers do what they do. When the lawyers present their evidence and make their arguments they are educating the court and helping craft the decision. This is true even when the decision is adverse to them. Looking back on my days as an advocate from my perspective as a judge, I realized that the judges I respected and revered required me, and allowed me to present my evidence and make my arguments. At times they did this because they needed the process of advocacy to help them make a decision.

However, at times they already knew the answer but entertained the arguments for the benefit of the lawyers. They did this to help us develop as advocates so that the next time they needed the process to make a decision, we, the lawyers, were better prepared to play our part. I try to model this behavior every opportunity I get.

Whether I do this job for another five years or another 15, I know I will never see myself in the same way that I do John Rolph or Linda Reade. I am perfectly fine with that. What I do hope, however, is that valuing advocates in my courtroom the way these great judges did in their courtrooms helps perpetuate the profession by making a positive impression on the lawyers who appear before me.

Black Robe Fever

Patrick H. Tott
Chief Judge, Iowa District Court

"Black Robe Fever" or "Robe-itis"—the syndrome from which elevation to a judicial position generates arrogance and disdain for the perspectives of others —is seldom addressed or corrected. But in fact, one jurist defined "Black Robe Fever" as the process by which "donning a 'judicial robe' brings out every latent character defect in an individual."[4]

After practicing law for over 20 years, during which I'd developed a working and personal relationship with many attorneys, I was told by many of my colleagues not to develop "black robe disease" after they learned of my appointment to the district court (trial court) bench nearly a decade ago. We had all had our experiences with various judges who never seemed to be wrong, at least in their own minds, and some of whom had no problem with trying to show how smart they were and how dumb you were. Practicing law is a demanding and challenging career path, which is only made more difficult when you have to deal with a judge suffering from "black robe disease."

As a law student and as an attorney, I always viewed myself as someone who, while zealously representing my client, tried to keep an open mind and view all issues from every angle. While I did not always agree with others' opinions on a topic or legal issue, I believed trying to understand someone else's opinion only helped me to better understand the strengths and weaknesses of my own opinions and how my positions might be attacked or supported. By showing respect for my colleagues and their opinions I developed a reputation of being a reasonable lawyer and a respectable and honorable person. Though as my older colleagues pointed out to me after my appointment to the bench, this was no guarantee that I would be immune from "black robe disease," as they had seen others with similar demeanors turn into judges that believed their opinions were the only ones that mattered.

During my investiture an error was made as I took my oath of office, which brought an air of levity to the ceremony. During my remarks, I referenced the advice I had received to remain humble and thoughtful as I began my career as a district court judge. I stated that I was glad that the "mistake" had happened as it was a good reminder for me of the need to remain humble.

At that time, I thought this would be easy to do. I soon learned that it would be more difficult than I thought.

As in all areas of life, no matter what job or position we might hold, we are required to deal with all kinds of people. The same is true of the practice of law or being a judge. We see all kinds of litigators, from the straightforward "just the facts" types who present their case in an analytical and logical fashion to the impassioned advocates whose clients are never wrong nor have ever done anything wrong, to those who tread on the border of unethical or outright dishonest presentations.

Within the first month on the bench, I was confronted with one of the second types. During the hearing, counsel made their impassioned plea in such a manner that the person hearing it could only conclude that they would have to be an idiot not to agree. Well, I did disagree, and after I issued my ruling counsel felt it would be a good idea to visit the "new judge" and point out how I had gotten it all wrong. Of course, my initial reaction was shock that someone would be so brash as to approach the judge about their ruling, and I started to bark back at them. I was not going to let them come in believing they could intimidate me. After a few moments, I realized that this was not a productive approach and simply pointed out to counsel, "Well if you do not agree with my ruling you are certainly free to file an appeal." They never did. This experience showed me how easy it would have been to become that judge who "knew it all" and deal with situations in that manner. That is not who I had been, nor was it who I wanted to be. As a judge there will be times despite your best efforts that you will get it wrong. This attorney apparently felt I had, but approached it in a clearly inappropriate manner. You quickly learn that some attorneys are performing, not necessarily for you but for their client. Both as an attorney and as a judge, you must learn that nothing is personal, or at least it should not be. People can legitimately disagree with you but that it is not meant as a personal attack. Sooner or later as a judge you will not only have a ruling appealed, but a higher court will tell you you were wrong.

While having an attorney come back to chambers to challenge a ruling has proven to be an isolated experience, observing attorneys "perform" for their clients or the public has not. As I had been more of the first type of attorney, using the "just the facts" analytical approach, the brash approach shown by many others tended to rub me the wrong way. The challenge presented then became to realize that as judges we must look beyond the manner of presentation and cut to the essence of the dispute, the facts involved, and the law that is to be applied, all the while ignoring any personal feelings you might have. In the early 1990's tennis star Andre Agassi starred in a television commercial for Canon Cameras, the theme of which was "Image is Everything." While that may be true in marketing, it is certainly not true for what we as judges must do every day. As judges, image must be nothing, while substance and the rule of law is everything. For the litigators, however, image does play a role as they must market themselves to potential clients.

As in every profession there are multiple ways to market your product or service. While the manner of presentation chosen may not appeal to everyone, as judges we must be able to look past the manner of presentation and focus on the substance of the facts and issues. This is not always easy to do but it is something that we must do.

Being a judge requires you to make tough decisions. Decisions that affect the day-to-day lives of the people that appear before you. As judges we are no longer advocates but arbiters, arbiters of the facts and the law. We must be able to see through the smoke and mirrors and bravado to reach a just decision. We must be able to put aside our personal opinions and beliefs and base our decisions on the law as it has been established, not what we believe the law should be or what a just outcome is. While this sounds easy in theory, it can be very difficult in practice. One of the very first cases I was assigned dealt with a post-conviction relief matter in which the defendant had been convicted a few years earlier of sexually abusing his three young children. The defendant had been convicted after a jury trial in which the children had been forced to go through the trauma of testifying. On post-conviction relief, the defendant alleged that his trial counsel was ineffective for having failed to file a Motion to Suppress the statements he had made to law enforcement. While it was clear to me based on the information available in the court file that the defendant was guilty, he was right, the circumstances surrounding his interrogation by police were such that his confession was not voluntary and should have been suppressed. As a father of young children myself, every fiber of my being told me that I needed to deny his request for post-conviction relief so that these children, who were now just a few years older, would not have to go through the trauma of having to testify at trial again. This was not, however, what the law and facts of the case required. I could have easily been that judge who let my own personal feelings take over and denied the request for relief as I personally believed would be the right thing to do. But I understood that the oath I had taken and my obligation to the system required me to make a decision that I not only did not like but abhorred. I did what the law required me to do. The right answer is not always the answer that I want but the answer the law requires. As I feared, the matter again proceeded to trial, the children were required to testify again, and even without the defendant's now suppressed confession, he was again found guilty.

As a judge you have the authority to make decisions that impact the lives of nearly everyone around you. You make rulings and control the manner in which the proceedings are conducted in front of you. It is not the authority that you have as a result of becoming a judge that is important, but how you choose to exercise that authority. Once you understand that it is not the robe, but the person wearing the robe, that makes all the difference.

Chapter 10

Difficult Decisions

Difficulty is in the Eye of the Beholder

Paul B. Ahlers
Judge, Iowa Court of Appeals

What makes a decision "difficult"? Does difficult refer to those cases that stretch our intellectual abilities, sometimes to the breaking point? As judges, we run across a fair number of those—legal tussles that don't lend themselves to clear answers. But we confront those cases head on, grappling with the issues with the hope that, with the right amount of research, reflection, and good old-fashioned effort, the legal answer will somehow materialize with clarity out of the fog of confusion. We naively jump into the fray on those cases with gusto, only to be disappointed because we forgot that, sometimes in the legal arena, there are cases for which there will never be a clear answer. Or does "difficult" mean something else? Does it mean making decisions in those cases in which the facts and the law require a certain outcome, but that outcome offends one's sense of justice? It is this latter type of difficult decision that came immediately to mind. And I knew exactly the case from my career that highlights the struggle.

It was early in my trial judge career, and the stakes couldn't have been lower. I drew a small claims case that pitted feuding neighbors against each other. Like the legendary feud between the Hatfields and McCoys, this feud involved an animal. Unlike the Hatfields and McCoys, the animal driving the wedge between the neighbors was not a pig. It was a cat. And if you're picturing some purring, fancy, purebred cat with a gleaming coat that radiates an aura of good health, the picture in your head is way off. This was a flea-ridden, matted, vagrant of a cat. (I remember the flea-ridden part because I vividly recall using my pen to slide the cat's collar back across my bench and kindly asking the party who, without invitation or permission, had just dropped it there to take it back right after that party had described the cat's flea problem. My germaphobia runs deep, and I recall struggling to resist the urge to scratch the psychosomatic itches from which I suffered the rest of the hearing.)

The feud developed because the neighbors across the street from the cat's owner had taken to feeding the cat, letting the cat in their house during inclement weather, and taking the cat to the veterinarian as needed. The evidence at trial suggested that the cat's owner was not inclined to provide any such services on a regular basis, if ever. Nevertheless, it was undisputed that the owner did, in fact, own the cat. The problem came to a head when the neighbors eventually refused to return the cat. So, the cat's owner filed a replevin suit seeking an order requiring the neighbors to return the cat. And that's where I came in.

The stark contrast between the parties was evident immediately upon entering the courtroom. The neighbors—the defendants in the replevin suit—were a kind, soft-spoken, polite, and affable retired couple. The cat owner plaintiff, on the other hand, was none of those things. She was a disagreeable, aggressive, loud, and argumentative younger woman. Based on the owner's attitude and demeanor in the courtroom, where she was presumably exhibiting her idea of best behavior, I had little difficulty believing the neighbors' testimony about their struggles when trying to calmly discuss issues about the cat with the owner. I could barely get the owner to listen to me during the hearing without her interrupting and arguing, so I could easily imagine that any efforts to talk rationally with her at home would have been a fruitless exercise. Although conducting the hearing was challenging due to some uncivil behavior and lots of detours into irrelevant matters, I eventually heard the evidence I needed to make a decision.

The neighbors presented evidence that the owner generally let the cat run loose, and it started showing up at their house more and more frequently, presumably because they gave the cat food and shelter. Eventually, the cat became a permanent fixture at their house, so they started taking the cat to the vet as needed, at considerable expense to them. This carried on for a period of time with no objection from the owner, so the couple was surprised when the owner demanded the cat back. Feeling like the cat was better off with them, the couple refused to return it. The evidence presented by the plaintiff? "I own the cat." That's it. She presented no contradictory evidence to the narrative given by the neighbors.

It was time to make a decision. Of course, making the decision pitted the disagreeable woman who had largely neglected her cat against the generous couple who had gone above and beyond the call of duty to look after the neglected pet. So, what to do? As a judge, one's job is to apply the controlling legal principles to the facts. And here, both the law and the facts were clear. It was a matter of property law—which doesn't provide for a "best interests of the cat" analysis—and that law required me to order the cat's return to its owner. So, that's what I did, even though my sense of justice strongly suggested the neighbors should be allowed to keep the cat. But judges aren't permitted to just assess the situation and rule based on their perceived notions of fairness and justice untethered to legal principles. What makes our system of justice so wonderful and credible is that it is governed by the rule of law, not by the whim or personal preferences of individual judges. It doesn't take much imagination to conceive of the chaos that could ensue if it were otherwise. In almost any given situation, reasonable minds could differ on what is "fair" or "just."

But the rule of law, which itself is based on principles of fairness and justice, provides the ground rules that guide us in our endeavors. Would we want it any other way?

When I tell this story about the cat case, I'm sometimes asked whether it was a "difficult" decision. Truth be told, the answer is "no." It wasn't a difficult decision. That's because I firmly believe that the essence of our justice system is this. The parties should be given a fair trial that permits the facts to be accurately determined. Once those facts are determined after a fair trial, a judge should apply the controlling legal principles to the facts and that application of the law to those facts dictates the outcome, whether the judge likes that outcome or not. Viewed through that lens, ordering the return of the cat to its owner was not a "difficult" decision.

But as I ponder the question of whether the cat case was "difficult," it occurs to me that my concept of "difficult" may have been too narrow. At the beginning of this piece, I posed the question of whether making "difficult" decisions refers to difficulty in determining the law and how to apply it to the facts in a challenging case or refers to the difficulty in making a decision when the outcome the law requires offends one's sense of justice. I'm convinced it refers to both of those. And under either of those concepts of "difficult," the cat case did not make for a difficult decision. But maybe the case reveals a third type of difficulty as well. Maybe "difficult" refers to the fact that making the decision that the law requires you to make leads to the realization that doing your job as a judge sometimes just plain stinks. And having the law require me to take that cat away from the kindly neighbors to return it to its neglectful owner was one of those times. In that sense, it was difficult.

So, does having at least three ways judicial decision making can be difficult make me wonder whether being a judge is worth it? Not at all. The difficulties create the challenges that make the job so rewarding. I wouldn't have it any other way.

Don't Be Afraid

Robert B. Hanson
Judge, Iowa District Court (Ret.)

When Jeff Goodman asked me to contribute an essay for this collection, he suggested that I reflect on the topic of making difficult decisions. In my more than two decades serving as a district court judge, I made hundreds if not thousands of rulings, and it's fair to say a great many—maybe most—of them were difficult. I strongly suspected, however, that Jeff had one particular decision in mind: my summary judgment ruling in the case of *Varnum v. Brien*, which struck down Iowa's statutory ban against same-sex marriage.

Varnum is probably the case most people want to hear about and, if so, that certainly comes as no surprise. If I recall correctly, by the time the case was assigned to my docket in 2005, marriage equality was already becoming a hot-button topic across the nation. However, only Massachusetts had actually legalized same-sex marriage—by judicial decision—while Vermont had legislatively provided for "civil unions." Most people probably didn't expect the next battleground for marriage equality to occur in Iowa, but *Varnum v. Brien* put Iowa—and thus my ruling—squarely in the national spotlight. Regardless of how I ruled, I knew my decision would be controversial, that it would be appealed, and that the outcome of that appeal would influence, to one degree or another, how other states addressed same-sex marriage. With all these factors in play, there was little question in my mind that it would likely be a career-defining case. I was also keenly aware that the decision would have both immediate and long-term effects on the everyday lives of same-sex couples right here in Iowa, as well as on their children and other loved ones. In short, *Varnum* was a high-profile, high-stakes case from the outset.

But none of that is what made *Varnum* difficult.

The difficulty stemmed from much more mundane reasons, reasons that will quickly become apparent to anyone who takes the bench in a district with a high-volume docket like Iowa Judicial District 5C (Polk County). *Varnum*, quite deservedly, took an extraordinarily long time to research and write, and abundant time is a luxury most judges with busy dockets simply do not have. Those dockets are always jam-packed, working on one case necessarily takes time away from the others, and at that time in District 5C, one law clerk typically supported three or more judges. At the time *Varnum* was assigned to me, I was already working between 10 and 12 hours each weekday, as well as 4-5 hours on Saturdays and Sundays. For most of my years on the bench, if anyone wanted to find me, they knew right where to look—the courthouse.

I felt I had no choice but to prioritize *Varnum*. It had to take precedence, not because it was a momentous case or one involving momentous issues, but because of the absolute certainty that it would go up on appeal before the Iowa Supreme Court. I needed to make sure that I wrote the best ruling I could so as to maximize the chances of it being affirmed on appeal.

And for *that* to happen, a lot of time-consuming painstaking work had to be done. Part of a judge's responsibility as a fair and impartial decision maker is to give thoughtful and open-minded consideration to all the submissions of the parties. Even though *Varnum* came before me on opposing motions for summary judgment rather than after a full trial on the merits, there was nevertheless a mountain of material to review and consider. It took months to review all the parties' motions, supporting statements of undisputed fact, affidavits, and briefs, as well as *amicus curiae* briefs submitted by a multitude of individuals and organizations, including legal and public policy organizations, child and family advocates, faith leaders, scholars, law professors, historians, and others who wished to voice their opinions. I wanted to be very careful that I didn't overlook any details and that I thoroughly addressed each and every argument presented by the parties. Compounding the difficulty of my task was that I didn't exactly consider myself a scholar when it came to constitutional law. Thus, my "staff" of one—my law clerk, Katie Naset, who I shared with two or three other judges—and I spent countless hours poring over every word of the parties' respective motions and supporting materials, including all applicable legal authorities cited therein.

As time-intensive and high-stakes as *Varnum* was, perhaps it is a supreme irony that, when it came to the ruling itself, determining the correct outcome was actually relatively easy. How was this possible? Simply stated, the plain wording of the Iowa Constitution made it so.

In the final analysis, *Varnum* was largely a case about equal protection under the law and, on that point, the Iowa Constitution was about as clear as it could be so far as the process of construction and interpretation of its language was concerned. Article I, Section 6 of the Iowa Constitution—its Equal Protection Clause—ensures that our state laws apply uniformly and impartially to all persons or circumstances under their purview, without unfair or arbitrary application that would benefit or disadvantage any citizen or class of citizens. By preventing same-sex couples from marrying, the state was effectively granting a privilege (the legal status and benefits of marriage) to one class of citizens (heterosexual couples) while denying it to another (same-sex couples) without, in my humble opinion, any justification, compelling or otherwise. To me, it was obvious that the law did not operate uniformly and equally and therefore violated the equal protection and uniform operation requirements of Article I, Section 6. Thus, I can honestly say that this decision was actually one of the easier ones of my career and that I certainly never lost one minute of sleep worrying about whether my ruling was the right one.

Of course, that wasn't the end of the story. Knowing that *Varnum* would immediately be appealed to the Iowa Supreme Court, the day after I entered my ruling and at the request of the defendant, I issued a stay on enforcement of the ruling pending appeal. (Though not before one alert same-sex couple from Ames obtained a marriage license and got married! And, I might add, they are still happily married and have a child.) And predictably, as soon as the ruling was announced there was an organized and vocal backlash from those who were unhappy with the outcome. I consider myself very fortunate that I experienced no personal repercussions other than the expected flurry of nasty letters and emails as well as a few voicemails—judges' phone numbers for their chambers were public knowledge as they were listed in the phone book—informing me where I should expect to spend eternity, in the callers' opinions.

Once the case was taken up by the Iowa Supreme Court, the matter was out of my hands. The seven justices of the Iowa Supreme Court were then tasked, as I was, with considering all of the legal arguments, applicable supporting authorities, and implications of their decision, and they obviously took great care to do so. They heard oral arguments in December, 2008, and after careful deliberation, issued their decision on April 3, 2009. All of the justices concurred that Iowa's statutory ban against same-sex marriage violated the Iowa Constitution. My decision was unanimously upheld.

As Connecticut had legalized same-sex marriage in the fall of the previous year, Iowa then officially became the third state in the nation to allow same-sex couples to marry. This was unquestionably a momentous occasion and one that has yielded significant happiness and fulfillment for so many over the ensuing years.

Of course, in the wake of the decision, local and national protest resumed, and I received a few more choice messages condemning my role in the legalization of same-sex marriage. That was nothing, however, compared to the treatment to which three of the *Varnum* appellate justices were eventually subjected.

In the months leading up to the general election in 2010, Iowa Supreme Court Chief Justice Marsha Ternus and Justices Michael Streit and David Baker were up for retention and all three became the primary targets of an unprecedented anti-retention campaign, organized and heavily funded by out-of-state groups who opposed same-sex marriage generally and the *Varnum* decision in particular. Sadly, all three justices lost their respective retention elections and were ousted from the Iowa Supreme Court, effectively ending their judicial careers. I can speak only for myself, but I am absolutely confident that the vast majority of those reading this essay will concur with me when I say that these developments will forever stand as an ugly stain on and a complete and inexcusable misuse—indeed, an absolute *abuse*—of the judicial retention process established by the Iowa Constitution.

Thankfully, this shameful turn of events did not further delay the recognition of same-sex marriage in Iowa, and the appellate ruling in *Varnum* helped pave the way for legalization of same-sex marriage nationally. Over the ensuing years, other states and, ultimately, the nation, via the United States Supreme Court's historic decision in *Obergefell v. Hodges*, have recognized the right of same-sex couples to marry. I unabashedly say that I am tremendously pleased and proud to have played some role—however large or small—in these developments.

Now, please forgive me but I must digress. About seven years after I entered my summary judgment ruling in *Varnum*, the case came back to me in an entirely unexpected—and very personal—way. The evening of January 1, 2014, my son Tom called me. He had just returned to his home in New York City after a visit to Iowa for the holidays, and it struck me as odd that he was calling so soon.

"Hey, T," I said. "Everything okay?"

"Dad," he said, "I have something to tell you."

I'm guessing many parents will identify with what I was experiencing at that moment. My son was pretty good about checking in on a regular basis—so good that we basically learned when to expect his calls. Suffice it to say this was not one of those times and my sense of foreboding was palpable.

"What's that?" I said, bracing myself.

"Dad," he said. "I'm gay."

I admit I was not expecting this and was completely silent for a moment as what he had just said sunk in. But what immediately followed was profound, albeit cautious, relief.

"T," I finally said. "Is *that* all you were going to tell me?"

We quickly shared a laugh. I had been fearing the very worst—that he was in jail or sick or whatever—but my son was only calling to tell me he was gay. I could not have cared less about his sexual orientation. I only cared that he was safe and in good health and that his life was happy and fulfilling. To this day, we both still get a chuckle out of this story.

I have always been proud of the role I've played in helping to establish marriage equality in Iowa. But not in a million years would I have guessed that, one day, my decision would be helping my own child. I am not a big believer in fate or destiny. But even I sometimes wonder if *Varnum* landing on my docket was more than mere coincidence.

Most judges won't see a case like *Varnum* in their entire careers. Even so, the ruling(s) in any case can, and probably will, be difficult in any one or more of a myriad of ways. This is something anyone who is considering the bench should be aware of...but not afraid of. Each case presents its own complexities and, at the time the parties appear before you, their case is one of the most important things in their lives, if not *the* most important thing. Some cases will have profoundly life-changing consequences. Custody decisions that will forever change the trajectory of a child's life, or the determination of whether someone is guilty of committing a crime based on the evidence presented, for instance, were far more difficult and weighed far more heavily on me than anything I encountered in writing the *Varnum* decision, where the law was unambiguous and the ruling was therefore obvious.

Whatever the nature of the case before you, the parties absolutely deserve your best efforts to make the correct ruling, i.e. the ruling that correctly applies the applicable law to the proven facts. The difficulty in accomplishing that, especially on a busy docket, lies in finding the time necessary to assure that a given ruling is indeed the product of your best efforts. And, unfortunately, the reality is that you will not always have enough time to assure that result. Part of being a judge is the realization and acceptance of the fact that, more often than you'd like, your rulings won't be all you'd hoped for. All you can do about it is keep plugging away, day after day, giving it your very best in the amount of time available to you.

I actually found that the overwhelming amount of work was a blessing in disguise in one important regard: I simply didn't have time to fret over my decisions. I couldn't spend time second-guessing myself or worrying about what would happen if I issued an unpopular opinion. I couldn't agonize over the times—and they happen to every judge—when what the law required didn't necessarily align with my own opinions or accomplish the outcome I personally would've preferred. I couldn't worry about future retention decisions or the prevailing political climate or allow myself to become overwhelmed by the never-ending docket. There just wasn't time.

Let me conclude by saying that, despite these challenges, serving as a judge was a great honor and privilege, and the most rewarding job that I ever held. Knowing that my decisions could and often would have a positive effect on the lives of the people I served was more gratifying than I ever could have imagined. Sometimes it was just a few people and at other times it was many, but having the chance to participate in protecting the rights of countless people, or in changing the laws of society to make life fairer and more equal for all made every hour worth it for me, and I'm certain it will be the same for you. So, don't be afraid....

High-Volume Dockets

Jeffrey D. Farrell
Judge, Iowa District Court

There was a point in time in my life when a couple of friends talked me into running a marathon. I was not excited. I had started running for exercise to lose a few pounds. Some friends joined me for the same reason. We ran local races to motivate ourselves . . . and maybe to have an excuse to drink beer afterward. I did not need to run a marathon to meet any of those goals.

I eventually capitulated and agreed to run. It was a struggle but I finished. I considered it an accomplishment and declared the end of my marathon career. Then the same two friends talked me into running the New York Marathon. I agreed because I had never visited New York. I got sick before the race and struggled again. For the second time, I declared an end to my marathon career.

A couple of years later, I decided to run another marathon. This time, I decided to do it on my own. I felt I could do better. This race was different. I had learned more about training and was healthy. My time was much improved. Upon reflection, I realized that I might be able to qualify for the Holy Grail of running—the Boston Marathon. Boston only accepted applications based on qualifying times. It is a point of honor to run Boston.

One lesson I learned was that, to run fast races, you have to run fast during training. Most marathoners do "speed training" to improve their times. Speed training involves running shorter intervals, e.g. a half mile or a mile, repeatedly at a hard pace. This builds lung capacity that helps to run longer distances at a faster pace.

At some point, I had learned about a speed training program referred to as the Yasso 800s. "Yasso" referred to Bart Yasso, who was a famous runner and a writer for *Runner's World* magazine. Yasso's program involved a build-up to running ten 800-meter intervals in succession during one training session. So, I would run hard for two laps around the track, then run a light recovery lap, then run hard for another two laps, and so on until I completed ten 800s. For those of you who do not know how hard that is, go to your local track, warm up with some light jogging, then run really hard for two laps. Then stop and think about doing that nine more times. Trust me, you won't want to do it. I didn't. But I did.

The selling point was that Yasso had discovered something special about his training program. He learned that the pace at which you ran the 800s was a very good predictor of your marathon time. For example, if you ran each 800 at or below a 3:30-minute pace, you should be able to run a 3:30-hour marathon. Or, if you ran each 800 at or below a 3:00-minute pace, you should be able to run a 3:00-hour marathon. This gave me a road map for how to qualify for Boston. I knew the qualifying time I needed. All I had to do was run ten 800s in a row at or below that time.

I did most of this training on my own, but my friend Michael Gould joined me for some of the Yasso training. Michael was a former track athlete at Nebraska. This was good and bad for me. It was bad because he had an easier time running the 800s. It was good because he pushed me. With Michael's help, I successfully completed the Yasso training. And when I approached the finish line in Grant Park in Chicago and saw that I was minutes ahead of my goal time, I was thankful to Bart Yasso and Michael Gould and everyone who had helped me on this quest.

In thinking about my assignment for this book, it occurred to me that difficult decision making is sometimes like training for a marathon. When we think about deciding hard cases, we often think about complex or high-profile cases or cases that challenge our sense of right and wrong. It is true that those cases often present us with difficult decisions, and some of my colleagues are writing about these topics. However, sometimes the greatest challenge in decision making occurs during a routine day taking on a routine case. When training for a marathon, you can't cheat on your training. If you do, you will pay for it on race day. Similarly, when performing the work of a district judge, you can't slack on cases some consider routine. If you do, you are not truly upholding your oath.

Let me give an example. In Polk County District Court, we are assigned to a specific docket that we manage for either one or two years. One of those dockets is referred to as the felony drug docket. This docket manages all pretrial matters for every felony drug case in the county. One responsibility is to take pleas and sentence defendants in these cases. Due to the volume, I might hold as many as ten in-person sentencing hearings on a day. This can feel like the mental and emotional equivalent of running ten 800-meter runs in one workout.

A sentencing decision in criminal cases is not like decision making in civil cases. The judge receives a presentence investigative report (PSI) describing the defendant's background a day or two before the hearing. When we have time, we read the PSI the day before the hearing. Sometimes we read it the day of the hearing. Then, we listen to arguments from the attorneys, a statement from the defendant, and possibly a victim impact statement. The judge then verbally pronounces sentence. There is no time to read case law or ponder the written information and the arguments of the parties. The judge has to rule and move on to the next case.

It can be very challenging to employ consistent decision making under these circumstances. Judges are people too. We have good and bad days. We get tired. We get bored. We get stressed. We have other things going on in our lives. An argument that sounds pretty good early in the day may not sound so good by the end of the day. Or, an argument that sounds questionable at the beginning of the day might sound a lot better at the end of the day.

As a judge, it is critical to remember that each case is important to each party. In other words, on those days we have ten sentencing hearings, we need to run the ninth and tenth hearing at the same speed (so to speak) as we run the first and second hearings. In the criminal context, it may mean the difference between sending a defendant to prison when drug and mental health treatment would have been a valid option. Certainly there are times when prison or jail or other consequences are warranted. The challenge is to remain consistent on busy dockets and treat each party the same in each case.

Prior to my appointment as a district judge, I served as an administrative law judge. I usually presided over self-represented litigants. Many felt they had no chance and that "the system was rigged" against them or "you are just going to rule for the State." I had a saying when faced with people who had that belief. I would tell them this: "There are two times when your case will be the most important thing in my life. The first is right now during this hearing. The second is when I am writing my decision. At both points, your case will be the most important thing I am doing."

I wasn't lying. I have a family, friends, other interests, and a challenging career. Any of these things could be considered more important than any particular case. But, I am a focused person. When I hear a case and write a decision, it actually is the most important thing in my life at that particular time. When making that statement, it seemed to alleviate the litigants' concerns and assure them that I was committed to treating them fairly.

I have been very blessed during my career. I have been fortunate to have argued or presided over many high-profile cases. Ironically, the only thank you letters I have received have been from unsuccessful self-represented litigants. In each case, they simply thanked me for listening to their claims. If we, as judges, can do that in each and every case, we have truly met our judicial oath and responsibilities.

Staying in the Judicial Lane

Dana L. Oxley
Justice, Iowa Supreme Court

One of the most common questions I have been asked since becoming a justice on the Supreme Court of Iowa almost five years ago is whether it is difficult to set aside my personal beliefs, experiences, and values when I am deciding cases. I generally have two responses: "yes" and "no."

First the "yes."

I came to the Supreme Court straight from private practice, so I did not bring with me the experience of deciding cases solo like district court judges do. Rather, my only judicial experience is as one of seven votes, and my goal is to convince at least three others to agree with my position. In that context, I believe the differing backgrounds and views each of the seven of us brings to the discussion are both healthy and invaluable.

I am a farm girl, raised in rural Iowa. That background gives me a different perspective from my colleagues. For example, Justice Mansfield grew up in Concord, Massachusetts outside of Boston, and his father taught political philosophy at Harvard University. Justice McDonald was a (self-proclaimed) army brat who spent his earlier-upbringing years living on bases across the globe, and the latter ones being raised on the south side of Des Moines by his Vietnamese mother who migrated to the United States as an adult. We each necessarily bring different views to the table by the very nature of our upbringings, if nothing else. From that perspective, I do not think it is really even possible for us as individual justices to set aside our personal experiences and views.

Nor do we necessarily want judges to completely set aside their personal experiences. Appellate courts sit as a panel—ranging from three to as many as 11 (or sometimes more) judges. The thought behind using a multi-member panel to decide the focused legal issues that arise in an appeal is premised on the idea that two (or seven) heads are better than one. Yet if the judges on a panel all have similar experiences and backgrounds, the panel risks losing the benefit of multiplicity.

Challenging—and considering—the views of six other legal minds as we discuss cases around our conference table has been one of the most stimulating (and sometimes frustrating) parts of this job. It is also—in my view—one of the most important parts of reaching the right decision in a particular case. I prepare for oral arguments on my own (with the help of my law clerk) without seeking the views of my colleagues until I have done my own review of the record and research of the legal issues. For me, that independent analysis is essential to ensuring I put in the work necessary to form my opinion not only about the resolution of a case, but also the reasoning needed to support it. Then, when I come together to discuss a case with my colleagues, it is equally important for me to consider their opposing views. They might identify a particular fact that I overlooked or minimized, not appreciating its significance to the legal issue. Or they may catch a nuance to a legal theory that needs to be further explored as applied to a unique set of facts. And I might do the same for them. Sometimes, they just read a legal doctrine differently than I do. But in all cases, objectively considering their points and positions is important for testing whether my own legal reasoning holds up.

This is all to say that bringing differing perspectives helps ensure that the correct decision is reached because presenting, and considering, different perspectives allows the weak points to be exposed and addressed. So from that perspective, the beliefs and values that have been shaped by my unique background and experiences should not be set aside—at least not entirely. That said, it can be difficult to recognize that someone else's perspective, shaped by their unique background and experiences, requires me to reconsider an issue from an unfamiliar perspective. And here, it is critical that I have an open mind when considering how the differing perspectives affect a particular issue before our court. I try to make a conscious effort to approach each case with that openness to hearing others' perspectives.

The discussion so far could apply to any decision-making process. But as judges, we aren't making just any decisions. We are making legal decisions about the issues raised in a particular case. This leads to my "no" answer to the question of whether it is difficult to set aside my personal beliefs and values in deciding cases.

Ours is a tripartite system of government, and the judiciary is one of the three, co-equal branches. While equal, we are also separate, each with our own unique role to play. In my view, that system operates best when each branch stays in its own lane. For me as a judge, that means applying the law to the issues that are raised in the case before me based on what the law is, not what I think it should be. Judges don't make law, but they do interpret it. To keep the judicial "interpretation" function within its proper lane, judicial philosophy becomes important—in the "small j," "small p" sense of judicial philosophy, not the categorical judicial philosophy that comes with titles such as liberal or conservative; activist or non-activist; deconstructionist or strict constructionist.

A judge's role is to resolve specific disputes between specific parties to a case based on the specific issues they raise. I took an oath to "support the Constitution of the United States and the Constitution of the State of Iowa, and that, without fear, favor, affection, or hope of reward, [I] will, to the best of [my] knowledge and ability, administer justice according to the law, equally to the rich and the poor." Iowa Code § 63.6.

In order to "administer justice according to the law," I approach each case by focusing on two objectives: being impartial and being principled in the process—both without giving thought to what outside interests might benefit, or suffer, from the outcome of the decision. My judicial philosophy, if you will. Approaching each case with these objectives helps me stay in my lane and gives me a clear(er) path to follow when hard cases come along.

Seeking to administer justice by being impartial means being blind not only to the personal characteristics of the parties that are irrelevant to the issues (a party's race or socio-economic status; a convicted criminal's horrendous crime), but also being blind to outside political and social interests. Here, it helps to stay focused on the specifics of the particular case. The parties decide which issues to raise, and those issues decide which facts and legal principles are relevant. Making a conscious effort to be impartial means keeping irrelevant factors irrelevant and letting the result work itself out. I tell my law clerks they have two primary jobs: make sure I get the law right, and don't let me be results-oriented.

Seeking to administer justice by being principled in the process means keeping an open mind while I follow the decision-making process until I reach the conclusion. I really don't know whether I will vote to affirm or reverse a district court's judgment until I have completed the process. I start with the record as developed in the district court. Then I move to the issues identified by the parties—and properly preserved for our review. Finally, I consider how the law applies to those issues—using rules, statutes, and precedent and then following the legal analysis to its conclusion.

I had the honor of serving as a career clerk for the Honorable David R. Hansen on the United States Court of Appeals for the Eighth Circuit for ten years. His directive in drafting an opinion was always: Get it Right, Keep it Tight. Getting it right means being intellectually honest about following the legal reasoning where it leads, not manipulating the reasoning to a predestined result. I recall more than one case that "just wouldn't write"—which meant changing the result, not the reasoning. Keeping it tight means deciding only the issues actually before the court, and then only those needed to resolve the appeal.

An example of how this has worked for me is reflected in *State v. Burns*, a case our court decided last year. Police officers used advances in DNA technology to solve a 40-year-old cold-case murder of an 18-year-old girl found stabbed to death on the floorboard of her car in a mall parking lot. The officers narrowed their search to the first cousins of a woman found through a genealogy website who had cooperated with the investigation. She had only three cousins—three brothers from Iowa. Investigators followed one of the brothers, Jerry Burns, to a Pizza Ranch restaurant and picked up the straw he left on the table after he finished his meal. They extracted his DNA from the straw and ultimately used it to get a conviction for the murder.

On appeal, Burns challenged the collection of his DNA without a warrant as a violation of the search and seizure clause of the Fourth Amendment. The majority of our court rejected the challenge, concluding Burns had abandoned any interest he had in his DNA when he discarded the straw, so a warrant wasn't needed. I dissented (as did Justice McDermott) based on my application of the United States Supreme Court's Fourth Amendment jurisprudence. I followed where I understood the precedent led, without letting the result manipulate the path.

I don't doubt the jury's conclusion that Mr. Burns committed the murder. But that is irrelevant to whether his Fourth Amendment rights were violated when his DNA was collected without a warrant. So in reaching my decision, I had to set aside the heinous nature of the crime; the 40 years Burns went on with his life while the victim's family was left without answers; and the fact that had a majority of our court agreed with me, the State would have had to retry Burns—likely without the DNA evidence that was so important to its case. It's not that I wanted Burns to go free. And I do empathize with the victim's family. But my job as a judge is to apply the law as I understand it to be—not the way I think it should be or the way that leads to a result I might prefer.

In this way—allowing the process to dictate the result instead of the other way around—it is not (as) difficult to set aside my personal views and beliefs when I recognize the lane I am in.

While we must stay in our own lane, we also have an obligation to fully occupy that lane. That can mean making hard decisions about controversial topics. Other authors in this chapter discuss what that looked like with respect to one such issue in recent times when our court decided *Varnum v. Brien.* I was not part of that court and cannot speak to the difficulty in deciding it. But I will no doubt face controversial cases—controversial from a political or societal standpoint—during my time on the court. And when I do, I will rely on my core objectives in addressing an appeal: being impartial and being principled in the process.

Without Fear, Favor or Hope of Reward

Marsha K. Ternus
Former Chief Justice, Iowa Supreme Court (Ret.)

On November 2, 2010, I lost my seat on the Iowa Supreme Court, a position I had held for more than 17 years. The 2010 election was my third retention election. The two previous ones in 2002 and 1994 were sleepy affairs, and each time the voters retained me for another eight-year term. But in 2009, the Iowa Supreme Court decided *Varnum v. Brien*, ruling that Iowa's statutory prohibition on same-sex marriage violated the equality clause found in the Iowa Constitution. That decision set the stage for a very different retention election in 2010—an election dominated by a challenge to the three justices on the ballot, a challenge motivated by retaliation and intimidation.

At the time of the *Varnum* decision, most Iowans opposed legalizing same-sex marriage, so it was not a surprise that there was a public outcry from those Iowans when the Iowa Supreme Court issued its unanimous decision in April 2009, which required county officials to issue marriage licenses to same-sex couples. In fact, the Court had a preview of that opposition in January 2008, when opponents of same-sex marriage organized a "prayer walk" at the capitol to launch an effort to amend the Iowa Constitution to prohibit same-sex marriage. This demonstration was timed to coincide with my 2008 State of the Judiciary address to the legislature, and the opponents of same-sex marriage packed the House galleries. As a *Des Moines Register* editorial stated at the time, opponents of same-sex marriage "delivered a subtle but menacing suggestion that judges who stray from popularly accepted rulings might face consequence."[1] That same legislative session, there was also an unsuccessful effort to encourage the legislature to impeach the trial judge who had ruled in 2007 that Iowa's ban on same-sex marriage violated Iowa's constitution, the decision that was on appeal to the Supreme Court.

Given the visible and vocal public opposition to same-sex marriage and the likelihood of efforts to punish justices who voted to legalize such marriages, one might think that the Court's decision in *Varnum* would be the consummate example of a tough decision. Whether same-sex couples should be allowed to marry was a polarizing issue. The few courts that had addressed this issue reached different conclusions, and even the courts that had allowed same-sex marriage did so with some justices dissenting. On a more personal level, a vote in favor of same-sex marriage was certain to generate disapproval from some of the justices' family members and friends, and most likely retribution by voters. The justices knew this. But the truth is: *Varnum* was not a tough decision. Not at all.

To explain why the *Varnum* decision was not difficult, I need to go back several years and talk about our Court's reaction to the increasing politicization of the American court system that began in the early 2000s. In the several years prior to our 2009 *Varnum* decision, our Court had become aware that political forces were increasingly working to undermine judicial independence in America's courts. In the 2008 judicial election in neighboring Wisconsin, "special interest groups... funded almost nine out of every ten dollars spent on television advertising."[2] Many of these ads were "criticized as misleading and unseemly."[3] In Chief Justice Lavorato's final State of the Judiciary speech to the legislature in 2006, he noted "[t]he current sport of lodging spurious and vitriolic attacks against the nation's judiciary" that were intended to make judges "servants of popular ideologies rather than servants of the law." He emphatically stated that judges were accountable to the constitution and the law, not political pressure.

I shared Chief Justice Lavorato's view of the role of the Court. When he retired later that year and I became the chief, I sought to confirm our Court's commitment to the rule of law. Rebecca Colton, who served as the chief justice's chief of staff, David Boyd, the state court administrator, and I planned the Court's annual retreat in 2007. We created an agenda I hoped would strengthen the Court's decision making and leadership. As I explained to my fellow justices:

> [F]or the past five years, we have used the retreat to discuss the day-to-day operations of the judicial branch.... This year, our retreat will be different. Because we have two new justices, this retreat is a good time for us to reflect on the supreme court as an institution and our roles as leaders of the judicial branch.

I added that we would begin our retreat with a discussion "that will focus on court culture: what it is and what we want it to be." For pre-retreat reading, I provided court members with a copy of an article written by Jeffrey Rosen, "Roberts's Rules."[4] I said, "This article is based on an interview of Chief Justice Roberts and provides an interesting perspective on how the court's collegiality, as reflected in its opinions, impacts public opinion of the court as an institution." Rosen had noted in this article that "Roberts praised justices who were willing to put the good of the Court above their own ideological agendas."[5]

Fortunately, our Court was like-minded. At our retreat discussion of court culture, we discovered the seven of us shared common values and beliefs regarding the role of the courts. We agreed we wanted to be a court that made principled decisions—decisions that were driven by the rule of law, not by political, ideological or personal agendas. We expressly affirmed the oath of office we had each taken upon joining the court, in which we promised to make decisions "without fear, favor, affection, or hope of reward."[6] Our discussion was more than aspirational: we committed to each other that we would adhere to this model in our future deliberations. And we gave each other permission to call out a colleague for failing to abide by our mutual commitment.

To bolster the court's ability to make collective decisions focused on what the constitution and law required, we engaged consultants to teach us the necessary skills. One set of consultants at our retreat taught us a communication process they named "dialogue." We learned to build a capacity to think and reflect on what others said; to respect and find value in differences in opinion; to make collaborative decisions upon which each of our seven diverse viewpoints was brought to bear; and to work together to reach a principled decision, namely, one based on the rule of law.

During my remaining years as chief justice, each member of the court kept a copy of the ten principles of dialogue we had learned in their opinion notebook that was brought to each opinion conference. Those dialogue principles were brought out from time to time and read aloud in our opinion conferences when court members became more focused on winning an argument than reaching the correct decision under the law. We also exercised our right to point out a stray court member who seemed to be espousing a view motivated more by what they wanted the law to be than what the constitution, statutes and precedent said the law was. None of us escaped correction, but this process strengthened our respect for each other and our commitment to the rule of law.

In 2008, the briefing in *Varnum v. Brien* was completed and the case was ready for submission to the Supreme Court. It was our practice to randomly assign an opinion writer for each case a month or two prior to the oral arguments. Generally, this assignment was completed by the chief's administrative assistant, but due to the importance of the *Varnum* decision, I decided that the random assignment would be made in one of our court conferences so all justices could participate and witness the process. Modeling the time-honored procedure of drawing names out of a hat, we wrote the name of each case to be submitted in December 2008, on a slip of paper and put the slips of paper in a small fabric bag. Justice Cady drew out the Varnum slip and became the designated author of the court's decision.

The appellate briefs in the *Varnum* appeal were voluminous. The court had been generous in allowing amicus briefs and those briefs filled an entire banker's box. Consequently, in the weeks leading up to the oral arguments, each court member worked diligently to read all the materials in preparation for the arguments and the court's deliberations. Our goal, and normal practice, was that each justice would exercise his or her independent judgment on each case. Justices were discouraged from privately lobbying other members to vote a certain way prior to the court conference. This practice ensured that all members would hear and benefit from each justice's distinct view of the issues, which in turn facilitated a robust discussion of the issues and a truly collaborative decision-making process.

I know from the court's later discussions that this practice was followed in the *Varnum* case. We walked into the conference room after the oral arguments in *Varnum* with no idea how the other court members would vote. I also know from our later discussions that we all expected that our court would be divided on the question of whether the legislative ban on same-sex marriage was constitutional. After all, public opinion was sharply divided, people held completely divergent views on this issue, and no court had issued a unanimous decision that such a statute was unconstitutional. We each entered the conference room wondering how divided our court would be.

Our procedure for the court's deliberation of an appeal was to allow each justice to state—without interruption—his or her opinion on how the case should be decided and why. We always started with the opinion writer and proceeded around the table with each justice in turn having the opportunity to speak. When all justices had expressed his or her views, a discussion would ensue where differences were discussed and, usually, consensus was reached. On that December day in 2008, we followed this procedure. Justice Cady gave an overview of the *Varnum* case, discussed the issues presented by the appeal, reviewed the applicable law and the parties' arguments, stated his opinion on whether the trial court's decision should be affirmed or reversed, and then explained the rationale for his opinion. Justice Cady announced he believed the trial court should be affirmed on the basis that the state law prohibiting same-sex marriage violated the Iowa Constitution's equality clause.

When Justice Cady finished, Justice Hecht shared his understanding of the issues and arguments, concluding, as had Justice Cady, that the trial judge was right and should be affirmed. From Justice Streit to Justice Baker to Justice Wiggins, although there were minor differences in their analysis of the issues, each had reached the same conclusion: the statute was unconstitutional.

It was my turn. In the weeks leading up to the submission of the *Varnum* appeal, I had worried whether the decision would be a difficult one to make, as the split decisions in other courts suggested. When I finally sat down with the voluminous briefs, read them and the authorities cited in them, I felt a flood of relief. The law was clear and pointed in one direction: the statute limiting marriage to a man and a woman denied same-sex couples numerous government benefits accorded to those who held civil-marriage status without substantially furthering any legitimate governmental interest. The statute violated Iowa's equality clause.

So when my colleagues turned to me to hear my view of the *Varnum* case, I without hesitation announced that I too believed the challenged statute violated the Iowa Constitution. Justice Appel, the final member of the court to state his position, concurred. The seven justices looked at each other in amazement. Each justice had independently reached the same conclusion, and our decision would be unanimous.

In retrospect, our unanimous decision was not surprising. We had committed ourselves to principled decision making, to following the rule of law, and to rendering decisions without fear, favor or hope of reward. That commitment allowed us to put aside the public opinion polls, the views of friends, colleagues and family members, possible repercussions from the legislature, and even the possibility that we would lose our jobs for voting as we did. We each focused solely on the governing legal principles and in doing so found that the outcome was clear. That's why the *Varnum* decision was an easy decision for our court. The law guided us, and nothing else mattered.

In time, some of us would, in fact, lose our jobs because of our votes in *Varnum*, but none of us ever regretted the principled approach we took in deciding this controversial case. And I know none of us considered our decision a tough one to make. Our oath of office required it.

Chapter 11

The Written Word

Writing for the District Court is a Balancing Act

Sarah E. Crane
Judge, Iowa District Court

A courtroom is a place where human problems are on display. To address this display of humanity requires a balancing act, including the way in which writing is employed. This is particularly true at the trial court level where I serve as a district court judge on a busy docket with hundreds of pending cases. As a general jurisdiction judge, I handle family law, criminal, and civil cases at all stages, including specialty business court cases.

One of the balancing acts for a busy district court judge is weighing the time it would take to draft a more academic piece of writing against the immediate need for the ruling itself. In many of the cases that come before me, the litigants may be better served by a clear and quick ruling than by a beautiful piece of writing that could take weeks to prepare. For example, in a family law case, parties who are struggling to co-parent and constantly engaged in schedule-related disputes, will be better served by a quick ruling that provides a clear schedule than a literary masterpiece.

The challenge is to recognize when efficiency is more important than a lengthy written opinion, and vice versa. At times, a judge may have an initial instinct on how to decide an issue, only for further research to reveal greater legal complexity. I try to balance the need or desire to explain a ruling in open court with the need to conduct a more thorough legal analysis. I believe speaking directly to the litigants from the bench is necessary and appropriate in many instances. However, it is also important not to rush into an announced decision that requires a more nuanced legal analysis. Every district court judge has probably made the wrong choice on occasion: (i) announced a ruling based on the belief that a straightforward fact-finding compelled the outcome only to discover upon further research that a more complex legal analysis was required; or (ii) taken a matter under advisement only to have the litigants' lives become even more complicated in the absence of a ruling. The goal is to accurately determine when you are prepared to announce a decision and when you must deliberate further. A district court judge must be able to downshift from quick decision making to the more deliberative, research-based process that leads to good writing.

Another balancing act for busy trial court judges is to be mindful of the impact a ruling will have on the litigants. Judges have the luxury of issuing an opinion and moving on to the next case. Litigants, by contrast, must live with the consequences of the decision. When writing an opinion, I try to set it aside for a day once it is completed so I can read for tone and clarity with fresh eyes before it is finalized. I am conscious that the way I describe litigants matters. It may be tempting to characterize one side harshly, particularly if the record shows that person has acted unreasonably. It is unlikely to be productive, however, to use pejorative labels. The basis for deciding for or against a litigant must be explained and judges shouldn't minimize or excuse behavior through passive language. I try to strike this balance by focusing on a person's actions rather than assigning broad character judgments. The litigants will have to read, follow, and live with the Court's order. I try to write in a way that might help them do so.

The third balancing act is to write for clarity and understanding, while also conveying the legal reasoning behind the decision. Judicial opinions must explain complex issues in a way that interested parties can understand, whether they be litigants, lawyers, other judges, or the general public. For me, the writing process is itself deliberative. I find that when I work to explain the legal analysis, it helps make the decision itself. A mentor once told me that if you are struggling to explain your ruling, it might mean you have it wrong. If there is a jump in legal reasoning as you work, it signals a need for greater research. Once I have an opinion drafted, I ask myself two primary questions: (i) is the outcome clear; and (ii) can a reasonable person understand the legal path to the decision?

As district court judges, we are providing a fundamental service to help resolve the human problems on display in our courtrooms. Considered use of the written word is a tool to do so effectively.

Was That Meant to be Funny? Humor in Judicial Writing

Stephen H. Locher
Judge, U.S. District Court, Southern District of Iowa

Judicial writing tends to be serious business. Depending on the court and case, you might be deciding if incriminating evidence should be suppressed in a gruesome murder prosecution, analyzing whether a statute requires someone to be sentenced to life imprisonment, or explaining why a parent's rights should be terminated. Hardly the time for jokes. Even in cases with less at stake, judges are usually explaining why one side wins and the other side loses, with the latter not terribly likely to be amused by a quip, no matter how clever. So should a judge *ever* try to be funny?

Reasonable minds can disagree, but I believe occasional attempts at humor have a place in judicial writing. Judges, after all, want to write in a way that is clear, engaging, and approachable. Humor—if judiciously employed—can help accomplish these goals. There are, however, certain rules that should be followed.

First, choose your time and place carefully. A sexual assault case, for example, is surely not the place for a witty aside. Nor is a case involving a long prison sentence, a victim who suffered a serious injury, or any other situation where someone has experienced trauma.

Second, just as you must consider your audience, you also must consider *yourself*. As in: are you a funny person? If not, it is probably best to stay away from attempts at humor in your judicial writing. Take Justice Elena Kagan—who is a funny person. She often sprinkles witticisms into her work, as she did in *Kimble v. Marvel Entertainment, LLC,* where she acknowledged the Supreme Court's authority to overturn well-established precedent but quoted Spider-Man (a Marvel character) to explain why such authority should be exercised sparingly: "[I]n this world, with great power there must also come—great responsibility." 576 U.S. 446, 465 (2015). Similarly, in *Kansas v. Nebraska,* Justice Kagan used several clever turns-of-phrase while analyzing a water rights dispute between two states, describing a brief détente as having failed because "there were more rapids ahead," noting that one side's argument "does not hold water," and explaining that the parties' relationship included complexities that "arise[] from water's . . . well, fluid quality." 574 U.S. 445, 452, 458, 467 (2015) (ellipses in original). The humor works for Justice Kagan because it comes across as natural, not contrived. She is not trying too hard.

Third, humor in judicial writing generally works best when it contributes to the flow of the decision and helps the reader understand the case. Consider the late Justice Antonin Scalia's discussion of the Second Amendment in *District of Columbia v. Heller*. The language of the Amendment is not a model of clarity, with a jumble of introductory clauses followed by the willfully insistent use of the passive voice: "A well regulated Militia, being necessary to the security of a free State, the right of the people to keep and bear Arms, shall not be infringed."

Prior to *Heller*, the Supreme Court interpreted the first introductory clause's reference to "Militia" as reflecting an intent to confer the right to bear arms only in connection with military service. Justice Scalia disagreed. In his view, the natural meaning of the words "the right to keep and bear Arms," as understood in the Founding era, conferred an individual right that did not need to be connected to military service. Justice Scalia recognized, however, that the words "bear Arms" also had an idiomatic meaning in the Founding era that *would* have been connected to military service. To explain his disagreement with a version of the idiomatic interpretation proposed by the dissenting Justices, he wrote:

> In any event, the meaning of "bear arms" that petitioners and Justice STEVENS propose is *not even* the (sometimes) idiomatic meaning. Rather,

> they manufacture a hybrid definition, whereby 'bear arms' connotes the actual carrying of arms (and therefore is not really an idiom) but only in the service of any organized militia. No dictionary has ever adopted that definition, and we have been apprised of no source that indicates that it carried that meaning at the time of the founding. But it is easy to see why petitioners and the dissent are driven to the hybrid definition. Giving "bear Arms" its idiomatic meaning would cause the protected right to consist of the right to be a soldier or to wage war—an absurdity that no commentator has ever endorsed. Worse still, the phrase 'keep and bear Arms' would be incoherent. The word "Arms" would have two different meanings at once: "weapons" (as the object of "keep") and (as the object of "bear") one-half of an idiom. It would be rather like saying "He filled and kicked the bucket" to mean "He filled the bucket and died." Grotesque.
>
> *Dist. of Columbia v. Heller*, 554 U.S. 570, 586–87 (2008) (internal citations omitted).

"He filled and kicked the bucket." *That's funny!* But it also serves the important purpose of explaining why, in Justice Scalia's view, alternative interpretations of a crucial phrase were grammatically unpersuasive.

Fourth, as Justices Kagan and Scalia illustrate, it is important to understand what "humor" means in judicial writing. It is not the slapstick humor one might find in a comedy movie, nor a riff on the absurdities of life like a stand-up comedian might use. Judicial opinions also are not the place for the setup/punchline structure you often hear in other contexts. ("An airline pilot, a college professor, and a grizzly bear walk into a bar…") Instead, effective judicial humor generally takes the form of Justice Kagan's plays on words or Justice Scalia's funny-but-illustrative explanations. They probably will not leave you rolling around on the floor in laughter, but they sometimes will make you smile while taking the edge off an otherwise dry subject—which, not incidentally, you might find yourself understanding better thanks to the lively writing.

For my part, I can only remember two times that I have intentionally tried to be witty when writing an opinion. The first was *Doe v. University of Iowa,* when I required the plaintiff to amend a prolix complaint that included, among other things, a single sentence running 178 words in length and a 443-word paragraph consisting of a "series of run-on sentences and sentence fragments." 2022 WL 4182196, at *3 (S.D. Iowa Sept. 2, 2022). After explaining that it was unfairly difficult for the defendant to respond to the complaint in its original form, I wrote: "Simply stated, the pleading needs more Hemingway, less Faulkner." *Id.,* at *4. Was I trying to be clever when I wrote that sentence? Yes. Did I also sincerely believe that Ernest Hemingway's writing style—with simple, concise sentences—is the model for drafting pleadings, particularly as compared to the often exhausting sentence structure of William Faulkner's work? Again, yes. My goal was not to be funny for the sake of being funny, but rather to illustrate what I wanted the plaintiff to do. And the message apparently landed: the amended complaint was much clearer and more succinct than the original version.

My second attempt to be witty was in *C.A. through P.A. v. Garcia,* when I had to decide whether Congress intended the phrase "medical assistance" to have a single, uniform meaning in a federal statute, or if the phrase meant different things in different places. In explaining why I thought it was the latter, I pointed out the incredible length of the statute in question, which contained "roughly 38,000 words and [ ] more than fifty subparts and hundreds (if not thousands) of sub-subparts." 673 F. Supp. 3d 967, 974 (S.D. Iowa 2023). To drive home just how long this was, I wrote: "If section 1396a were a book, it would be approximately as long as *The Lion, the Witch, and the Wardrobe* and considerably longer than *The Old Man and the Sea* and *Of Mice and Men.* Given section 1396a's incredible length, it is easy to understand why the phrase 'medical assistance'—which appears 280 times—might not have a single, uniform meaning throughout the statute." *Id.* Again, I confess: I was trying to be clever. In context, however, I also believed the reader would have a better understanding of how long "roughly 38,000 words" is if I compared it to the length of well-known works of literature. I wanted the reader to know that Congress did not write a statute, it wrote a *book*. No wonder the meaning of certain phrases changed from one "chapter" to the next.

Readers may not find my attempts at humor clever. They're probably right. I am steadfast, however, in my belief that humor can play an important role in judicial writing if used in the right times and places. All the better if it's genuinely funny.

Some Thoughts on Judicial Opinion Writing

Matthew C. McDermott
Justice, Iowa Supreme Court

How an appellate judge thinks about writing a judicial opinion often depends on the judge's ideas about the potential audience. A judge might assume, for starters, that the lawyers for the litigants in the case will read the opinion. The parties' lawyers have usually developed some expertise in the legal issues and are always assumed to have a deep fluency with the facts of the case. If judges wrote only for the lawyers in a case, opinions would probably look much different than they do, both in their length (since minimal recitation of facts would be necessary) and verbiage (since the audience would consist of expert insiders).

Having previously represented clients in cases before I became a judge, I know that the litigants themselves will ordinarily be interested in reading the opinion. The litigants in a case also tend to be familiar with the facts of their cases, often having lived through the events in some way. But as nonlawyers, they generally lack expertise in the legal doctrines in play.

Beyond the lawyers and clients, who else might be part of a judicial opinion's audience? The answer involves some speculation. With appellate opinions, lower court judges who must treat the opinion's holding as binding precedent in a sufficiently comparable case might be part of the audience.[1] In newsworthy cases, members of the media might not only read the opinion but need to summarize it for a general audience. Academic researchers in a subject involved in the case might be part of the audience. Members of the bar seeking to stay abreast of recent developments in the law generally, or in the legal issues in the case specifically, might be part of the audience. And in some cases, particularly in high-profile cases, members of the general public might be an audience.

My default is to attempt to write so that a nonlawyer party in the case—who I assume to be an adult of reasonable intelligence with the reading ability of a high school graduate—can understand it. This stereotype doesn't always hold. In criminal appeals, for instance, defendants often skew younger and sometimes under-educated, and thus even greater attention to simplicity in explanation becomes necessary. But in general, writing for an intelligent nonlawyer audience will usually satisfy the needs of most potential audiences too, including other lawyers and judges, the media, and researchers.

Despite requiring more diligence and time, attempting to write for a nonlawyer audience ultimately serves judges well. Perhaps counterintuitively, this is particularly true in cases dealing with technical subjects or arcane areas of the law. A judge's inability to explain a complicated subject in simple and concrete terms probably means that the judge insufficiently understands the subject. And if the judge doesn't really understand the case, the reader doesn't stand a chance. Writing for nonlawyers forces judges to grapple with a complicated concept to the point that the judge can reframe it in simpler language.

Writing style matters too. Professor William Popkin's research on judicial writing describes a divide between two stylistic camps.[2] On one side are the "authoritative" writers. These judges often employ a technical or professional voice, coming across as an expert in the internal workings of the law. These opinions are formal in tone and often heavy in legal jargon (including Latin words), long quotations, and string citations. Authoritative writing often includes words that have long appeared in legal writing but that you would never use in a conversation with your aunt or your nephew over lunch, such as "subsequently," "aforesaid," "moreover," or "such person."

On the other side are the "personal" writers. These judges often use a conversational style that seeks to minimize the gap between the judge and the reader through simpler and livelier prose. The writing is less formal, less solemn, and perhaps less pompous. Legal jargon is replaced with plain English whenever possible. Stilted phrases such as "prior to" are replaced with "before" and "subsequent to" with "after."[3] Contractions are common while footnotes, long quotations, and string citations are shunned.

In my view, judicial opinions written in a personal style are the most edifying to read, perhaps because they're also the most enjoyable to read. Although I'm still a long way from having perfected the personal voice as a writer, I strive for it in my own opinion writing.

This subject is not without controversy. Some commentators have criticized judicial writers employing the personal style.[4] These critics contend that a judge's conversational style can come off as glib or insufficiently serious-minded, particularly considering the stakes for parties in cases. These critics advocate that judicial opinions conform to a more restrained, institutional style.

As in most things, there's a balance to be struck. Deciding cases requires sober and serious consideration, and those attributes need to come through in any opinion. An informal style taken to its ultimate exaggeration could indeed leave a reader wondering. A judicial opinion necessarily has a certain form with certain boundaries. Opinions are not presented in the form of epic poems or comic strips or screenplays or cookbooks or instruction manuals or travel guides. Opinions most closely resemble in form a persuasive essay whose purpose is to explain why and how the court reached its decision.

A personal writing style does not preclude sober and serious consideration. Richard Rhodes, winner of the Pulitzer Prize for his scientific and historical epic *The Making of the Atomic Bomb*, derides the notion that nonfiction writers should avoid the power of animated prose in educating readers. Rhodes says that stripping a nonfiction text of its resonances and rhetoric doesn't make the text clearer; it just makes it deader. There is perhaps no more serious subject than nuclear war, yet I doubt any readers have come away from reading the book's lively prose questioning Rhodes's seriousness—about his writing or the subject.

When asked to define good writing, David Foster Wallace, a gifted writer of both fiction and nonfiction, gave this answer: "In the broadest possible sense, writing well means to communicate clearly and interestingly and in a way that feels alive to the reader. Where there's some kind of relationship between the writer and the reader—even though it's mediated by a kind of text—there's an electricity about it."[5] Writing well is hard work. Writing in an informal style—one that by design seeks to draw the reader in with its language and tone—can undoubtedly help judges better communicate with their audience, just as it has in other species of nonfiction.

A judge's writing process also matters. Many writing teachers advise that you prepare a written outline before beginning. Although I always have an outline *concept* in my head, I almost never prepare a written outline before writing an opinion. The cliché that "writing is thinking" holds true for me. The process of writing an opinion forces a confrontation with facts and law that clarifies and organizes my thoughts in ways that other preparation simply does not. Because this approach is how I operate best, I'm generally unable to prepare an opinion by editing a draft prepared by a law clerk. I'm aware of no cliché that similarly holds "editing is thinking." What's more, by the time I edit a clerk's draft opinion to state the facts and law as I contemplate them, I usually would have been better off if I had just written the first draft myself.

Bruce Springsteen has said that when he and his band begin a concert, they do so in a protective crouch, never sure at the outset that the ingredients will come together for a satisfying performance. As the show goes on and the crowd comes alive, the band loosens up and they come out of the protective crouch. There is a hint of this protective crouch when I'm starting a judicial opinion. At the outset, my goal is always to write an opinion as succinctly and simply as I can. Get in, explain the *why* and *how* of the decision, and get out. I write most efficiently when under a deadline, whether externally imposed (rarely) or self-imposed (typically). A writing trip that has little time for detours usually results in a shorter and cleaner opinion. Additions can always be made in later drafts if necessary.

I almost always start by writing the most limited scope of facts that will be necessary to apply the legal rules in play. The advice attributed to Chekhov that a loaded gun introduced in the first act needs to go off in the third act should have some currency with judges in stating the facts in an opinion. Mentioning a fact signals the fact's importance. When we ask readers to digest loads of facts but then never draw a connection between those facts and the legal analysis later in the opinion, we leave the audience wondering. Most judges (and I confess my own sins here) frequently venture far too deep into background narratives with pages of facts that have no discernable tie to why or how the court reached its decision in the case.

I then write the legal analysis. Whenever possible, I try to explain legal concepts in plain English. With so few people today having learned Latin, I'm puzzled by its continued appearance in so much legal writing. Legal writers would do well to obey Orwell's advice to "[n]ever use a foreign phrase, a scientific word or a jargon word if you can think of an everyday English equivalent."[6] We have instinctual comprehension of simple English words. Why would we say "*inter alia*" when we can say "among other things" or "*ab initio*" when we can say "from the beginning"? Sometimes the Latin term for a legal concept seems so ingrained in legal usage that its appearance is unavoidable.[7] But even when we need to refer to, say, *habeas corpus* or *res ipsa loquitur*, there's no reason we can't also explain what the term means for those who wish to understand our opinions but didn't minor in Latin or go to law school.

As I type my opinions, I have at my fingertips PDFs of the parties' briefs, a bench memo from my law clerk, my notes from my own reading of the briefs and other materials, my notes from the conference with the other justices, and any highlighted cases, statutes, or law reviews that I'd read. The rough draft I give my law clerk often notes places where further research is necessary. But beyond research, I also rely on my clerk as a sounding board for the draft's tone, organization, accuracy, sufficiency, and whatever other input my clerk might offer. After my clerk provides comments, I'll revise the draft and send it back to the clerk for further comments. This back-and-forth exchange continues until we have a document that we feel sufficiently good about it to circulate to the other justices.

I try to avoid using footnotes in opinions. Some nonfiction writers use them to great effect, adding to the power of the piece.[8] But I can think of few judicial opinions that have been improved much by their inclusion. If a particular comment merits inclusion in an opinion, then it almost always should be granted a seat on the main deck, not the boiler room, so put it in the main text. Part of my contempt for footnotes is simply the difficulty in reading them. Eyes must leave the main text for the bottom of the page, only to have to search back in the main text for wherever I left off.

I try to be mindful of the advice that Steven Spielberg is said to have offered a young director about filmmaking: never tell the audience the same thing twice. Sometimes that isn't practical or advisable, of course; some facts, for instance, are so important that they determine the outcome of multiple lines of argument in a case and thus demand repetition. But we as judges could do much better. Repetition invites the reader to skim—a skill judges learn quickly from reading poorly written briefs from parties, which sometimes revel in repetition. The last thing any writer wants is to compose skim-worthy material.

I usually save the opinion's introduction and conclusion for last. (If there is an introduction; sometimes starting straight with the facts sufficiently orients the reader without the need for a separate introduction.) I have wasted many precious hours by starting my writing with the introduction, only to come back after completing the rest of the opinion to find my introduction failed to capture what turned out to be a central property of the finished opinion. Also, I do not like to announce the result (affirmed, reversed, etc.) until the end of the opinion. As Judge Posner puts this point, when judges announce the result at the beginning, "the impression conveyed is that what follows is simply the rationalization of a result reached on undisclosed grounds."[9] Although I will have already determined the result, at least tentatively, before writing the opinion, I fear that stating the result at the outset can give the impression that the rest of the opinion is all just an effort to justify what has already been decided. The reader moves from a fellow traveler in exploring the factual and legal analysis, to someone pushed or pulled to see the correctness of the court's outcome. I think the reader learns and engages more, because more is asked of the reader, under an approach that waits to disclose the conclusion.

My court works on a September-to-June term system in which every case we take during the term is decided by the end of the term (in other words, by June 30). But beyond this backstop of a deadline, we know that our job involves deciding real cases for real parties. We thus work hard to get opinions out as reasonably promptly as possible so the parties can get their decision and move on to whatever comes next. Regardless of whatever else an opinion might be destined for—precedent for a future case, the basis for a newspaper story, research for a student note in a law review, or perhaps none of these things—one hopes that any reader grasps both that the court cared deeply both about the soundness of the decision and the quality of the writing that delivered it.

The Parallels Between Legal Writing and News Reporting

Mary E. Tabor
Chief Judge, Iowa Court of Appeals

Aside from serving as a judge, I view my time as editor-in-chief of *The Daily Iowan* newspaper as my finest professional achievement. After that college experience, I worked as a reporter for United Press International and then the Associated Press before entering law school. So it follows that, to this day, when I'm sorting through résumés from law-student applicants, if they worked as a journalist, they hop to the top of the stack. Many attributes drive that affinity. Like judges, journalists face deadline pressures and strive for independence. But most importantly, they both tell people's stories.

Speed Versus Precision

True, the urgency of the storytelling differs between news and law. Journalists pride themselves on reporting breaking stories as fast as possible. Judges are more deliberate. Yet the adage "justice delayed is justice denied" motivates courts to decide cases as expeditiously as possible. Which brings me to the first of my five parallels between journalism and judging: the trade-off between speed and precision vexes both professions. How should judges strike the balance? Here's my suggestion: Sweat every detail while drafting an opinion, then develop a tolerance for imperfection.

An example stands out from my newspaper days. My crew was covering a big downtown fire. Our reporters and photographers were on scene overnight to capture the story. Bleary-eyed, we dashed off the copy and met our deadlines. Only the next morning did I see the caption on the front-page photo: "Firefighters distinguish the flames." Obviously, it was supposed to say "extinguish" the flames. A glaring error still emblazoned on my brain. But this far removed, I give myself some grace. The important part was that we told the story, even with flaws.

The same is true today. As much as I try to thoroughly research, deftly analyze, and competently proofread, I later find silly mistakes in my judicial decisions. Our high caseload contributes to the pressure. Indeed, the mission of the Iowa Court of Appeals is to "dispose of a high volume of cases justly." It is inevitable when our court is issuing more than one thousand opinions per year that a few errors will slip through the editing process. But the cases must be resolved—and the stories must be told—sooner than later.

Besides, endless tinkering isn't guaranteed to improve judicial writing. Consider this memorable scene from the movie *Six Degrees of Separation*. Donald Sutherland's character asks his child's second-grade teacher why all her students are geniuses with finger paints. "Look at the first grade—blotches of green and black, the third grade—camouflage. But the second grade—Matisses, every one. You've made my child a Matisse. Let me study with you. Let me into the second grade, what is your secret?" The teacher replies: "I don't have any secrets. I just know when to take the paintings away from them." Knowing when to stop editing is an art unto itself.

The Inverted Pyramid

From timing to structure, the second parallel I see between the j-school lesson plan and judicial writing is reliance on the inverted pyramid. One of the first things budding journalists learn is to go top-heavy with their writing. A good opening paragraph strives to answer the who, what, where, when, and why of the story. Sir Harold Evans, former editor of *The Times* of London, agrees these questions must be answered, "but not in the lead, which demands a short, sharp sentence carrying a maximum impact with a minimum of phrase." In his book, *Do I Make Myself Clear*, Evans recognizes the evolution of communications: "Cyberspace is indulgent, but attention spans are shorter. We appreciate conciseness." Today, the derisive verdict, TL;DR, may doom online articles.

But print journalists have long tried to deliver their key points up front. And the best lead may feature a tantalizing quote or an enticing detail to keep the reader reading.

In the world of judicial decisions, legal-writing guru Ross Guberman suggests four possible openings: (1) "the teaser" (a short brisk statement of the issue before the court leaving resolution for later in the text); (2) "the trailer" (a narrative that grabs the reader's attention and parades key facts still leaving the outcome unresolved); (3) "the sound bite" (a compressed statement of the issue and outcome); and (4) "the op-ed" (a free-form thought piece on the legal issues before the court, complete with answers). True to its journalistic name, the fourth option comes closest to the classic inverted pyramid. And it's my favorite opening when drafting a decision. Like news consumers, readers of legal opinions appreciate conciseness.

Here's an example of an op-ed opening from the 2017 case of *State v. Retterrath*:

> Sex acts, vengeance, and castor beans. After digesting salacious testimony offered by prosecution witnesses on these subjects, a jury convicted Mark Retterath of sexual abuse in the third degree, solicitation to commit murder, and attempted murder. Retterath appeals the three guilty verdicts, challenging the sufficiency of the evidence and alleging a number of errors by the trial court.

> When viewing the proof in the light most favorable to the State, we find substantial evidence to support the convictions for sexual abuse and solicitation to commit murder. But because the State did not prove Retterath performed an act that met the statutory definition of assault, we reverse and remand for dismissal of the attempted-murder count. We find no grounds for reversal in Retterath's remaining issues, though we do remand for an in camera review of the counseling records of two witnesses whose credibility was critical to the State's case on solicitation to commit murder.

This opening tells who (witnesses, jurors, and the defendant), what (sex acts and castor beans), when (at trial), where (the courtroom) and why (vengeance). The whole story emerges from these two paragraphs. While the parties will likely travel down to find details at the tip, casual readers will learn all they need from the bottom of the pyramid.

Attention to Tone

From timing to structure to tone. The third parallel between journalism and judicial decisions is the risk of disparaging the people in the stories we're telling. In my first year of j-school, Don Henley had a popular song on the radio called "Dirty Laundry" bemoaning the callousness of tabloid journalism. The lyrics described an anchor making "a living on the evening news. Just give me something I can use. People love it when you lose.

They love dirty laundry." The chorus repeated: "Kick 'em when they're up. Kick 'em when they're down. Kick 'em all around." The careful reader of this essay will stop here and say: "Wait? Aren't sex acts and castor beans sensationalized details?" Fair question. But my advice is not to sanitize the facts. Stories are not told well without any color or depth. Legal readers will not understand why we reach our results if our opinions whitewash the events. Rather, I am advocating for something more nuanced: Tell their stories without dehumanizing the people who end up before the courts. During my years on the bench, I have been lucky to work with talented staff attorneys and law clerks who aren't afraid to warn me if the tone of a decision is too harsh. Nothing good comes of tearing people down gratuitously. Parents whose children are removed, criminal defendants convicted of crimes, quarreling siblings in estate cases, angry spouses getting divorced, disgruntled parties to a contract, feuding neighbors in property disputes. Few parties in our appeals are having their best days. Better not to kick 'em when they're up, and especially not to kick 'em when they're down. Being sensitive to people's struggles will strengthen a judge's writing and decision making.

Maintaining Objectivity

From timing to structure to tone to objectivity. The fourth parallel I see between journalism and judging is the enduring importance of staying objective. Just after I left journalism and went to law school, a book came out called *The Journalist and the Murderer* by Janet Malcolm.

Malcolm questioned the ethics of journalist Joe McGinnis, who wrote the book *Fatal Vision* about Army doctor Jeffrey MacDonald, who was convicted for killing his pregnant wife and their two daughters. During MacDonald's criminal trial, McGinnis lived with him and convinced him they were friends. After McGinnis published his scathing book, MacDonald sued him for fraud, alleging the journalist—to maintain access—had pretended to believe in his innocence long after concluding that he was guilty. One takeaway from Malcolm's critique is that the image of the objective reporter doesn't hold up. In her words, "Every journalist who is not too stupid or too full of himself to notice what is going on knows that what he does is morally indefensible. He is a kind of confident man, preying on people's vanity, ignorance, or loneliness, gaining their trust and betraying them without remorse." Even if Malcolm's provocative hypothesis is overstated, it aptly warns of the ease of slipping into dodgy relationships with sources.

By contrast, judges don't rely on interviewing sources. The raw material for our storytelling comes from court records. But the loss of objectivity remains a danger. Judges have a responsibility to maintain the public's trust by evaluating those factual records and the applicable law from a neutral standpoint. When I transitioned from assistant attorney general to appellate judge, I worked hard to stop looking at cases through a pro-prosecution lens. And I still try to communicate through my writing that our court is operating from an impartial position—not reflecting our past careers nor beholden to any benefactors. Easier said than done in this political climate. Indeed, recent polling shows public confidence in our nation's highest court is at an all-time low. And that distrust trickles down to state courts. But like journalists trying to deliver on the promise of fair reporting, judges need to keep practicing objectivity in their decision making to preserve the rule of law and preserve public trust.

Avoiding Arrogance

As a fifth and final parallel between my judicial writing and my days at *The Daily Iowan*, I would point to the need for humility. We had a couple self-deprecating mottos for the newspaper. First, "All the News That Fits We Print." (Of course, a take-off on *The New York Times* slogan "All the News That's Fit to Print.") Second, "If It Happens It's News to Us." Which is still my favorite t-shirt. Both playful puns underscore the value of not taking yourself too seriously. Journalists who realize that they don't have all the answers will ask better questions.

The same is true for lawyers and judges. Often in oral arguments I will remind myself of the quote attributed to Mark Twain: "It is better to keep your mouth closed and let people think you are a fool than to open it and remove all doubt." But then I throw caution to the wind and ask a question anyway. I feel better about this habit after reading *Doing Justice*, a book by former U.S. Attorney Preet Bharara. He discusses "the utility of dumb questions" and suggests that "curiosity and query" ensure getting to the right answer. I wholeheartedly agree. No doubt, sometimes a dumb question is just a dumb question. But often revealing my stupidity will prompt the lawyers to clarify their positions. And that clarification will help the court reach the best result. I recognize the irony of quoting Shakespeare after warning against arrogance, but the bard said it best: "The fool doth know that he is wise, but the wise man knows himself to be a fool." In that spirit, the best judges will channel the curiosity of journalists.

Chapter 12

Being a Good Colleague

Disagreeing Without Being Disagreeable

Gina C. Badding
Judge, Iowa Court of Appeals

"You can disagree without being disagreeable."[1] This quote is often attributed to Justice Ruth Bader Ginsburg, who once said the United States Supreme Court was the most collegial workplace she had. And it perhaps explains why she and Justice Antonin Scalia were close friends despite their sharply different ideologies. I've had the same collegial experience on the Iowa Court of Appeals, and I think it's because all of us understand the importance of being able to disagree with one another without being disagreeable.

Before being appointed as a judge on the Iowa Court of Appeals, I was a district court judge presiding over my own busy docket. While I often talked through tough cases with my colleagues, the final decisions were my own—a sometimes lonely endeavor. That all changed once I became a judge on our state's intermediate court.

Our court of nine judges decides cases in three-judge panels. One judge is assigned to author the case, with the other two left to concur or dissent. While concurring is the norm, dissents happen. And even concurrences sometimes require compromise. The result is a better opinion and a closer relationship with my fellow judges, who are willing to share their opposing viewpoints with me.

One of the first opinions that I authored as a judge on the court of appeals was a criminal case with a tough evidentiary issue. I started a draft to affirm the district court before changing my mind and writing the opinion to reverse. After I circulated the draft—our term for notifying the panel members that the opinion is ready for their vote—I received an email from one of the other judges on the panel. The email very thoughtfully explained why that judge disagreed with me, before offering to write a dissent if I was committed to a reversal. I wasn't. The points my colleague raised were the same that had led me to think about affirming in the first draft. Seeing my initial reasoning laid out in that judge's email made me rethink my position and rewrite the draft to affirm.

Reaching out to the authoring judge with points of disagreement—by email, phone, or Zoom—is something that all of us on the court do routinely. Jumping to a dissent before discussing the points of disagreement would, in my view, lead to hard feelings and weaker opinions. Each of us, of course, strives to produce the best opinion that we can. And having differing viewpoints involved in the drafting process helps get us there.

In my almost three years on the court, I have started around six dissents but filed none. Some of my dissents turned into the majority opinion, while other points of disagreement were addressed by the authoring judge in a way that garnered my agreement. This collaborative process is key to the success of our court. I always value the insight of my colleagues, taking their questions and comments seriously. I rely on them to spot weaknesses in my analysis so that we can reach the right result for the litigants before us based on the applicable law and facts. Being open to a discussion about how an issue might be resolved differently is an important part of the process—and something I learned from one of my mentors on the court, Judge Anuradha Vaitheswaran. She has such an ability to see the strengths on each side of an issue that she would sometimes write both the majority and dissenting opinions. I think that is the mark of an exemplary jurist because to get to the correct answer, you must be able to understand where the other side is coming from.

Beyond our court's willingness to talk through disagreements with one another, we make it a point to get together outside the workplace. We take walks together after work, and we arrange fun outings for our court staff—baseball games and bowling parties. Maybe most importantly, we have monthly dinners together where work is seldom discussed. Instead, we talk about what books we've been reading, the latest Netflix show that's gripped our attention, our travel plans, and how our families have been. We know each other's partners, children, and grandchildren. And we care about what's happening in one another's lives. I always knew my court family was there for me, but that was never more apparent than when my father passed away last December. He went into the hospital the weekend before our court was scheduled to hear oral arguments, and we knew that he would not be coming home. I called our chief judge, Thomas Bower, on the phone from the hospital waiting room to tell him what was going on. I was worried that I wouldn't be able to attend the arguments that week, where I was scheduled to hear six cases. Without hesitation, Judge Bower told me to stay with my family, and he would take care of things at work. He and another one of my colleagues then covered my cases that week on top of their own—a kindness that I will never forget.

I am fortunate to be a part of a court that values collegiality because it allows us to have open and honest dialogues with one another despite our different backgrounds, experiences, and philosophies. Some of us were trial court judges. Others were government attorneys or defended insurance companies. We are spread across the state, with a few living in small, rural towns like me and others living in larger, metropolitan cities. Yet we listen to each other, appreciating the viewpoints each of us brings to deciding cases. Even when those viewpoints lead to different opinions, we are agreeable in the disagreement. As Scalia said when a former law clerk questioned him about sending two dozen roses to Ginsburg for her birthday, even though she rarely voted with him in split decisions, "Some things are more important than votes."[2] So true. The friendships that I have with my fellow judges—the respect, kindness, and support that exist among us—are the most important part of our daily work on what we like to call the court of collegiality.

The Best Colleagues

Thomas N. Bower
Former Chief & Senior Judge,
Iowa Court of Appeals

When I was asked to pen an essay for *The Book of Judges* I thought, "What a great idea…and I wonder why a book like this hasn't been written before." It is certainly a book I would have sought out to make myself a better judge, colleague, and person.

Initially, I was enthusiastic about participating, but as the submission deadline approached I began to feel uneasy. Would my background as a judge and pseudo-supervisor give me suitable material to draw from on the topic of "How to be a Good Colleague"? But having served on the Iowa Court of Appeals for 13 years (five as the Chief Judge), where I continue to work in a part-time capacity, two years on the Associate Court, and 16 years as a District Court Judge in and for the First Judicial District State of Iowa (two as Chief Judge), I realized my biggest struggle would be what to share—or maybe more correctly, what not to share. The challenge would be choosing from an abundance of material.

For those less familiar, the Iowa Court of Appeals is considered by many as the most collegial court in Iowa. Even though we review cases in three-judge panels in search of a majority—or unanimity—we try to do so with the utmost respect and good humor. In my experience, the Iowa District Court for the First Judicial District is also composed of many collegial and professional people.

To complete my assignment, I wrote down the names of many of the colleagues who'd had an impact on my views on what makes a good colleague—and honestly, I added a few who were not good colleagues as well. Of these 40 or so people, I completed a sentence or two about each and then tried to distill down those characteristics for this essay.

Before I share the characteristics of a good colleague or a collegial person, however, let's try to define the term collegial. Some people believe the terms cordial and collegial are synonyms—I do not. To me cordial means being friendly and courteous with others to some degree. Being collegial is understanding "the mission" and approaching the mission with unity and cooperation. A good colleague can be both.

Understand the Organization and Yourself

First, understanding the organization you are a part of or hope to become a part of is essential. It is my firm belief that unless you have a good grasp of the organization, including its parts, subparts, and goals, you may struggle to be a good colleague. I also believe nobody is born to be on the bench or born to be a leader. Sure, you may be intelligent, a hard worker, and possess other attributes which many judges and leaders share. But I believe your climb to the bench or leadership is a result of understanding the organization and learning from those who helped shape you into the person you have become. Hopefully, everyone reading this knows who Fred Rogers (Mr. Rogers) was. If not, please do some research. Mr. Rogers's thoughts were simple but profound. He reminded us that few people can remember who won the World Series, the Super Bowl, or even the gold medal at the most recent Olympics, but everyone can remember those who helped guide or shape them in pursuit of their aspirations. I can easily name 20 people going back more than 50 years who helped shape me. Whether it is your parent(s), sibling(s), spouse, children, coworkers, teachers, or friends, many have played a role. Take a moment and think of those people and how they helped. Also, your role in the organization and the organization itself are not static; both will change. However, change is not needed simply for change's sake. But adaptation is essential to becoming or remaining a good colleague.

Understand the Other Side

Next, to be a good colleague you should be able to see and understand the other side of an argument, position, or policy even though you may disagree. A good colleague doesn't have to convince others they are wrong and they are right—it is okay to have a difference of opinion. Maintaining your position without throwing havoc into the organization and isolating yourself or others as a result is extremely important. If you later determine your position was correct, the worst thing a good colleague can do is celebrate their shallow victory. We should remember that the body of law a judge relies upon is the result of people who disagreed on things. A collective approach to resolving problems generally results in a better outcome and everyone feeling as though they contributed. A good colleague is not an autocrat. If you have such a personality, please find another profession.

Solutions-Based Colleague

Be a solutions-based colleague. Many colleagues are quick to point out problems in an organization, but few bring with them solutions to the problem. Having assumed several leadership positions throughout my life I can assure you someone who complains about issues without some type of solution can be exhausting and at times burdensome. For example, maybe within your organization there is a staff member who easily gets bogged down or there is something within the organization causing a kink in the smooth flow of the work product. Going to your colleagues and identifying the problems is the easy part. Coming up with solutions is the hard part. A person who presents a problem with a variety of solutions allows everyone to be a part of the decision making. Also, be patient when complaining. Remember, sometimes problems that are resolved quickly may not be what is best for everyone and the organization. Your concern will often resolve itself without intervention. As a trial judge once told me, "Sometimes the best decision is no decision at all." In other words, be patient, if possible.

Slow to Criticize

In a related area, be slow to criticize others and if you must, remember your audience. It is a difficult colleague who goes public in the organization with criticism when only a few people need to know. Criticism is rarely appreciated but constructive criticism delivered in an appropriate way with the appropriate audience may reap rewards. Think back to how you felt when someone criticized or disparaged your idea or thought in a large group or in an inappropriate or aggressive manner. The humiliation you felt, and that others likely felt for you, is still palpable. Always remember your audience. That thought not only applies to your organization but in life. Certainly, some of the things you might say in front of your friends are not the same as you would say to colleagues. In my opinion, little good ever comes from public criticism.

Understand There Is a Place for Kindness

I found that colleagues who showed kindness helped me be a better colleague. These colleagues were from varied backgrounds with many different talents and strengths. Colleagues who were kind not just to each other but to litigants, staff, and the public seemed to be the best. You might be the smartest person in the room, but you are unlikely to be the smartest person in the organization. Those who can show their intelligence while understanding their colleagues and help others solve problems will go far in their career. Remember that no matter how insignificant a case or problem is before you, it is the most important thing to those who will be impacted by your decision. One need not be cruel, degrading, or mean-spirited to show how smart you are. Kindness can help soften the blow to those who are adversely impacted by your decision.

Build Consensus

Being able to build consensus is another characteristic of a good colleague. You may think a judge only has to decide that one case before them, and thus wonder why they need to be a consensus builder. Building consensus helps you and the organization grow. It allows everyone to feel a part of the organization and encourages participation. Building consensus takes time and patience. It is impossible to build consensus in your organization if you always work alone or without input from others. Being able to convey your thoughts and build consensus is a good way to encourage others to participate and know that their ideas are important and valued. After all, the concept of stare decisis is based largely on consensus.

Give Credit to Others

Don't be afraid to give others credit for what might have originally been your idea. After all, it is more often the collective members of the organization rather than the individual that lead to collegiality. When given the opportunity to lead organizations from my time in retail before law school to being the chief of the court of appeals, I truly tried to give others credit when good things happened, and take the blame when bad things occurred. I always tried to follow what President Harry Truman once said: "The buck stops here." I know it goes against much of how we are raised and develop, but it worked for me. It allowed colleagues to have confidence in their thoughts and ideas. Remember, those in the organization will likely recall whose initial idea it was.

Commit to the Organization

Another good characteristic is committing to the organization. There are many positions in the legal profession or any organization that may require you to refine your skills before you are recognized or qualified for another position. Using one position to acquire another might be what is necessary in the long run for your goals, but understanding and working towards a common goal or outcome in the organization you are currently working in should always be your primary focus. Not only should you understand the organization, you should also understand the people within it. This should not be limited to those in your office or on your team. Please try to understand the macro-organization, not just the micro-organization. An organization is made up of many people. Recently many have tried to magnify our differences, but a good colleague recognizes our similarities. Most people I have worked with over my entire legal career of almost 40 years are good people. How about taking a few minutes and getting to know these folks, their interests, and their goals. I have always been of the belief that if you want to have a conversation with someone just ask them about themselves. Obviously, those questions should not be overly personal. I have been "accused" by a dear colleague of being able to talk to just about anyone, and I suspect he is right. I believe that engaging with others even outside your organization will be both personally and professionally rewarding. Finding the similarities and differences in people will help you become a colleague who is understood and respected. In this area I think of the example set by the late United States Supreme Court Justices Ruth Bader-Ginsburg and Antonin Scalia. The former was thought of as a liberal and the latter a conservative. However, they often went to the opera and the symphony together, and shared many non-legal interests. Although their judicial beliefs were often at odds their human interests were similar. Certainly, you don't need to hang out with others to make the organization better, but be aware and embrace the differences and similarities we have.

Be Kind

You may think from what you have read that one must be kind and empathetic to be a good colleague. Although those characteristics can help a person, many of my great colleagues could be a bit "in your face" at times. However, they are not "in your face" all the time. In my opinion there is a time and a place to be brash and aggressive, but those should be for short periods and quickly forgotten. Over the years I remember having those moments when I felt I needed to be a little aggressive to make my point, but I was never mean-spirited. In looking back, I really don't remember the particulars of these aggressive conversations. Although passionate about my point I don't believe I was ever nasty. Sure, you can be brash and aggressive all the time, but what is the cost to you, others, and the organization?

In closing, I want to thank all my colleagues over the last several years for hopefully making me a better coworker and more importantly, a better person. I also want to thank Jeff Goodman for approaching me regarding this project, and for his encouragement in assuring me that I had something to offer. As my number of years left in the profession lessens, seeing what is important and best for the greater good is even more vital to me. I challenge you to be a mentor, a leader, a person who can help others be their best. Be the person who engages with the custodian and not just the partners, say hi to the cashier or maybe offer just a simple smile. All of those things help. Please don't always be about what is best for you. Implementing some or all my observations is one of many steps to making you a better colleague and adding to the overall success or your career and organization.

Those Were the Days

Michael J. Moon
Judge, Iowa District Court (Ret.)

I spent my undergraduate days at the University of Iowa in the mid-1960's. The dark cloud of Vietnam and the draft cast its shadow over my senior year. In the second semester of that year, I enlisted in the Army on the delayed entry program. That committed me to three years of active duty instead of the two-year stint for draftees. The advantage was putting off the inevitable for several months while giving me options for special military training.

Upon graduation in May of 1968, I went to work at Collins Radio in Cedar Rapids. I was able to delay reporting for active duty until October 31, 1968, and tested well enough to go to the Army Intelligence School in Baltimore and the Defense Language Institute in Washington, D.C. I once boasted that I could say "Don't shoot, I am your friend" in seven different languages. I was discharged from the Army three months early to enroll in Drake Law School. After graduating and passing the bar, I was finally poised to begin my legal career. My first day on the job as a brand-new attorney was June 17, 1974.

I thought I would impress the partners on my first day by showing up early. I pulled into a full parking lot at 7:30 that morning and found that all of the partners had been at their desks for some time. I was welcomed by everyone and then shown to my office. I vividly remember one of the partners stopping by that morning just to say, "Remember, the practice of law is first and foremost a business."

I spent my first day sorting through a stack of files with memos attached to get a rough idea of what I was being asked to do and the nature of the legal issues involved. When 5:30 eventually rolled around I straightened my desk, turned out the lights and headed toward the door. I quickly noticed that all of the attorneys were still working. I sheepishly retreated to my office and waited until I heard people actually leaving the building. I heard one of the senior partners remark to another, "I'll see you back here tonight." I soon learned that we worked long hours each day and that Saturday mornings were a regular working day.

The second day I was taken to the courthouse by John Veldey, an old friend from the University of Iowa whom I had met at Donnelly's Pub in Iowa City in 1962. As it turned out, I had attended church camp with his wife in the mid 1950's—small world. John introduced me to each official in the courthouse as well as the members of their respective staffs. He also took me to the basement where I was introduced to the maintenance staff. We then went to the Sheriff's Office, where I met the Sheriff, several of the deputies, and the jail staff. I remember John saying that these were the most important people I would work with as an attorney and that they were all to be treated with courtesy and respect.

John's sage advice was spot-on. Over the years, I learned firsthand how important it was to have a good personal and professional relationship with those people. As an example, our office was corporate counsel for Lennox Industries. We represented Lennox in collective bargaining, and from time to time there would be a strike. The picketing UAW members occasionally blocked the entrances to the manufacturing plant, thereby bringing business to a halt. It was probably just coincidental that blocking the gates usually occurred after the close of business on a Friday. Under ordinary circumstances, that would preclude seeking legal redress until the courthouse opened the following Monday.

George Fagg, the resident judge, however, worked on Saturdays, and granted us a temporary injunction. And as our firm had an excellent relationship with the Clerk of Court and her staff, she graciously opened her office on Saturday to allow the filing of the petition for temporary injunction, the court order, and directions to the sheriff for serving the injunction. None of this would have been possible without relationships built on mutual trust and respect. I dare say that quality of service would not be obtainable in today's legal environment.

The rest of my first week was spent researching and learning how to dictate to a secretary who sat across from me on a straight chair with a legal pad and pencil. On Friday afternoon, Rex Ryden, a senior partner, brought a probate file to me with a fee order attached. He directed me to take the order to the courthouse the following Monday during order hour (8:00 a.m. to 9:00 a.m.) and get it signed. I had no idea what to do, so I asked John. He said to take the order to the courthouse, obtain the court file from the Clerk, then take the order and court file to the judge and explain what the order was and how much we were requesting for fees. Once signed, I was to file the order and return file-stamped copies to the office. I figured that if I could take apart and reassemble an M-14 blindfolded, I could do that. After all, I knew where the Clerk was, I had met the employees there, and I had a Post-it note with the amount of requested fees.

That Monday was a pleasant summer day, so I packed my brand-new briefcase with the office file and headed to the courthouse. I stopped at the Clerk's office and got the Court file then went to the visiting judge's chambers. There was a line of distinguished-looking gentlemen holding briefcases and court files of varying colors in the hallway outside the door.

Fortunately, the attorney at the end of the line was Les Smaha, whom I had met at the University of

Iowa in 1963 and with whom I had consumed a beer of two over the years. We chatted a bit as the line slowly progressed, and Les introduced me to the other attorneys standing in line. It was yet another invaluable opportunity to meet my colleagues and begin establishing professional relationships, some of which would last for decades.

Fortuitously, Les was also there for a fee order. Now all I had to do was follow his example. I listened carefully as Les presented his order to Judge Ed Kelly, who was from Ames. I later found out that he had the reputation of being rather gruff and ornery. He also had had his larynx removed because of throat cancer, and communicated by belching his words. No one had informed me about that, but I quickly got a feel for his speech pattern and could understand him.

Les handed his order to Judge Kelly and informed him that all heirs had signed receipts and waivers, all statutory requirements for closing the estate had been met, and the fee requested of $2,250.25 was the statutory fee. Judge Kelly said everything seemed to be in order and then said, "I approve your fees in the amount of $2,250 and *no* cents." I thought that was strange but certainly being no fool, I went to school on that bit of information.

I went into chambers next and introduced myself. I presented the court file and the proposed order. Judge Kelly asked me what the fee was, and I told him it was $1,750.25, but that we would waive the $0.25. Judge Kelly looked at me and then looked at the order and said, "Fees approved in the amount of $1,750." He then looked up at me and said, "And 25 cents." That was my first court appearance.

This story, however, is not so much about Judge Kelly as it is the attorneys who were there for orders. Mondays were known as "court service days," which provided attorneys with an excellent opportunity to visit with each other, sit and chat, and of course, tell stories while we waited for our hearings or orders. We all got to know each other and learn about each other's families.

Those days, unfortunately, are gone, taking with them the sharing of stories that represent an integral part of our history. Our legal folklore is replete with extremely interesting stories not captured in official court records.

I recall attorney Harry Druker telling the story of his representation of a Marshall County man on a criminal charge of theft. The defendant had been accused of stealing his neighbor's chickens, which in the late 1930's and early 1940's was tantamount to taking food off the table of the neighbor and his family.

Listening to Druker tell this story, which he did often and with high drama, I had vivid images of early black-and-white movies with courtroom scenes—*Twelve Angry Men*, *Inherit the Wind*, *To Kill a Mockingbird* and the like.

The trial lasted a day and a half. The judge asked the jury if they had reached a verdict, and the foreman acknowledged that they had. The bailiff took the verdict from the foreman and gave it to the judge. After reading it to himself, the judge looked over his spectacles at the defendant, then returned the verdict form to the bailiff, who handed it to the foreman. The judge then inquired, "Mr. Foreman, what is your verdict?"

"We find the defendant not guilty," came the reply.

Unfortunately for the defendant, who was an older man, the words were lost in the cavernous Marshall County grand courtroom. He turned to Druker and asked, "What did he say?"

The judge heard the question and replied in a loud voice, "Sir, you have been exonerated!"

The defendant, obviously perplexed, turned back to Druker and asked, "Exonerated—does that mean I have to give those chickens back?"

A more recent Marshall County anecdote involves attorney Barry Kaplan, who was trying a divorce case in front of Judge George Fagg. Suddenly the Court Bailiff, Duane Johnson, who had served in the Navy during World War II and had a military bearing such that he was affectionately call "Sergeant Major," entered the courtroom and proceeded in his military fashion to the front of the bench, stood at attention and announced, "Sir, the President of the United States is on the telephone for you." Judge Fagg excused himself and returned to the bench a few minutes later. Without explanation, he asked his court reporter to read back the last question and answer, then proceeded with the trial. We all later found out that he had been appointed Judge of the United

States Court of Appeals for the Eighth Circuit by President Ronald Reagan.

Three and a half years later, Barry was trying a divorce case before Judge David R. Hansen. The proceedings were interrupted by the Bailiff, who announced that the President was on the telephone. It was President Reagan again, who informed Judge Hansen that he had been appointed Judge of the United States District Court for the Northern District of Iowa. Judge Hansen was later appointed to the Court of Appeals for the Eighth Circuit by President George H.W. Bush, and in 2002 became the Chief Judge of that Court.

The good luck of having Barry in your courtroom was not yet over. Barry was trying a case in the Sixth Judicial District before Judge Mary Chicchelly in 2021. Again, the proceedings were interrupted by a telephone call for the Judge. This time it was Iowa Governor Kim Reynolds, who informed Judge Chicchelly that she had been appointed to the Iowa Court of Appeals. Unfortunately for those judges aspiring to higher office, Barry has retired.

Druker's vignette and Barry's experiences are both part of the legal culture that is now in danger of being lost as attorneys seldom communicate with one another on a personal level anymore, let alone take time to tell stories.

We enjoyed a certain camaraderie in the old days when we interacted face to face, which was evident in the ways we helped each other out from time to time and extended professional courtesies to each other. Most of the younger attorneys in Marshall County, for example, when confronted with a particularly complex title issue, had no problem seeking advice from Ed Adams, who was an attorney and owner of Central Abstract Company and old when I met him in 1974. Ed would take time out of his day to visit about the issue and give advice. Further, if you went to his office for any reason, you were treated to stories about the practice and a fair amount of Marshall County legal history.

Today there is also a stark disconnect between members of the bar and the judiciary. We simply do not know each other like we used to. I was the presiding judge in Story County and scheduled to take a guilty plea from a defendant who had been charged with burglary in the third degree, a Class D felony. The court attendant opened court and commanded all in attendance to rise. I was astonished when I looked down to see who would be participating in the hearing. I knew my court reporter Jane, of course, who was with me from the day I was sworn in until my retirement. I also knew the court attendant and jailor. But that was it. I did not know the people in the back of the room and to my surprise, I did not know either the prosecutor or the defense attorney.

As I addressed the defendant, though, I recognized him. I had sentenced him to prison years earlier. Therefore, of the three major players in this hearing, the only one I knew was the defendant.

Practicing in a rural county as I did, I had many cases in adjoining counties, and Marshall County was ideally located for contact with attorneys from other judicial districts. In those days, court proceedings were not conducted by electronic means but were held in person. The beauty of that was that I met attorneys face to face with whom I had cases all over the state. Positive relationships developed from that type of contact. Certainly, there were a few obstreperous attorneys who had neither the time nor the inclination to sit and chat, but those were few and far between. I found it difficult to be a jerk to an attorney whom I knew on a personal level, and I am sure this is true of others.

Marshall County's geography was also ideally located for local attorneys to become acquainted with judges in adjoining districts. During a lunch break on a court service day in Tama County, I wandered into the Maid Rite. I did not notice Chief Judge William Eads of the Sixth District sitting at a table by himself, but he spotted me and asked me to join him. Judge Eads had the reputation of being somewhat eccentric and standoffish, and I wondered what I was about to get myself into.

Any qualms I had quickly subsided. Judge Eads and I talked about our career paths and learned a little bit about each other. I soon discovered that he took great pride in his grandchildren. He carried pictures of them in his wallet, which he showed me. Thereafter, whenever I saw Judge Eads I would ask him about his grandchildren. He would smile and show me their photos, all to the chagrin of opposing counsel.

Not all contacts with nonlocal judges were as positive, however. Barry Kaplan and I had the first trial assigned to Judge B.C. Sullivan in Marshall County, who was there as part of the yearly exchange program. It was a routine divorce case with no child issues, just property division and alimony. (The kinder and gentler term "spousal support" was not in vogue then.) All litigants and counsel were seated in the courtroom and ready for trial. The court reporter entered and said that the judge wanted to see counsel in chambers.

Judge Sullivan remained seated as we introduced ourselves. He did not introduce himself or extend a hand. Rather, he said, "I do not know who represents the husband, but he has a tough row to hoe in this case." I represented the wife and perked up at this statement. Barry was taken aback. The Judge then added, "I would suggest that you talk to your client about paying alimony and get this case resolved."

"Judge," Barry said, "I believe you have judged this case without hearing the evidence. I would like to make a record regarding your statements. The Iowa Supreme Court has held that—"

He was cut off in mid-sentence by Judge Sullivan. "Young man, I do not give a damn what those people in Des Moines have to say! If they want to come here and listen to this crap day in and day out, they are welcome to do so. Until then you must deal with me. I will tell you for the last time that your client will be better served if you get this case settled."

The case settled. Word quickly spread about this encounter on the first day of a five-week term with Judge

Sullivan. An inordinate number of motions to continue quickly followed.

As much as attorneys swapped stories, much of the legal oral tradition was kept alive by district court judges. They were generally older individuals who had been raised in the community where they presided, or at least had spent their professional careers in those counties. Today, with electronic filing and hearings that are conducted via Zoom, telephone, and other non-personal means, the storytelling judges can do is greatly diminished. This is especially true since judges have become physically isolated by security measures that prohibit anyone from going into their chambers without first passing through a series of secure doors, locks, and security personnel. Gone are the days, for example, when a visiting judge would be interrupted by a resident who would suddenly appear unannounced in chambers and ask where he could renew his boat license or pay property taxes!

I do not mean to cast aspersions on electronic filing, courthouse security, or the modern way of transacting legal business. These are necessary developments and have certainly enhanced efficiency. My only concern is that we must not lose sight of what has occurred in the past, as our tradition is rich and full of fabulous stories.

My thoughts on the subject can be summed up with this final story. There was a hog farmer in Marshall County who raised somewhere around 5,000 hogs per year, farrow to finish. As he got older, he decided to turn the farming operation over to his son, who had a degree in Ag Business from Iowa State University. The old farmer kept a hand in the business, though, and had the final say in business decisions.

The son wanted to introduce artificial insemination into the business as the means of propagation of the herd. The old farmer was against it but did agree to attend a seminar at Iowa State on the topic. He spent the day listening intently to the presentations and at the end of the day the moderator, who knew the old farmer, asked if he had any questions about the process or the program. The old farmer thought for a while then said, "No, I think I understand everything you're saying, but you know, I think I prefer the old-fashioned way better and I'm damn sure the hogs do, too!"

I am not advocating a return to doing legal business the way we did 50 years ago. Like all professions, the practice of law must change with the times. Personally, though, I prefer the old-fashioned way, when there was time and opportunity for everyone, from clerks to bailiffs to attorneys to judges, to get to know each other better, and in some cases, to cultivate professional relationships that spanned one's career. Those were the days.

How Empathy Made Me a Better Colleague

Shawn R. Showers
Judge, Iowa District Court

I have been fortunate to work with outstanding colleagues. Most are friends and mentors. The best colleagues can teach while they listen. It is an excellent skill to possess. Good colleagues are humble. They share resources. A great coworker is generous with his/her time and respectful of others' time.

Being a good colleague to all who work in or with the Iowa Judicial Branch will always be a paramount goal for me. To achieve this goal, it is essential to show appreciation for everyone's contribution in the justice system, from buildings & grounds staff, clerks of court, court administrators, law enforcement, court reporters, schedulers, litigants/defendants, county employees, attorneys, fellow judges, court attendants, jurors/prospective jurors, and so on. This is vital to the administration of justice.

Empathy is one of the most important judicial qualities. The best judges I know are innately, remarkably empathic. Genuine people care a great deal about and for others. It is as the adage goes, "Don't judge a man until you have walked a mile in his shoes." A good colleague considers his fellow judges and coworkers' thoughts and feelings. A great colleague prioritizes them.

Chris Ware, a cartoonist, said: "There is absolutely no single aspect of one's personality that is more important to develop than empathy, which is not a skill at which men typically are asked to excel. I believe empathy is not only the core of art, literature, and music, but should also be at the core of society, from ethics to economics."

Great mentors of mine, such as Iowa's Eighth Judicial District Chief Judge Myron Gookin, Senior Judge Michael Schilling, and Senior Court of Appeals Judge Mike Mullins, have led by example in several pivotal ways, with the first being listening (and hearing). But additionally, these skilled judges possess marked empathy.

As a new and youthful-looking judge, these experienced and respected judges' simple act of listening was immeasurably valuable to me. Their generosity in listening to my questions and their wise counsel bolstered my confidence as a new judge and assisted in the transition from non-judge to judge. The message for any new judge is clear: "You belong and your opinion matters."

Judge Mullins's office was next to mine when I became a judge. He has always taken the time to ask how I was doing and talk to me about various subjects. The world can be a lonely place for a judge. Very few have the honor of experiencing this adjustment. Judge Mullins understood this, and his door was always open for professional questions and discussions, or just to have another human being in the Washington County Courthouse to have a conversation with.

Being a good colleague can also mean saying yes, even though your life is hectic. My children were very young when I became a judge. In my first full month on the job, I was presiding over a jury trial. During the late night/early morning hours prior to the second day of trial it became clear that I was ill and would not be able to make it the 53 miles from Washington to Ottumwa.

It was very early. I messaged Judge Joel Yates, another great mentor and friend. Without Judge Yates's support and encouragement, I never would have had the confidence to become a judge, or even apply. He is also a notorious early bird so I knew he would be up. We talked on the phone, and I told him the situation. Judge Yates was an experienced judge, and when he took the bench, he and his wife were the parents of six-month-old triplets. He understood. He had empathy.

Judge Yates called Court Administration for me and managed the situation. He prioritized my situation and drove to Ottumwa that day. I will always appreciate this more than I can explain. From the beginning, the other judges I work with demonstrated what being a good colleague was. Empathy was not an abstract concept; it was actively on display.

We live in an instant gratification culture. The new reality is an immediate response in both our home and work environments. When another judge simply offers to cover your work queues while you are in a lengthy trial or away from the office, that is what being a good colleague looks like. After I was appointed, former Chief Judge Mary Ann Brown wisely assigned Judge Gookin to be my mentor. I am forever grateful to both for this. Judge Gookin showed me how to use our judicial interface computer system, allowed me to shadow him on a busy court service day, and, like Judge Mullins, is always responsive to my questions.

The Iowa Code of Judicial Conduct, Rule 51:2.5 (B) requires, "A judge shall cooperate with other judges and court officials in the administration of court business." Comment 3 of this rule states:

> Prompt disposition of the court's business requires a judge to devote adequate time to judicial duties, to be punctual in attending court and expeditious in determining matters under submission, and to take reasonable measures to ensure that court officials, litigants, and their lawyers cooperate with the judge to that end.

The Judicial Canons are rules that all judges are obligated to abide by. Judges and attorneys live by statutes and rules. But, just like the litigants, jurors, and lawyers, judges are just human beings. Judges have weaknesses and bad days. The black robe does not inoculate us from mistakes. It is common to feel overwhelmed by the weight of decision making. I have observed other judges, despite the challenges of vicarious trauma fatigue, operate at remarkably high levels during cases.

It is easy to become jaded and cynical in this career. Much of a trial court judge's time is spent presiding over child custody disputes, domestic abuse allegations, family feuds involving money, and serious criminal matters, from burglary to sex abuse to murder. I have observed burnout and annoyance in the Iowa Judicial Branch.

But the sense of duty, oath, and empathy from my colleagues, such as Judge Gookin, Judge Schilling, and (now-retired Judge) Lucy Gamon, provides motivation for me to embrace this challenge and obligation. I learned from these mentors that ensuring a litigant's day in Court is the most sacred and fundamental commitment we have. To fairly judge, applying the facts of the case to existing law equally to all litigants, requires careful judicial restraint. But that does not equate to losing our humanity and empathy.

In Iowa, a full-time judge must retire at the age of 72. Judges may continue as senior judges. Judge Michael Schilling is as intelligent, both intellectually and emotionally, as any person I have ever met. He is an extremely wise mentor to other judges and attorneys. I sensed that

Judge Schilling's transition from full-time to senior judge weighed on him. We were working on a presentation for the local Eighth District Bench Bar Conference. It was a great opportunity for me to learn from Judge Schilling what being an elite judge meant.

I really got to know Judge Schilling during this time. I marveled at his commitment and the care he took in making decisions. Judge Schilling's retirement party was packed with the people whose lives he had impacted. This included not only his family and coworkers, but the participants in his drug treatment program, community members, and at least one man he had sentenced to prison. They came and when he identified everyone by name, it was because he cares.

This is a difficult job, but we all signed up for it because we were called to serve. The combination of legal scholarship and intellectual curiosity does lead many to the law and bench. Judges pledge to uphold the Constitution and laws and administer this application equally to the rich and the poor. Logical thinking, keen legal interpretation, and hard work are obvious qualities good judges possess.

But we serve the citizens of our communities. I believe the public expects judges to bring their humanity to the bench. This obligation can be overlooked when we are bogged down in pedantic or menial tasks. While judges are restrained by what the law permits us to rule or order, the way an empathetic judge approaches the task and interacts with those in the justice system leaves a lasting mark.

Chapter 13

Judicial Philosophy

Why Having a Judicial Philosophy Matters

David L. D. Faith II
Judge, Iowa District Court

I am not the most obvious person to write about judicial philosophy. I am not a Supreme Court justice or a law professor or someone who regularly has to grapple with undecided constitutional issues. I am a district court judge in a mostly rural district where my decisions are more often rooted in factual specifics than in ruminations on historiography.

Therefore, a question may fairly be asked, do I even need a judicial philosophy? Indeed, should I have a judicial philosophy? It is a fair question. I have met judges who profess not to have a judicial philosophy and who regard the whole concept as suspect. While I do not doubt their sincerity, I think we may be talking about different things. Judges who disclaim judicial philosophy tend to regard the concept as a form of bias and therefore anathema to the impartiality required of our profession. I think having a judicial philosophy does just the opposite. It is a conceptual framework for interpreting the law that, if rigorously and honestly applied, helps prevent judicial biases of all kinds.

Having a judicial philosophy matters to me because it provides an intellectual scaffolding that serves the same purpose that physical scaffolding does in construction. That is, it provides a support structure on which to hang my mental tools and offers a stable platform to ensure I do not become unbalanced and fall off. In this case, to fall off means allowing my intuitive biases of how things ought to be to lead me to inconsistent and unjust results. In the absence of a judicial philosophy any attempt to simply "decide each case on its merits" will inevitably degenerate to applying my personal likes and dislikes to the facts and law in any given case.

The concept of implicit bias has become so widely accepted that Iowa's model jury instructions include an admonition to jurors about it. In every jury trial I instruct the jury that everyone, including me, has hidden or implicit thoughts, generalizations, gut feelings, prejudices, fears, sympathies, stereotypes, or inward and outward biases. Jurors are told that they must disregard such gut feelings and decide solely on the basis of the facts and the instructions of law I provide. My instructions of law help the jury stay objective. The jury need not decide intuitively what they feel is right; they just need to follow instructions. But who instructs the instructor? What helps a judge to apply the law in a way that avoids allowing sometimes unconscious feelings to corrupt the impartiality of the process? The answer, again, is judicial philosophy.

To illustrate I'll use my own judicial philosophy since that is what I am most familiar with. My judicial philosophy is what is commonly referred to as textualism, or sometimes "original public meaning." This is a fancy way of saying that in interpreting any legal text, whether constitutional, legislative, or contractual, I seek to decipher the meaning by looking first to the text itself. What do the words, fairly understood, actually mean? It is the specific words chosen, after all, that reflect the political compromise or contractual agreement between the people who wrote those words. Moreover, it is how the people who agreed to the words would have understood them that matters, not their subjective motivations or my feelings about what the words should mean. This shields me from my own biases. As with the jurors following my instructions, it does not matter what I think the law ought to be; all I need to do is follow instructions (i.e., the reasonably understood contemporary meaning of the words).

To be clear, no judicial philosophy is a panacea. This includes my own. Legal texts are often ambiguous or fail to anticipate certain circumstances. To further extend the analogy, the instructions are sometimes missing a page. In those situations, I have to reach for other interpretive tools like extrinsic evidence to try and fill the gap. If I can find objective evidence of, for instance, legislative intent that is consistent with the words actually written then I may be able to expand the meaning to unanticipated scenarios. But the further I stray from the text the greater the risk my own prejudices will color my decision. I am accordingly cautious to distinguish between applying the words as written to unanticipated scenarios, a core judicial function, vs. re-writing the words through interpretation, which intrudes into the proper realm of legislatures, constitutional convention delegates, and contracting parties.

Since the discussion so far has been on a largely theoretical level, it may be helpful to illustrate how this plays out in a specific case. I recently had to rule on a motion for summary judgment that centered around the interpretation of a written subrogation clause. The clause in question included language waiving any claims the parties may have had against each other to the extent covered by the proceeds of certain types of insurance. Those types were defined in another section of the contract to mean builder's risk policy or any other property or equipment insurance in force for the project. The issue was whether a commercial general liability policy that paid out in that case fell within the meaning of the subrogation clause. Following my intuition, I would have said it probably should. But the words as written failed to address a commercial general liability policy or whether this would have been reasonably understood to be included within the meaning of "other property or equipment insurance" in force for the project. I therefore concluded the meaning of the words written was facially ambiguous and therefore subject to extrinsic evidence not yet available at the summary judgment stage, and accordingly denied the motion. It is possible that extrinsic evidence might show that the contracting parties would have understood the "other property or equipment insurance" to include commercial general liability insurance, and thereby fill in a gap in the written language, but the evidence was not there yet. Following my judicial philosophy prevented me from going down the rabbit hole of interpreting the contract according to what I feel it ought to mean and thereby overstepping my proper role as the interpreter and not the maker of that contract.

The savvy reader will note that what I have described as judicial philosophy is, in contract cases, simply an application of precedent. Indeed, the principles of textualism are embedded into long-standing precedent regarding how contracts should be interpreted, i.e., first applying the unambiguous meaning of the text and then (and only then) looking to extrinsic evidence to find what the contracting parties meant. This is not controversial and yet when you apply the same principles to interpreting statutes or constitutions it may become so. This has always seemed odd to me. If hewing to the contemporary understanding of written words makes the most sense when interpreting a contract why should the same principles not apply when interpreting law? Applying textualism to interpretation of law keeps the judge grounded in the proper interpretive role of seeking to understand what the drafters understood their writing to mean in exactly the same way it does when interpreting a contract.

While I have made a pitch for the judicial philosophy I believe is most correct, I do not contend the benefits of having a judicial philosophy are limited to my own. Any philosophy of judicial interpretation, if honestly and rigorously applied, provides the judge with a standard against which to measure the consistency of his or her interpretations of law. It allows the judge to ask, "is this correct, according to standard," as opposed to "does this feel right?" The former ties the judge to the role of interpreter of law whereas the latter invites a judge into the role of lawmaker or, worse yet, king. Solomon may have had the wisdom to rule by moral intuition. I do not.

I started this essay by saying I am not the most obvious person to write about judicial philosophy, but that should not be the case. It should be obvious that every judge, at every level, should have a judicial philosophy because judicial philosophy is just the term we use for any consistent approach to interpreting legal writing—something every judge does for a living. James Madison famously said that "if angels were to govern men, neither external nor internal controls on government would be necessary." One might just as easily say that if judges were angels, then no judicial philosophy would be necessary. Since we are not angels, holding ourselves to the standard of a consistent judicial philosophy keeps us honest. The single most important promise I made when I decided to become a judge was to render equal justice before the law. My judicial philosophy helps me keep that promise.

Your Judicial Philosophy is a Work in Progress

Roger L. Sailer
Judge, Iowa District Court

A foolish consistency is the hobgoblin of little minds, adored by little statesmen and philosophers and divines. With consistency a great soul has simply nothing to do. He may as well concern himself with his shadow on the wall. Speak what you think now in hard words, and tomorrow speak what tomorrow thinks in hard words again, though it contradict everything you said today.

~ Ralph Waldo Emerson, *Self-Reliance*

Many esteemed judges, scholars, and other great thinkers have penned their lofty thoughts through the years on the subject of judicial philosophy. Every one of those minds is far greater than mine, and I do not presume to believe that I might spar with them here. However, I do have my own humble ideas about "having" a judicial philosophy and how one might approach the subject, and I intend to offer the somewhat radical suggestion that having a judicial philosophy may actually be more of a detriment than an asset.

Now, to be clear: In the narrow, literal sense, there is certainly great importance to having some sort of judicial philosophy from which to begin, as opposed to a legal professional who gives the matter no thought whatsoever. That person is floating rudderless and lacks not only direction to know where he or she is going, but also lacks any landmarks or sources of navigation to even know where he or she is at any given time. Do not misunderstand me to be advocating for such an approach, which would result in a scattershot application of ideas and would render a person, at best, like the broken clock that is right only twice per day by happenstance.

The problem for me is that to speak of "having" a judicial philosophy suggests that one has settled upon and adopted some sort of fixed framework, whether legalistic, philosophical, political, or otherwise, within which one operates when rendering judicial decisions. The temptation for a new or aspiring judge is to browse through the various ideas that are floating about and to treat them as a sort of catalog, selecting those ideas that seem most sensible or appealing, perhaps even mixing and matching, in order to create such a framework for oneself, and then to apply it in practice. I believe this approach is wrong-headed because a sound judicial philosophy must be grounded in experience and real-life utility.

I submit that to declare, "I have a judicial philosophy," particularly at the outset of one's judicial career, is to take a bold step down the road toward the land of dogmatism, where concepts and ideas become the ends rather than the means, leading to blind application and foolish consistency in the face of real, substantive problems and issues. Anyone who travels that road may as well stop thinking and "may as well concern himself with his shadow on the wall," as Emerson put it.

In order to be effective judges and attorneys, we must never lose sight of the fact that we are resolving the real-life problems of the real-life people standing before us, to whom the issues matter greatly. The ultimate purpose of the law itself, at least in my view, is to allow citizens to order their affairs and conduct them with repose, knowing what the parameters are, and to protect those who might be wronged at the hands of others who might violate those parameters. This is a profound, nearly sacred trust that is placed in our hands as judges every time we put on our robe or pick up our pen. This is not an abstract intellectual game or an interesting exercise in legal theory, which it can too easily become in the hands of a dogmatic judge adhering to his or her "judicial philosophy."

In my view, what is truly beneficial, indeed essential, is not for any of us to say, "I have a judicial philosophy," but instead for all of us to firmly commit ourselves to the ongoing process of developing a judicial philosophy and, most importantly, to firmly commit ourselves to continuing that development throughout our careers in the law, conceding that there is no endpoint to the process at which we might rightly proclaim to "have" a judicial philosophy. It is a truism in life that the more we learn, the more we realize how much we still have to learn, and the realm of judicial philosophy is no exception.

Consider for a moment the long-entrenched legal principles of "Ripeness" and "Standing." With few exceptions, courts in general refuse to consider or decide any matter that is not a "real controversy in interest" brought by "real parties in interest." These concepts are based on solid principles. To consider an issue hypothetically, in a vacuum, may have certain benefits. But it is not generally conducive to the creation or administration of good law. Likewise, to consider one's "judicial philosophy" in the abstract, even if based upon good scholarship and sound reasoning, is not generally conducive to making sound judicial decisions. It is only in the crucible of real controversies, brought by the real parties in interest with significant issues in their lives hanging in the balance, where one's judicial philosophy is tried, tested, and forged, only to be retried, retested, and reforged again and again in the same crucible.

In the sports world, there is a common adage that "iron sharpens iron," which means that only by continually pitting ourselves against the stiffest competition available can we hope to develop to our full potential. The same is true, in my opinion, with respect to one's judicial philosophy. Only by pitting ourselves against real-world controversies, in which we confront the sometimes horrific clash of mutually exclusive but equally meritorious claims, can we hope to eventually develop a sound judicial philosophy in the moment. And only by continuing to do so over and over again, acknowledging and accepting that our thoughts tomorrow may be entirely different, can we hope to see our judicial philosophy develop into the kind of genuine, deep, mature, and nuanced understanding of legal decision making that we strive for, and which might even eventually approach the ultimate goal of "wisdom" from the bench. "But what about *stare decisis*?" you might ask. And rightly so. Consistency, in and of itself, is a fundamental and essential aspect of the law, and here I sit advocating against it. To that question I give two answers.

First, do not confuse consistency in the law with consistency of personal thought or philosophy. Consistency is important in the law itself because it is essential to achieving the law's ultimate goal, as discussed above, of allowing citizens to order their affairs and conduct them with repose, knowing what the parameters are. If the parameters are constantly shifting, there can be no repose. The citizens cannot know what the parameters are and the law fails miserably in its fundamental function. In such a circumstance, there might as well be no law at all and one could reasonably argue that there isn't. But that is an entirely different matter from seeking consistency for its own sake in our thoughts and philosophies, which would necessarily include a corresponding resistance, or even outright refusal, to evolve, adapt, improve, and mature our legal thoughts and mental frameworks.

Second, I would point out that Mr. Emerson's caution in the quote above, and my caution in this essay, is against "a foolish consistency." A general policy of upholding the precept of *stare decisis* in order to provide consistency in the law has solid underpinnings and cannot be said to be a "foolish" consistency (unless it reaches untenable extremes, and our law has the necessary provisions to recognize such a circumstance as foolish and to correct it). Whereas in the realm of judicial philosophy, there is nothing at all foolish about seeking consistency of thought, particularly across boundaries of issues, but adherence to consistency for its own sake closes minds rather than opens them and has a sneaky way of becoming foolish rather quickly and easily and the perpetrator is always the last to detect it.

We should, in my opinion, avoid being "little statesmen, philosophers and divines" who adore foolish consistency by adopting and clinging to a "judicial philosophy" that we treasure but which comes with the danger of ruling us rather than serving us. We should, rather, embrace a process of judicial development that continually leads us to ever-greater wisdom in our decision making, even if that means that the "hard words" we speak today may be different from "tomorrow's truth."

But all of this begs the obvious question of how to go about it. Obviously, we should be reading and thinking. If you are a legal professional—judge, attorney, or otherwise—and you have never given serious thought to the broader ideas of judicial philosophy, you should get busy thinking and reading about it. There is no shortage of excellent material, written over the course of centuries, that is easily accessible to all of us in this digital information age. There are books and essays galore from judges, legal thinkers, and philosophers both ancient and modern. There are restatements of the law, written by legal scholars, that go out of their way to explain the reasoning behind the law and delve into the pros and cons of alternative legal ideas.

There is also, of course, a never-ending stream of appellate court opinions in every jurisdiction, and it is not difficult to find the ones that wax poetic on issues of judicial philosophy. For an attorney or a trial court judge such as myself, I strongly suggest that it's an excellent idea for all of us to become familiar with the judicial philosophies of those who sit on the appellate courts in our own jurisdictions. As we read the opinions that are handed down on a weekly or monthly basis, rather than skipping to the "nuts and bolts" of the ruling, we should perk up our ears and pay attention when they turn philosophical. This is not only useful in a practical sense to know how our own decisions are going to be received and reviewed from above, but it is also an invaluable tool in formulating our own ideas, whether we agree or disagree with what's written.

However, as I've hopefully convinced you above, all of this reading and thinking in the abstract should be only a starting point, not the formative point. The formative point should come as we practice in the crucible of real-life cases. And in order to do this, we must practice purposefully and mindfully. As we grapple with the facts and the law of a given case, we must constantly keep an eye toward the larger questions, such as "why?" and "what do I think about that?"

We must purposefully build habits that lead to our philosophical development as legal professionals. We all deal with the application of legal rules every day, whether they are constitutional, statutory, or judicially created. As we do the everyday work of interpreting those rules and applying them to the facts in front of us, we should build the habit of constantly questioning their underpinnings.

Build the habit of asking, "What are the policy reasons for this rule? What was it put in place to foster or prevent?"

Build the habit of considering alternatives to the rule and whether they would be better or worse than the rule we have.

Build the habit of testing the rules by considering extreme applications: "What if [x] happened? Would this rule still hold, or would sticking with it become foolish?" I use this technique often in my own rulings to test legal arguments offered by the attorneys. Great insight can often be gained by asking, "If what this attorney is saying about the law were accepted as true, what would that lead to under other facts that are more extreme or more difficult?"

Build the habit of broadening your view to consider not only your own role in the legal machinery, but also the roles of others. As a trial court judge, consider the roles of the attorneys, the roles of the appellate courts, and the roles of the other branches of government. This can have profound implications with regard to judicial philosophy. Are you improperly legislating from the bench? Are you improperly performing an appellate function through your own interpretation of the law? Are you improperly performing an executive function when deciding cases in which government entities are parties?

My father used to say, "Successful people build habits." I believe that these habits of broadening our view of the daily work in front of us are the key to the successful development of sound judicial philosophy. Thoughtful consideration of the "whys and wherefores" of the rules leads to better application of them and also provides a solid basis of support if and when you should decide to depart from them.

So, "speak what you think now in hard words, and tomorrow speak what tomorrow thinks in hard words again, though it contradicts everything you said today." When faced with a difficult decision, relish the opportunity for growth. Do not fear inconsistency or confuse growth with inconsistency. Make the best decision you can in the moment as you are presently equipped to make it. Then move on, wiser for having faced it, and continue to grow and make better decisions.

Consider the possibility that some day you may be a litigant (or, God forbid, even a criminal defendant). Who would you rather have decided your fate? The judge who has followed this prescription of fearless personal growth and purposeful evolution of thought for years? Or the judge who declared at the outset of their career, "I have a judicial philosophy!"?

Developing and Applying Your Judicial Philosophy

Samuel A. Thumma
Judge, Arizona Court of Appeals, Division One

Introduction

"Judicial philosophy" can mean many things. For a supreme court nominee, it may mean an approach to interpreting the law, invoking originalism, textualism, living constitutionalism, pragmatism, or even calling balls and strikes. But for most judicial officers, their judicial philosophy is different and more basic. It is less abstract, and more gritty. Particularly for a busy trial judge, it is more about how to best get through a bloated daily calendar. For an appellate judge, it may be more about how to plow through ponderous briefs that misstate the record and avoid hard legal issues.

Building on my experiences as a state trial and intermediate state appellate judge, this article advocates developing and applying a judicial philosophy. More accurately, I highlight ten judicial philosophies that have helped me. Judicial philosophies are wildly personal, so what follows are examples based on my experiences, errors, and successes, showing why having a judicial philosophy matters.

Ten Judicial Philosophies That Have Helped Me

1. Be candid and honest.

I began my judicial journey as a trial judge on a juvenile rotation. I knew nothing about juvenile law, having spent more than 15 years in civil litigation in private practice. And the brief juvenile training I had didn't stick. But then someone gave me the keys to the courtroom and basically said, "Don't mess it up." Gulp.

My first juvenile court hearings started with me telling the lawyers and parties that, although I thought I was a quick learner, I did not yet know juvenile law and asked them to keep that in mind. I then paused, not quite knowing what to expect. But three things seemed to follow: (1) an almost audible sigh of relief from the lawyers, who knew juvenile law; (2) me not betraying anything (it quickly would have been obvious that I did not know juvenile law even without my disclaimer); and (3) some immediate credibility and trust by the attorneys given that I was being candid with them. I've tried ever since to be candid and honest with counsel and the parties.

2. Let the hearing come to you.

In another early case, I read the filings, saw the issues, and identified a resolution before I took the bench. To speed things along, as I called the hearing, I summarized things, suggested a resolution, and waited for someone to compare my wisdom to Solomon. Wrong. I quickly learned that the parties, in the hallway before the hearing, had agreed to a far better resolution. Now, nearly 20 years later, I recall spending the rest of the hearing trying to get the parties *back* to their far better hallway resolution, and I think we got there. But it would have been far, far better if I had let the hearing come to me.

I am not suggesting judges should allow parties to run hearings, endure filibusters, or cede control over the courtroom. But serving as a judge presiding over a hearing is (and should be) very different than being an attorney advocating at a hearing. There is great wisdom and value to not think as a judge that you have all the answers. As a judge, it is important to let the hearing come to you.

3. I want to get it right. And I want to do it once.

All good judges want to get it right and, when another court says we made a mistake, we feel bad. But I also try to resolve issues so that, if another court rejects one basis for a ruling, I will not need to revisit things on remand. If there were several possible reasons for a ruling, I could stop with the first one and leave the others unresolved. If I was correct, that would be just fine. But if I was wrong, and I got reversed, I would have the "privilege" of addressing the other reasons a year (or more) later, long after my memory had faded. In juvenile court, that could mean that children may have been avoidably in foster care during that time. In criminal court, that someone was in custody longer than they should have been. So particularly where multiple reasons supported the same conclusion, I learned to address them all in my ruling. And on the appellate court, I continue to generally follow this approach. I want to get it right. And I want to do it once.

4. Everyone has a right to a level, calm judge presiding over their case.

Juvenile court was where I heard the most matters in a day; the largest calendar I remember was 37 hearings one day. It was a time management exercise. I was delighted to have the attorneys appear before me. But there was the occasional sharp and pointed hearing. If that was the last hearing of the day, fair enough. But if a sharp hearing was early in the calendar, I needed to get back to a level, calm place within seconds before I called the next hearing. That took real effort, and I cannot say with confidence that I always succeeded. I did, however, work hard to do so. And I know that I did better by realizing that everyone has a right to a level, calm judge presiding over their case.

5. Every litigant has a right to think that their case is the most important case you will hear.

I was in trial most every day while serving on a criminal rotation. When that happened, I needed to finish with my pretrial calendar (pleas, sentencings, motions and other non-trial hearings) by 10 a.m. so my trial defendant, who almost always was in custody, could be dressed into civilian clothes and trial could start back up by 10:30 a.m. If that didn't happen, my trial participants (including the jury) would wonder why they were waiting and why I was wasting their time.

In the middle of a murder trial that had as many complications as I could imagine, we had what I thought was a manageable pretrial calendar. I was wrong. A victim spoke for nearly an hour about a physical injury that could be viewed as minor. I struggled, and likely failed, to be patient. But the victim's statement was critical to and for her. I learned from that. And I tried my best to recognize that all participants have a right to think their case was the most important case I will hear.

6. Cases have numbers but are about people.

Serving as a trial judge is dealing with the human condition. You see crying, furrowed brows, puzzled squints, and other emotions almost every day. The interactions are raw, with instant reaction and feedback. That is less true as an appellate judge. The communication is largely one way, through written opinions, often without oral argument. Seldom do I interact with the parties on appeal.

Particularly as an appellate judge, on my best days, I work hard to remember what I experienced as a trial judge. That effort does not, I hope, alter my view of the legal merits. But it does, I hope, influence the tone and language I use, how I address the parties' arguments, and how I phrase things, particularly in ruling against a party. I always try to remember that cases have numbers but are about people.

7. Less is (or at least generally can be) more.

I could never figure out when, for example, I wrote a lengthy decision as a trial judge, including weighing and assessing conflicting evidence, why about a year later I would receive an equally long appellate decision doing similar work affirming what I did without apparent struggle. Given that experience, as an appellate judge, I try to have the length of my decision reflect whether the appeal is comparatively easy (aka short) or hard (longer). There are exceptions, of course, including appeals by self-represented litigants who struggle with the law. But this approach also furthers my view that, for every additional word used in a decision, the possibility of ambiguity or error increases, even if just by a bit. For these and other reasons, I firmly believe that less is (or at least generally can be) more.

8. Consistency is important.

These days, for decisions where I am the primary author, I get drafts from several sources: my recent law school graduate law clerks; externs who are law students;

staff attorneys who have been with the court for years, and me (and, yes, I do draft some of my decisions). Each drafter brings their own experience, education and perspectives. And they all have at least somewhat different approaches, different go-to authorities, and different views of the world. When I am the primary author of a decision, it is fair to expect that I will use the same general approach, not varied and different approaches depending on who was the initial drafter. I recognized that expectation pretty early on, and I work to make sure that my final decisions use the same approach, no matter who prepared the original draft. Not infrequently, this takes substantial additional time to make sure I do so (what I call "Thumma-izing" a draft). But the effort is worth it in my attempt to reflect that consistency is important.

9. The abuse of discretion standard is the best friend of both the trial judge and the appellate judge.

As a trial judge, I always tried to know when I had discretion and then apply it. I am positive those rulings were the beneficiary of the deferential abuse of discretion standard of appellate review. Now, as an appellate judge, I appreciate that the deferential abuse of discretion standard of review is much more forgiving than the de novo standard of review applicable to legal issues. I also know that the abuse of discretion standard on appeal is not "what would Sam do?" Instead, it focuses on whether the trial judge's ruling was within a zone of reasonableness.

Correctly applied, this deferential standard of review honors the challenging role of a trial judge in weighing disputed evidence, determining credibility, and making judgment calls. It reflects that factual disputes are resolved in trial courts, and that appellate courts review issues for legal error. It also means that I have affirmed, on an abuse of discretion standard, rulings I never would have made as a trial judge. In these respects, I firmly believe that the abuse of discretion standard is the best friend of both the trial judge and the appellate judge.

10. People have to respect the judicial office, but a judge must earn respect.

People stand when a judge enters the room, use honorifics, and usually show deference to a judge in and outside the courtroom. They respect the judicial office.

But there is a difference between respecting the office and respecting the person holding the office. I do my best to earn the respect of the individuals that appear before me. It takes a lot to earn that respect, which is the way it should be. And in many ways, an individual judge is only as good as that judge's worst hearing, meaning respect earned over years can be lost in minutes. That's scary and daunting. But I try, every day, to remember that people have to respect the judicial office, but as an individual judge, I need to earn their respect.

Conclusion

These ten "judicial philosophies" are based on my experiences, errors, and successes while serving as a state court trial and appellate judge. Although they are wildly personal, they have served me well. I hope that they will help others develop their own, best judicial philosophies. There is no doubt that having a judicial philosophy matters.

Chapter 14

Persistence and Perseverance Pay Off

Einstein and the Sanity of Relentless Pursuit

Mary E. Chicchelly
Judge, Iowa Court of Appeals

Albert Einstein once said, "The definition of insanity is doing the same thing over and over again but expecting different results." These words hold true for many things, but they miss the mark when discussing the judicial application process in Iowa. If you hope to become an Iowa judge, persistence is not just sane, it is essential. In fact, most who have pursued the bench here had to apply multiple times. Persistence and perseverance are, for better or worse, an integral part of this journey.

I have no recollection of exactly when I first thought about becoming a judge. Since my early childhood, growing up in a family of attorneys, I always knew I wanted to be a lawyer. My dad was the head of the legal department at a large casualty insurance company, and three of my older siblings followed him into the law. As a result, from when I was young, the stories around our dinner table were lively and intriguing and involved terrible things happening to good people. The world was turned upside down, and through a child's eyes, I saw lawyers as capeless superheroes who helped right it again. For me, choosing to be a lawyer was less a decision and more just a commitment to an ideal set forth by my ancestry.

As I viewed it, the law was a well-trodden path, and the journey along that path was interesting, dependable, challenging and comforting all at once. For years, this chosen route provided a wealth of experience, accomplishment, and a reliable income. But there came a time when the path began to feel too easy and too safe, as though what I had garnered from this path demanded more from me in return. I knew I was serving my clients well, but I began to ask if that was enough. I felt the pull to serve the greater good—to try to improve justice from the other side of the bench. I never had a "magical moment" or epiphany so much as there were these nagging thoughts, accompanied soon after by numerous gentle nudges from judges and other lawyers, suggesting I "toss my hat in the ring" for district court openings.

In 2011 I deviated from the safety of what I always thought would be my professional trajectory, and I applied for a district court opening. Right off the bat I was a finalist, which I saw as a sort of validation. And while validating at first, it was no less crushing when the governor did not select me. If you are good at what you do, chances are high that you almost always enjoy success. Here I was at the top of my professional game, and I had been told I did not have what it took to get the job.

Or had I? As I thought about this initial selection process and the ensuing rejection, I realized I had a great deal of respect for the newly selected judge. So, I pivoted from self-pity to chalking the experience up to the quality of the competition.

Another judicial opening soon followed, and this time I was not a finalist. Thoughts of inadequacy again crept in, and I tossed my application materials in the trash. The universe had spoken, and it was telling me that I was not a good fit for the bench. But the judge chosen by the governor that time around happened to be a close colleague of mine, and after he took the bench, he encouraged me to keep applying. So, at the next opportunity, thinking more about the "nagging thoughts" and "gentle nudges" and less about the agony of defeat, I blindly heeded his advice. And on Valentine's Day of 2013, the third time was the charm. I started my work on the District Court bench soon after and began forging a new and different path upon which I sought to make the judicial process a better, more comfortable place for litigants.

Fast forward to 2018. By this point, I had hit my stride. I felt that the work I was doing on the district bench was important, and I enjoyed the hands-on nature of the courtroom. As a member of the Iowa Judges Association, I was working with the other branches of the Iowa government to help ensure that the courts had the support and funding necessary to best serve Iowans. This new path seemed a great fit, and I moved along it without design or endeavor to abandon it. But then came another nudge. A retirement on the Iowa Supreme Court had created an opening. I had no intention of applying—in fact it hadn't even crossed my mind—until I got a call from Judge Rebecca Ebinger from the federal bench. She asked if I had ever considered appellate work. I truly had not. She suggested that perhaps I should apply for the opening. She would encourage others as well, but I was on her list. I did not take that lightly.

After some soul-searching and numerous conversations with colleagues and my siblings, I ultimately gritted my teeth and sat down at my desk to start getting my application put together. I figured that at the very least, my participation in the process would make it more robust and give the commission and the governor one more candidate to draw from. With the application filed, I then put over a thousand miles on my car traveling throughout Iowa to meet with the State Selection Commissioners. In the end, there were over 30 applicants, and I was not a finalist. While I was disappointed, I found myself also strangely relieved. This foray into the appellate bench had felt like a stretch for me, and I had a "soft landing" from the process right back in district court. I made peace with how things worked out.

But in 2019, another opening came up, this time on the Court of Appeals. And once again, there were emails, texts, calls, and other nudges. Would I apply? A lot of people seemed to think it was a good idea, so I had to decide whether I agreed with them. I made a list of pros and cons. On one hand, I was comfortable and happy on the district court bench, but on the other hand I still wondered if I should be doing more. By this point, the judiciary was in crisis. We were battling skimpy budgets, losing court reporters, and dealing with an increasingly skeptical public. As a result, fewer people were applying for judicial positions throughout the state. Nonetheless, with the sting of rejection front of mind, I was hesitant. But I knew that my application was essentially already complete from the year before and would require only a small update and a little polish, and I recalled that traveling the state and meeting the commissioners was actually quite interesting and fun. So, with more pros than cons on my tally, I applied.

In March 2019, I became a finalist for the Court of Appeals for the first time. Spoiler alert: I didn't get the job. Again. But even in my disappointment, I again experienced a deep sense of validation that the commission had chosen me as one of three finalists. I didn't hesitate to apply again later that year when a similar opening came about. But this time I was not a finalist. I had barely begun to grieve the loss that time around when yet another opening came up. By this point, I think muscle memory had set in. My application was still in good shape and ready to file, so I just went ahead and filed it. More meetings with commissioners ensued. All were positive. I felt good about participating, even though I had begun to feel that success was unlikely. At least my involvement would enrich the selection process. Much to my surprise, the commission sent me forth as a finalist again. And yet again, the governor did not select me.

To spare all the gory details, I became a finalist for Iowa's appellate courts three more times after that, once for the Supreme Court and twice more for the Court of Appeals. By the numbers, between 2018 and 2021, in all I applied for eight appellate openings and interviewed with the governor five times. I got four rejection calls from the governor's senior legal counsel, and grappled with self-pity, self-doubt, and frustration each and every time. So much so that I almost didn't apply the final time. Even my own daughter told me the governor would never hire me. Talk about a punch in the gut.

But two things kept me going. The first was the unrelenting challenge that the judiciary was continuing to face in getting qualified applicants to apply. It wasn't getting any better, and application numbers continued to tank. More applications simply helped create a credible and reliable selection process. It was hard to argue against that logic.

The second thing that kept me going was something one of the commissioners said to me. In a moment of vulnerability, I had told him what my daughter had said, and I wasn't sure I wanted to endure another rejection. His response surprised me. He pointed out that as he saw it, I had never been "rejected." Sure, I didn't get the job, but that didn't speak to my qualifications or fitness for the position. If there was no intention of considering me, I would have already heard about it. He also pointed out all of the excellent jurists that had been appointed at the times that I wasn't. Touché.

On the morning of December 7, 2021, I was in the middle of a trial in Tama County when a message flashed across my Garmin watch face—the governor's office was calling. I had just interviewed the day prior, so this was fast. Normally several days would pass before a decision was made. I called a quick recess and ducked into my chambers to take the call. I braced for impact. *This time, it was the governor's voice I heard.*

In the wake of my tumultuous journey, I impart some bits of residual wisdom. First, deciding to apply for the bench requires some self-reflection. Are you well-accomplished as a judge or attorney? Do you feel the draw to serve others? Do you have a sound judicial temperament? Are you patient, kind, and empathetic? Do you have a strong work ethic and an even stronger sense of integrity? Do you write well? If you are thinking about appellate work, do you work well with others? Do other lawyers and judges whom you respect "nudge" you to apply? If after considering all of this you ultimately think you are a good fit for the bench, apply. If you aren't selected, apply again. And if again you aren't selected, apply again. And again. And again. The selection of good judges depends entirely on the quality of those who step up for consideration, and the very process itself gains credibility and reliability the more candidates that step forward.

Second, if you do not find success the first or even fifth time around, remember that this is not a reflection on you, your fitness, or your accomplishments. It simply means that someone else was selected. Like the lottery where you can't win if you don't play, you can't become a judge if you don't apply, and sometimes that means you have to apply multiple times. If you self-select out, you can never know what might have been.

And so on that December morning, I presided over my final trial in district court. My persistence had finally paid off, and the rest is history. At my investiture for the Iowa Court of Appeals a few months later, Chief Judge Bower joked that my theme song would be Chumbawamba's "I Get Knocked Down, But I Get Up Again." And he wasn't wrong about that at all. Einstein, eat your heart out.

Testing Before Trusting

Susan L. Christensen
Chief Justice, Iowa Supreme Court

I know now that I began my journey to become a judge long before I was qualified. In the fall of 1995, after I had been practicing law in Harlan for four years, Judge Leo Connolly announced his retirement. My application was short and sweet—not much to brag about that early in my career. Because Judge Connolly was the most senior judge in the fourth district, he presided over the nominating commission. After my interview with the commission, he delivered the news to me in person: "Suzy, maybe someday you'll become a judge. But not today. You need to have a little gray in your whiskers." I knew what he meant. I needed more experience. Little did I know that the "no" I received that day would be the first of 14 no's in my journey to become a judge at one level or another.

For years, I repeated the process, applying every time a judge in my district retired. In 2005, ten years after my first attempt to become a judge, I finally made it out of commission and into an interview with Governor Tom Vilsack. As the Governor's deadline to fill the vacancy approached, I received a Saturday-morning phone call from a woman who identified herself by saying she was calling from the Governor's office. I immediately knew I didn't get the job before she confirmed what I feared. Everyone knows the Governor only calls the person he is appointing, and the female voice on the other end gave it away. I tried my best to maintain a measured tone in my voice and told her that I was honored to even be in the hunt. I lied.

After we hung up, I dropped to my knees and wept as the weight of rejection hit me. I was devastated. Not only did I put a ton of effort into the post-commission process, but I even allowed myself to daydream about how I would wrap up my private practice before taking the bench.

On Monday morning, I drove from my home in Harlan to Council Bluffs and personally congratulated the man Governor Vilsack had chosen instead of me to be the newest district court judge in my district. It wasn't easy, but it felt important. I didn't cry in his office, but that was only because I rehearsed what I would say, blinked a lot, and didn't stick around for small talk that might betray my true feelings.

The Governor's "no" in 2005 was a punch in the gut. It felt different than all the other no's delivered to me by the judicial nominating commission. I never considered giving up, but I was certainly wounded more than I had been before. A few days later, I received a handwritten letter from one of my dad's best friends, David Harris. He served on the Iowa Supreme Court with my dad, Jerry Larson. Justice Harris's one-page letter of encouragement included the following phrase which has been indelibly marked in my memory:

> *Life has a way of testing us with disappointment, before trusting us with sought after responsibility.*
>
> —*Justice David Harris*

When I read those words for the first time, it stung. It stung because I knew it was true. Every time an opening was announced in my district, my updated application became more and more robust with experience and examples of my skills as an attorney and community member. Whether I wanted to admit it or not, I should not have been chosen to replace Judge Connolly with only four years' experience. But day by day, I was becoming a stronger and stronger candidate.

While I was committed to applying for district court judicial openings, it never occurred to me that I would be interested in a district associate judge position because I would have been required to live in Pottawattamie County. I never considered moving from my beloved hometown of Harlan in Shelby County. But in 2007, Chief Judge Charles Smith called to encourage me to apply for a new district associate position created by the legislature. This new position was different than the other associate positions—it would include jurisdiction in all nine counties and the judge could live anywhere in the district. I applied for this position and was chosen. I was thrilled to take my first step into the judicial branch.

Throughout my time on the district associate bench, I continued to apply for district court positions. I also started looking into appellate positions. Once in 2011 and then again in 2012, I got out of commission for openings on the Iowa Court of Appeals but was told "no" both times by then-Governor Terry Branstad. By this time in my journey, I had learned to receive "no" as meaning "not now."

In 2015, I applied for and was chosen to fill a vacancy created by the retirement of Judge Timothy O'Grady. I found it poignant that Judge O'Grady had been chosen to fill Judge Connolly's position 20 years earlier. Judge Connolly was right—maybe I didn't have gray whiskers, but by the time his own replacement retired, I had 20 years' experience under my belt and a résumé that looked much different than it had in 1995.

I was rewarded for this experience again in 2018, when Justice Bruce Zager announced his retirement from the Iowa Supreme Court. At the time, Justice Zager was the only member of the court with recent experience as a district court judge, and my own experience as both a district associate judge and district court judge was crucial to my application. I may never have had these experiences had I not been rejected in the past, and they helped lead to my appointment to fill Justice Zager's vacancy—an appointment that would ultimately lead to my current position as the Chief Justice of the Iowa Supreme Court.

Just like Justice Harris said in his handwritten letter, life had certainly disappointed me many times prior to being trusted with a position of great responsibility. As painful as those rejections were, they also gave me the opportunity to grow into a more qualified individual prepared to take on a judicial position of great responsibility through my additional years of experience. In the end, my experience serves as a reminder that rejection is not where your story ends, but where another chapter in your tale begins.

Chapter 15

Deciding Whether the Robe is a Good Fit

The Incurable Advocate

Michael R. Mullins
Senior Judge, Iowa Court of Appeals

So, you are a pretty good lawyer, perhaps a great lawyer. You provide zealous representation of the interests of your clients. Opposing attorneys respect you, your ethics, your professionalism, and your passion for representing your clients. You now have several years of experience and think you may be ready for your career to take another path. You are contemplating applying to become a judge, presumably a trial judge.

As you consider whether you should seek nomination and selection as a judge, perhaps you reflect on your attributes and consider the qualities you admire in judges before whom you have practiced. You also consider what you believe to be the positive prospects for your selection, and the hurdles or the competition. Is the bench a good fit for you? Are you a good fit for the bench? Is your personality suited to be non-adversarial, a non-advocate? Can you put aside your competitive nature? Are you going to find satisfaction in remaining a neutral fact finder and decision maker? What will happen to your neutrality when, as a judge, a party appears before you in a difficult case and you see a lawyer bumbling in the representation of a client who needs more skilled counsel? Are you going to be tempted to interject yourself in an effort to level the litigation playing field? How are you going to handle deciding a case that is "exactly like" one in which you were counsel, but where the lawyering in the case before you seems to be taking it to a different outcome than you achieved and believed was correct?

It is easy to get wrapped up in "what if's." As you share your thoughts about a career change with others, you will likely receive encouragement and information about the pluses of being a judge. But, I suggest you hit the "pause" button and first examine your current career. Think about the positive aspects of your situation, and what currently gives you professional satisfaction and pride.

For example, how do you feel when you meet a new client who has been referred to you by an existing client? Think about the interesting cases in which you have provided representation. Reflect on the difference you have made in the lives of those clients for whom you obtained a positive result. Remember an excellent trial strategy or cross examination that advanced your client's cause during a trial. And what about the legal theories you have woven together to support your client's proposition or to defeat the claims of the client on the other side of the case?

Are you going to find satisfaction as a judge? Or are you going to find frustration? Unfortunately, I know of circumstances in which a judge could not refrain from interjecting self into the trial process. In one such criminal case, the judge was convinced the lawyer had incompetently failed to file a motion to suppress evidence. So, the judge sua sponte declared a mistrial based on the judge's perception that the defendant was receiving ineffective assistance of counsel. Defense counsel was furious: he had intentionally not filed the motion on the belief it would be unsuccessful, and that if he had filed it, the prosecution would have been tipped off to a strategic defensive plan he had for the evidence. In that case, after the sua sponte dismissal, the prosecution sought to begin a new trial, prompting the defendant to file an appeal claiming double jeopardy. The Iowa Supreme Court agreed with the defendant and dismissed the State's case—all because the judge was convinced he *knew* how the defense should have been trying the case, and could not resist interfering in the advocacy of the case.

That is a dramatic—but very real—example of the problem; but less dramatic events present themselves regularly in the life of a judge. Those circumstances occur at all stages of litigation: scheduling, pretrial motions and conferences, identification of disputed issues, jury selection, examination of witnesses, and so forth. It is one thing for a judge to quietly, reflectively ponder the strategies of lawyers as an academic exercise, but quite another thing for a judge to interject self into the pretrial or trial strategy of a lawyer. And yet another thing for the judge to so greatly want to interject self that the judge is frustrated with the experience. Some judges who were great advocates are able to "flip the switch" to the academic exercise, but others find frustration that is not conducive to job satisfaction or quality judging.

You should also consider the changes in work-life balance and work-life control that you will experience if appointed to the bench. In your practice, you may sometimes feel as though you have little control in balancing your work and personal life. You get phone calls when you take vacation. You can never/rarely disengage from the electronic connection to your office, clients, opposing counsel, electronic filings, etc. You have responsibilities for office expenses and management. Ah, to be a judge and not have those worries. Not so fast. As with many things in life, there are tradeoffs.

As a judge, your schedule will be dictated by court administration and case schedulers. You may know a few days in advance where you will be working or on what type of case, but you may not know until 4 p.m. the day before. I had more than one occasion on which I received a call early in the morning and was told I needed to go to a different courthouse than I had been told the day before. Once, I was called about 7 a.m. and told they needed me at a courthouse a full hour away to commence a three-day speedy jury trial, to replace a judge whose car had broken down while the judge was returning from an out-of-state vacation. I did not mind that kind of situation. Can you be satisfied with relinquishing control of your daily schedule to a case coordinator? Or do you prefer control over your schedule?

As a lawyer, you no doubt deal with several different clients and cases every day. You may find it exhausting to change directions multiple times daily. But realize that most of the time, you know who your client is and have some idea what their expectations are, and so forth. You have some control to decide whether to take a call, accept a new client or case, schedule an appointment or leave work early. As a judge, especially on a court service day (in rural counties) or during an order "hour," you will have a carousel of cases, parties, lawyers, areas of the law, and so forth. Often you would be looking at a file cold, with little introduction or prior knowledge, and perhaps not knowing any of the people appearing before you. You will not have control over whether you want to hear a case or not.

And you may soon realize that as a lawyer you had more freedoms and controls over your life and schedule than you realized. As a lawyer, you may not appreciate the flexibility you have to decide what hours you work and when you take time off work. You have certain control of your physical environment. You get to choose your clients and choose your staff support.

Before my first day as a district court judge, my mentor-judge explained that I would be a judge everywhere I was to go, not just in the courthouse (but not at home!). I would be expected to behave like a judge while at the grocery store, on the golf course, at the YMCA, at a ball game, etc. Just this last summer, a baseball mom came up to me during one of my grandson's baseball games and apologized for her husband's crude language at a previous ball game, explaining that she had reminded him that he was standing by a judge when he made those remarks. It was a stark reminder that people still have expectations of me, even as I have retired from full-time judging and now serve as a senior judge. My wife and children faced similar scrutiny, with certain members of the public imposing expectations on them. Just be aware: you, your spouse or significant other, and your children may not like those expectations.

If you are appointed as a judge, there are many ethical limitations to your involvement in the community and in organizations. If you are now politically active, that will all change. No, you cannot even silently attend a political party caucus. If you have been an important part of fundraising or promoting certain activities in your community, not anymore. If you have been outspoken about issues in your community, muzzle it. This list only touches the surface of Iowa Court Rules chapter 51, Iowa Code of Judicial Conduct, which constrains activities of judges in order to help preserve the dignity, impartiality and independence of the judiciary.

Before my appointment to the bench, I practiced law in a typical county seat practice. I enjoyed practicing law. I enjoyed researching and studying the law in order to apply it to addressing the problems or issues of my clients. I viewed myself as a problem solver. I used the law to help solve problems for my clients. I still remember the excitement of planning and presenting evidence in a few cases that called for some creativity. I loved arguing legal issues in cases, whether to a district court judge, a jury or an appellate court. After I argued a case to the Iowa Supreme Court promoting expansion of a legal principle, my client and I were walking down the steps of the State Capitol and I remember turning to him and saying, "That is about the most fun a lawyer can have!" (I must add that my client did not share my excitement; and ultimately, the supreme court ruled against my client.) That was about 30 years ago, and I still remember the feeling.

You likely have had moments like that: dramatic, emotional. I can tell you that as a judge, you do not experience dramatic moments like that. Judges see and hear drama. Judges rein in drama. The job of a judge is to avoid creating or being drawn into drama or emotional experiences. Judges try not to show emotion. In 20-plus years as a judge, I have never walked off the bench and declared, "That is the most fun a judge can have!" (There is only one close exception: the occasional adoption proceeding.)

As a lawyer, I enjoyed preparing to try a case and going to trial against a very good advocate on the opposite side of the case. I did not give much thought to the big-picture significance of good lawyering. When I became a district court judge, I soon appreciated the value and importance of great advocacy in the delivery of judicial services and judicious outcomes. On several occasions, when I was presiding over a case in which both sides were represented by excellent lawyers, I would tell them that as a judge, I liked nothing better than to watch good lawyers at work. For one thing, good lawyers make the job of the judge easier. But, more importantly, good lawyers help make certain that justice—be it in civil or criminal cases—prevails. Excellent advocates are necessary for the wheels of justice to turn smoothly.

Conversely, lawyers who lack strong advocacy skills make it more difficult to achieve the fairest results. I have not used the term "adversarial" in this essay, until now. Some lawyers equate adversarial with advocacy. My view is that while the judicial process is by nature and design an adversarial process, the art of advocacy—great advocates—remain focused on advocacy of their own client's cause and less on the defeat of an adversary.

If you are a skilled advocate, we need you representing clients, pursuing remedies and defenses. I have always believed we should each use our God-given talents to the best of our abilities. Justice is admirable. It is a goal worth pursuing. But we judges are constrained to only consider the evidence and arguments presented to us as we deliberate a disputed case. Without competent advocacy and solid legal arguments, we lose the ultimate benefits of an adversarial process that leans on the promise of strong, meaningful representation of all parties in order to sharpen the edges of the steely legal issues and factual determinations that must be made.

So, as you consider whether to be a judge or remain an advocate, carefully consider where you and your family can experience peace and satisfaction and where the use of your talents can be most valuable to the greatest system of justice in the world!

Good luck as you contemplate and make your decision.

Traits of a Great Advocate and Why Perhaps You Should Remain One

David W. Nelmark
Judge, Iowa District Court

You are almost certainly a great lawyer. Whether you practice in civil or criminal or family or some other type of law, the fact that you're reading this book likely means someone has encouraged you to think about being a judge. That means you're doing terrific work.

Unfortunately, being a great lawyer is no guarantee that you'll be a great judge. Some of the traits that make a great advocate translate well to the bench. Other traits can be counterproductive. One that is a double-edged sword is ego.

As a judge you have to have *enough* ego, but not too much. Some ego is required because judges must make difficult decisions. Many involve exercising discretion rather than just researching the right answer in a code book or case law. If you do not trust yourself, it can be paralyzing. Once you do make a decision, you may still engage in second-guessing. To move forward, you have to remember that no one is perfect, and someone has to make the call.

Self-confidence is also required because judges get surprisingly little feedback. Attorneys may tell you that you're doing a good job, but once you put on the robe, all positive feedback from attorneys needs to be taken with a healthy grain of salt. (Also, the jokes that kill in your courtroom may be decidedly less funny in other settings.) You probably have a Chief Judge and may technically answer to your state's Supreme Court, but those folks have a lot more on their plate than making sure you progress in your development. At the end of the day, you just need to be able to sleep well at night knowing that in your own mind you did the best you could do.

Lacking self-confidence can be a problem. But a little ego goes a long way. Having a tremendous ego, as many great trial lawyers do, is the bigger danger. Most great trial lawyers command the courtroom. They like to be in the spotlight with all eyes on them. A great advocate steals the show. After a transition to the bench, that approach needs to change.

As a judge, you are literally the center of attention. You get the elevated seat in the middle of the front of the room. You are the only one with the special outfit. But it's not *about* you. For you, it's another day at the office. For the parties appearing in front of you, it is likely one of the most important days of their lives. Their livelihood, their children, their freedom may hang in the balance of the proceedings.

"Black Robe Syndrome" can afflict people who would otherwise be great judges. The litigants in the courtroom will sense if you think you're better than they are. You must be able to judge without being judgmental. Attorneys will spread the word, quickly, if you're too high and mighty to respect their requests for continuances or fail to show understanding for the mistakes everyone makes.

Apart from the negative impact on others, having too much ego can also be internally damaging for a judge. Even if you are the smartest person present for a hearing, it will be on one of the 400 cases on your docket. The attorneys will have lived and breathed the matter for months and you may not have even been assigned to cover the hearing until one of your colleagues left to pick up a sick child 20 minutes ago.

You likely had expertise in one or even a few subjects while serving as a lawyer. Perhaps you will be fortunate and will see those types of cases on the bench. But you will also see many others. You will have to interpret laws that you didn't know existed before a particular case came across your docket. The attorneys, who are likely experts in the type of case you're seeing, will know more than you do.

You will misspeak. You will get things wrong. You will be criticized—in the courtroom and in the press. And you will be unable to respond to it. Usually, one side leaves your courtroom unhappy. Sometimes it's both sides. You will get reversed. That is all part of the job. But you have to be able to deal with it. If your ego is such that mistakes are a serious blow to your psyche, you won't last.

Great advocates are also usually very competitive. They work hard because they want to do a good job for their clients, but they also care greatly about the results from an internal perspective. It's worth staying up late and making other sacrifices in order to get that victory at the end of the trial, or the end of an appeal. Whether the outcome is fair, you can still relish a verdict that goes your client's way. Unlike many professions, trial lawyers get a scoreboard. And the rush of winning can be addictive. But the need to win can be problematic for a judge. Judges rarely have "wins" and "losses." Of course, appellate courts tell you when you got things right or wrong. But only a small percentage of cases are appealed, and that feedback may come years after your decision was made. And the reversals tend to be bigger stories than the affirmances. Any contemporaneous feedback you receive is usually negative. Parties will ask you to reconsider your rulings. The media and the public will criticize your decisions (even though they often know very little about the case or the law).

You have no clients. In some cases, there is no good solution. No matter what you do, it won't feel like a victory. Getting too competitive can mean getting too combative. You are in high-stakes situations with people who are often very nervous or emotional. If you put out the vibe that you're looking for a fight, you'll probably get it.

Having hyper focus can help make someone a great advocate, in multiple ways. First, you can identify with your client and become emotionally invested in his case. You can become a true believer and do everything to help her win. Your passion will be obvious to the jurors, and it may persuade them to also side with your client.

On the bench you have to work hard to *not* identify with one side or the other. You have to set aside biases. Your primary goal is a just outcome—which is not always a fair outcome.

Trial preparation is intense, and trial lawyers are notorious for having poor work-life balance. Having hyper focus aids in advocacy in that it allows an attorney to focus on a client's needs to the exclusion of everything else. It may not be good for one's family or health, but it can be effective.

A judge can almost never give a single case her full attention. During the throes of a trial, motions in other cases keep coming in and some of them are time sensitive. Further, even within the confines of a trial, the legal matter at hand cannot be a judge's sole focus. You need to watch the jurors to make sure they are alert and comfortable. You need to watch the gallery to make sure no one looks like they will cause an outburst. You need to observe the parties to see if anyone is going through trauma. You need to be aware of whether your assistant is passing you a note about a fire in another matter that you need to put out. You need to be aware of your own reactions, lest they influence the jury.

Great advocates generally like to be in control. That may seem like it translates well to the bench. But it does not. Judges have power *in the courtroom*. After all, we can throw someone in jail for contempt. Yet power is not the same as control.

I rarely knew my own schedule until 4 p.m. the day before when Court Administration tells me what trial is being dumped into my lap. The days I do think I know what I'm going to be doing, things often change. Other judges get sick, and you have to step in. Emergencies happen on your own docket and schedules have to be adjusted.

I don't even have full control over my staff. My assistant or court reporter might get called to a different courtroom for the day. As a state judge, I have access to law clerks in theory but there are six clerks serving 17 district court judges and 13 district associate judges. Thus, in most cases, I'm on my own. I don't get to choose what cases I take. I can't fire a client who gets difficult. I can't put the rest of the docket on hold just to focus on a challenging trial.

If you can't handle being told what to do, where to go, or what time you need to be there, this is a tough profession. You also don't get to finish your work a little early and go to lunch or play a round of golf. Unless you're on vacation, you're in the courthouse when the courthouse is open.

Great advocates are often stars and expect to be treated as such. Being elected or appointed to be a judge may seem like a status boost. But being a judge is also not as glamorous as it may seem. There are few perks. You can't even accept gifts above a certain limit. (Iowa's is $3.) Sure, my government ID occasionally gets me a hotel discount, but when I'm traveling for work my lodging reimbursement gets capped at $80 per night plus tax. In Iowa, we do have a nice pension system and benefits. But we rarely get raises. Because our mandatory pension contribution went up last year, our take-home pay actually went *down*. Further, in a 2024 survey put out by the National Judicial College, more than 90% of the judges who responded felt that the public's esteem for judges had declined in the last decade.

Whether you possess all, some, or none of the above traits, it is difficult to know when you're "ready" to be a judge. Make sure you have not only the requisite experience but also the emotional maturity. If people start suggesting it as a career move, it's a good sign. But be aware of the challenges of changing into an entirely new job. It's hard to move from one you may have mastered to one where you are starting at ground zero. For years, you will be doing things for the first time. If you've ever suffered from imposter syndrome, it's quite likely to rear up. And don't overlook how draining it is to go through the process of attempting to become a judge, whether or not you are successful.

Even after you feel comfortable with the job itself, there are days that are very draining. Judges can be subject to burnout and experience vicarious trauma. We often see people at their worst.

But it's a terrific job. You have the best seat in the house to observe top-notch advocacy. You get to do meaningful and interesting work. As long as you are pursuing it for the right reasons, I encourage you to do so.

Not All Barristers Belong on the Bench

John M. Sandy
Judge, Iowa Court of Appeals[1]

Immediately upon my graduation from high school I attended Saint John Vianney College Seminary (SJV) located on the campus of the University of St. Thomas in St. Paul, Minnesota. While not all Catholic college seminaries across the United States—and the world—are the same, SJV had a reputation for very good academics and structured formation. For example, a typical day at SJV would begin as follows: wake at 5:30 a.m. Holy hour and confession in the chapel (conveniently located on the first floor of the dormitory) at 6:00 a.m. Morning prayer and mass at 7:00 a.m. Breakfast at 7:45 a.m. Class from 9:00 a.m. until 12:00 p.m. Lunch at 12:00 p.m. Class from 1:00 p.m. until 4:00 p.m. Evening prayer at 4:45 p.m. Dinner at 5:30 p.m. Mandatory study hours (painfully memorizing and declining Latin nouns) from 7:00 p.m. until 9:30 p.m. Night prayer at 9:30 p.m. Lights out at approximately 10:15 p.m. and repeat. Scattered in such a schedule were weekly formation and spiritual direction meetings as well as various other non-negotiable activities like exercise and community social justice outreach. And of course: no girlfriends. I devoted the first three years of college to this routine. It was both wonderful and, at times, trying.

Why am I boring you with this information in a book about judges? Because my college seminary experiences provided me with the opportunity to do what most other college-aged men were not doing at that time—self-integration. Iron sharpens iron. Almost every day I was confronted with the reality that I am not as great as I may think I am. Living in a residence with 125 other men and five priests who continuously challenged and evaluated our progress resulted in a development of keen self-awareness. Examinations of conscience and self-inventories occurred not just daily, but multiple times throughout the day. Those who could not undertake such brutal realism left in short order. Every lawyer desiring to become a judge better make sure they are self-aware before they make such a leap. Without self-awareness, one is unable to know whether they possess the temperamental attributes required of a good judge.

"Know thyself" is a philosophical maxim which was inscribed upon the Temple of Apollo in the ancient Greek precinct of Delphi. In Latin works, the phrase is commonly translated *nosce te ipsum.* The phrase has been quoted and analyzed by numerous authors throughout history and has been applied in many ways. However, in the 4th century B.C. the maxim was interpreted by Plato, who understood it to mean "know your soul." Students of Plato and Socrates such as St. Thomas Aquinas connected this knowledge as the cornerstone of humility.

Humility is born out of knowing God and knowing oneself.[2] Put differently, "Humility is not about having a low self-image or poor self-esteem. Humility is about self-awareness."[3] Humility reflects one's understanding of self—one's strengths, shortcomings, and limitations. And this self-understanding allows insight as to why some outstanding litigators are best left at that—litigating.

Of course, we want judges who possess a robust practice background. What better basis of knowledge than experience? Indeed, rough seas make a smooth sailor. However, being a judge requires more than just experience. It requires the right temperament. Temperament refers to an individual's natural disposition or inherent personality traits. Good judicial temperament is not learned in law school but innately possessed. Certainly, there is room for diversity of varying temperaments on the bench (sanguine, choleric, melancholic, phlegmatic, and the static range that exists therein). Thankfully, no one judge is the same. Yet it has been my observation that, in some instances, the very temperament that makes a litigator great would be disastrous on the bench. Three examples readily come to mind: competitiveness, belonging, and patience (or lack thereof).

Competitiveness

Some of the best advice I received upon taking the bench was not to compete with the lawyers. There is an old story about a lawyer who, after the judge had questioned a witness, pleaded with the judge that if the judge was going to try his case for him, not to lose it. The lawyers can see that you have a black robe and they don't. There is no need to demonstrate that you're smarter or that you can try their case better. You aren't, and you can't. You are likely to make a fool of yourself if you try. Judges should never try to compete with the lawyers.

Yet good litigators are often competitive. It is what fuels the fire. Michael Jordan is now known to have created false narratives of opponents disrespecting him to fuel his competitive drive. He did so to try and gain every competitive edge he could. Litigators thrive in a "me vs. world" mentality. It is what endears them to their clients. It is also the mark of a terrible judge. Think about it. We all have experienced the judge that screwed up the deal the lawyers made for their clients. The judge does not know the attorneys' case or clients better than they do. Yet some judges routinely refuse stipulations. This is an area that should be tread very lightly. Indeed, a judge should not abandon their responsibilities. However, the judge's responsibility is to the law and the standards of the community—not their personal preferences.

If a lawyer cannot rid him or herself of that competitive nature—at least in the professional arena—they should seriously consider whether an appointment to the bench is for them.

Belonging

It still amazes me how many well-intended folks from my community assume that I am still an attorney, and I sometimes do the "judge thing." Those who knew me as the main street lawyer, who are not otherwise well versed in civics or how the legal world operates, assume I only moonlight as a judge. Perhaps the part-time magistrate system used in Iowa adds to such confusion. However, it is a continuous reminder that I am still a lawyer. And yet, I am not.

Paradoxically, good judges would do well to never forget that they are lawyers and always remember that they are not. This is to say, though not simply, that a judge will always be a lawyer, even though a judge is no longer an advocate. A judge is no longer "one of the guys" or "one of the girls." There is a boundary here that isn't precisely defined. A judge has the same education, experience, friends, and identity as a lawyer. Lawyers expect you to understand where they come from and to help them out when you can do so without doing harm to the other side. Our livelihoods and theirs are interdependent. I could not be retained (or appointed) without them; they cannot make a living without me. On the other hand, I am not one of them, can never be one of them again, and should not try. If a judge is unable to draw that boundary, at best, they will not be respected. And at worst, the board of judicial standards will be in touch with them.

For some advocates, this sense of belonging is paramount to their professional identity. Don't believe me? Think of how many state and national lawyer "clubs" exist. Iowa Association of Justice, Iowa Defense Counsel Association, Iowa State Bar Association, Iowa County Attorney Association, Iowa Organization of Women Attorneys, National Association of Criminal Defense Lawyers, DUI Defense Lawyers Association, the Trial Lawyers College: the list is endless. And if that is not enough, we even have more "exclusive" clubs to combine competitiveness and a sense of belonging like ABOTA, Super Lawyers, Best Lawyers in America, Society of Outstanding Lawyers in America, Million Dollar Advocates, and various specialized certifications by illustrious groups which make a lawyer even more prestigiously cliquish. To say attorneys are tribal would be an understatement.

Good judges should not be tribal. Judges resolve disputes between parties who are represented by lawyers because they couldn't resolve it themselves. It is not an opportunity for a judge to prove that they are tough on crime (tribe Iowa County Attorney Association) or the champion of the underdog (tribe Iowa Association of Justice) or anything else a judge would like people to think about them. Judges should not make rulings because they want to be regarded in a certain way. When a judge wants to be known for ruling in a certain way, he or she is likely to rule that way whether or not the case warrants it. That is an injustice and a violation of our oath to "administer justice without fear, favor, affect, or hope of reward."

No matter how hard a judge may try to "temper the wind to the shorn lamb," nobody likes losing. The parties and their lawyers will often blame the judge. If they thought they were wrong, they would not have taken the case. The worst thing a judge can do is "throw people bones" or try to make every case come out exactly even. If they do, lawyers with good cases will avoid them, and lawyers with bad cases will seek them out. The former because they know their good case will be cut in half, and the latter because they know they'll be rewarded no matter how bad their case. Either way, they won't respect the judge or the office.

If a lawyer cannot rid him or herself of a desire for belonging—at least in the professional arena—they should seriously consider whether an appointment to the bench is for them. While judges do share some collegiality and "war stories" at annual judicial seminars, my experience is that this sense of belonging has not been the same since I left private practice. And it shouldn't be. While advocates do have to play by the rules as officers of the court, they do not have to be neutral. It is ok if they champion certain causes—we expect it. They belong to those causes which animate their passions. When judges are invested they are divested from such belonging.

Patience

Of course, all legal eagles have good analytical skills. However, the temporal processing of those skills varies depending on the need. It has been my experience that some of the very best litigators are not just analytical thinkers, but *quick* analytical thinkers. They see the chess pieces four steps ahead with little forethought, in real-time, and mid-trial. Then they adjust accordingly and strike. They relish the unpredictable because they know they can rely on quick wit and analytical prowess in the unforeseen to their persuasive advantage. No doubt, they also anticipate and prepare for the unforeseen. Yet there is still a "quick on the feet" component that has less to do with preparation and more to do with intuition. That comes with a cost. Those same litigators often have little patience. Their mind races at a different pace than most. Conclusions are made faster than premises given. They don't like waiting for *all* the facts to come in before reaching an opinion.

Waiting for all the facts to come in prior to reaching an opinion is paramount for a judge (and juror). Candidly, this is the area I struggled with my first few years on the bench. While it served me well in litigation, it betrayed me on the bench. It is not so much that a judge will miss something because they were not listening. It is that the judge will have moved onto a resolution before all facts are before them. For me, this rush to judgement happened less in trial while hearing live testimony and more in reading motions, briefs, summary judgment filings, and various other pleadings.

But for trial attorneys, more grace is given with such lack of patience. The adversarial process rewards aggressively quick thinkers more handsomely. Timely well-placed objection? You either won or at least preserved error. Timely well-placed "gotcha" question not previously thought of? You persuasively impeached. Turned opposing counsel's prose to your client's benefit? You just won the jury. Yet, that same benefit does not exist on the bench. In fact, just the opposite. It catches you making bad decisions or not weighing arguments/evidence as you otherwise ought.

If a lawyer cannot rid him or herself of such lack of patience—at least in the professional arena—they should seriously consider whether an appointment to the bench is for them.

Conclusion

Jeffrey L. Goodman

I trust that you have found the real-life stories, advice, questions for self-reflection, and deep insight offered by judges who heard and heeded the call to serve the public from the bench both edifying and illuminating. If, after reading this book, you too are contemplating a call to the bench, I offer the following points to ponder as you assess your path forward.

- Serving on the bench isn't for everyone. It's a calling. The first step is to test your commitment to determine whether you are *the one among the many*. If the answer isn't apparent, reexamine your motivations. Are you being called to the bench from a sense of purpose, or are you merely curious about the position? Are you responding to an inner prompting, or are you attracted to the power that comes with a judicial appointment? Do you feel drawn—perhaps even compelled—to serve the public from the bench, or are you simply seeking a career change or treating the judiciary as a next logical step?
- Inventory and rigorously evaluate your skills and experiences to determine whether you possess what it takes to serve on the bench. Conduct an honest and thorough self-assessment. There is

nothing wrong with deciding that your skills are better applied elsewhere—or that you are not ready to serve *yet*, but you may be better prepared for a future vacancy. Remember: timing is everything, and readiness is key.

- Picture yourself in the role. Ask yourself: "What kind of judge would I strive to be?" Try to visualize yourself after 25 years of service and ask: "What would my legacy as a judge be?" If you need further insight into these questions, review what you have accomplished as a lawyer and how you have comported yourself. Ask family, friends, colleagues, and other judges for their candid thoughts on your serving in this new and different role. For example, you may believe you are an effective listener, but do others perceive you that way?
- Serving on the bench is both an honor and a sacrifice. Carefully weigh the obligations and expectations that will be placed on you, and by extension, your loved ones. Realize that if you are nominated and appointed, your personal life will likely change in ways you cannot fully anticipate. Devote some careful thought to the potentially life-changing aspects of becoming a judge.
- Remain clear-eyed about the professional challenges that await you—for instance, the quick transition from advocate to umpire, high-volume dockets, pushy and demanding lawyers and liti-

gants, increasingly common pro se litigants, navigating unfamiliar areas of the law, and having to rule under the pressures of time constraints and inadequate support. There will be a perpetual balancing act between the need to issue clear, well-reasoned and timely decisions and the time needed to craft them.

- Be prepared for the full consequences of having the final, fate-determining word with your rulings. Instead of staking out and forcibly advocating for a position, you are now the decision maker. Everyone else can help persuade, inform, or offer an opinion, but you must carefully weigh every fact and come to an informed conclusion. As a judge, you will not have the luxury of being wrong.
- Understand that fealty to the law takes precedence over any personal opinion, conviction, or stance you might otherwise be able to express. There will be times when you would prefer a different outcome, but you must adhere to the rule of law—and still be able to live with the consequences. For example, could you take a guilty plea in a criminal case, dissolve a marriage and divide parties' lifetime assets, separate a child from a parent (permanently or temporarily), or preside over a complex, multimillion-dollar case? Are you ready for all that entails?

- Once you heed the call, assess how you are different from others who have applied, either for current or prior vacancies. What sets you apart? Can you distinguish yourself as *the one among the many*? Why you and not another worthy contender?
- Avoid the temptation to apply for any or every vacancy. Do not be the person who says, "Well, I heard Judge Smith was retiring, so why not throw my hat in the ring and see what happens?" Or "My law partners thought I would be a good judge, so I decided to give it a shot." Instead, pick your moment carefully. Is the timing right for you, your firm, and your loved ones? Will you be competitive among the current group of applicants? Is today's cultural climate conducive to your success as a judge?
- Get a trusted advisor or two and enlist others to help you prepare. Ask friends and colleagues to rigorously challenge you and to practice interviews with you. Learn from other judges who have been through the process. Those with experience are the best instructors.

None of these points are meant to discourage you. To the contrary, they should help you determine whether you are truly ready and, most of all, well-suited to face the challenge of being the one among the many—and if you are, to then become the best prepared applicant you can possibly be, and ultimately the best-prepared judge.

The decision to pursue the bench is one that should be made only after honest self-study and deep and honest introspection. If you are truly called to serve, you'll be responding to an urge from deep within that points you to something far greater than yourself. You'll be acting out of an inner conviction that you have something to offer that no one else does. Your decision should stem from a candid self-assessment that includes a full reckoning of your strengths and weaknesses—not from hubris, but from a true and trustworthy belief in your ability to contribute meaningfully to the judiciary. If all of this is so, heed the call because a just and well-ordered society needs you.

Wherever your professional future lies, I hope this book proved both informative and inspiring.

Notes

Chapter 1

[1]While the *Blue Book* is tremendously useful in giving us subtle and nuanced language, it is unreasonable to expect the public to know or care about the shadings between *cf.* and *but cf.* Similarly, Law Latin and Law French should be eschewed when possible.

Chapter 2

[1]https://www.uscourts.gov/about-federal-courts/educational-resources/supreme-court-landmarks/nomination-process/chief-justice-roberts-statement-nomination-process.

[2]Major League (Paramount Pictures, 1989); https://www.youtube.com/watch?v=g_wc9JvTXGc ("Just a bit outside" as Bob Uecker's character told his radio listeners who couldn't see how badly Vaughn's pitches were missing the strike zone.)

[3]https://www.washingtonpost.com/sports/2021/08/16/worst-strike-zones-data/. (Information about umpire biases, the impact of bad calls, and the emergence of robotic umpires comes from this article.)

[4]https://www.newyorker.com/magazine/2021/08/30/invasion-of-the-robot-umpires.

[5]"Poker face" means "an inscrutable face that reveals no hint of a person's thoughts or feelings." https://www.merriam-webster.com/dictionary/poker%20face.

[6]"TL;DR." https://www.merriam-webster.com/dictionary/TL%3BDR.

[7]https://www.iowabar.org/?pg=JudicialEvaluations. (Temperament, demeanor, clarity and quality of written opinions, decides cases on basis of applicable law and fact, not affected by outside influence, treats people equally and demonstrates an awareness of the influence of implicit bias are some other categories.)

[8]https://www.sportsbusinessjournal.com/Daily/Issues/2023/05/30/Leagues-and-Governing-Bodies/mlb-robot-umpires-coming-up-from-milb.aspx.

[9]Iowa Court Rules Chapter 51: Iowa Code of Judicial Conduct. Preamble.

[10]This concept is used in a secular sense and not intended to be confused with the Christian notion of transfiguration.

[11]I retired in 2021 and took senior status. As a senior judge I am responsible for writing 25% of the number of opinions an active judge annually writes.

Chapter 3

[1]For another excellent discussion of a similar nature, see C. J. Williams, A View from the Well: One Trial Lawyer's Observations About Attributes of a Good Judge, 63 MAY Fed Law 58 (2016).

[2]See Gina M. Messamer, Iowa's All-Male Supreme Court, 98 Iowa Law Review 421 (2012).

[3]See generally Bure, K., Leben, S, Rottman, D., Tyler, T. Procedural Fairness for Judges and Courts (2022).

[4]Nourit Zimmerman & Tom R. Tyler, Between Access to Counsel and Access to Justice: A Psychological Perspective, 37 Fordham Urb. L. J. 473, 483 (2010).

[5]See generally Anna E. Carpenter, Active Judging and Access to Justice, 93 Notre Dame L. Rev. 647 (2017).

[6]See e.g. Charles M. McGee (Retired) and Anna Fine, Keeping Our Porticos Accessible, Open, and Relevant: A Frank Discussion By A Retired Judge Regarding the Remarkable Features of Nevada's Justice System and a Couple of Challenges That Lie Ahead, 32 Nevada Lawyer 22 (2024); Anna E. Carpenter, Active Judging and Access to Justice, 93 Notre Dame L. Rev. 647 (2017), Russell Engler, Turner v. Rogers and the Essential Role of the Courts in Delivering Access to Justice, Harv. Law & Policy Rev. 31 (2013) Scott W. Skavdahl, Access to Justice: A Judge's Perspective, 32 Wyoming Lawyer 28 (2008); Hon. Patrick C. Bowler, Access to Justice—The Judge's Role, 79 Mich. B. J. 79 (2000).

[7]The role of trial courts as case managers has been recognized for a number of years. See Peckham, R.F., The Federal Judge as a Case Manager: The New Role in Guiding a Case from Filing to Disposition, 69 Calif. L. Rev. 770 (1981).

[8]Elizabeth G. Thornberg, The Managerial Judge Goes to Trial, 44 U of Rich. L. Rev. 44 (2009).

[9]Jerry Kang and Kristin Lane, Seeing Through Colorblindness: Implicit Bias and the Law, 58 U.C.L.A. L. Rev. 465, 503 (2010).

[10]J.J. Rachlinski, et al., Does Unconscious Racial Bias Affect Trial Judges, 84 Notre Dame L Rev. 1195, at 1221 (2009).

[11]Id. See also Haney Keith, Latonia, Cultural Competency in a Post Model Rule 8.4(g), 25 Duke J. Gender L & Pol'y 1, 40 (2017-2018).

[12]See Jerry Kang, What Judges Can Do About Implicit Bias, 75 Court Review 78 (2021).

[13]See Latonia Haney Keith, Cultural Competency in a Post Model Rule 8-4(g) World, 25 Duke J. Gender L. & Pol'y 1 (2017).

[14]Tusan, Hon. Gail S., and Sharon Obialo, Cultural Competence in the Courtroom; A Judge's Insight, From the Bench, 39 (2010).

[15]See discussion in Marie A. Failinger, Can A Good Judge Be A Good Politician? Judicial Elections From a Virtue Ethics Approach, 70 Mo. L. Rev. 433 (2005).

[16]Victor Eugene Flango, State Supreme Court Opinions as Law Development, 11 Journal of App. Prac. & Pro. 105, 106 (2010).

[17]See Youngstown Sheet & Tube Co. v. Sawyer, 343 U.S. 579, 634 (1952)(Jackson, J., concurring).

[18]See The Slaughter-House Cases, 83 U.S. 36 (1872)(narrow interpretation of privileges and immunities clause not supported by historical record); Prigg v Comm. Of Pennsylvania, 41 U.S. 539 (1842)(deal breaking significance to fugitive slave clause not supported by historical record).

[19]See Amir H. Ali, An Appeal to Books, 121 Mich. L. Rev. 871, 872-73 (2023), Saul Cornell, Heller, New Originalism, and Law Office History: "Meet the New Boss, Same as the Old Boss," 56 UCLA L Rev 1095, 1098 (2009); J. Harvie Wilkinson III, Of Guns, Abortions, and the Unraveling Rule of Law, 95 Va. L. Rev. 253, 269 (2009).

[20]Oliver Wendell Holmes, Jr., The Common Law 1 (1881).

[21]See e.g. Laurence H. Tribe, Reaching the Limits of Traditional Constitutional Scholarship Constitutional Choices (1985); Erwin Chemerinsky, Getting Beyond Formalism in Constitutional law: Constitutional Theory Matters, 54 Okla. L. Rev. 1, 2 (2001) (asserting constitutional law is about value choices).

[22]See generally H. L. A. Hart, The Concept of Law (2nd Ed. 1994).

[23]See William L. Reynolds, William M. Richman, The Non-Precedential Precedent—Limited Publication and No-Citation Rules in the United States Court of Appeals, 78 Columbia La Review 1167, 1174-1176 (1978).

[24]See Noah Feldman, Scorpions: The Battles and Triumphs of FDS's Great Supreme Court Justices (2011).

[25]Henry Wadsworth Longfellow.

[26]Margaret Chase Smith.

Chapter 4

[1]See *I Love Lucy*, "Job Switching", Season 2, Episode 1 (CBS television broadcast September 15, 1952).

[2]Rudyard Kipling and T.S. Eliott, A Choice of Kipling's Verse Made by T.S. Eliot (Faber and Faber, Ltd.)(1941).

[3]See Jonathan O'Neill, Federalist Society, Volume 24 (December 20, 2023), https://fedsoc.org/fedsoc-review. ("Originalism has substantially reoriented constitutional discourse since it first reemerged in response to the Warren Court of the 1960s"; "Originalism has also come to better acknowledge that original meaning will not always be clear or available to answer contemporary questions"; "Numerous versions of originalism have

proliferated amid these general trends. Theorists differ in their understanding of how precisely to define the original meaning sought, the appropriate methodology for finding it, and the normative justification for doing so at all, however originalism might be defined or practiced"; "Despite widespread acceptance of the ideas of fixation and constraint, theoretical developments and new originalist labels continually appear.")

[4]Law, Justice and the Holocaust, William F. Meineke Jr. and Alexandra Zapruder, United States Holocaust Museum, May 2017, page 7.

[5]Law, Justice and the Holocaust, William F. Meineke Jr. and Alexandra Zapruder, United States Holocaust Museum, May 2017, page 74.

[6]Law, Justice and the Holocaust, William F. Meineke Jr. and Alexandra Zapruder, United States Holocaust Museum, May 2017, page 8.

[7]Law, Justice and the Holocaust, William F. Meineke Jr. and Alexandra Zapruder, United States Holocaust Museum, May 2017, page 8.

Chapter 5

[1]In rare circumstances, federal appellate judges may be appointed to serve on three-judge panels that include trial judges and hold evidentiary hearings. See, e.g., 28 U.S.C. § 2284(b)(1). Also, some state supreme courts hear evidence when resolving attorney disciplinary matters.

Chapter 6

[1]Marcus Welby, M.D., was an American medical drama television series that aired on ABC from September 23, 1969, to May 4, 1976. It starred Robert Young as the title character, a family practitioner with a kind bedside manner, who made house calls and was on a first-name basis with many of his patients.
See Wikipedia, Marcus Welby, M.D., https://en.wikipedia.org/wiki/Marcus_Welby,_M.D. (as of Mar 8, 2024, 15:59 GMT).

[2]I have served with the following justices who were appointed to the court directly from private practice: David Wiggins, Brent Appel, Dana Oxley, and Matthew McDermott, as well as these justices who were first appointed from private practice directly to the court of appeals before their appointment to the supreme court: Daryl Hecht and Edward Mansfield. I filled the vacancy of Chief Justice Marsha Ternus who was also appointed to the supreme court directly from private practice.

Chapter 7

[1]See Iowa Code section 331.756.

[2]District court is court of general jurisdiction, and as such it is empowered by Constitution to hear all cases in law, equity, or special proceedings. Schrier v. State, 573 N.W.2d 242 (Iowa 1997).

[3]See Comment 1, Iowa R. Prof. Resp. 32:3.8.

[4]Oath of office Iowa Const. art. XI, § 5; Iowa Code sections 63.10 and 63.6.

[5]National Center for State Courts, found at: https://ccj.ncsc.org/news/judicial-securityupdate.

Chapter 9

[1]In a jury trial, the same "guidance" can be given to counsel in a sidebar.

[2]I have often thought there is a special place in Hell for judges.

[3]Bob Woodward & Scott Armstrong, The Brethren: Inside the Supreme Court (1979).

[4]Black Robe Fever: The Role of the Judge in American Society, by Steven I. Platt (2023).

Chapter 10

[1]*The Des Moines Register*, 18 January 2008, p 8. Editorial.

[2]Buying Time 2008: Wisconsin, Brennan Center for Justice (May 12, 2008), found at https://www.brennancenter.org/our-work/research-reports/buying-time-2008-wisconsin

[3]Id.

[4]"Roberts's Rules," *The Atlantic* (January/February 2007).

[5]Rosen wrote:

> In Roberts's view, the most successful chief justices help their colleagues speak with one voice. Unanimous, or nearly unanimous, decisions are hard to overturn and contribute to the stability of the law and the continuity of the Court; by contrast, closely divided, 5-4 decisions make it harder for the public to respect the Court as an impartial institution that transcends partisan politics.

[6]Iowa Code section 63.6 states:

All judges of courts of record shall qualify before taking office following appointment by taking and subscribing an oath to the effect that they will support the Constitution of the United States and the Constitution of the State of Iowa, and that, without fear, favor, affection, or hope of reward, they will, to the best of their knowledge and ability, administer justice according to the law, equally to the rich and the poor.

Chapter 11

[1]See Frederick Schauer, Thinking Like a Lawyer: A New Introduction to Legal Reasoning 57 (2009).

[2]William D. Popkin, Evolution of the Judicial Opinion: Institutional and Individual Styles 143–51 (2007).

[3]See Bryan A. Garner, Legal Writing in Plain English 34–35 (2001); see also Bryan A. Garner, "Legalisms and Lawyerisms" in Garner's Dictionary of Legal Usage 531–32 (3d ed., 2011).

[4]See, e.g., Nina Varsava, Professional Irresponsibility and Judicial Opinions, 59 Hous. L. Rev. 103 (2021).

[5]Bryan A. Garner, Quack This Way: David Foster Wallace & Bryan A. Garner Talk Language and Writing 26–26 (2013).

[6]George Orwell, "Politics and the English Language" in The Collected Essays, Journalism, and Letters of George Orwell (vol. 4) 139 (1946).

[7]Bryan A. Garner, "Latinisms" in Garner's Dictionary of Legal Usage 517–18 (3d ed., 2011).

[8]See, e.g., David Foster Wallace, "A Supposedly Fun Thing I'll Never Do Again," in A Supposedly Fun Thing I'll Never Do Again (1997); see also Grant Gilmore, The Ages of American Law (1977).

[9]Richard Posner, Reflections on Judging 256 (2013).

Chapter 12

[1]Abraham Lincoln expressed a similar sentiment more than a century earlier in a letter that he wrote to his friend, Joshua Speed, on the issue of slavery: "If for this you and I must differ, differ we must." Yet after laying out the reasons for their disagreement, Lincoln ended the letter with, "Your friend forever." Collected Works of Abraham Lincoln, edited by Roy P. Basler et al.

[2]Antonin Scalia, The Essential Scalia: On the Constitution, the Courts, and the Rule of Law, Forum Books (Sept. 15, 2020).

Chapter 15

[1]The inspiration for my essay is taken from retired Minnesota Judge Bernard Boland. In 2002, Judge Boland wrote an article for the Minnesota State Bar Association "Bench & Bar" publication on ten judicial aspirations for new judges. It has helped shape many judicial practices including my own.

[2]St. Josemaría Escrivá, The Forge, at 184.

[3]Erwin Raphael McManus.

Biographical Notes

Paul B. Ahlers was appointed to the bench in 2011 and to the Iowa Court of Appeals in 2019. He earned his bachelor's degree from Iowa State University in 1991 and his law degree from the University of Iowa College of Law in 1994. Prior to his appointment, from 1994 to 2008 Judge Ahlers practiced in a private law firm. From 2008 to 2011, he served as claim counsel in the bond and financial products claim group for the Travelers Companies. Judge Ahlers is a member of the Iowa State Bar Association.

Lars G. Anderson was appointed to the bench in 2014. He earned his bachelor's degree from Luther College in 1992 and his law degree, with distinction, from the University of Iowa College of Law in 1995. Prior to his appointment, Judge Anderson was in private practice in Iowa City from 1995-2014 and was an adjunct professor at the University of Iowa College of Law in 2014. Judge Anderson served as an alternate Judicial Hospitalization Referee for Johnson County from 1997 to 2001 and as a Judicial Hospitalization Referee from 2003 to 2014. Judge Anderson is a member of the Johnson County Bar Association, the Iowa State Bar Association, and the Dean Mason Ladd American Inn of Court.

Brent R. Appel was appointed to the Iowa Supreme Court in 2006. He earned his bachelor's degree and master's degree from Stanford University in 1973 and his law degree from the University of California, Berkeley School of Law in 1977. Prior to his appointment, Justice Appel was First Assistant Attorney General of Iowa, Deputy Attorney General, and then worked in private practice until 2006. Justice Appel is currently a professor of law at Drake University Law School. He is a member of the Iowa State Bar Association and the American Bar Association. He is married and has six children.

Gina C. Badding was appointed to the Iowa Court of Appeals in 2021. Judge Badding received her bachelor's degree with honors from the University of Iowa in 2001, and her law degree with distinction from the University of Iowa in 2004. Prior to her appointment, Judge Badding worked as an associate attorney and partner in private law, as well as a staff attorney for the Iowa Court of Appeals. She was appointed a district court judge in April 2019. She is a member of the Iowa State Bar Association, the Carroll County Bar Association, and the Iowa Judges Association. She is married and has four children.

Joel W. Barrows was appointed to the bench in 2012. He earned his bachelor's degree from Coe College in 1983, a master's degree from Southern Illinois University in 1986, his law degree from Drake University Law School in 1989, and his Master of Laws degree, with distinction, from Georgetown University Law Center in 1993. Prior to his appointment, Judge Barrows worked as a child support recovery attorney for Clinton, Jackson, and Cedar Counties. He also served as an Assistant Polk County Attorney in Des Moines and as an Assistant United State Attorney in Des Moines and Davenport, Iowa. He is a member of the Scott County and Iowa State Bar Associations, as well as the Iowa Judges Association. He is married and has two children.

Romonda D. Belcher was appointed to the bench in 2010. She earned her bachelor's degree with honors from Howard University in 1990 and her law degree from Drake University Law School in 1995. Prior to her appointment, Judge Belcher was an assistant Polk County attorney. She is a member of the Iowa State Bar Association and the Polk County Bar Association. In 2024 she received the Alumna of the Year award from Drake University Law School, which recognizes alumni who have demonstrated outstanding service to the legal profession, the community, and the law school.

Mark W. Bennett was appointed to the bench in 1994 by President Bill Clinton. He earned his bachelor's degree from Gustavus Adolphus College in 1972 and his law degree in 1975 from Drake University Law School.

Prior to his appointment, Judge Bennett began his own firm, Babich, Bennett, & Nickerson, now known as Babich Goldman. He was in private practice in Des Moines, Iowa from 1975 to 1991 and also served as general counsel to the Iowa Civil Liberties Union from 1975 to 1989. From 1991 to 1994, Bennett was a United States magistrate judge for the United States District Court for the Southern District of Iowa, until his nomination to the United States District Court for the Northern District of Iowa. After retiring from the federal judiciary, Bennett joined the faculty of Drake University Law School, where he is Director of the Institute for Justice Reform and Innovation. He is also a fellow of the New York University School of Law's Civil Jury Project.

Richard G. Blane, II was appointed as a district court trial judge in 1995, where he served for 20 years. He then served as a senior judge on the Iowa Court of Appeals for another nine years. He earned his bachelor's degree from Drake University in 1970 and his law degree at Drake University Law School in 1973. Prior to his appointment, Judge Blane was an assistant county attorney with the Polk County (Iowa) Attorney's Office, and later became first assistant United States Attorney for the Southern District of Iowa until he joined a Des Moines law firm specializing in trial practice. For 20 years Judge Blane was an adjunct professor at the Drake Law School teaching trial advocacy. He is a member of the Polk County Bar Association and the Iowa Judges Association.

Robert J. Blink was appointed to the bench in 1995. He earned his bachelor's degree in English and Speech Communications from North Central College in 1972 and his law degree from Drake University Law School in 1975. Prior to his appointment, Judge Blink was a trial lawyer for 20 years. He litigated as an assistant Polk County Attorney, Assistant Iowa Attorney General, Special Deputy United States Attorney and product liability counsel in private practice. He has also served as a Trial Advocacy professor at Drake University Law School for 37 years. Judge Blink is a member of the Polk County and Iowa State Bar Associations, the Iowa Judges Association and an Honorary Member of the Order of the Coif and the Order of Barristers. Judge Blink and his wife have five children and eight grandchildren.

Thomas N. Bower was appointed to the Iowa Court of Appeals in January 2012. In 2019 he was selected by his colleagues to be Chief of the Iowa Court of Appeals until he became a senior judge in 2024. Chief Judge Bower received his bachelor's degree from Illinois State University in 1984 and his law degree from Drake University Law School in 1987. He was appointed to the district associate court bench in 1993 and the district court bench in 1995. In 2010, Chief Judge Bower was appointed chief judge of the First District. Prior to his appointment, he served as an assistant city attorney for the city of Ames and as an assistant Black Hawk County Attorney. Chief Judge Bower helped to establish the Black Hawk County Adult Drug Court program in 2006, a mental health court program in 2009, and secured funding for a court ordered domestic violence prevention program. Additionally, Chief Judge Bower has dedicated his career to the prevention of child abuse and domestic violence, having presented to local, regional, and national conferences. He has also presented on the topics of restorative justice and collegiality in the courts. Chief Judge Bower has been an adjunct professor at the University of Northern Iowa teaching Constitutional and Business Law and an adjunct professor teaching criminal law and American politics at Upper Iowa University. He is a member of the Iowa State Bar Association, the Black Hawk County Bar Association, and the Iowa Judges Association.

Tyler J. Buller was appointed to the Iowa Court of Appeals in 2022. He earned his undergraduate degree from Drake University and graduated Order of the Coif from the University of Iowa College of Law. Before his appointment, Judge Buller prosecuted criminal trials and appeals as an Assistant Attorney General in the Iowa Department of Justice.

Andrew B. Chappell was appointed to the bench in 2017. He earned his bachelor's degree with high honors from James Madison College at Michigan State University in 1994 and his law degree with Honors from the University of Iowa College of Law in 1997. Prior to his appointment, Judge Chappell was in private practice in Iowa City from 1997-2000 and was an Assistant Johnson County Attorney in the Civil Division from 2000-2017. Judge Chappell is a longtime member of the Iowa State Bar Association and has served on numerous ISBA Committees over the years, including the ISBA Jury Instructions Committee which he currently co-chairs. Prior to his appointment, Judge Chappell also served on the Iowa Supreme Court Attorney Disciplinary Board. He is married and has one child.

Mary E. Chicchelly was appointed to the Iowa Court of Appeals in 2021. She earned her bachelor's degree from the University of Iowa in 1989 and her J.D. from the University of Iowa College of Law in 1992. Prior to her appointment, Judge Chicchelly served as a judicial clerk for Iowa Judicial District 2A from 1992-1993, practiced law in Fort Dodge from 1993-1995 and then in Waterloo from 1995-1997. She was a partner in the law firm of Seidl & Chicchelly in Cedar Rapids from 1997 until her appointment to the Iowa District Court for Judicial District 6 in March 2013. Judge Chicchelly served in that role until her appointment to the Court of Appeals. She is a member of the American Bar Association, the Iowa State Bar Association, the Linn County Bar Association, and the Judge David R. Hansen American Inn of Court (Emeritus). Judge Chicchelly previously served as a member and past delegate to the ABA National Conference of State Trial Judges, is a past president of the Iowa Judges Association and current member of the Iowa Judges Association Board. She is married and has two children.

Susan L. Christensen was appointed to the Iowa Supreme Court in 2018. The members of the court selected her as chief justice in February 2020. She earned her bachelor's degree from Judson College in 1988 and her law degree from Creighton University School of Law in 1991. Prior to her appointment to the Iowa Supreme Court, Chief Justice Christensen was appointed a district associate judge in 2007 and a district court judge in 2015. Before becoming a judge, she practiced law in Harlan for 16 years. Chief Justice Christensen chaired the Children's Justice State Council and the Family First Task Force and served on the Supreme Court's Family Law Pro Se Forms Committee, Child Support Guidelines Review Committee, Parents Representation Standards Committee, and Guardianship/Conservatorship Task Force as well as the Children's Mental Health and Wellbeing Advisory Committee. She is a member of the Iowa Judges Association, the Iowa State Bar Association, the Southwest Iowa Bar Association, and the Shelby County

Bar Association. She is married with five children and nine grandchildren.

Sarah E. Crane was appointed to the bench in 2018. She was also appointed as a member of the Iowa Business Specialty Court in November 2019. Judge Crane received her bachelor's degree *summa cum laude* from Gustavus Adolphus College in 2004 and her law degree from the University of Chicago Law School in 2007. Prior to her appointment, Judge Crane started out in private practice at a firm in Chicago, but she returned to Iowa and served as a law clerk for the Iowa Supreme Court. Judge Crane also worked in private practice at the Davis Brown Law Firm in Des Moines. She is a member of the Iowa State Bar Association, the Polk County Bar Association, the Iowa Organization of Women Attorneys, and the Polk County Women Attorneys. She is married and has four children.

Richard H. Doyle was appointed to the Court of Appeals in 2008. He retired in 2021 and became a senior judge on the court. He earned his bachelor's degree from Drake University in 1971. He then served in the United States Army for two years before attending Drake University Law School, earning his law degree in 1976. Prior to his appointment, Judge Doyle served for a year as an assistant attorney general in the Criminal Appeals Division of the Iowa Attorney General's office. He was in private practice in Des Moines from 1977 until his appointment to the Court of Appeals. Judge Doyle is a member of the Polk County and Iowa State Bar Associations, the Iowa Academy of Trial Lawyers, the Iowa Judges Association, and Lincoln Inne. He co-authored "History of the Iowa Court of Appeals," 60 *Drake L. Rev.* 1 (2011). He is widowed and has two children and four grandchildren.

David L. D. Faith II was appointed to the bench in 2023. He earned his bachelor's degree from Concordia College in 2001, his master's degree in history from Syracuse University in 2004, and his law degree from the University of Iowa College of Law in 2008, where he was inducted into the Order of the Coif. Prior to his appointment, Judge Faith worked in private practice at Dorsey & Whitney LLP, as an Assistant and later Deputy Attorney General for the State of Iowa, and as an Assistant United States Attorney. He has also served in the Iowa Army National Guard as a member of the United States Army Judge Advocate General's Corps. He is married and has one child.

Jeffrey D. Farrell was appointed to the bench in 2013. He earned his bachelor's degree in 1986 from the University of Iowa and his law degree from the University of Iowa College of Law in 1989. Prior to his appointment, he was a law clerk for the Fifth Judicial

District from 1989-1991. Judge Farrell served for 12 years as an assistant attorney general and ten years as an administrative law judge before being appointed to the bench. He is married with two children.

Arthur E. Gamble was appointed to the bench in 1983. He attended the University of Iowa where he earned his bachelor's and law degrees. Prior to his appointment, Judge Gamble worked in private practice. Judge Gamble is a member of the Polk County and Iowa State Bar Associations. He is also the past president of the Iowa Judges Association and of the C. Edwin Moore American Inn of Court. Judge Gamble retired and became a senior judge in January 2019. He is married with four children.

Myron L. Gookin was appointed to the bench in 2011. He received his bachelor's degree with distinction from Iowa State University in 1980 and his law degree with honors from Drake University Law School in 1983. Prior to his appointment, Judge Gookin was in private practice with Foss, Kuiken, Gookin & Cochran P.C. in Fairfield, Iowa beginning in July 1983. He is a member of the Iowa State Bar Association and the Iowa Judge's Association. He has served on many boards and commissions including the IJA Board of Directors, the Iowa Supreme Court Criminal Rules Advisory Committee, the Iowa

Supreme Court Client Security Commission, the Iowa Supreme Court CLE Commission and the Iowa State Bar Association Jury Instruction Committee. In January 2022, he was appointed Chief Judge of the 8th Judicial District of Iowa and serves on the Iowa Judicial Council.

John J. Haney was appointed to the bench in 2014. He earned an AA degree with honors from Marshalltown Community College in 1991, a bachelor's degree with honors from Grinnell College in 1993, and his law degree from the University of Iowa College of Law in 1996. Prior to his appointment, Judge Haney was in private practice and also served as a Marshall County magistrate from 2007. He is a member of the Marshall County Bar Association, the Iowa Judges Association, and the Iowa State Bar Association. He is married with four children and ten grandchildren.

David R. Hansen first took the bench in 1969 as a police court judge in Iowa Falls, Iowa. In 1976, Governor Robert Ray appointed him as judge for Iowa's District 2B. In 1986, he was appointed by President Ronald Reagan to the Northern District of Iowa, and in 1991, President George H.W. Bush appointed him to the Eighth Circuit. He earned his bachelor's degree from Northwest Missouri State University in 1960 with highest honors and his law degree, with honors, from

George Washington University Law School in 1963. Prior to his appointment to the bench, he served with the U.S. Army JAG Corps from 1964-1968. He also engaged in private practice from 1968 until his appointment to the Iowa District Court in 1976. He is a widower with two adult sons, three grandsons and three great-grandchildren.

Robert B. Hanson was appointed to the bench in 2003. He earned his bachelor's degree from Stanford University in 1978 and his law degree from the University of Iowa College of Law in 1981. Prior to his appointment, Judge Hanson worked as a judicial law clerk for the late Justice K. David Harris of the Iowa Supreme Court in 1981 and then enjoyed a 21-year career in private practice until his appointment. He is a member of the Polk County Bar Association, the Iowa State Bar Association, and the American Bar Association as well as the Iowa Judges Association.

Alan T. Heavens was appointed to the bench in 2019. He earned his bachelor's degree *cum laude* from the University of St. Thomas, Minnesota in 2007 and his law degree from St. Thomas in 2010. Prior to his appointment to the bench, he served as Clayton County attorney from 2010 until 2019 and was also engaged in private practice at McClean Law Office in Dyersville. Judge Heavens is the administrative judge for Allamakee

County and Clayton County and a member of the Iowa Judges Association, the Iowa Bar Association and the Clayton County Bar Association, which he was President of for six years prior to becoming a judge. He is married with four children.

Randy V. Hefner was appointed to the bench in 2010 and retired in 2023. He earned his bachelor's degree from the University of Northern Iowa in 1975 and his law degree from Drake University Law School in 1978. Judge Hefner worked at Shaff, Farwell & Senneff in Clinton for one year and then practiced law in Adel from 1979 until his judicial appointment. During his years of practice, Judge Hefner served on the governing boards of numerous organizations, including the ADM Scholarship Foundation, Dallas County Care Facility, Dallas County Compensation Committee, Adel Enterprises, Adel Rotary Club, ACLU of Iowa and Iowa Association for Justice. He coached little league baseball and local mock trial teams. He and his wife Connie were married in 1975 and have one son, Mark, who is married to Nichole. Following the birth of twin granddaughters Judge Hefner retired, and he and Connie moved to Minnesota to help care for the twins.

Zachary S. Hindman was appointed to the bench in 2018. He earned his bachelor's degree *summa cum laude* from Morningside College in 2007 and graduated Order of the Coif from Drake University Law School in 2010. After law school Judge Hindman clerked for the Honorable Steven M. Colloton, circuit judge on the United States Court of Appeals for the Eighth Circuit. He then worked in private practice in Sioux City until his appointment. Judge Hindman is a member of the Iowa State Bar Association and the Iowa Judges Association. He is married and has three children.

Duane E. Hoffmeyer was appointed to the bench in 2001. He earned his bachelor's degree from the University of Northern Iowa in 1979 and his law degree from Creighton University Law School in 1982. Prior to his appointment, Judge Hoffmeyer engaged in private practice at Vakulskas & Hoffmeyer. He is a member of the Iowa State Bar Association, the Iowa Judges Association, and the Woodbury County Bar Association. He is married with two adult children.

Michael D. Huppert was appointed to the bench in December of 1999. He earned his bachelor's degree in 1979 from Drake University and his law degree from Drake University Law School in 1982, Order of the Coif. Prior to his appointment, Chief Judge Huppert was a partner with the Patterson Law Firm in Des Moines. He is a member of the Iowa State and Polk County Bar Associations. He is a member and former director of the

Iowa Judges Association. He is also a Master of the Bench (Emeritus) and former president of the C. Edwin Moore American Inn of Court.

John A. Jarvey was appointed to the bench in 2007 by President George W. Bush. He earned his bachelor's degree from the University of Akron in 1978 and his law degree from Drake University Law School in 1981. Prior to his appointment, Judge Jarvey served as a law clerk to Judge Donald E. O'Brien of the United States District Court for the Northern District of Iowa from 1981 to 1983. He was a trial attorney of the Criminal Division of the United States Department of Justice from 1983 to 1987. As a prosecutor, he specialized in fraud in the pharmaceutical industry. He taught trial advocacy at the University of Iowa College of Law and mock trial at Cedar Rapids Washington High School. Judge Jarvey was a United States Magistrate Judge of the United States District Court for the Northern District of Iowa from 1987 to 2007. As a Magistrate Judge, Jarvey conducted over 400 mediations until his nomination in 2007. Judge Jarvey served as Chief Judge from 2015 until 2022 and retired from active service on March 18, 2022. He is married with three sons.

Stephen H. Locher was appointed to the bench in 2022 by President Joe Biden. He earned his bachelor's degree from the University of Notre Dame, *magna cum laude*, in

2000 and his law degree from Harvard Law School in 2003. Prior to his appointment, Judge Locher worked as an associate at Goldberg Kahn in Chicago from 2004 to 2008. From 2008 to 2013, he was an Assistant United States Attorney in the U.S. Attorney's Office for the Southern District of Iowa. From 2013 to 2021, he was a partner at Belin McCormick, P.C. Judge Locher was selected to serve as a United States magistrate judge in 2020 and nominated to serve as a United States district judge for the Southern District of Iowa in 2022. He is a member of the Iowa State Bar Association and the American Bar Association. He is married with four children.

Edward M. Mansfield has been a judge since 2009, when he was appointed to the Iowa Court of Appeals. In 2011, he was appointed to the Iowa Supreme Court where he currently serves. Justice Mansfield earned his bachelor's degree from Harvard in 1978 and his law degree from Yale in 1982. He spent 26 years in private practice before becoming a judge. In addition to his judicial duties, Justice Mansfield teaches as an adjunct professor of law at Drake Law School, where his courses have included contracts, civil procedure, election law, federal jurisdiction, and sports and antitrust law. Since 2023, Justice Mansfield has been a member of the Standing Committee on the Federal Rules of Practice and Procedure. Justice Mansfield is married and has three children.

David N. May was appointed to the bench in 2016. He earned his bachelor's degree from the University of Missouri-Columbia, his Master of Public Health degree from the University of Oklahoma Health Sciences Center, and his law degree with high honors from Drake University Law School. Prior to his appointment, Justice May practiced law with Hawkins & Norris, P.C. from 1998 to 2001. From 2001 to 2016, he practiced with Bradshaw, Fowler, Proctor & Fairgrave, P.C. He was appointed to the Iowa Court of Appeals in 2019 and then to the Iowa Supreme Court in 2022. Justice May is a member of the Iowa State Bar Association, the Polk County Bar Association, the C. Edwin Moore Inn of Court, the Lincoln Inn of Court, the Iowa Judges Association, and the Drake Law School Board of Counselors. He is married and has two children.

Matthew C. McDermott was appointed to the Supreme Court in 2020. He earned his bachelor's degree from the University of Iowa in 2000 and his law degree from the University of California, Berkeley, in 2003. Prior to his appointment, he was a partner at Belin McCormick, P.C., where he had a trial and appellate practice in commercial litigation, criminal law, and administrative law. He is a former member of the Iowa State Bar Association's Board of Governors, former chair of its Judicial Administration Committee, and past president of its Young Lawyers Division. Justice McDermott previously served on the board of directors and as board president for Iowa Legal Aid, the Iowa Lottery Authority, the Polk County Homeless Continuum of Care Board, and Central Iowa Shelter and Services. He chairs the Iowa Supreme Court's Access to Justice Commission. He is married and has three children.

Patrick A. McElyea was appointed to the bench in 2017. He received his undergraduate degree in History and Political Science from Central College and his law degree from Drake University Law School. He previously served as a Special Assistant United States Attorney in the Southern District of Iowa, and as an Assistant County Attorney in Iowa, Wapello, and Scott Counties. He is a member of the Iowa Bar Association and the Iowa Judges Association.

Kevin McKeever was appointed to the bench in 2015. He earned his bachelor's degree from Northwestern University in 1991 and his law degree from the University of Iowa College of Law in 2001. Prior to his appointment, Judge McKeever was an Officer with the United States Navy (1991-1998), an Assistant Ramsey County Attorney (2001-2007), a Staff Attorney with ACT Inc. (2007-2011), and an Assistant Muscatine County Attorney (2011-2015). Judge McKeever serves as a board member of the African American Museum of Iowa, and he enjoys bicycle riding and reading books about history.

Sean W. McPartland was appointed to the bench in 2008 and became a senior judge in 2024. He received his undergraduate degree from the University of Iowa in 1981, with distinction, and his law degree in 1984, with distinction, from the University of Iowa College of Law. Prior to his appointment, Judge McPartland practiced in general civil litigation with law firms in Kansas City, Missouri (1984-1989) and in Cedar Rapids, Iowa (1989-2008). After his appointment to the bench, Judge McPartland served on the Iowa Civil Justice Task Force Steering Committee from 2009-2012 and contributed to the 2021 report of the Task Force. Judge McPartland also served as a member of the Advisory Committee Concerning Certain Civil Justice Reform Task Force Recommendations beginning in 2012. Judge McPartland was appointed in 2017 to serve as a judge on the Iowa Business Specialty Court, served in that capacity until 2020, and continues to serve as a settlement judge in some business court cases. Judge McPartland also served regularly as a faculty member in orientation programs for new judges presented by the Iowa Judicial Branch.

Michael J. Moon was appointed by former Governor Tom Vilsack and served as a judge for the 2nd Judicial

Court of Iowa until his retirement in September 2017. Prior to his appointment, Judge Moon was an attorney in private practice in Marshalltown. Additionally, he served as magistrate for the 2nd Judicial District Court in Marshall County from 1993-2000. Moon earned a bachelor's degree from the University of Iowa in 1968, and after serving in the United States Army, earned his J.D. from Drake University Law School in 1974.

Michael R. Mullins was appointed to the Iowa Court of Appeals in 2011, and took senior status upon his retirement in 2022. He received his bachelor's degree from Southwest Baptist University, Bolivar, Missouri, in 1974; his M.S.W. from the University of Iowa in 1976; and earned his Juris Doctorate, with honors, Order of Coif, from Drake University Law School in 1982. Prior to his appointment, Judge Mullins spent 19 years in private practice in Washington, Iowa. He was appointed to the district court bench in District Eight in January 2002. He is a former member of the Judicial Technology Committee and the Business Advisory Committee for the Electronic Document Management System (EDMS). He is a faculty member for new judge orientation and has often been a presenter for continuing legal education on the topic of sentencing issues. Judge Mullins developed the Iowa Criminal Statutes Summary Chart used by judges and lawyers throughout Iowa. The Chart is now part of the Sentencing Project under the direction of Drake University Law School and the Drake Legal

Clinic, in consultation with Judge Mullins. He is a member of the Washington County Bar Association, Iowa Judges Association, Iowa State Bar Association, and the American Bar Association. Judge Mullins is married and has two married children and four grandchildren. His current term of office expires in January 2026.

Thomas P. Murphy was appointed to the bench in 2017. He earned his bachelor's degree as a Distinguished Military Graduate from Marquette University in 1985. He then served four years on active duty in the United States Army. In 1992, he earned his law degree with Honors from Drake University Law School. Prior to his appointment, Judge Murphy practiced as an attorney for 25 years, including private practice at Hopkins & Huebner, P.C. beginning in 2002. He is a member of the Iowa State Bar Association and the Dallas County Bar Association.

David W. Nelmark was appointed to the district court bench in 2019 and the Iowa Business Specialty Court in 2021. He earned his bachelor's degrees from Drake University in 1999 and his law degree from Stanford Law School in 2005. Prior to his appointment, Judge Nelmark worked for Gislason & Hunter, L.L.P., as well as Belin McCormick, P.C. He is a member of the Iowa State Bar Association and the Polk County Bar Association as well as a past president of the Polk County Bar Association and the American Mock Trial Association. He is the coauthor of *Championship Mock Trial: The Guide for Students and Coaches.*

David P. Odekirk was appointed to the bench in 2014. He received his bachelor's degree with honors from the University of Iowa in 1989 and his law degree from the University of Iowa in 1993. Prior to his appointment, Judge Odekirk practiced law in Waterloo, Iowa for over 20 years in the areas of civil litigation and trial work involving a wide variety of civil matters. He is currently the immediate past President and member of the Iowa Judges Association as well as a member of the Black Hawk County Bar Association, the Iowa State Bar Association, and the American Bar Association. He is married with three children.

Eliza J. Ovrom was appointed to the Iowa district court bench in 1999. She served as assistant chief judge of the 5th Judicial District from 2014 to her retirement in 2018. Prior to her appointment, she served as a First Assistant Polk County Attorney for the civil bureau, and as an assistant Iowa Attorney General. Judge Ovrom has been active in many state and local bar associations. She is a founding member of the Iowa Center for Children's Justice. She is a recipient of the Willie Stevenson Glanton Award and the Arabella Mansfield Award. She earned her bachelor's degree from Coe College in 1975 and her law degree from the University of Iowa College of Law in 1979.

Dana L. Oxley was appointed to the Iowa Supreme Court in 2020. She earned her bachelor's degree in accounting from the University of Northern Iowa in 1990 and was a bank auditor before earning her law degree from the University of Iowa College of Law in 1998, Order of the Coif. Following law school, Justice Oxley served as a one-year term clerk for the Honorable David R. Hansen on the Eighth Circuit Court of Appeals and later returned to serve as a career law clerk for Judge Hansen until 2011. Prior to being appointed to the Supreme Court, Justice Oxley practiced with Shuttleworth & Ingersoll PLC in Cedar Rapids. Justice Oxley has taught as an adjunct professor at the University of Iowa College of Law, is a past president of the Eighth Circuit Bar Association and is an editor of the Eighth Circuit Appellate Practice Manual. She is a member of the Iowa State Bar Association, the Eighth Circuit Bar Association, and the Linn County Bar Association. She is married and has two children.

Christopher C. Polking was appointed to the bench in 2019. He earned his bachelor's degree from Tufts University in 1994 and his law degree from the University of Minnesota in 2001, graduating *magna cum laude*,

Order of the Coif. Prior to his appointment, Judge Polking worked as an attorney in private practice, as well as the Carroll County Magistrate. He is a member of the Carroll County Bar Association, the Iowa State Bar Association, and the Iowa Judges Association.

Robert W. Pratt was appointed to the bench in 1997 by President Bill Clinton. He graduated from Loras College with a bachelor's degree in 1969 and received his law degree from Creighton University Law School in 1972. Prior to his appointment, Judge Pratt was a staff attorney of Polk County Legal Aid Society from 1973 to 1974, during which time his colleagues included future Senator Tom Harkin. He was in private practice in Des Moines, Iowa from 1975 to 1997 at Funaro, Brick, & Pratt, then at Hedberg, Brick, Tann, Pratt & Ward, and then as a sole practitioner. He served as chief judge of the Southern District of Iowa from 2006 to 2011, assumed senior status in 2012, and became inactive senior judge in 2023. Judge Pratt is a member of the Iowa State Bar Association and an elected member of the American Law Institute. He is married with three children and seven grandchildren.

Dustria A. Relph was appointed to the bench in 2014. She graduated from Iowa Methodist School of Nursing in 1988, Mercy College of Health Sciences in 2003, and earned her law degree from Drake University Law

School in 2006. Prior to her appointment, Judge Relph was in private practice at Chambers & Relph, P.C. She is a member of the American Bar Association, the Iowa State Bar Association, the Judicial District 5B Bar Association, the Iowa Judges Association, and the National Association of Women Judges. She is married and has four children.

Margaret J. Reyes was appointed to the bench in 2018. She earned her bachelor's degree from Creighton University in 1990 and her law degree from Creighton University Law School in 1993. Prior to her appointment, Judge Reyes worked as an Assistant Pottawattamie County Attorney in charge of the office's Civil Division. She is a member of the Iowa Bar Association including the Criminal Law, Employment/Labor Law, and Government Sections, and a member of the Criminal Law Legislative Subcommittee. She is a member of the Iowa County Attorneys Association, the Government Practice Committee, the National Association of District Attorneys and the Pottawattamie County Bar Association.

Karen A. Romano was appointed to the bench in 2001 and became a senior judge in 2019. She earned her bachelor's degree from Creighton University in 1983 and her law degree from University of Iowa College of Law in 1986 with distinction. Prior to her appointment, Judge Romano worked for a private law firm before serving as an Assistant Polk County Attorney from 1987 to 1996. She served as a District Associate Judge from April 1996 until her appointment as a District Court Judge. Judge Romano is a member of the Polk County, Iowa State, and American Bar Associations. She is also a member of Polk County Women Attorneys, Iowa Organization of Women Attorneys, Iowa Judges Association, and the National Association of Women Judges. Prior to retiring, Judge Romano served as the chair of the Polk County Courthouse Security Committee and was a member of Court Interpreter Policies Advisory Committee.

Robin S. Rosenbaum was appointed to the bench in 2011 by President Barack Obama. She earned her bachelor's degree from Cornell University and her law degree *magna cum laude* from the University of Miami School of Law in 1991. Prior to her appointment, Judge Rosenbaum was a trial attorney in the Federal Programs Branch of the United States Department of Justice, served as staff counsel for the United States Office of the Independent Counsel, and worked as a litigation associate at Holland & Knight. Rosenbaum then clerked for Judge Stanley Marcus of the United States Court of Appeals for the Eleventh Circuit in 1998. From 1998 to 2007, she served as an Assistant United States Attorney in the Southern District of Florida. In 2007, Rosenbaum was selected to be a United States magistrate judge of the U.S. District Court for the Southern District of Florida. Her service as a magistrate judge ended on June 27,

2012, when she was elevated to district court judge. In 2013, she was elevated to the United States Court of Appeals for the Eleventh Circuit. She is a member of the Florida Bar Association and the American Bar Association.

Roger L. Sailer was appointed to the bench in 2019. He earned his Bachelor of Arts in English from the University of Nebraska in 1987 and his Bachelor of Science in Journalism from the University of Colorado in 1994. He earned his J.D. from Creighton Law School in 2007. Prior to his appointment, Judge Sailer worked as the Crawford County Attorney, Assistant Crawford County Attorney, and Associate Attorney at Mundt, Franck, and Schumacher Law Firm.

John M. Sandy was appointed as the 38th judge of the Iowa Court of Appeals in June 2024. He filled the vacancy created by the retirement of Chief Judge Thomas Bower. Before his appointment, he practiced law with his family at Sandy Law Firm, P.C. where he maintained a busy trial practice. Judge Sandy loved civil litigation and the courtroom. He also previously worked as a public defender for the State of Minnesota and served as a law clerk to the Office of the Federal Public Defender in Minneapolis, Minnesota. Judge Sandy earned his law degree with dean's honors from the University of St. Thomas in 2010, where he served as editor-in-chief of the *Journal of Law & Public Policy* and was awarded the law school's scholarly engagement and societal reform award. Judge Sandy earned his undergraduate degrees in Philosophy and Latin from the same institution, graduating *cum laude* in 2007. He was raised and graduated from high school in Spirit Lake.

Michael J. Schilling was appointed to the bench in 2006. He served close to nine years as a specialty drug court judge before taking senior status in September 2023. He earned his bachelor's degree with honors from the University of Iowa in 1973 and his law degree, with distinction, from the University of Iowa College of Law in 1976. Prior to his appointment, Judge Schilling served as a VISTA volunteer lawyer on the three Native American reservations in Nebraska. He also served as an Assistant Public Defender before entering private practice. Judge Schilling is a member of the Des Moines County, Iowa State, and American Bar Associations, the American Judicature Society, and the Iowa Judges Association. As a senior judge, he is serving on the Iowa Specialty Business Court, as well as handling assignments in the Eighth Judicial District. He is married with three children.

Julie A. Schumacher was appointed to the Iowa Court of Appeals in 2019. She earned her bachelor's degree from the University of South Dakota in 1990 and her law degree from Creighton University Law School in 1993. Prior to her appointment, Judge Schumacher spent nearly 20 years in private practice in Denison, Iowa, and also served as a prosecutor for Crawford County, an assistant city attorney for Denison, and a hospitalization referee. Prior to her current appellate court position, Judge Schumacher was selected to serve as a district associate judge in 2012 and was appointed as a district court judge in 2017. She is a member of the Iowa State Bar Association, the Iowa Judges Association, and the Crawford County Bar Association.

Paul D. Scott was appointed to the bench in 2014. He earned his undergraduate degree from Drake University in 1984 and his law degree from Drake University Law School in 1987. Prior to his appointment, he was in private practice. Judge Scott practiced in the state and federal courts of Iowa, as well as the Eighth Circuit Court of Appeals. He is a member of the Iowa State Bar Association, the Polk County Bar Association, and the Iowa Academy of Trial Lawyers. Judge Scott is a past president of the Iowa Judges Association. He is married and has three children.

Joseph W. Seidlin was appointed as a District Court Judge in 2018, after serving as a District Associate Judge since 2013. Before that, he served as a Polk County Magistrate for eight years. Judge Seidlin attended Drake

University where he earned his undergraduate degree in 1982 and his law degree in 1985. Prior to his appointment, he was in private practice for 28 years before taking the District Associate bench in 2013. Judge Seidlin is a member of the Polk County and Iowa Bar Associations, as well as the C. Edwin Moore and Jack D. Levine Inns of Court.

Shawn R. Showers was appointed to the bench in 2016. He earned his bachelor's degree from the University of Iowa in 2004 and his law degree from Washburn University School of Law in 2008. Prior to his appointment, Judge Showers worked as an assistant county attorney in Cerro Gordo County and Washington County. He also worked as an assistant public defender in Ottumwa before being elected Washington County Attorney in November 2014. Judge Showers is a member of the Washington County Bar Association, the Iowa Bar Association and the Iowa Judges Association. He is married with two children.

Michael J. Shubatt was appointed to the bench in 2008. He earned his undergraduate degree in 1987 from the University of Iowa and his law degree in 1990 from the University of Iowa College of Law. Prior to his appointment, Judge Shubatt was a shareholder in the Dubuque law firm of Fuerste, Carew, Coyle, Juergens & Sudmeier, P.C., and served clients for 18 years as a general practitioner with an emphasis in civil litigation and trial work. Judge Shubatt also practiced in the state and federal courts of Iowa and Illinois, as well as the Eighth Circuit Court of Appeals. He is a member of the Dubuque County, Iowa State and American Bar Associations, and currently serves as the Administrative Judge for Dubuque and Delaware Counties.

Sharon Soorholtz Greer was appointed to the Iowa Court of Appeals in 2019. She earned double undergraduate degrees in Psychology and Child Development from Iowa State University and her law degree from the University of Iowa College of Law. Before her appointment, Judge Soorholtz Greer practiced law with Cartwright, Druker & Ryden in Marshalltown. She holds membership in the Iowa Judges Association, the Marshall County Bar Association, and the Iowa State Bar Association. She is a recipient of the University Iowa Law Review Distinguished Alumni Award.

Leonard T. Strand joined the federal bench in 2012 as a U.S. Magistrate Judge. In 2016, he was appointed as a U.S. District Judge for the Northern District of Iowa by President Barack Obama and later served as the Chief Judge of that court. Judge Strand earned his bachelor's degree from the University of Iowa in 1987 and his law degree from the University of Iowa College of Law, Order of the Coif, in 1990. Before becoming a judge, he was a civil trial attorney at Simmons Perrine Moyer & Bergman in Cedar Rapids, Iowa. Judge Strand has been a member of various professional organizations, including the American Bar Association, the Federal Judges Association, the Iowa State Bar Association, the Iowa Defense Counsel Association, the Linn County Bar Association and the Woodbury County Bar Association.

Mary E. Tabor was appointed to the Court of Appeals in 2010. She earned her bachelor's degree from the University of Iowa in 1985 and her law degree from the University of Iowa College of Law in 1991. Prior to her appointment, Judge Tabor worked as a staff attorney in the Office of General Counsel for the Federal Election Commission in Washington, D.C. from 1991 to 1993. She joined the Iowa Attorney General's Office in 1993 and served as director of the Criminal Appeals Division from 1999 to 2010. Judge Tabor is a member of the Polk County Bar Association, the Iowa State Bar Association, the Iowa Judges Association, the American Law Institute, the Blackstone Inn of Court, the Iowa Organization of Women Attorneys and the Polk County Women Attorneys. Judge Tabor is married and has three children.

Marsha K. Ternus was appointed to the Iowa Supreme Court in 1993. Her term on the court ended on December 31, 2010, after voters failed to retain her in the 2010 retention election. Chief Justice Ternus earned her bachelor's degree with honors and high distinction, Phi Beta Kappa, from the University of Iowa in 1972 and earned her law degree with honors, Order of the Coif, from Drake University Law School in 1977. Prior to her appointment, she worked in private practice in the Des Moines law firm of Bradshaw, Fowler, Proctor and Fairgrave, with a primary emphasis on civil litigation and insurance law. Since leaving the court, Chief Justice Ternus serves as an arbitrator and legal consultant.

Ian K. Thornhill is a native of Ida Grove, Iowa, and has lived in Cedar Rapids since 2002. He was appointed to the 6th District bench in 2009. Judge Thornhill earned his bachelor's degree in 1989, his M.B.A. in 1991, and his law degree with High Distinction in 1998, all from The University of Iowa. Prior to his appointment to the state court bench, Judge Thornhill served as Assistant United States Attorney and as an active-duty U.S. Navy J.A.G. Corps Attorney. Upon leaving active duty in 2002, Judge Thornhill remained in the Navy Reserve. He was recalled to active duty and deployed to Baghdad, Iraq from November 2007 to May 2008 in support of Operation Iraqi Freedom. Judge Thornhill has also served as both a Reserve trial and appellate court judge in his over 25-year Navy career.

Samuel A. Thumma was appointed to Arizona Court of Appeals, Division One, in 2012. He earned his bachelor's degree from Iowa State University in 1984, where he was a Harry S. Truman Memorial Scholar. Judge Thumma earned his law degree from the University of Iowa College of Law in 1988, Order of the Coif, and his Master of Laws from Duke University School of Law in 2020. Prior to his appointment, Judge Thumma was an AV Peer Review Rated Lawyer and a partner at Perkins Coie Brown & Bain, P.A., in Phoenix, and an associate at Arnold & Porter in Washington, D.C. He served as a law clerk for Arizona Supreme Court Chief Justice Stanley G. Feldman and Judge David R. Hansen, then on the United States District Court for the Northern District of Iowa. From 2007 to 2012, he served as a Judge on the Arizona Superior Court in Maricopa County, on juvenile and criminal rotations. In 2023, he received the James A. Walsh Outstanding Jurist Award from the State Bar of Arizona, and, in 2021, he was named the Judge of the Year by the Arizona Supreme Court.

Patrick H. Tott was appointed to the bench in 2014. He earned his bachelor's degree from Creighton University in 1989 and his law degree magna cum laude from Creighton University Law School in 1991. He served as a part-time Associate Juvenile Judge from 1994 to 2001 and as a part-time magistrate for Woodbury County from 1999 to 2014. Immediately prior to his appointment, Judge Tott worked at Buckmeier & Daane, P.C., in Sioux City, Iowa. He is a member of the Nebraska State Bar Association and the Iowa State Bar Association. He is married with seven children.

Thomas D. Waterman was appointed to the Iowa Supreme Court in 2011. He earned his bachelor's degree from Dartmouth College in 1981 and his law degree from the University of Iowa College of Law, Order of the Coif, in 1984. Before his appointment, Justice Waterman was in private practice at Lane & Waterman L.L.P. in Davenport, beginning in 1984. Justice Waterman was active in numerous organizations including the Jury Instruction Committee of the Iowa State Bar Association, the American College of Trial Lawyers, and the Iowa Academy of Trial Lawyers. He was a member of the State Judicial Nominating Commission from 1999-2005 and is also an elected member of the American Law Institute. He is married with four daughters.

C. J. Williams was appointed to the district court bench in 2018. He earned his bachelor's degree from the University of Iowa with high distinction in 1985 and his law degree from the University of Iowa College of Law, with high distinction, in 1988. He also received his Master of Laws with a specialization in criminal law from the University of Missouri-Kansas City School of Law.

Prior to his appointment, Judge Williams worked as a trial attorney for the United States Department of Justice Criminal Division from 1990-1992. From 1992 to 1997, he engaged in private practice at Lathrop & Gage in Kansas City, and from 1997 to 2016, he was an Assistant United States Attorney for the Northern District of Iowa. From 2016 to 2018, he served as a magistrate judge for the Northern District of Iowa until his appointment. Judge Williams became chief judge on February 12, 2024. He is a member of the Iowa State Bar Association and the American Bar Association.

Index

www.ingramcontent.com/pod-product-compliance
Lightning Source LLC
LaVergne TN
LVHW051059210926
848486LV00025B/427/J

* 9 7 9 8 2 1 8 6 1 5 4 1 3 *